sweetness & lightning

11

Gido Amagakure

c o n t e n t s

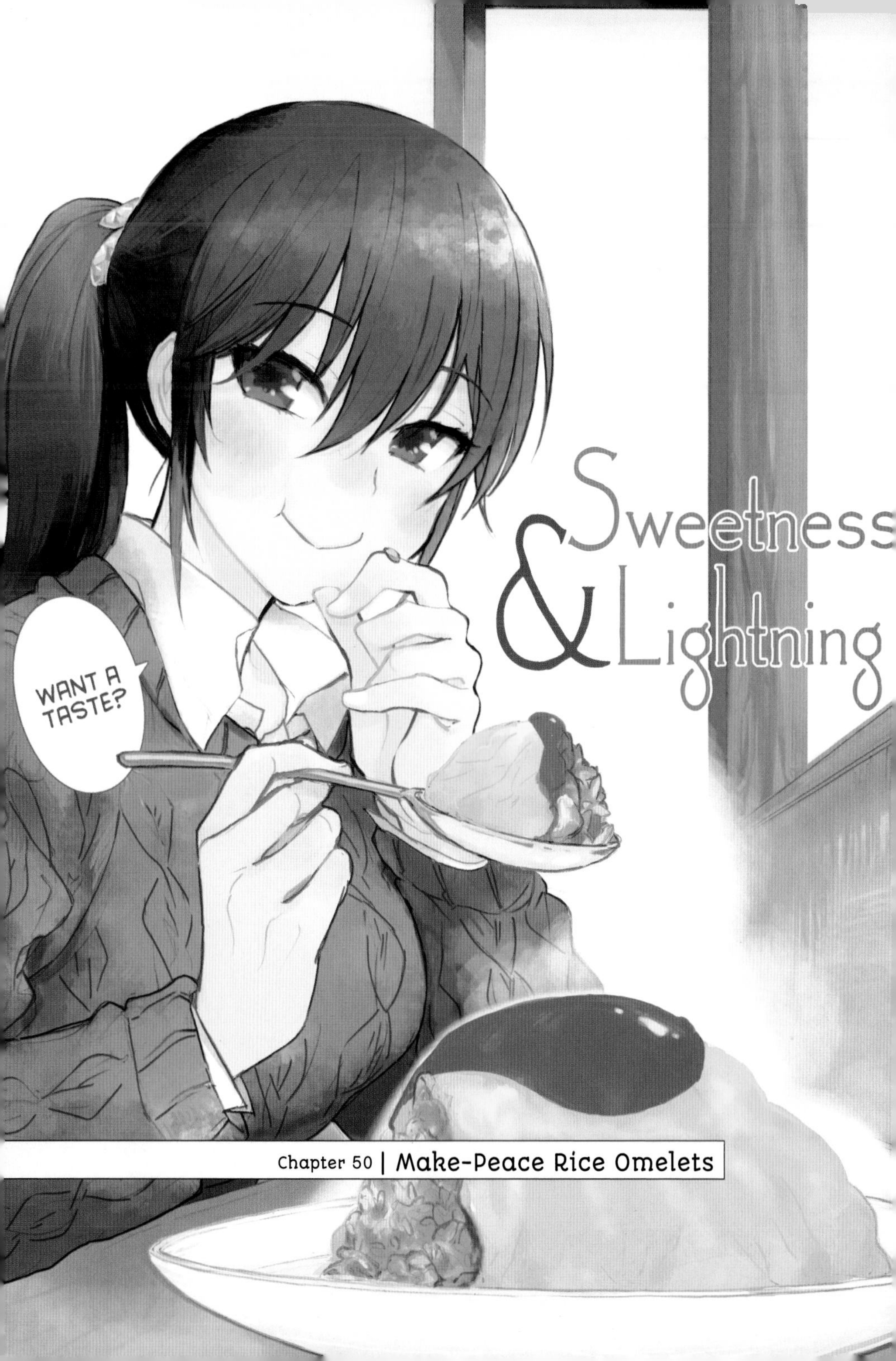
Sweetness & Lightning
WANT A TASTE?

Chapter 50 | Make-Peace Rice Omelets

sweetness &
lightning

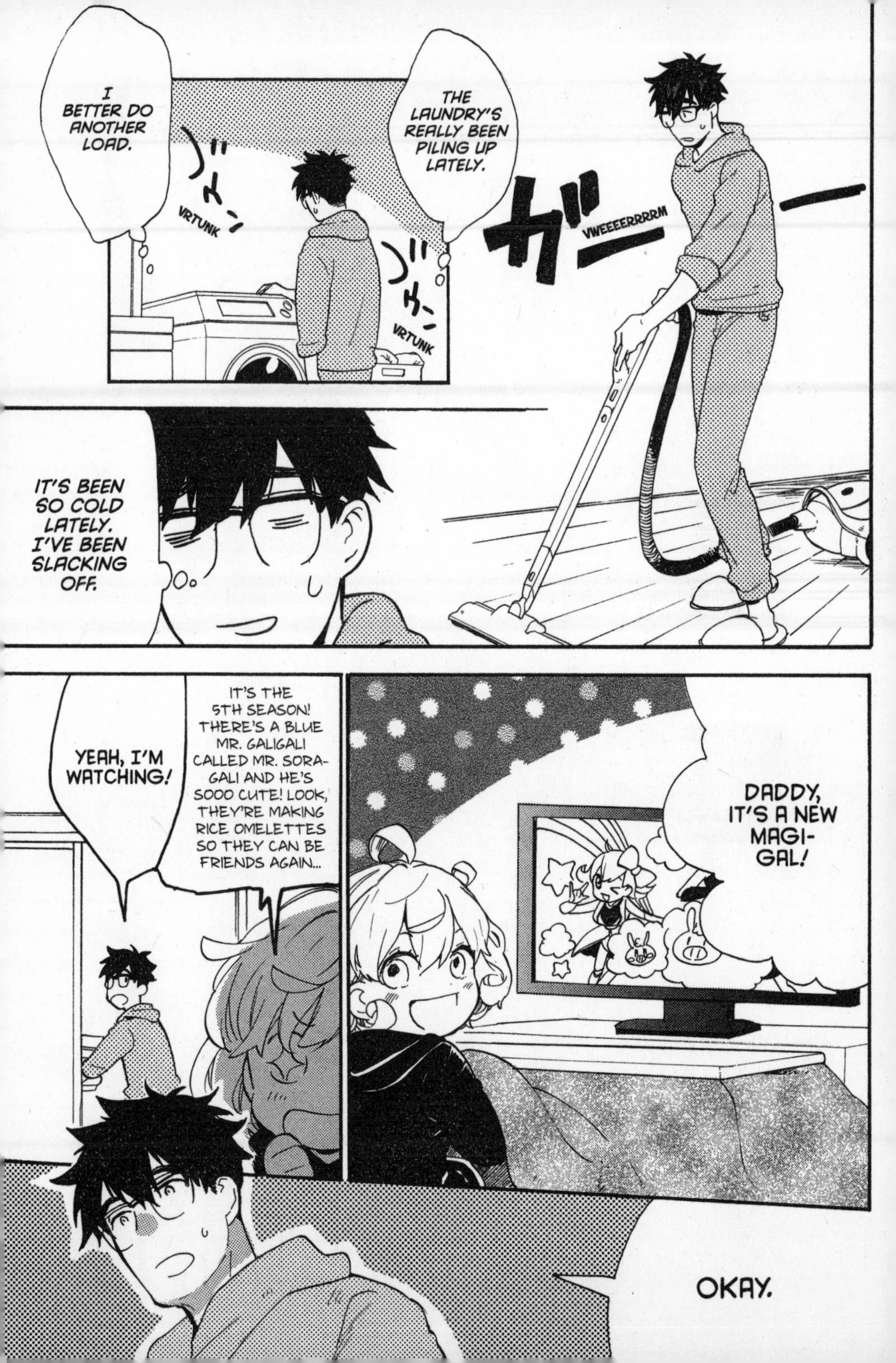
VWEEEERRRRM
THE LAUNDRY'S REALLY BEEN PILING UP LATELY.
VRTUNK
I BETTER DO ANOTHER LOAD.
VRTUNK
IT'S BEEN SO COLD LATELY. I'VE BEEN SLACKING OFF.
DADDY, IT'S A NEW MAGI-GAL!
IT'S THE 5TH SEASON! THERE'S A BLUE MR. GALIGALI CALLED MR. SORA-GALI AND HE'S SOOO CUTE! LOOK, THEY'RE MAKING RICE OMELETTES SO THEY CAN BE FRIENDS AGAIN...
YEAH, I'M WATCHING!
OKAY.

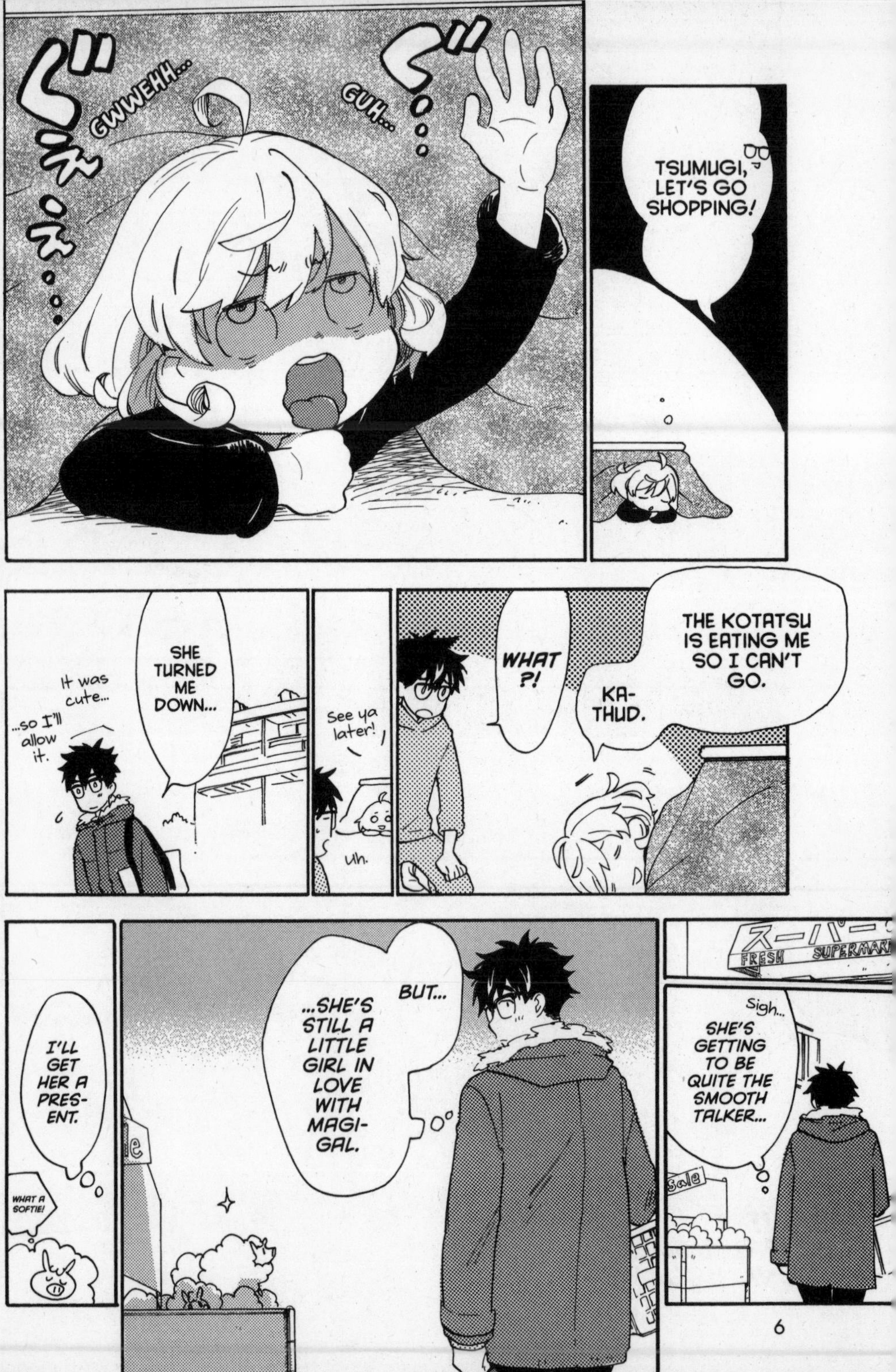
TSUMUGI, LET'S GO SHOPPING!
GUH...
GWWEHH...
THE KOTATSU IS EATING ME SO I CAN'T GO.
KA-THUD.
WHAT?!
See ya later!
uh.
SHE TURNED ME DOWN...
It was cute...
...so I'll allow it.
FRESH
Sigh...
SHE'S GETTING TO BE QUITE THE SMOOTH TALKER...
Sale
BUT...
...SHE'S STILL A LITTLE GIRL IN LOVE WITH MAGI-GAL.
I'LL GET HER A PRES-ENT.
WHAT A SOFTIE!

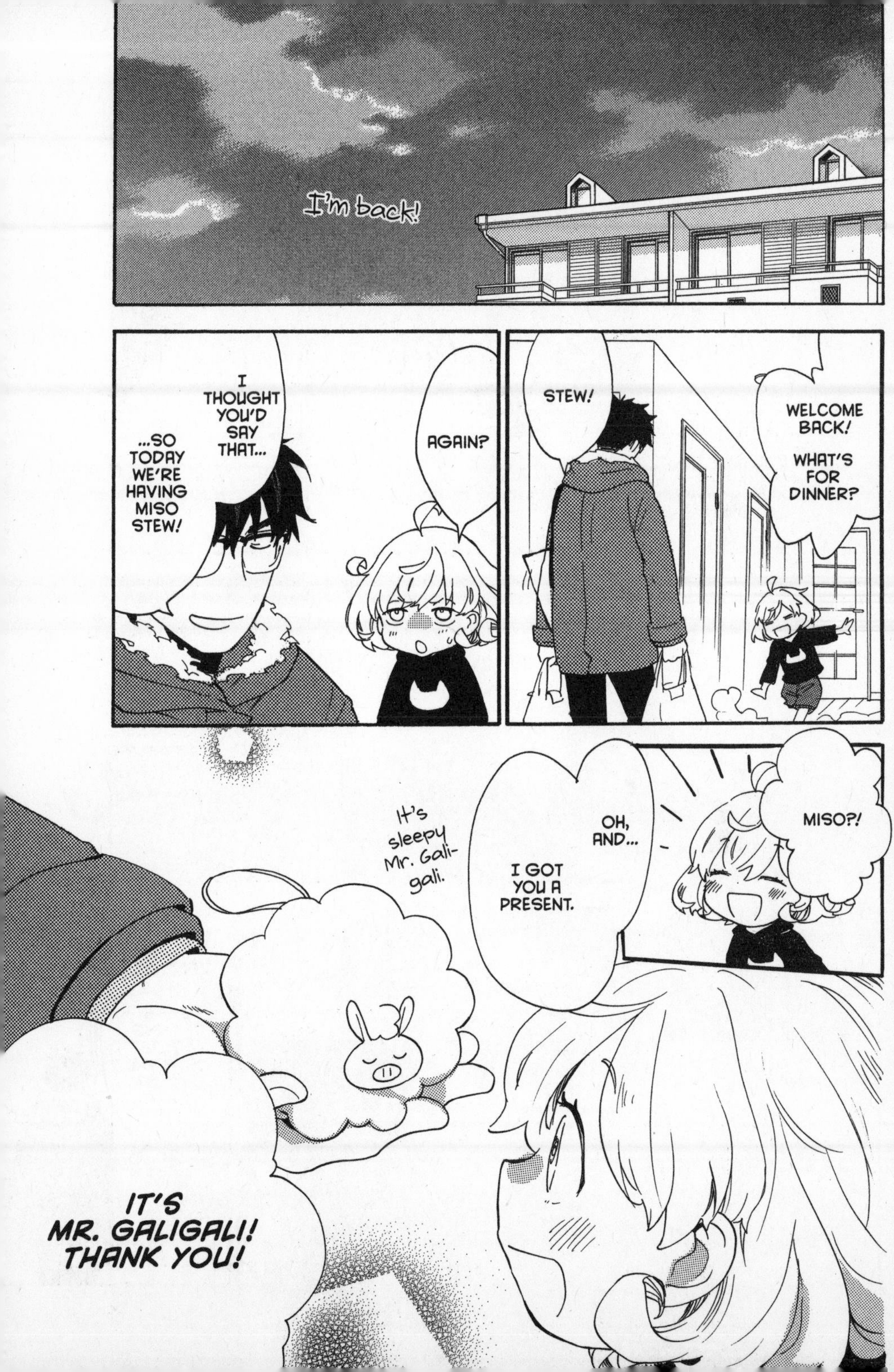
I'm back!
WELCOME BACK!
WHAT'S FOR DINNER?
STEW!
AGAIN?
I THOUGHT YOU'D SAY THAT...
...SO TODAY WE'RE HAVING MISO STEW!
MISO?!
OH, AND...
I GOT YOU A PRESENT.
It's sleepy Mr. Gali-gali.
IT'S MR. GALIGALI! THANK YOU!

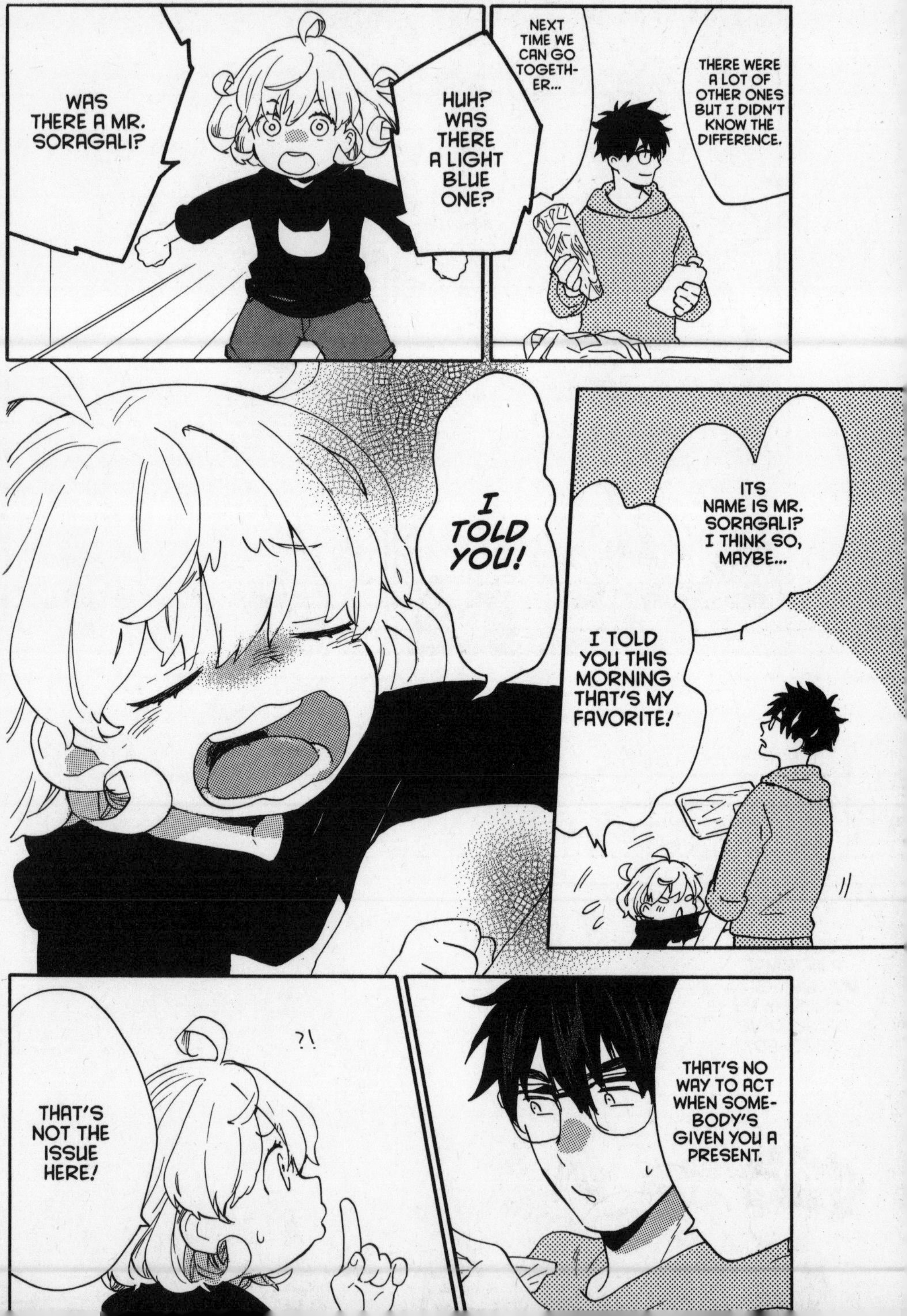
THERE WERE A LOT OF OTHER ONES BUT I DIDN'T KNOW THE DIFFERENCE.
NEXT TIME WE CAN GO TOGETH-ER...
HUH? WAS THERE A LIGHT BLUE ONE?
WAS THERE A MR. SORAGALI?
ITS NAME IS MR. SORAGALI? I THINK SO, MAYBE...
I TOLD YOU THIS MORNING THAT'S MY FAVORITE!
I TOLD YOU!
THAT'S NO WAY TO ACT WHEN SOME-BODY'S GIVEN YOU A PRESENT.
?!
THAT'S NOT THE ISSUE HERE!

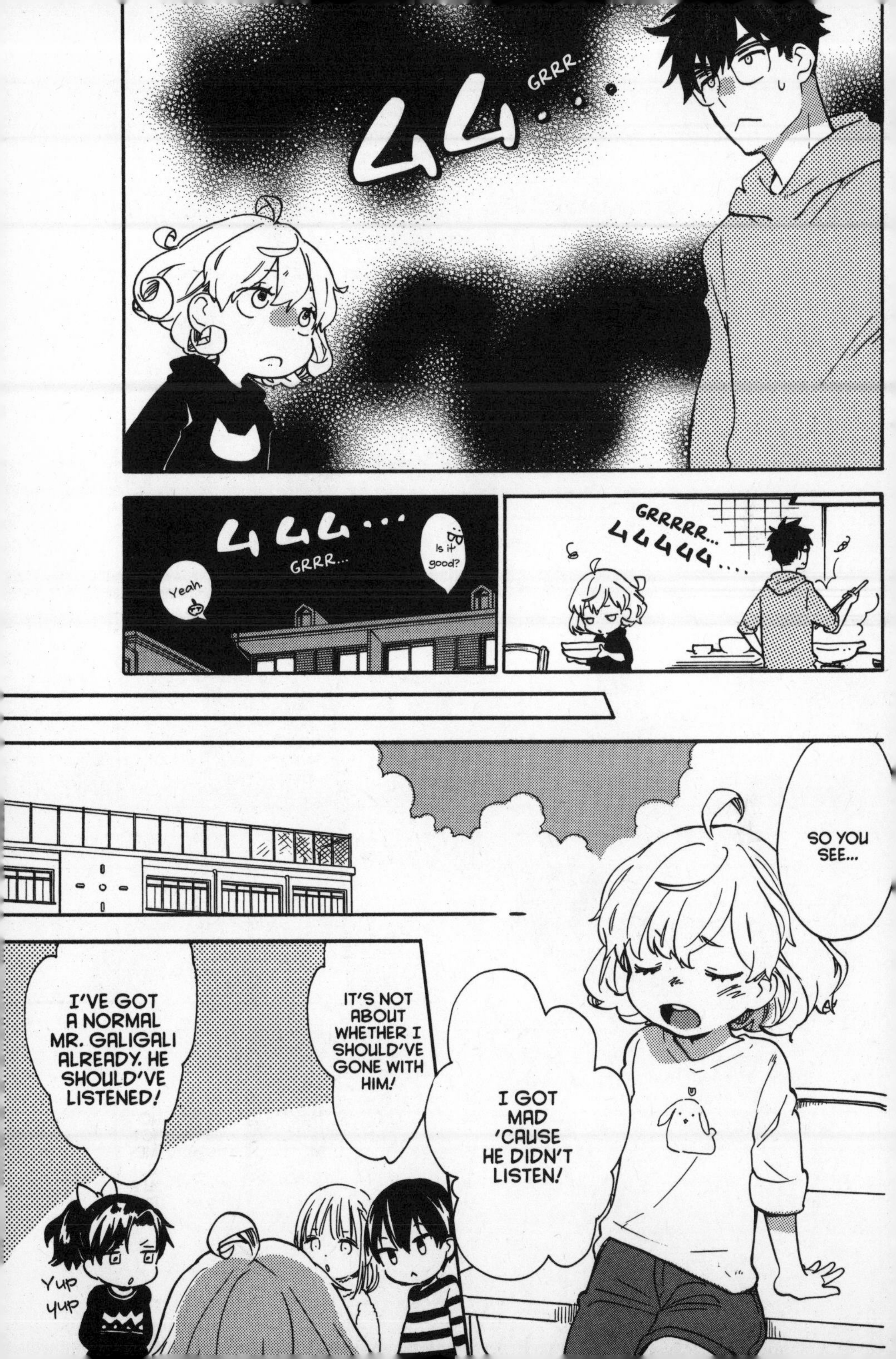
ムム...
GRRR...
GRRRRR...
ムムムム....
Is it good?
ムムム...
GRRR...
Yeah.
SO YOU SEE...
I GOT MAD 'CAUSE HE DIDN'T LISTEN!
IT'S NOT ABOUT WHETHER I SHOULD'VE GONE WITH HIM!
I'VE GOT A NORMAL MR. GALIGALI ALREADY. HE SHOULD'VE LISTENED!
Yup yup

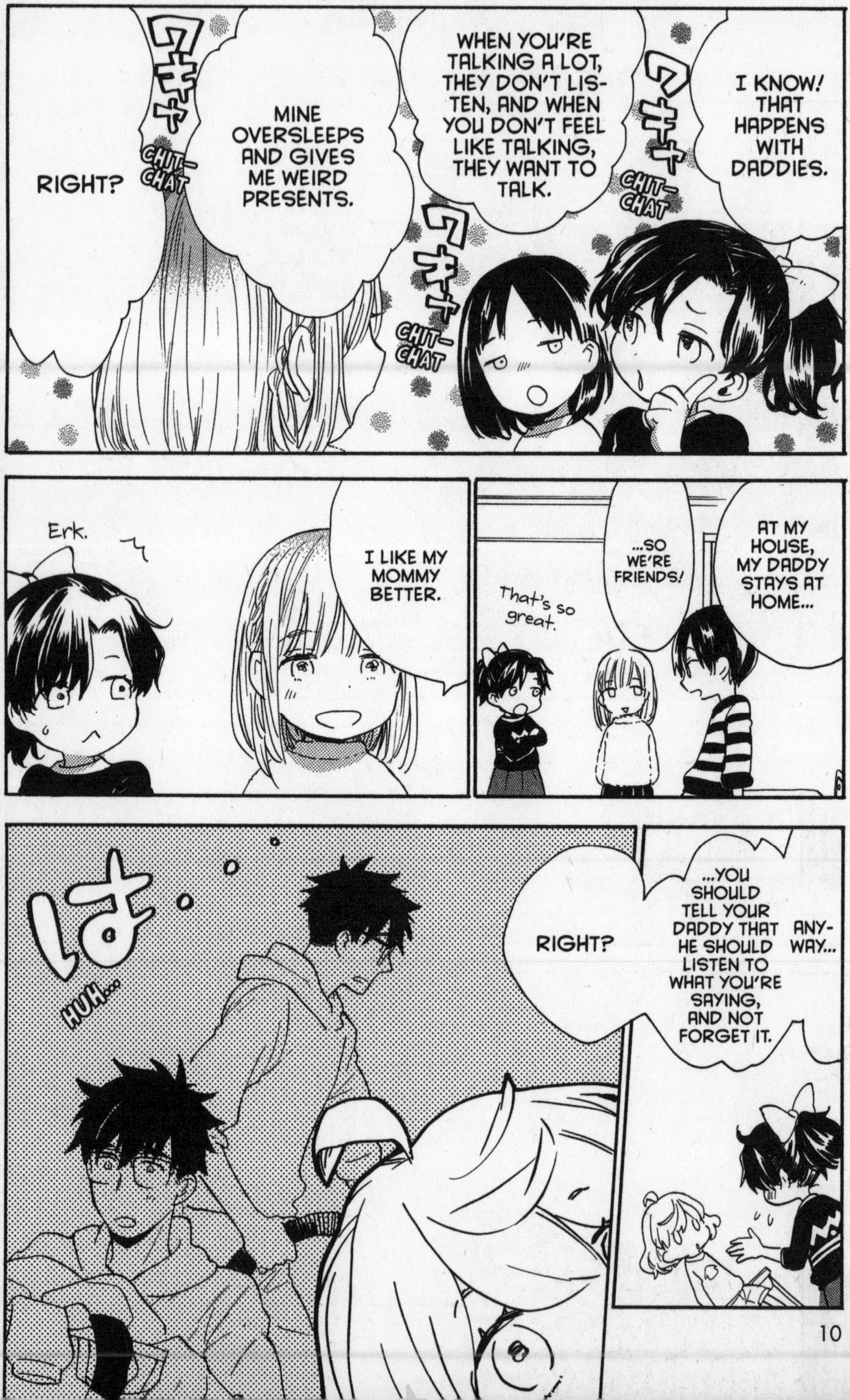
I KNOW! THAT HAPPENS WITH DADDIES.
ワキャ
CHIT-CHAT
WHEN YOU'RE TALKING A LOT, THEY DON'T LIS-TEN, AND WHEN YOU DON'T FEEL LIKE TALKING, THEY WANT TO TALK.
ワキャ
CHIT-CHAT
MINE OVERSLEEPS AND GIVES ME WEIRD PRESENTS.
ワキャ
CHIT-CHAT
RIGHT?
AT MY HOUSE, MY DADDY STAYS AT HOME...
...SO WE'RE FRIENDS!
That's so great.
I LIKE MY MOMMY BETTER.
Erk.
ANY-WAY...
...YOU SHOULD TELL YOUR DADDY THAT HE SHOULD LISTEN TO WHAT YOU'RE SAYING, AND NOT FORGET IT.
RIGHT?
は
HUH...

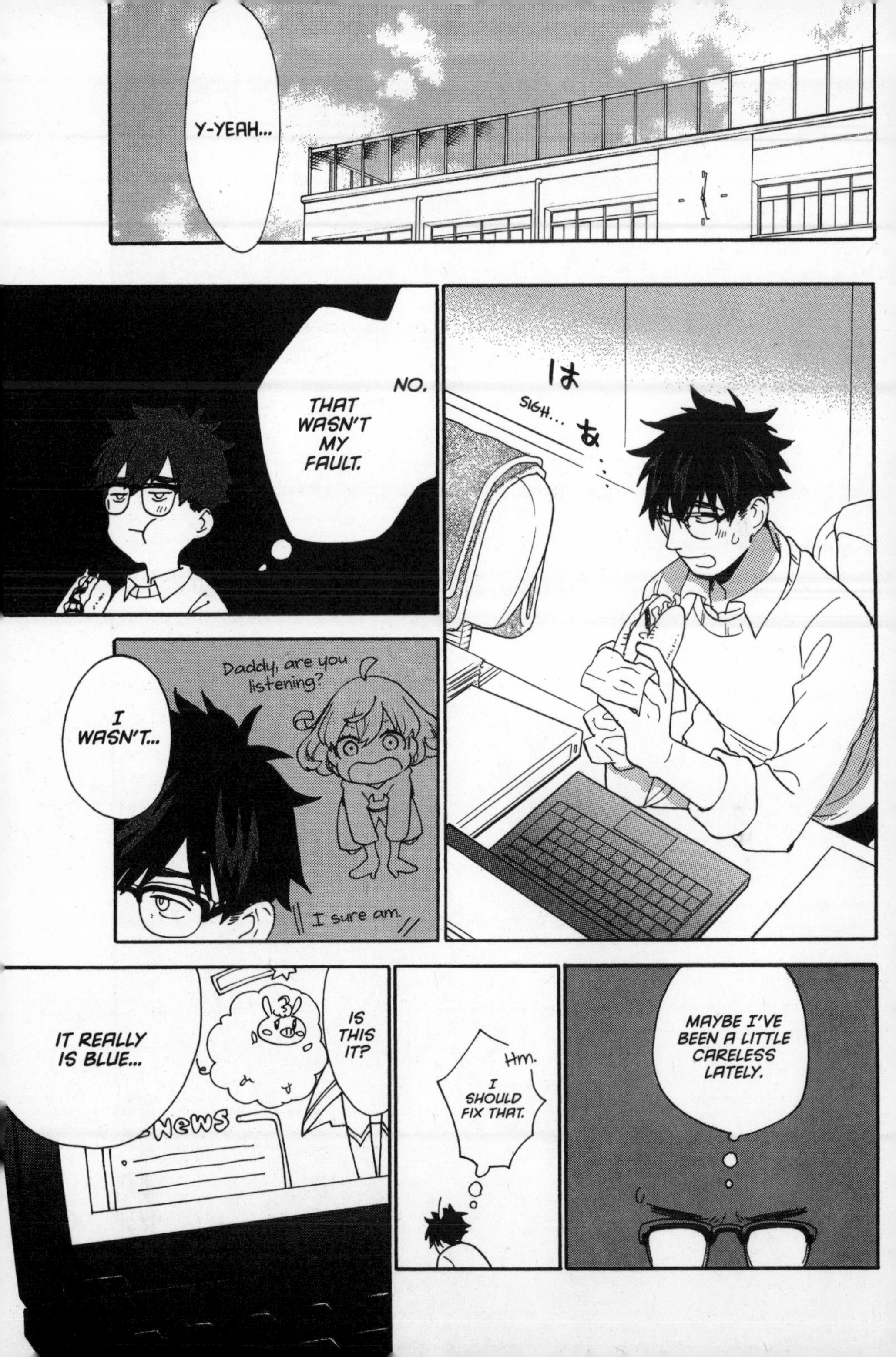
Y-YEAH...
は あ
SIGH...
NO. THAT WASN'T MY FAULT.
Daddy, are you listening?
I WASN'T...
I sure am.
MAYBE I'VE BEEN A LITTLE CARELESS LATELY.
Hm. I SHOULD FIX THAT.
IS THIS IT?
IT REALLY IS BLUE...
News

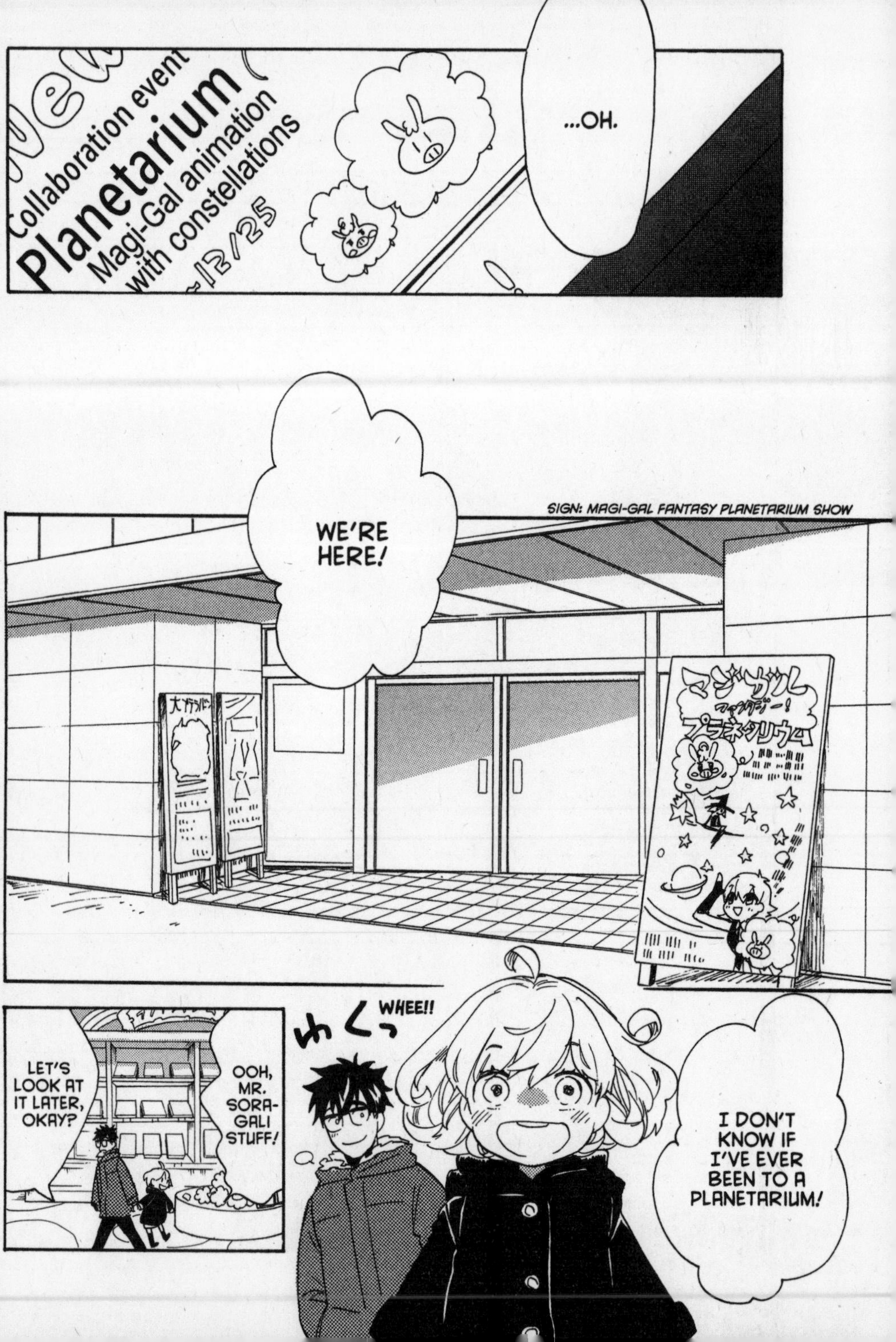
Collaboration event
Planetarium
Magi-Gal animation with constellations
~12/25
...OH.
SIGN: MAGI-GAL FANTASY PLANETARIUM SHOW
WE'RE HERE!
I DON'T KNOW IF I'VE EVER BEEN TO A PLANETARIUM!
わくっ
WHEE!!
OOH, MR. SORA-GALI STUFF!
LET'S LOOK AT IT LATER, OKAY?

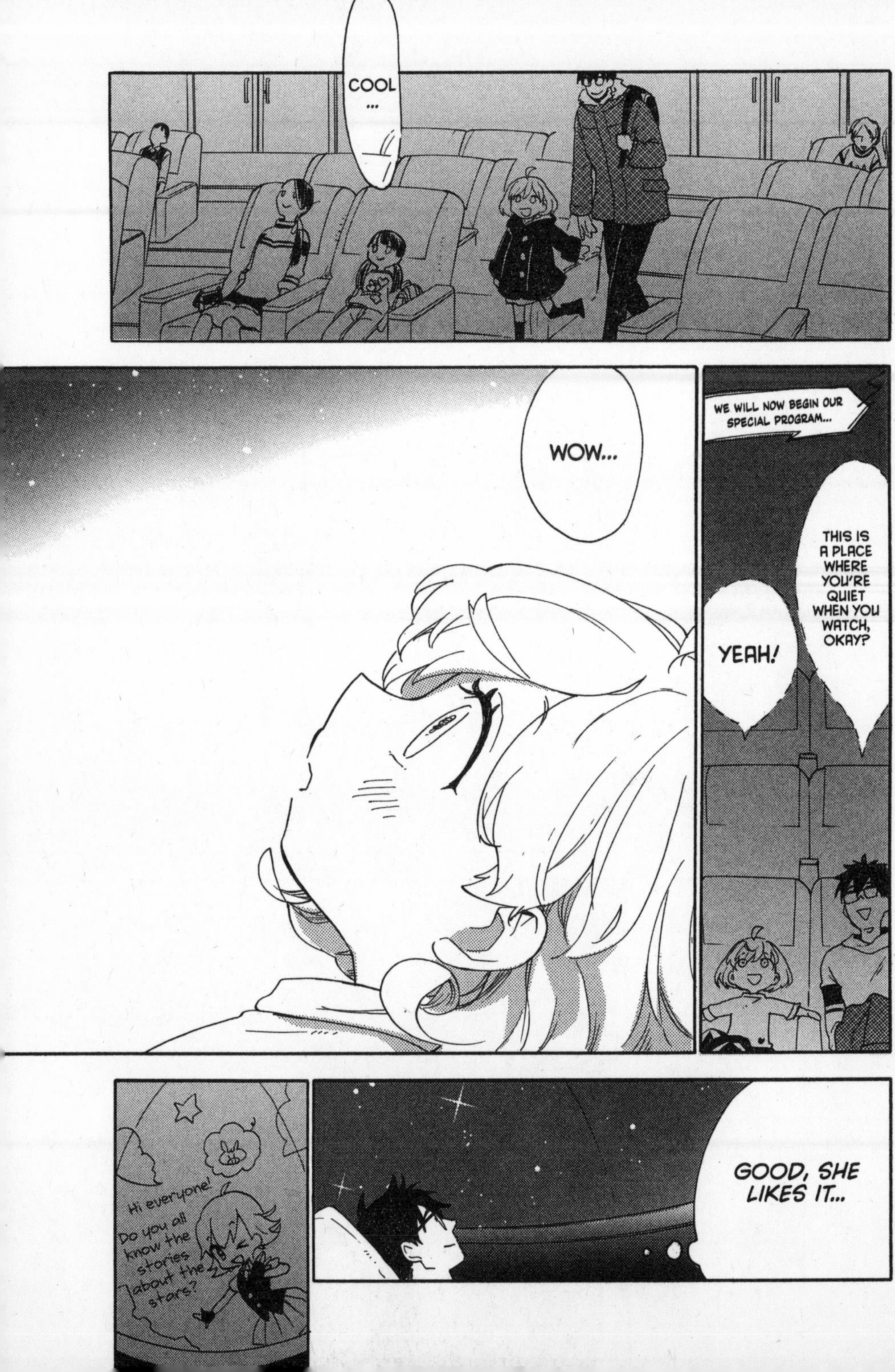
COOL ...
WE WILL NOW BEGIN OUR SPECIAL PROGRAM...
THIS IS A PLACE WHERE YOU'RE QUIET WHEN YOU WATCH, OKAY?
YEAH!
WOW...
GOOD, SHE LIKES IT...
Hi everyone! Do you all know the stories about the stars?

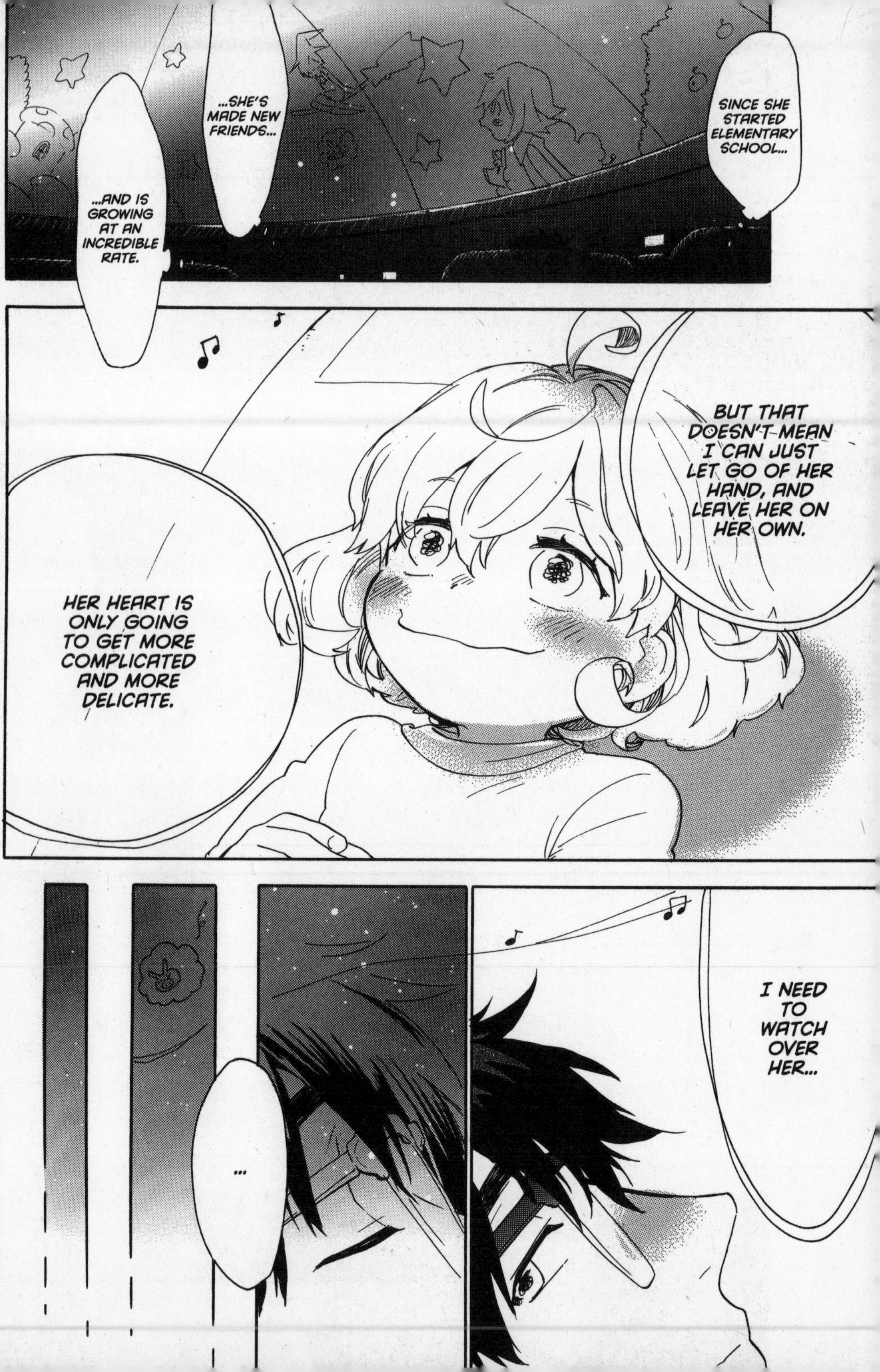
SINCE SHE STARTED ELEMENTARY SCHOOL...
...SHE'S MADE NEW FRIENDS...
...AND IS GROWING AT AN INCREDIBLE RATE.
BUT THAT DOESN'T MEAN I CAN JUST LET GO OF HER HAND, AND LEAVE HER ON HER OWN.
HER HEART IS ONLY GOING TO GET MORE COMPLICATED AND MORE DELICATE.
I NEED TO WATCH OVER HER...
...

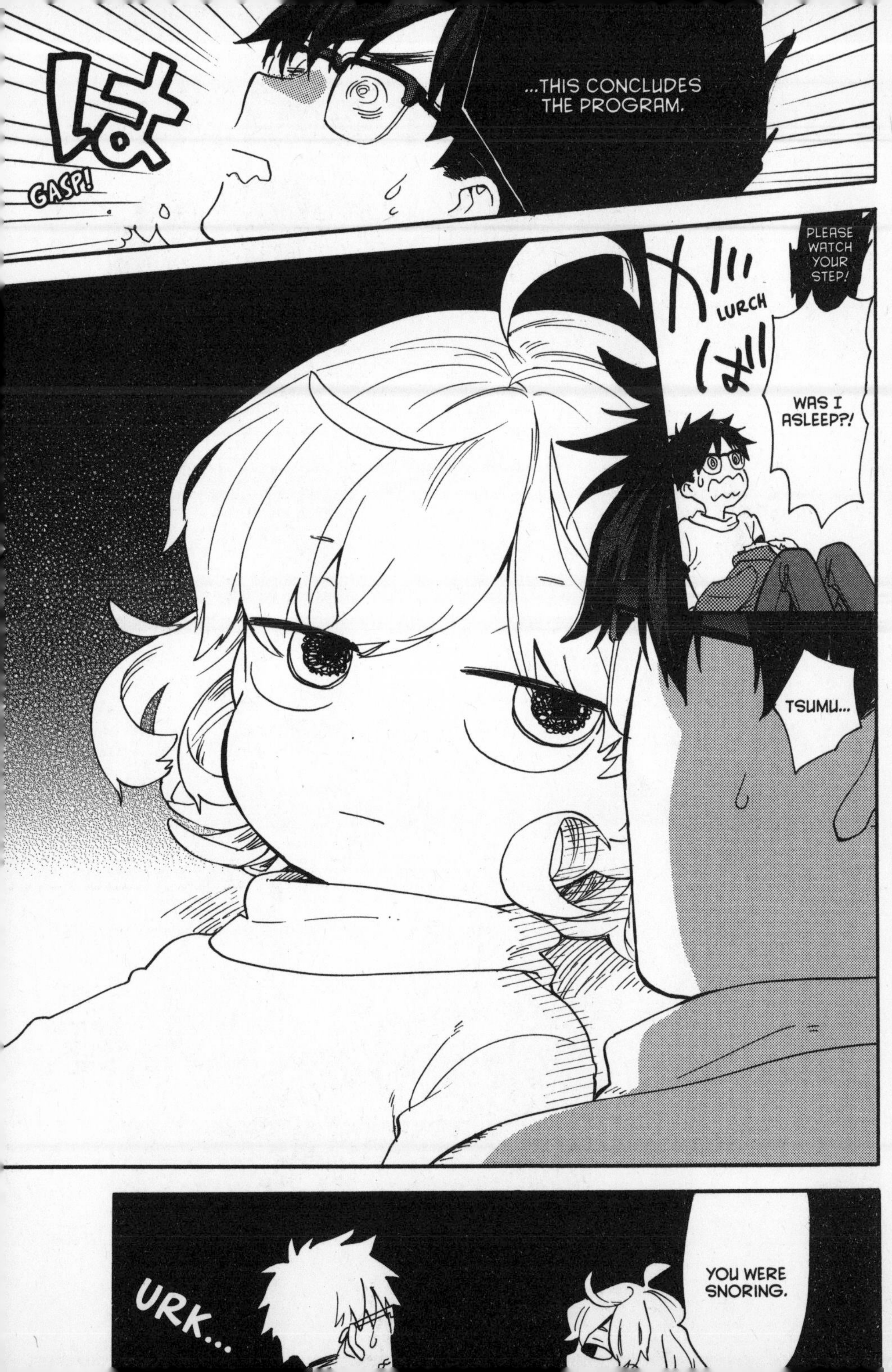
...THIS CONCLUDES THE PROGRAM.
はっ
GASP!
PLEASE WATCH YOUR STEP!
LURCH
WAS I ASLEEP?!
TSUMU...
YOU WERE SNORING.
URK...

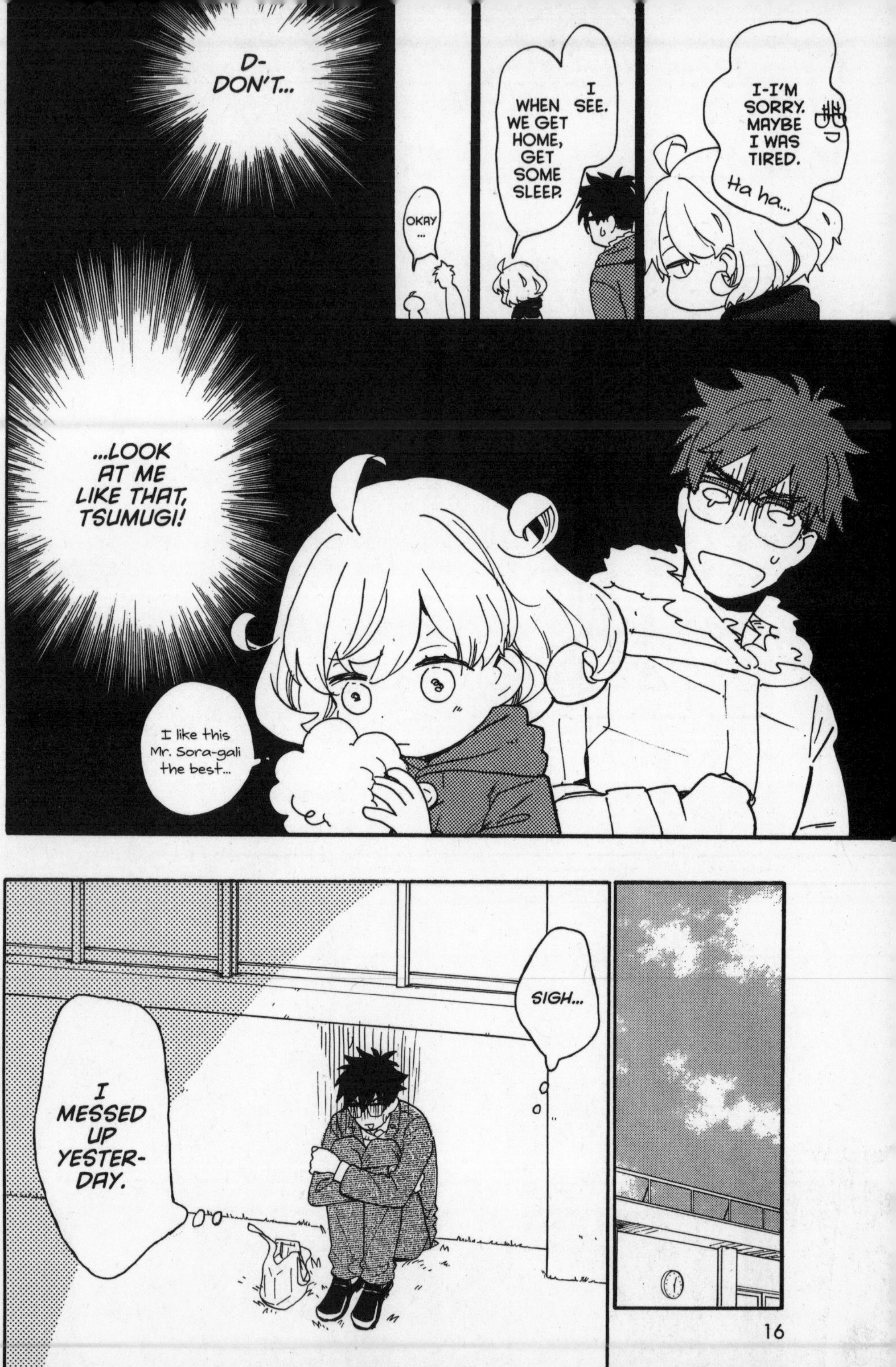
I-I'M SORRY. MAYBE I WAS TIRED.
Ha ha...
I SEE.
WHEN WE GET HOME, GET SOME SLEEP.
OKAY...
D- DON'T...
...LOOK AT ME LIKE THAT, TSUMUGI!
I like this Mr. Sora-gali the best...
SIGH...
I MESSED UP YESTER-DAY.

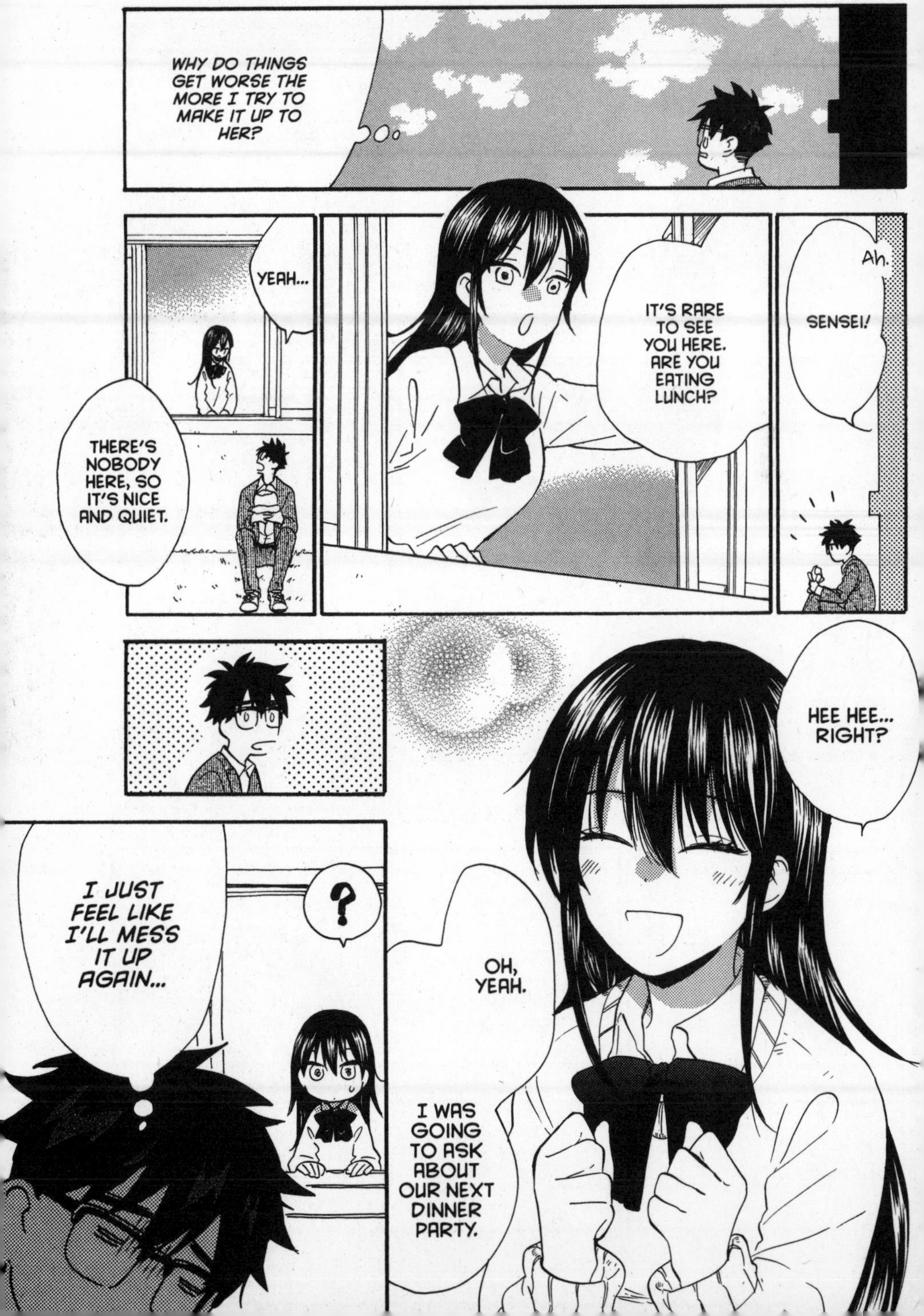
WHY DO THINGS GET WORSE THE MORE I TRY TO MAKE IT UP TO HER?
Ah.
SENSEI!
IT'S RARE TO SEE YOU HERE. ARE YOU EATING LUNCH?
YEAH...
THERE'S NOBODY HERE, SO IT'S NICE AND QUIET.
HEE HEE... RIGHT?
OH, YEAH.
I WAS GOING TO ASK ABOUT OUR NEXT DINNER PARTY.
?
I JUST FEEL LIKE I'LL MESS IT UP AGAIN...

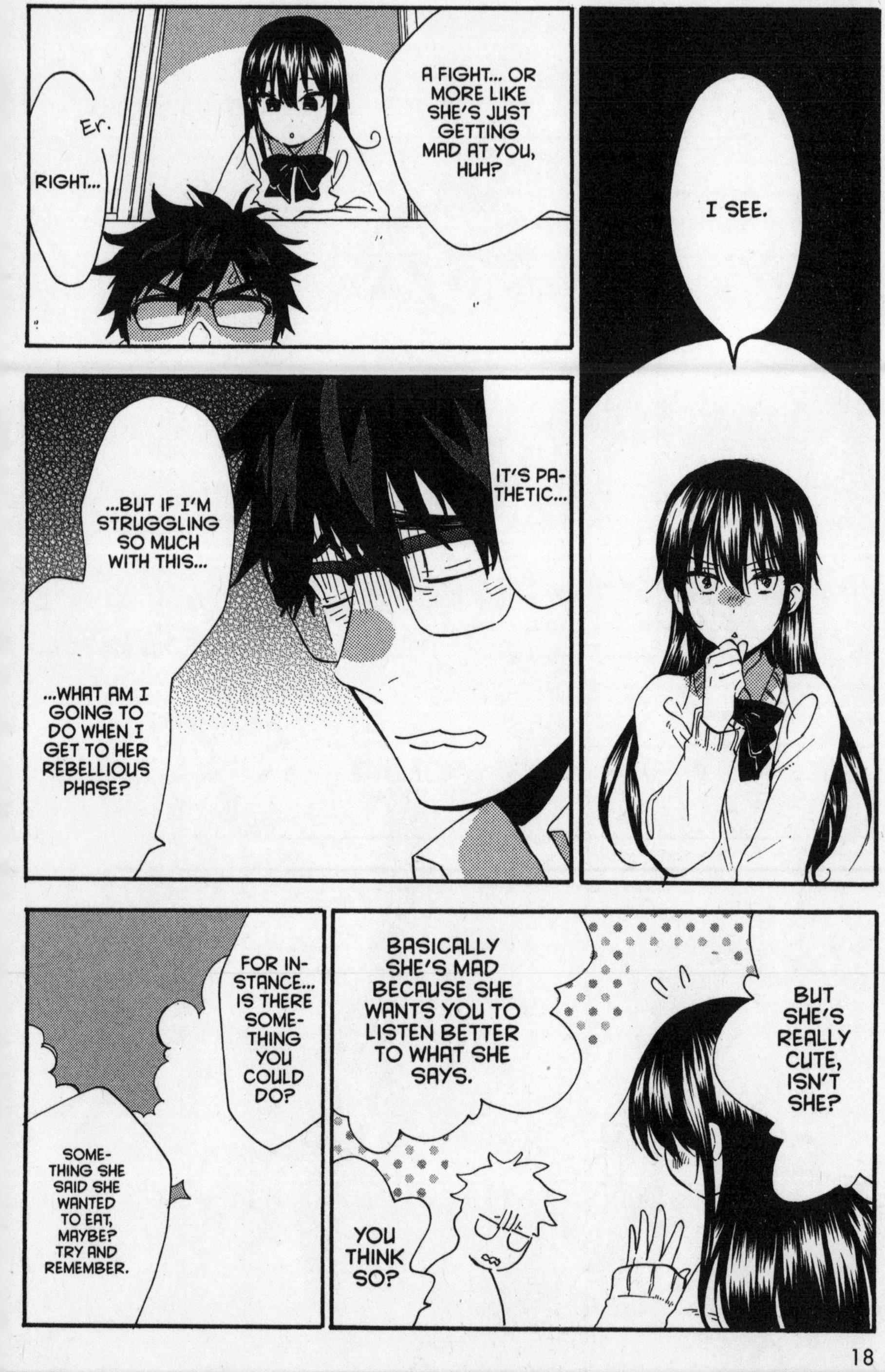
I SEE.
A FIGHT... OR MORE LIKE SHE'S JUST GETTING MAD AT YOU, HUH?
Er.
RIGHT...
IT'S PA-THETIC...
...BUT IF I'M STRUGGLING SO MUCH WITH THIS...
...WHAT AM I GOING TO DO WHEN I GET TO HER REBELLIOUS PHASE?
BASICALLY SHE'S MAD BECAUSE SHE WANTS YOU TO LISTEN BETTER TO WHAT SHE SAYS.
BUT SHE'S REALLY CUTE, ISN'T SHE?
YOU THINK SO?
FOR IN-STANCE... IS THERE SOME-THING YOU COULD DO?
SOME-THING SHE SAID SHE WANTED TO EAT, MAYBE? TRY AND REMEMBER.

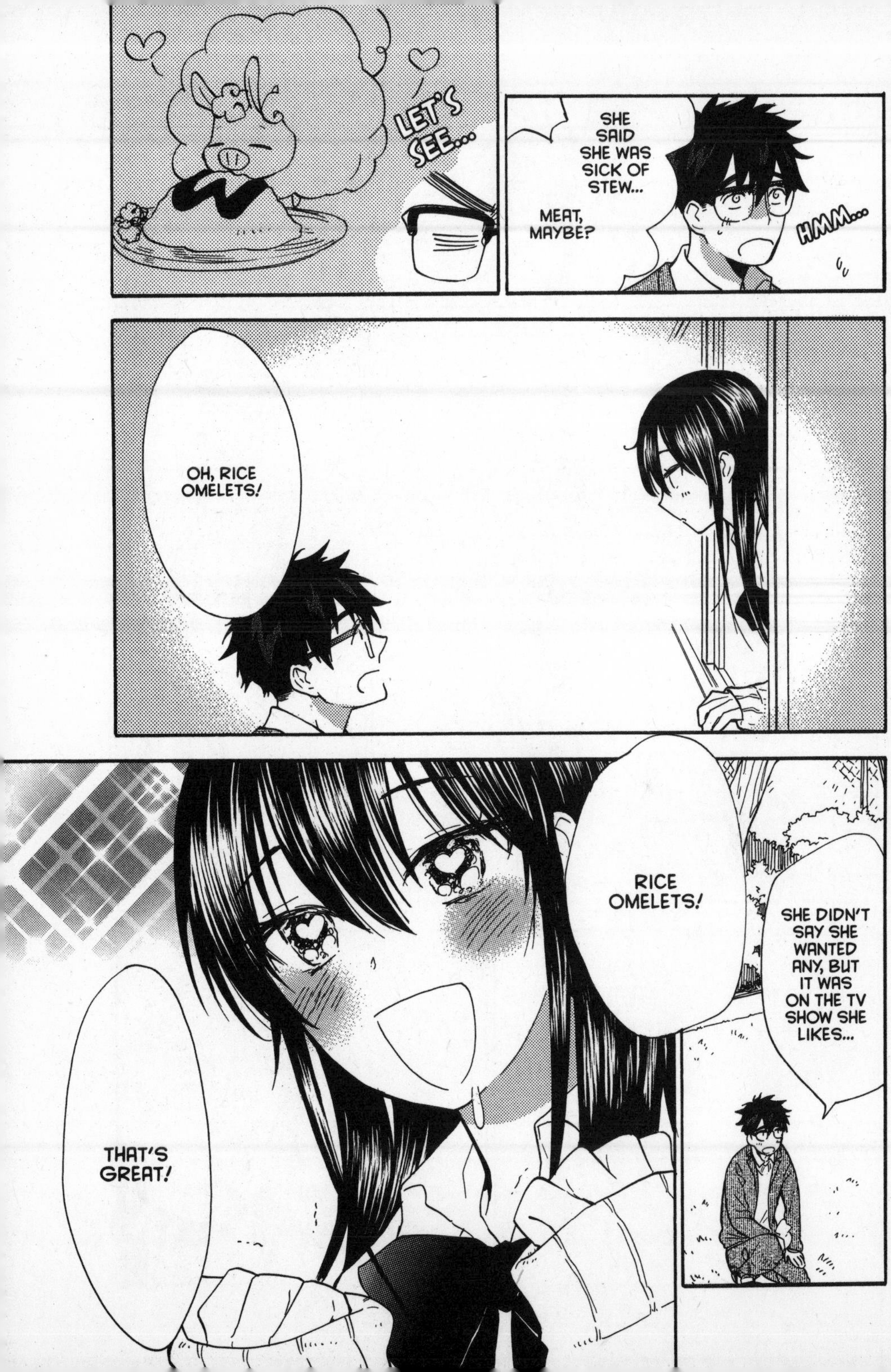
SHE SAID SHE WAS SICK OF STEW...
MEAT, MAYBE?
HMM...
LET'S SEE...
OH, RICE OMELETS!
SHE DIDN'T SAY SHE WANTED ANY, BUT IT WAS ON THE TV SHOW SHE LIKES...
RICE OMELETS!
THAT'S GREAT!

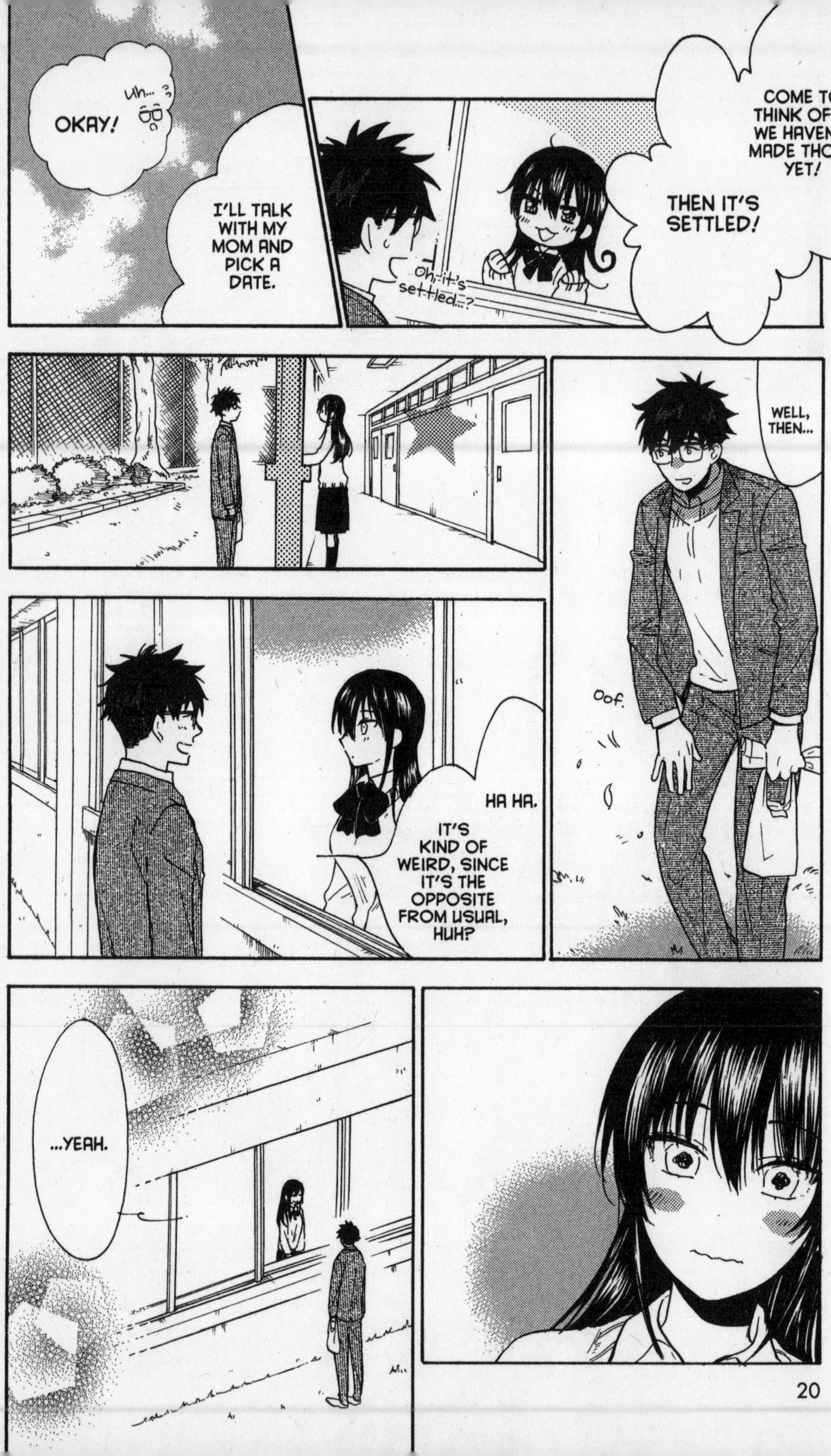
COME TO THINK OF IT, WE HAVEN'T MADE THOSE YET!
THEN IT'S SETTLED!
Oh, it's settled...?
I'LL TALK WITH MY MOM AND PICK A DATE.
OKAY!
Uh...
WELL, THEN...
Oof.
HA HA.
IT'S KIND OF WEIRD, SINCE IT'S THE OPPOSITE FROM USUAL, HUH?
...YEAH.

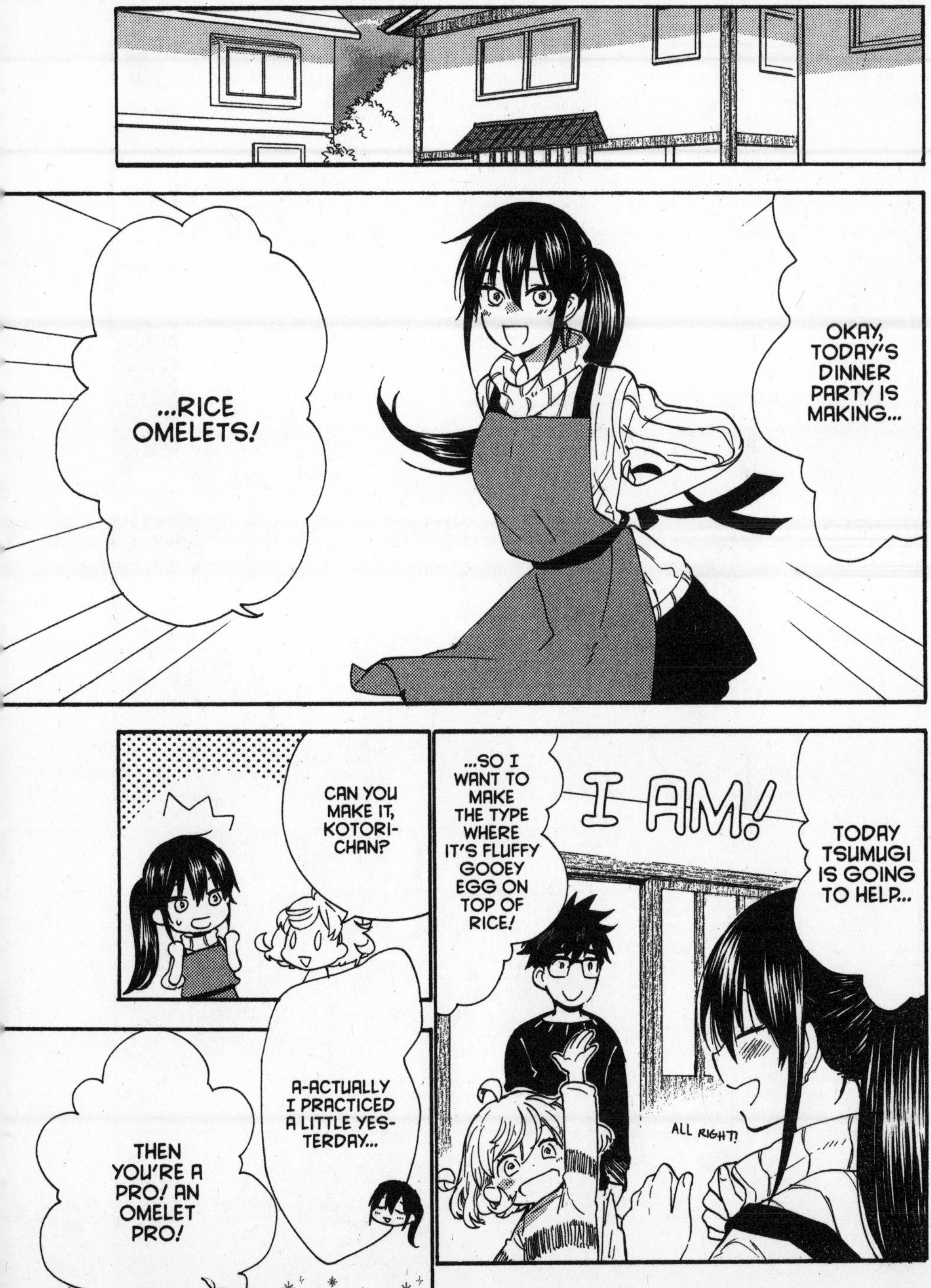
OKAY, TODAY'S DINNER PARTY IS MAKING...
...RICE OMELETS!
TODAY TSUMUGI IS GOING TO HELP...
I AM!
ALL RIGHT!
...SO I WANT TO MAKE THE TYPE WHERE IT'S FLUFFY GOOEY EGG ON TOP OF RICE!
CAN YOU MAKE IT, KOTORI-CHAN?
A-ACTUALLY I PRACTICED A LITTLE YES-TERDAY...
THEN YOU'RE A PRO! AN OMELET PRO!

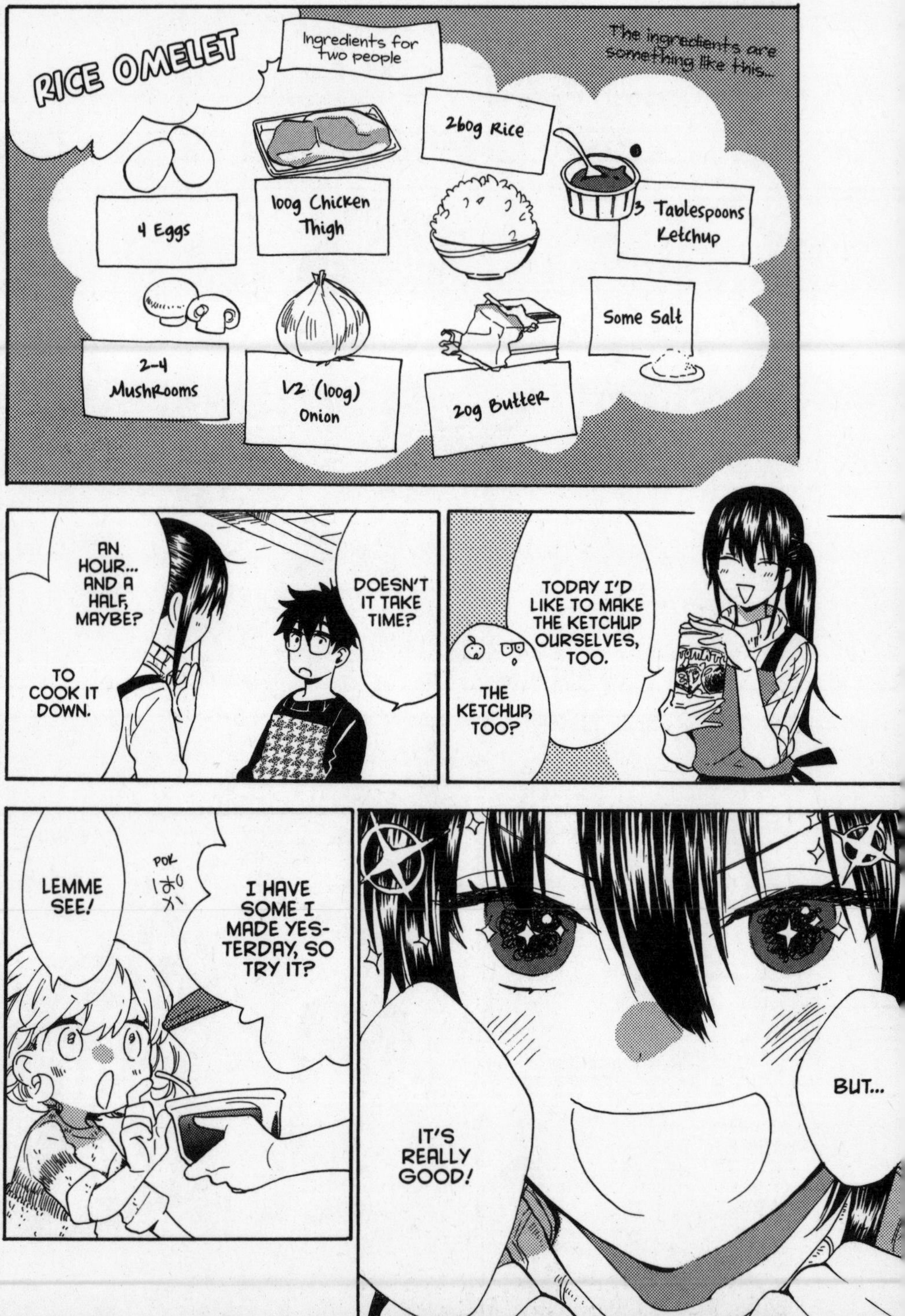

The ingredients are something like this...
Ingredients for two people
RICE OMELET
260g Rice
3 Tablespoons Ketchup
100g Chicken Thigh
4 Eggs
Some Salt
20g Butter
1/2 (100g) Onion
2-4 Mushrooms
TODAY I'D LIKE TO MAKE THE KETCHUP OURSELVES, TOO.
THE KETCHUP, TOO?
DOESN'T IT TAKE TIME?
AN HOUR... AND A HALF, MAYBE?
TO COOK IT DOWN.
BUT...
IT'S REALLY GOOD!
I HAVE SOME I MADE YES-TERDAY, SO TRY IT?
POK
ぱか
LEMME SEE!

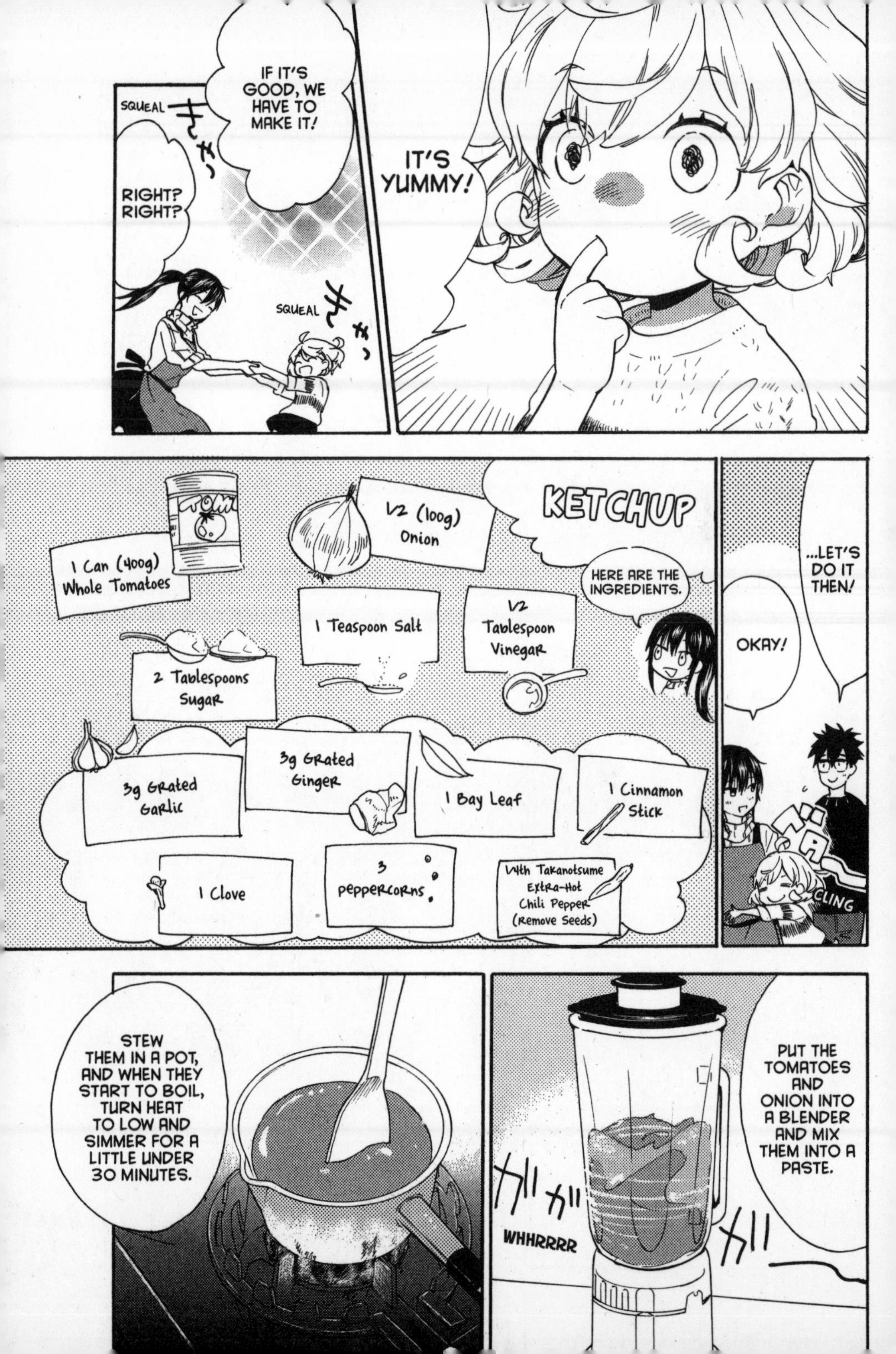
IT'S YUMMY!
IF IT'S GOOD, WE HAVE TO MAKE IT!
SQUEAL
RIGHT? RIGHT?
SQUEAL
...LET'S DO IT THEN!
OKAY!
CLING
KETCHUP
HERE ARE THE INGREDIENTS.
1/2 (100g) Onion
1 Can (400g) Whole Tomatoes
1/2 Tablespoon Vinegar
1 Teaspoon Salt
2 Tablespoons Sugar
1 Cinnamon Stick
1 Bay Leaf
3g Grated Ginger
3g Grated Garlic
1/4th Takanotsume Extra-Hot Chili Pepper (Remove Seeds)
3 peppercorns
1 Clove
PUT THE TOMATOES AND ONION INTO A BLENDER AND MIX THEM INTO A PASTE.
WHHRRRR
STEW THEM IN A POT, AND WHEN THEY START TO BOIL, TURN HEAT TO LOW AND SIMMER FOR A LITTLE UNDER 30 MINUTES.

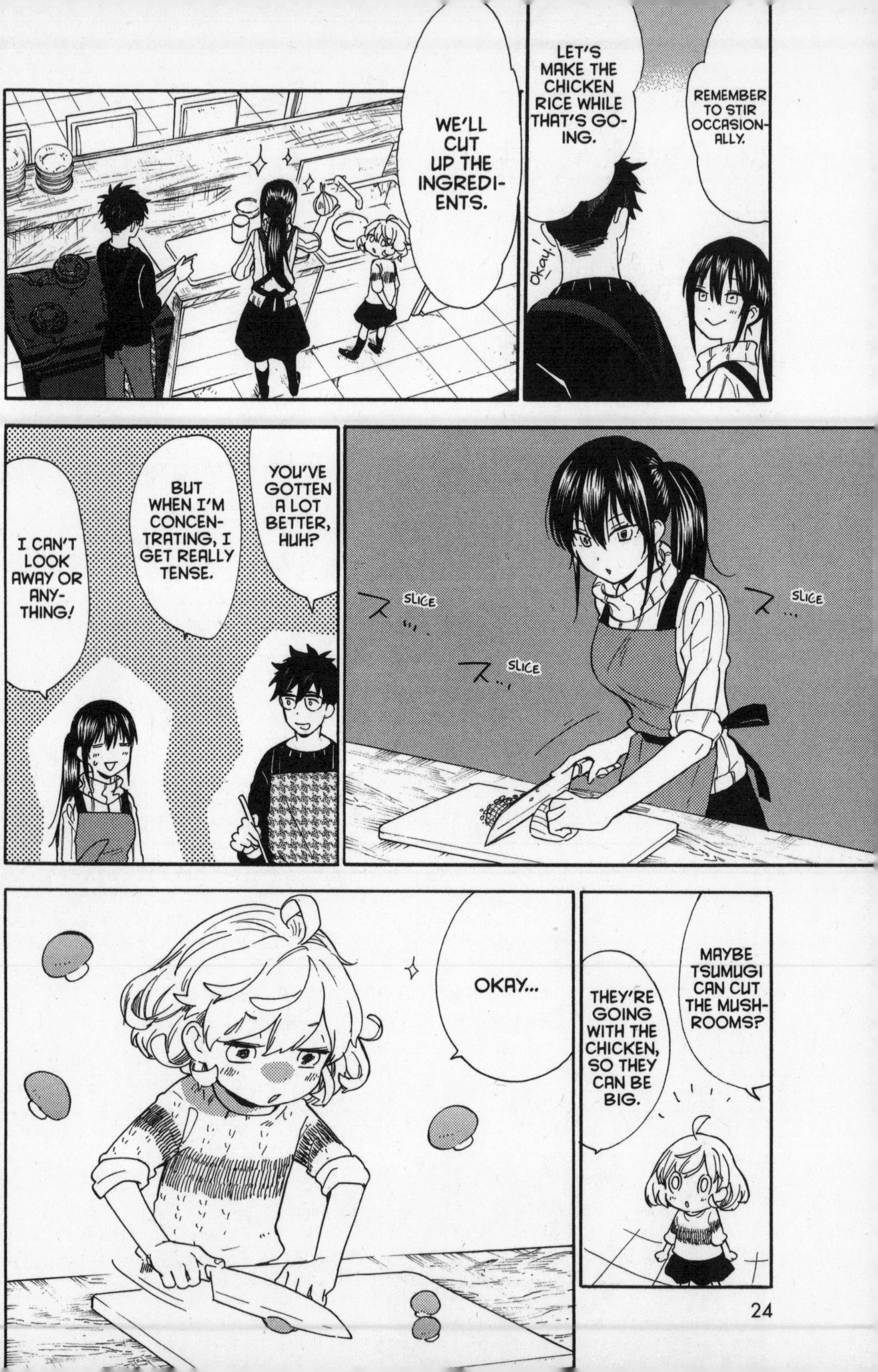
REMEMBER TO STIR OCCASION-ALLY.
LET'S MAKE THE CHICKEN RICE WHILE THAT'S GO-ING.
Okay.
WE'LL CUT UP THE INGREDI-ENTS.
SLICE
SLICE
SLICE
YOU'VE GOTTEN A LOT BETTER, HUH?
BUT WHEN I'M CONCEN-TRATING, I GET REALLY TENSE.
I CAN'T LOOK AWAY OR ANY-THING!
MAYBE TSUMUGI CAN CUT THE MUSH-ROOMS?
THEY'RE GOING WITH THE CHICKEN, SO THEY CAN BE BIG.
OKAY...

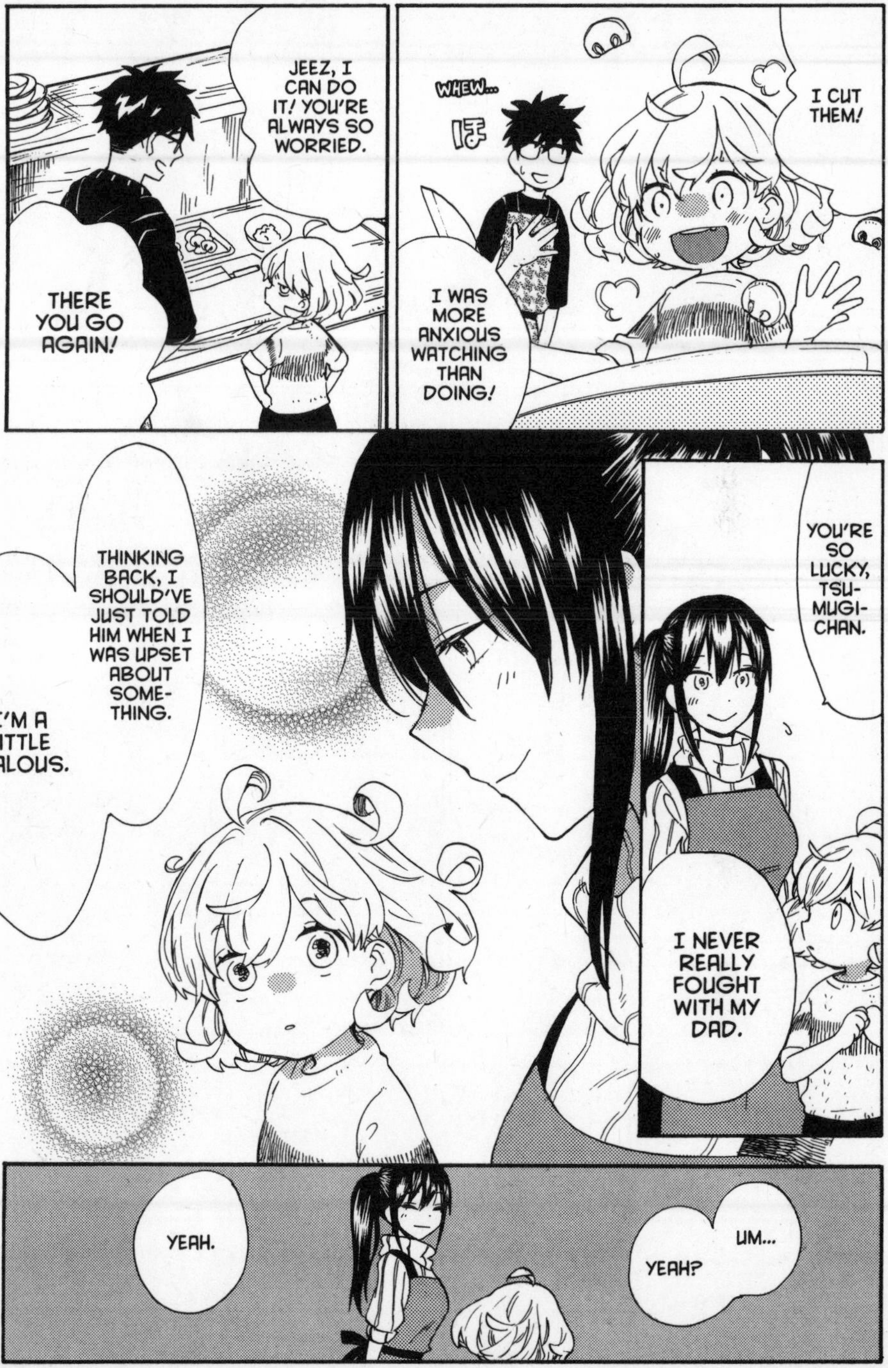
I CUT THEM!
WHEW...
ほ
I WAS MORE ANXIOUS WATCHING THAN DOING!
JEEZ, I CAN DO IT! YOU'RE ALWAYS SO WORRIED.
THERE YOU GO AGAIN!
YOU'RE SO LUCKY, TSUMUGI-CHAN.
I NEVER REALLY FOUGHT WITH MY DAD.
THINKING BACK, I SHOULD'VE JUST TOLD HIM WHEN I WAS UPSET ABOUT SOMETHING.
I'M A LITTLE JEALOUS.
UM...
YEAH?
YEAH.

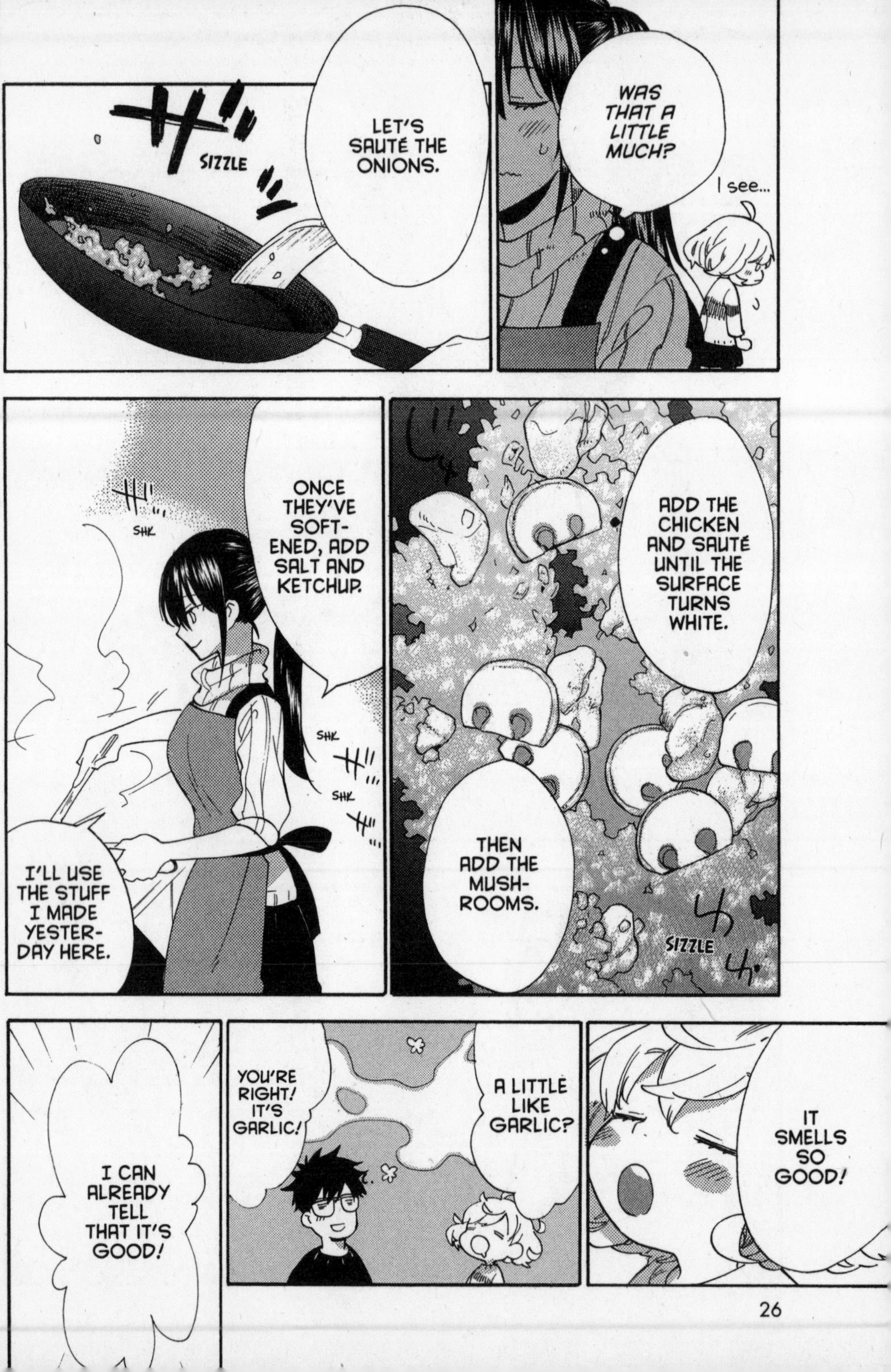
WAS THAT A LITTLE MUCH?
I see...
LET'S SAUTÉ THE ONIONS.
SIZZLE
ADD THE CHICKEN AND SAUTÉ UNTIL THE SURFACE TURNS WHITE.
THEN ADD THE MUSH-ROOMS.
SIZZLE
ONCE THEY'VE SOFT-ENED, ADD SALT AND KETCHUP.
SHK
SHK
SHK
I'LL USE THE STUFF I MADE YESTER-DAY HERE.
IT SMELLS SO GOOD!
A LITTLE LIKE GARLIC?
YOU'RE RIGHT! IT'S GARLIC!
I CAN ALREADY TELL THAT IT'S GOOD!

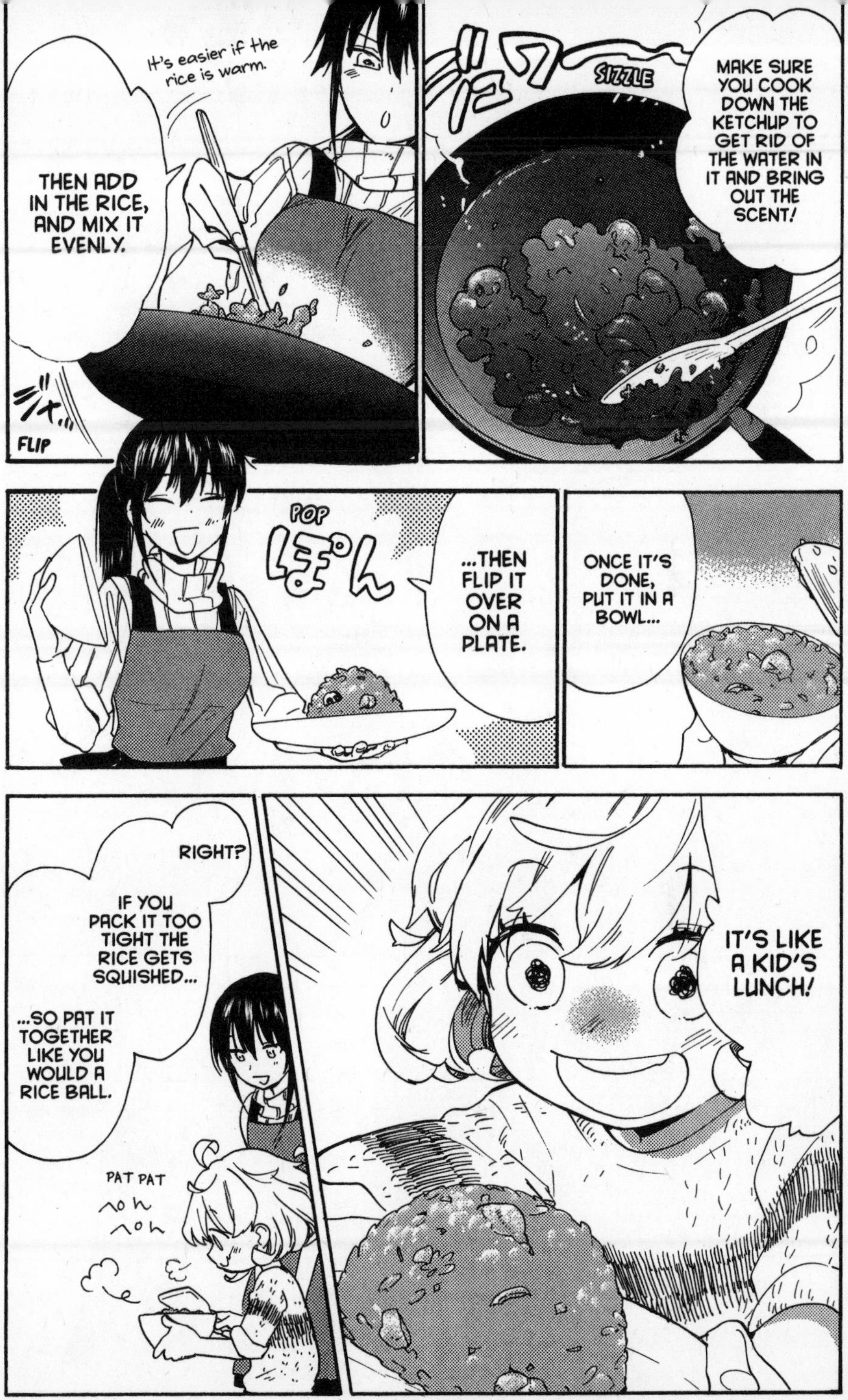
SIZZLE
MAKE SURE YOU COOK DOWN THE KETCHUP TO GET RID OF THE WATER IN IT AND BRING OUT THE SCENT!
THEN ADD IN THE RICE, AND MIX IT EVENLY.
It's easier if the rice is warm.
FLIP
ONCE IT'S DONE, PUT IT IN A BOWL...
...THEN FLIP IT OVER ON A PLATE.
POP
ぽん
IT'S LIKE A KID'S LUNCH!
RIGHT?
IF YOU PACK IT TOO TIGHT THE RICE GETS SQUISHED...
...SO PAT IT TOGETHER LIKE YOU WOULD A RICE BALL.
PAT PAT

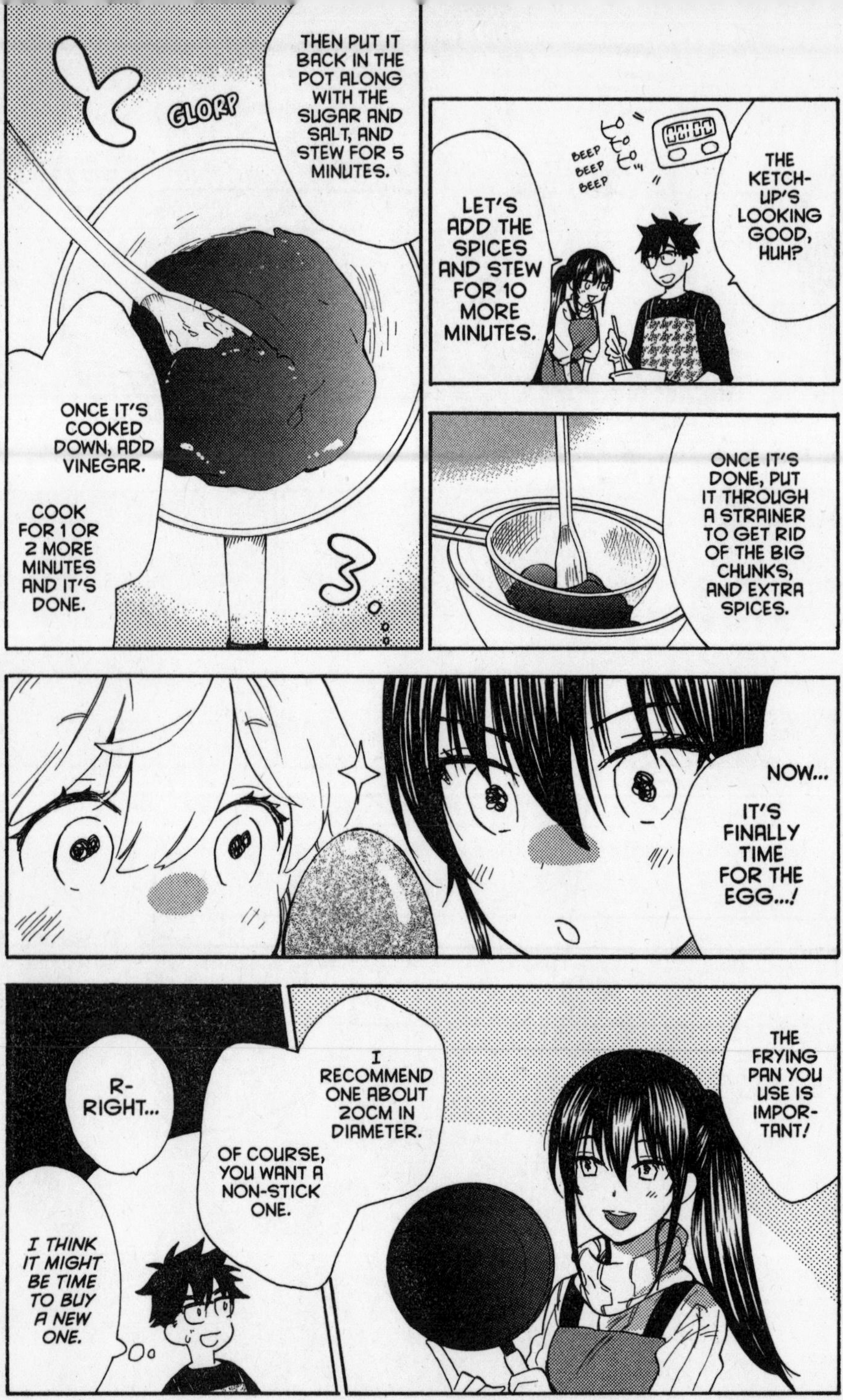
THE KETCH-UP'S LOOKING GOOD, HUH?
BEEP BEEP BEEP
LET'S ADD THE SPICES AND STEW FOR 10 MORE MINUTES.
ONCE IT'S DONE, PUT IT THROUGH A STRAINER TO GET RID OF THE BIG CHUNKS, AND EXTRA SPICES.
THEN PUT IT BACK IN THE POT ALONG WITH THE SUGAR AND SALT, AND STEW FOR 5 MINUTES.
GLORP
ONCE IT'S COOKED DOWN, ADD VINEGAR.
COOK FOR 1 OR 2 MORE MINUTES AND IT'S DONE.
NOW...
IT'S FINALLY TIME FOR THE EGG...!
THE FRYING PAN YOU USE IS IMPOR-TANT!
I RECOMMEND ONE ABOUT 20CM IN DIAMETER.
OF COURSE, YOU WANT A NON-STICK ONE.
R-RIGHT...
I THINK IT MIGHT BE TIME TO BUY A NEW ONE.

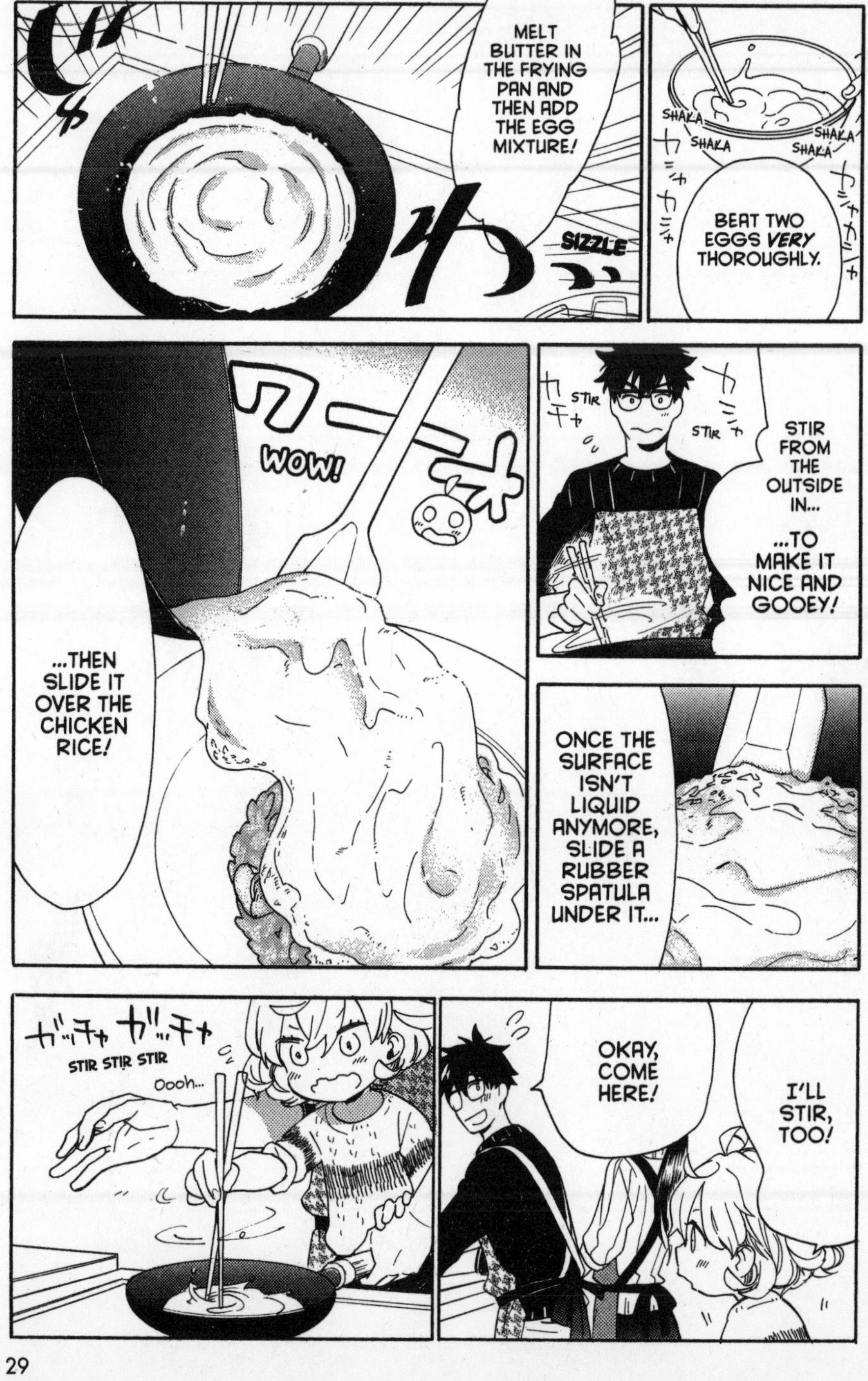
SHAKA SHAKA SHAKA SHAKA
BEAT TWO EGGS *VERY* THOROUGHLY.
MELT BUTTER IN THE FRYING PAN AND THEN ADD THE EGG MIXTURE!
SIZZLE
STIR STIR
STIR FROM THE OUTSIDE IN...
...TO MAKE IT NICE AND GOOEY!
ONCE THE SURFACE ISN'T LIQUID ANYMORE, SLIDE A RUBBER SPATULA UNDER IT...
WOW!
...THEN SLIDE IT OVER THE CHICKEN RICE!
OKAY, COME HERE!
I'LL STIR, TOO!
ガッチャ ガッチャ
STIR STIR STIR
Oooh...

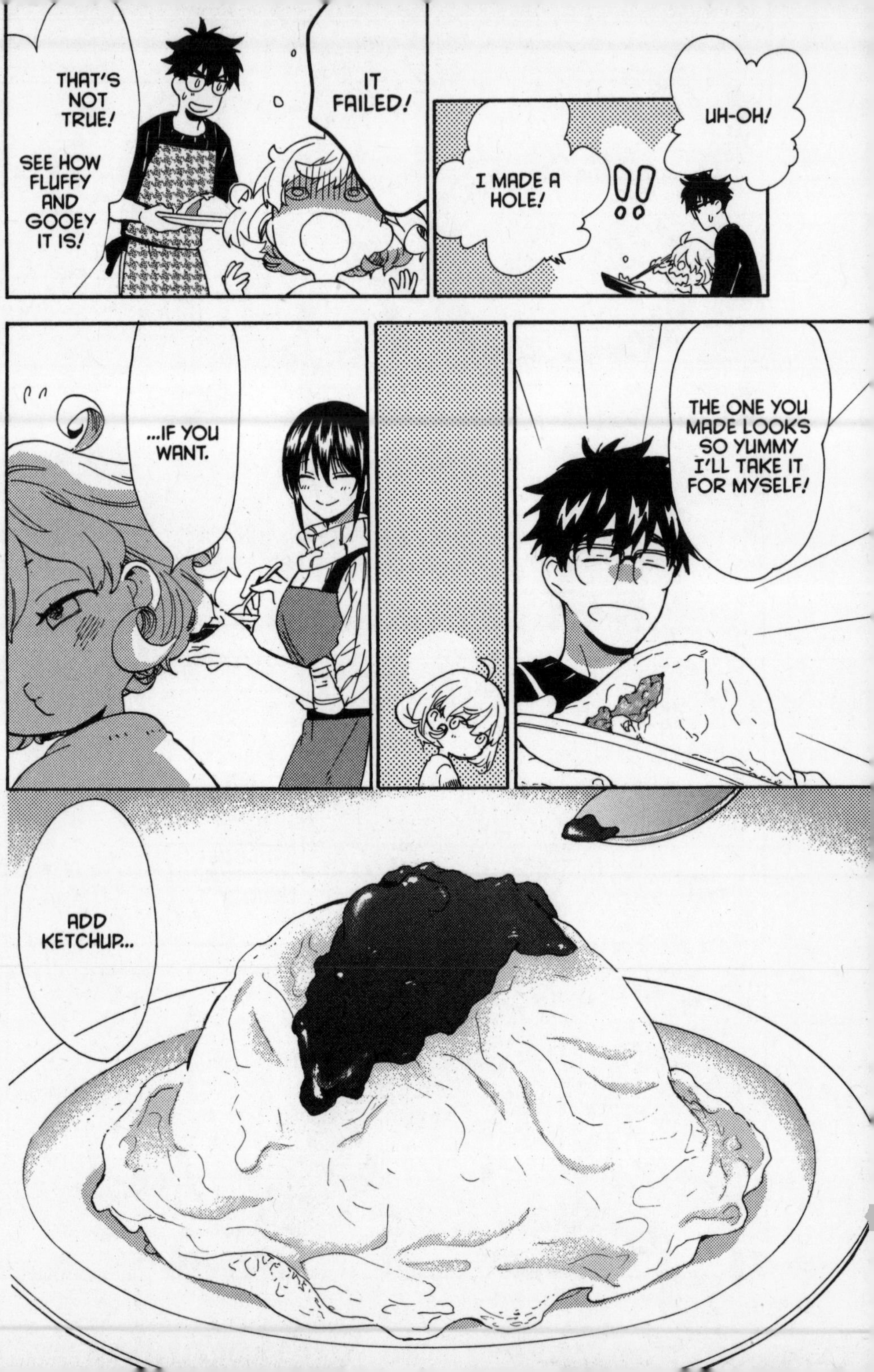
UH-OH!
I MADE A HOLE!
!!
IT FAILED!
THAT'S NOT TRUE!
SEE HOW FLUFFY AND GOOEY IT IS!
THE ONE YOU MADE LOOKS SO YUMMY I'LL TAKE IT FOR MYSELF!
...IF YOU WANT.
ADD KETCHUP...

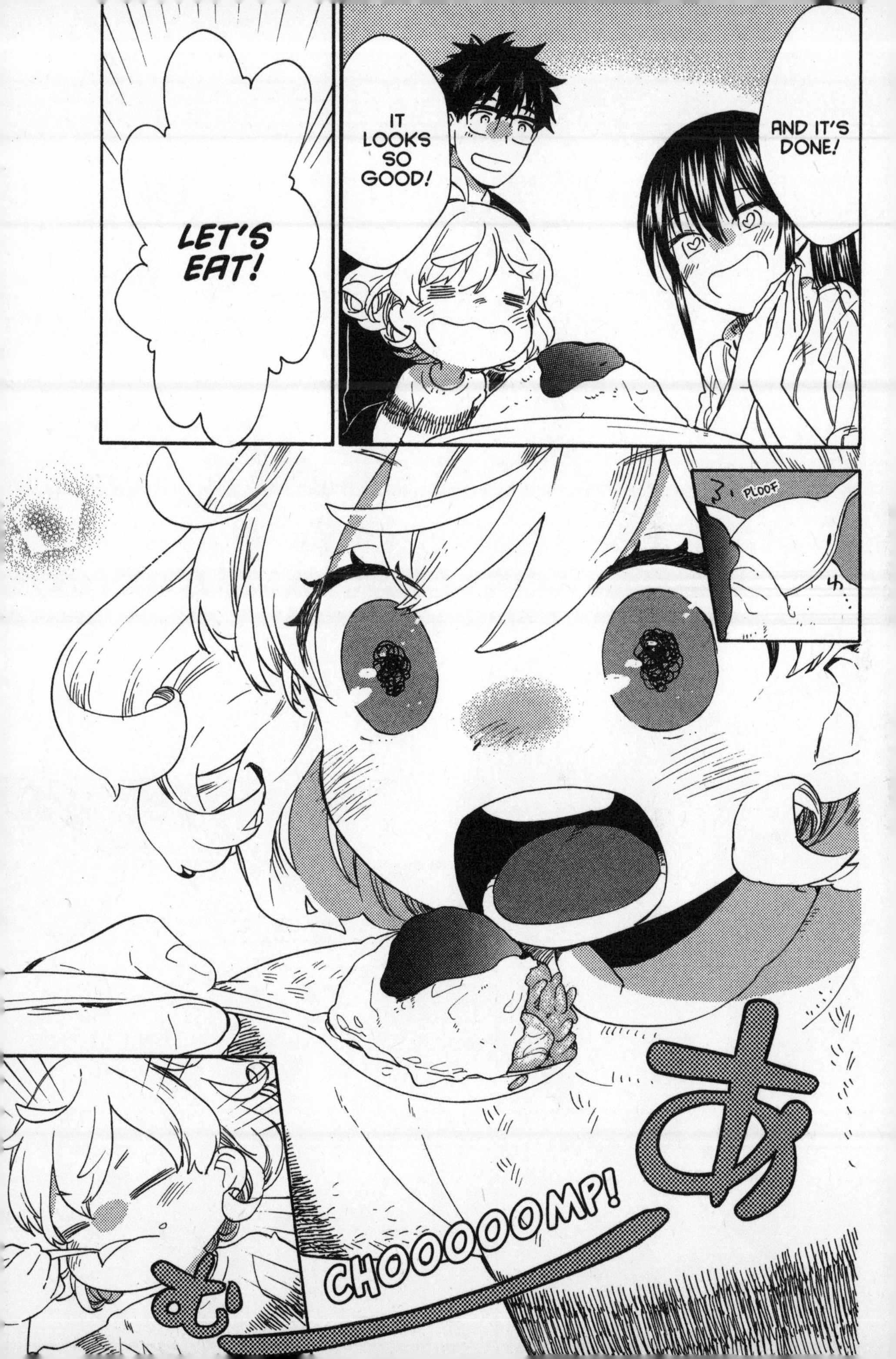
AND IT'S DONE!
IT LOOKS SO GOOD!
LET'S EAT!
PLOOF
あーむ
CHOOOOOMP!

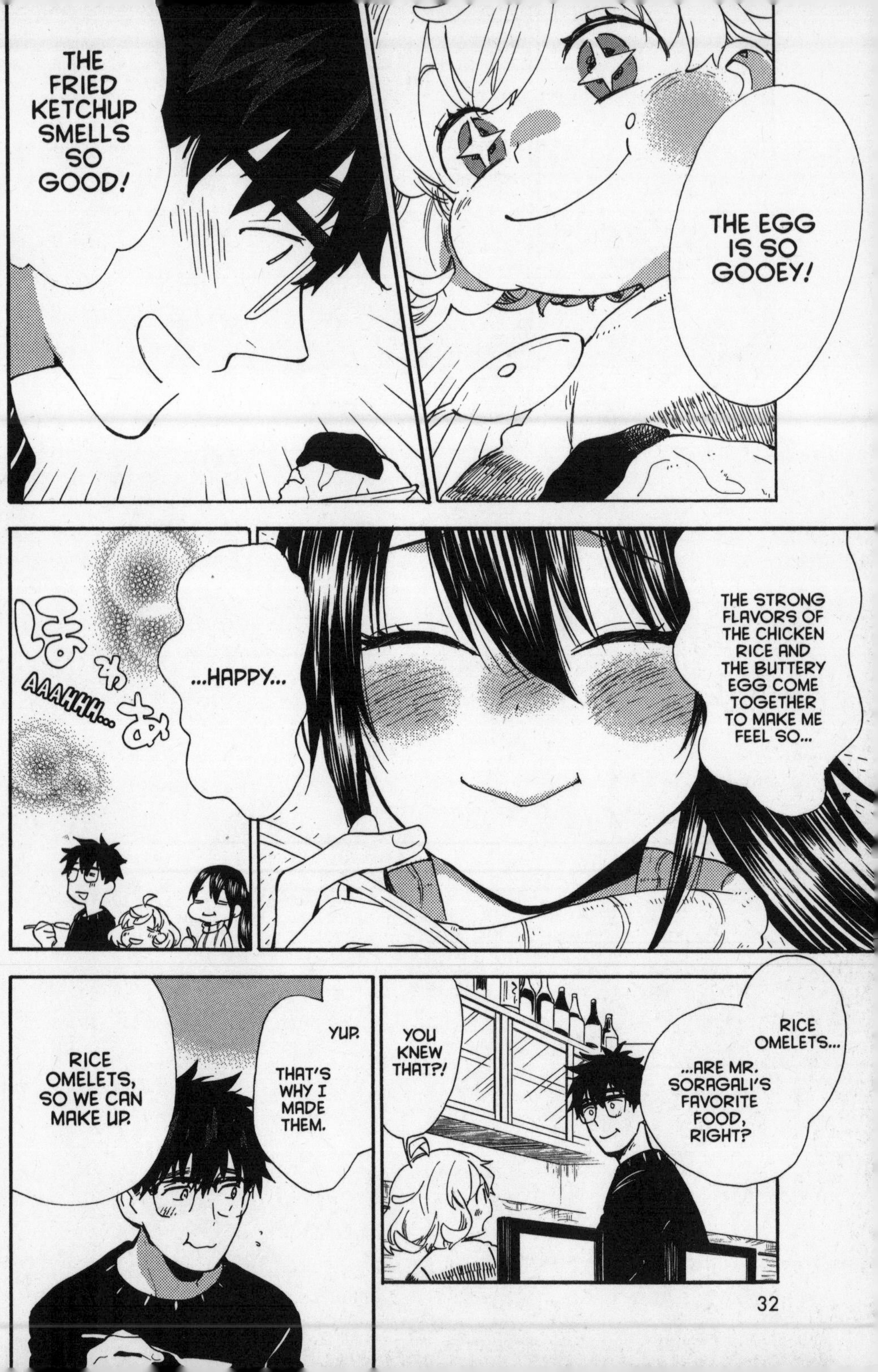
THE EGG IS SO GOOEY!
THE FRIED KETCHUP SMELLS SO GOOD!
THE STRONG FLAVORS OF THE CHICKEN RICE AND THE BUTTERY EGG COME TOGETHER TO MAKE ME FEEL SO...
...HAPPY...
ほわあ
AAAHHH...
RICE OMELETS...
...ARE MR. SORAGALI'S FAVORITE FOOD, RIGHT?
YOU KNEW THAT?!
YUP.
THAT'S WHY I MADE THEM.
RICE OMELETS, SO WE CAN MAKE UP.

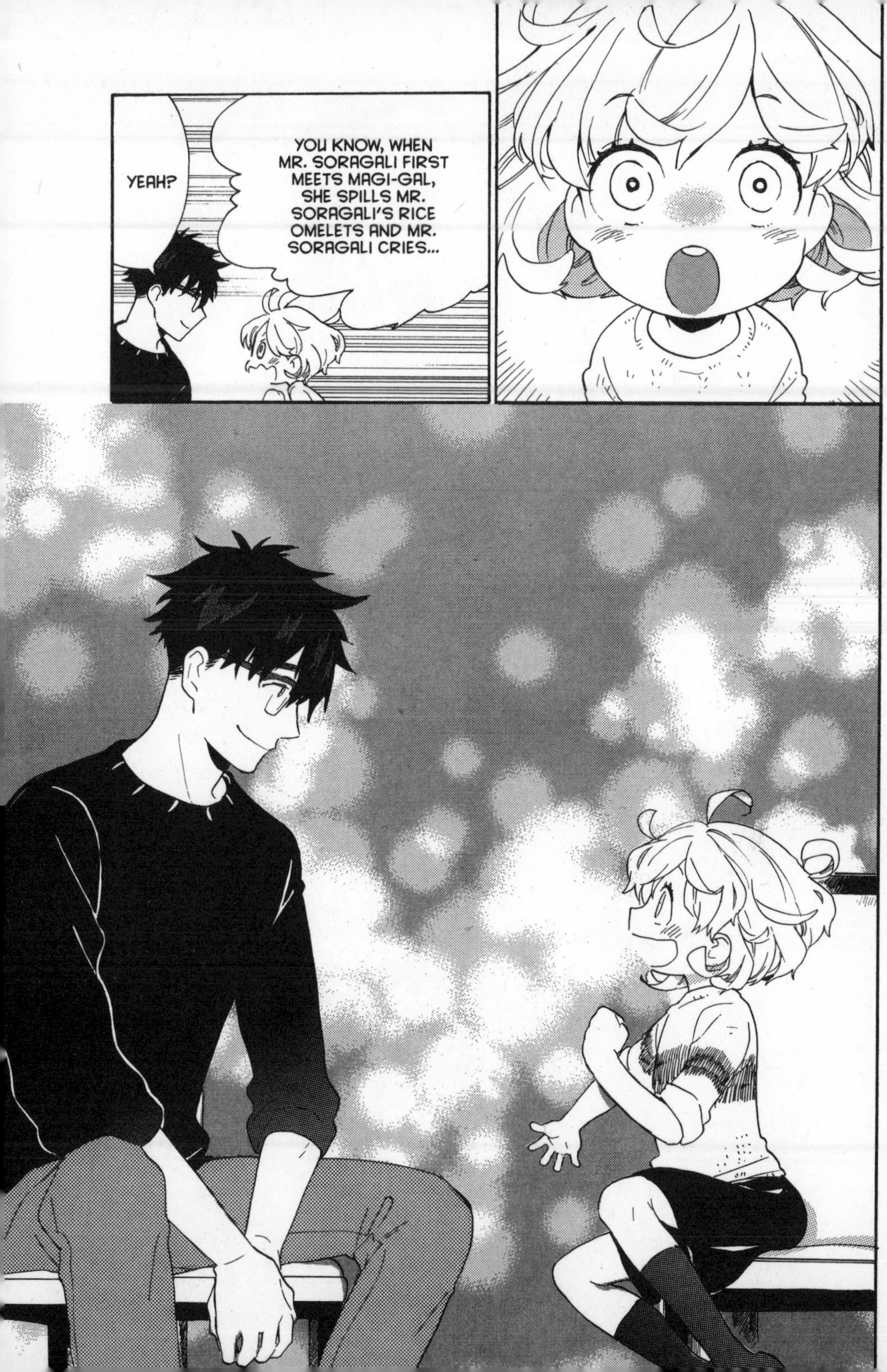

YOU KNOW, WHEN MR. SORAGALI FIRST MEETS MAGI-GAL, SHE SPILLS MR. SORAGALI'S RICE OMELETS AND MR. SORAGALI CRIES...
YEAH?

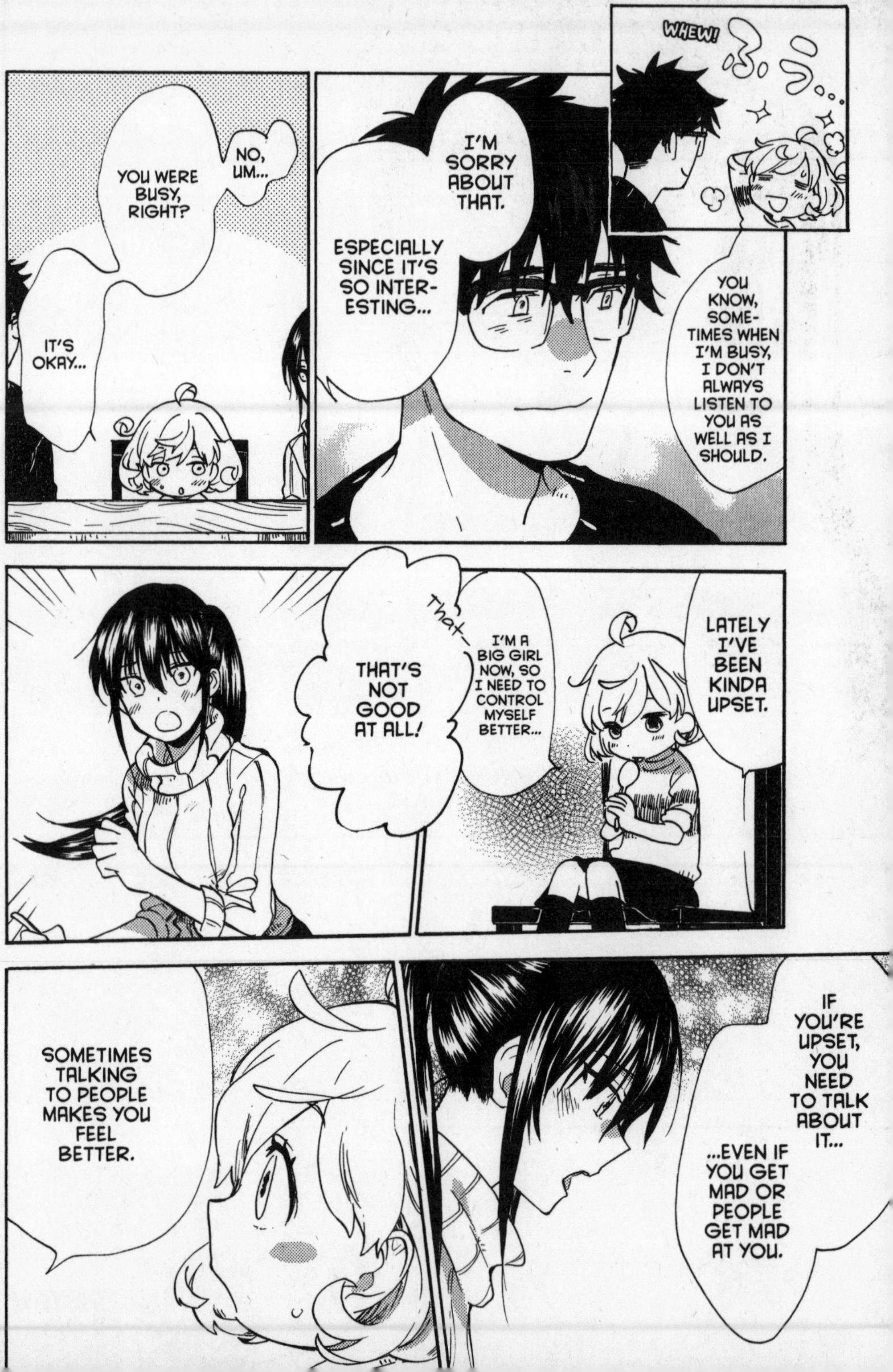

WHEW!
ふぅ...
YOU KNOW, SOMETIMES WHEN I'M BUSY, I DON'T ALWAYS LISTEN TO YOU AS WELL AS I SHOULD.
I'M SORRY ABOUT THAT.
ESPECIALLY SINCE IT'S SO INTERESTING...
NO, UM...
YOU WERE BUSY, RIGHT?
IT'S OKAY...
LATELY I'VE BEEN KINDA UPSET.
I'M A BIG GIRL NOW, SO I NEED TO CONTROL MYSELF BETTER...
That—
THAT'S NOT GOOD AT ALL!
IF YOU'RE UPSET, YOU NEED TO TALK ABOUT IT...
...EVEN IF YOU GET MAD OR PEOPLE GET MAD AT YOU.
SOMETIMES TALKING TO PEOPLE MAKES YOU FEEL BETTER.

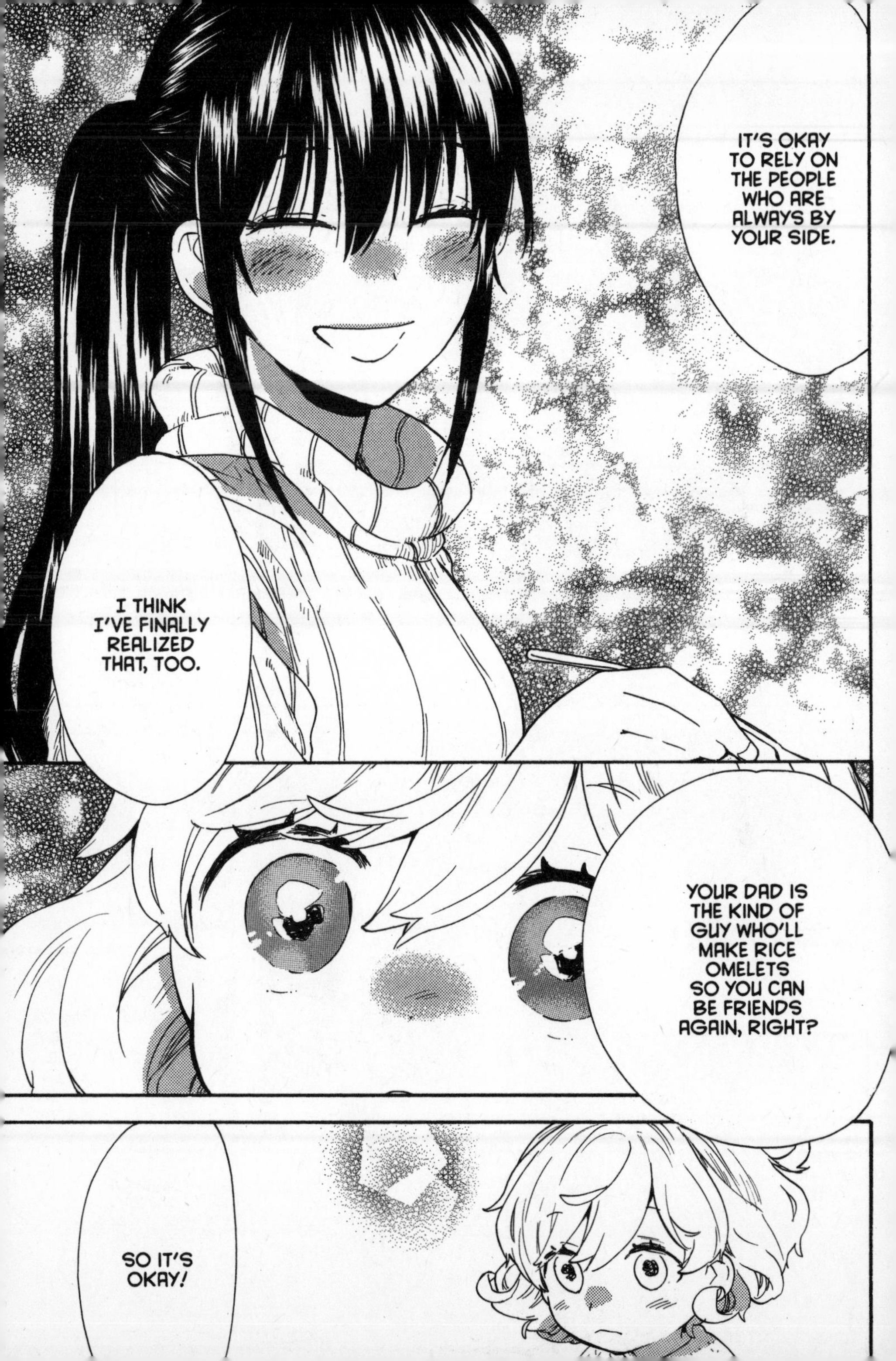
IT'S OKAY TO RELY ON THE PEOPLE WHO ARE ALWAYS BY YOUR SIDE.
I THINK I'VE FINALLY REALIZED THAT, TOO.
YOUR DAD IS THE KIND OF GUY WHO'LL MAKE RICE OMELETS SO YOU CAN BE FRIENDS AGAIN, RIGHT?
SO IT'S OKAY!

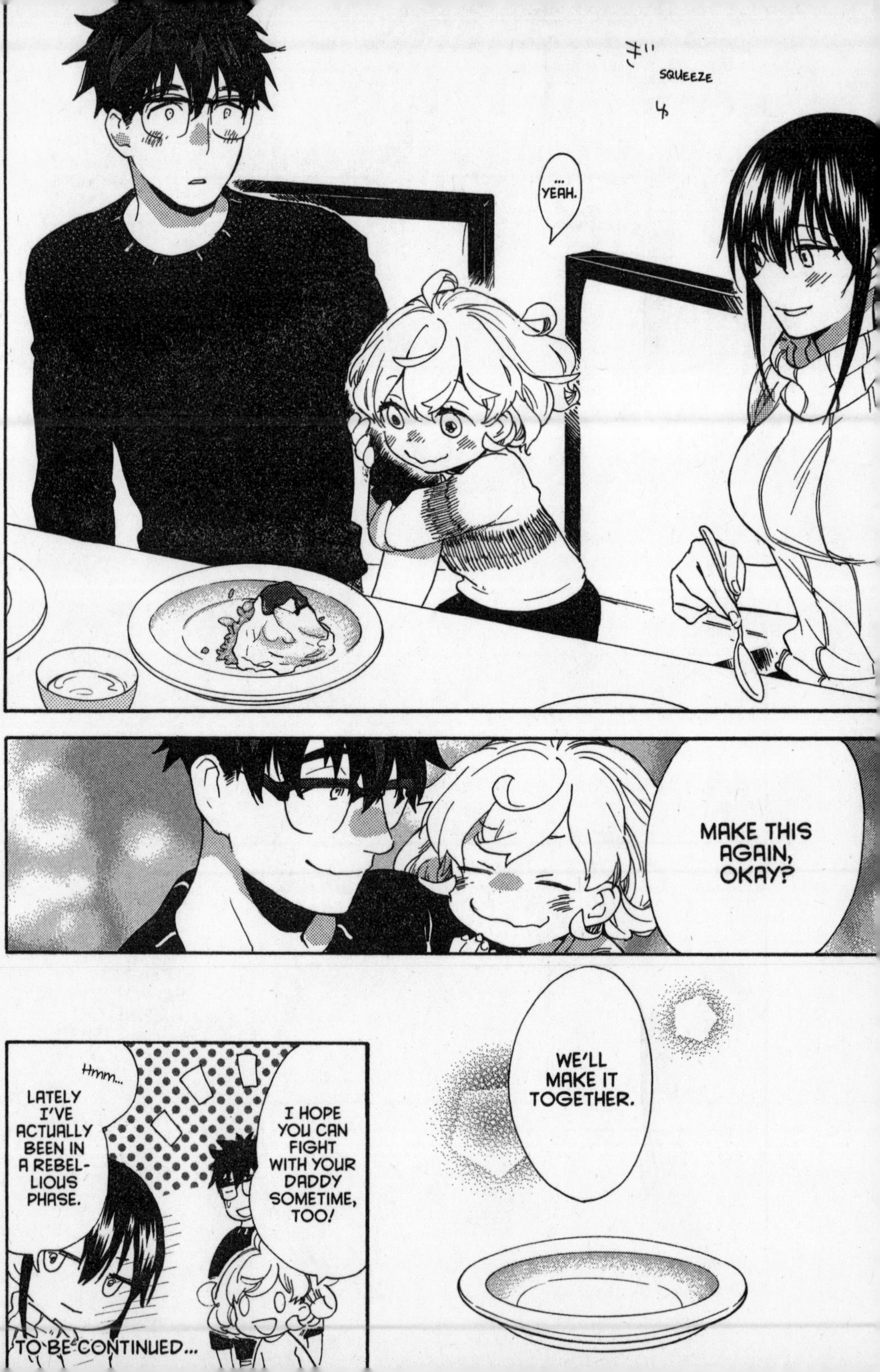
ぎゅ
SQUEEZE
...YEAH.
MAKE THIS AGAIN, OKAY?
WE'LL MAKE IT TOGETHER.
I HOPE YOU CAN FIGHT WITH YOUR DADDY SOMETIME, TOO!
Hmm...
LATELY I'VE ACTUALLY BEEN IN A REBEL-LIOUS PHASE.
TO BE CONTINUED...

OMELET RICE

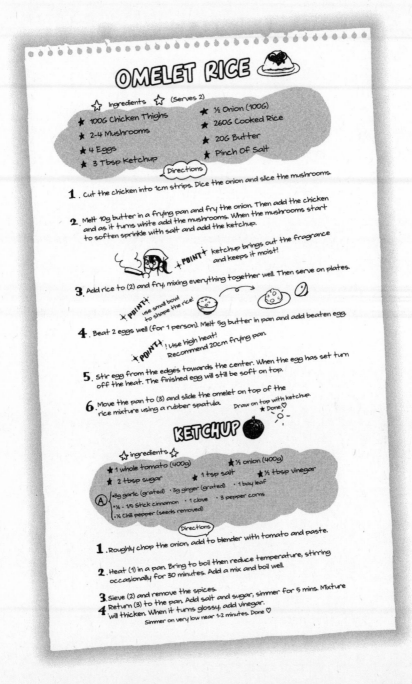

☆ Ingredients ☆ (Serves 2)

★ 100G Chicken Thighs
★ 2-4 Mushrooms
★ 4 Eggs
★ 3 Tbsp Ketchup

★ ½ Onion (100G)
★ 260G Cooked Rice
★ 20G Butter
★ Pinch Of Salt

Directions

1. Cut the chicken into 1cm strips. Dice the onion and slice the mushrooms.

2. Melt 10g butter in a frying pan and fry the onion. Then add the chicken and as it turns white add the mushrooms. When the mushrooms start to soften sprinkle with salt and add the ketchup.

POINT ketchup brings out the fragrance and keeps it moist!

3. Add rice to (2) and fry, mixing everything together well. Then serve on plates.

POINT use small bowl to shape the rice!

4. Beat 2 eggs well (for 1 person). Melt 5g butter in pan and add beaten egg

POINT Use high heat! Recommend 20cm frying pan.

5. Stir egg from the edges towards the center. When the egg has set turn off the heat. The finished egg will still be soft on top.

6. Move the pan to (3) and slide the omelet on top of the rice mixture using a rubber spatula. Draw on top with ketchup.
★ Done. ♡

KETCHUP

☆ Ingredients ☆

★ 1 whole tomato (400g)   ★ ½ onion (400g)
★ 2 tbsp sugar   ★ 1 tsp salt   ★ ½ tbsp vinegar

Ⓐ · 3g garlic (grated) · 3g ginger (grated) · 1 bay leaf
· ¼ - ⅕ stick cinnamon · 1 clove · 3 pepper corns
· ¼ chili pepper (seeds removed)

Directions

1. Roughly chop the onion, add to blender with tomato and paste.

2. Heat (1) in a pan. Bring to boil then reduce temperature, stirring occasionally for 30 minutes. Add a mix and boil well.

3. Sieve (2) and remove the spices.

4. Return (3) to the pan. Add salt and sugar, simmer for 5 mins. Mixture will thicken. When it turns glossy, add vinegar.
Simmer on very low near 1-2 minutes. Done ♡

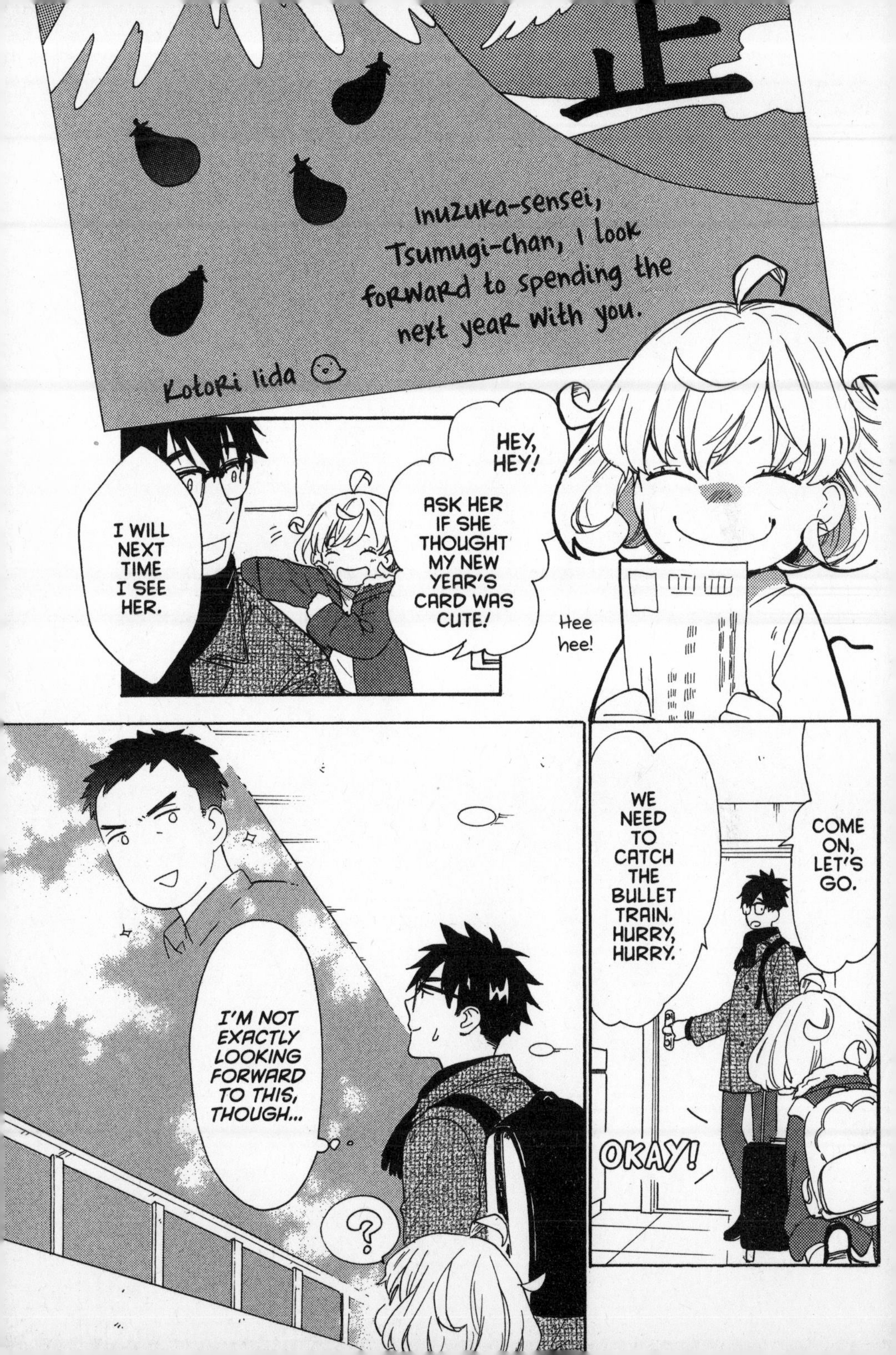

上
Inuzuka-sensei, Tsumugi-chan, I look forward to spending the next year with you.
Kotori Iida
Hee hee!
HEY, HEY!
ASK HER IF SHE THOUGHT MY NEW YEAR'S CARD WAS CUTE!
I WILL NEXT TIME I SEE HER.
COME ON, LET'S GO.
WE NEED TO CATCH THE BULLET TRAIN. HURRY, HURRY.
OKAY!
I'M NOT EXACTLY LOOKING FORWARD TO THIS, THOUGH...
?

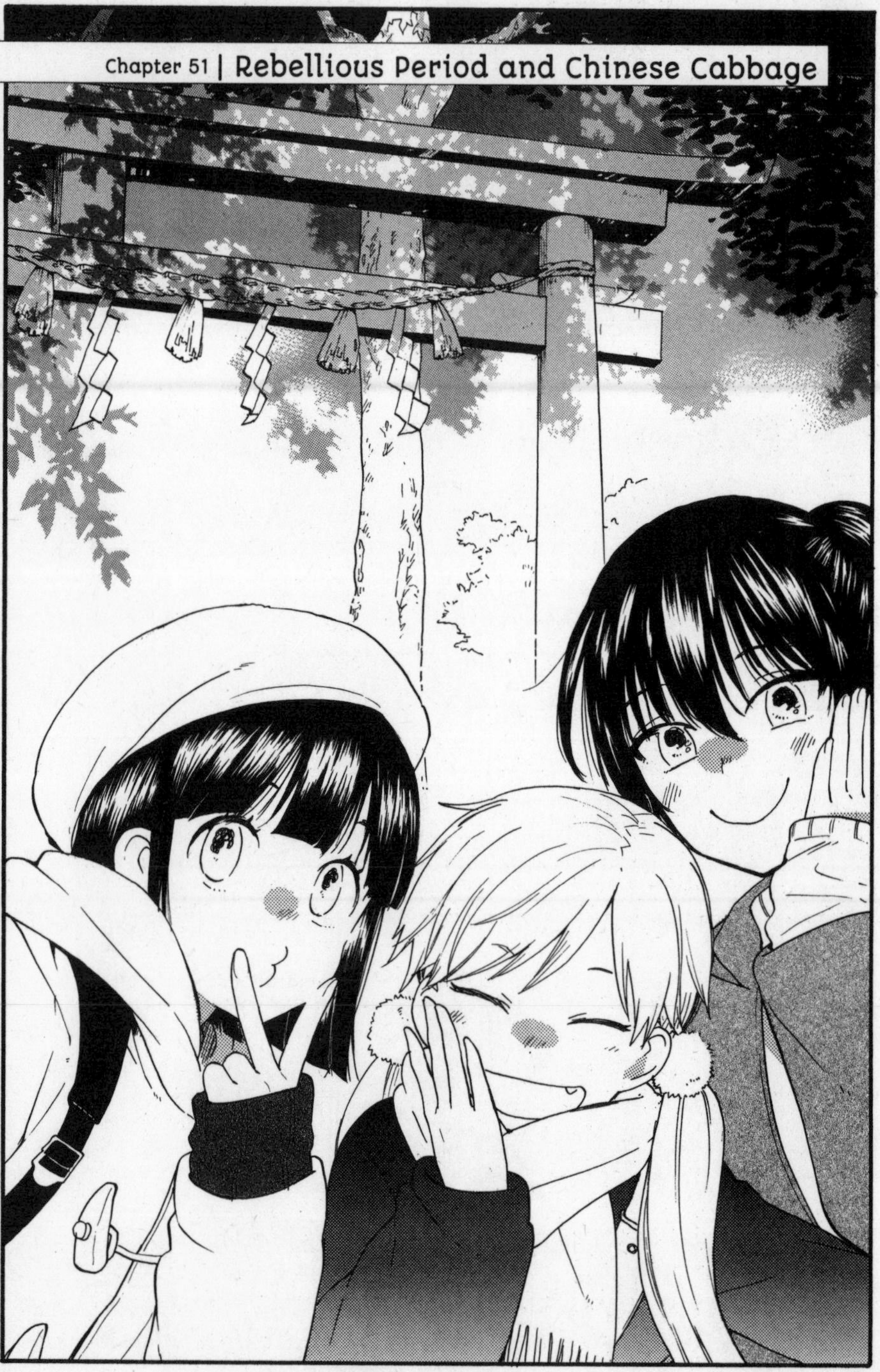
Chapter 51 | Rebellious Period and Chinese Cabbage

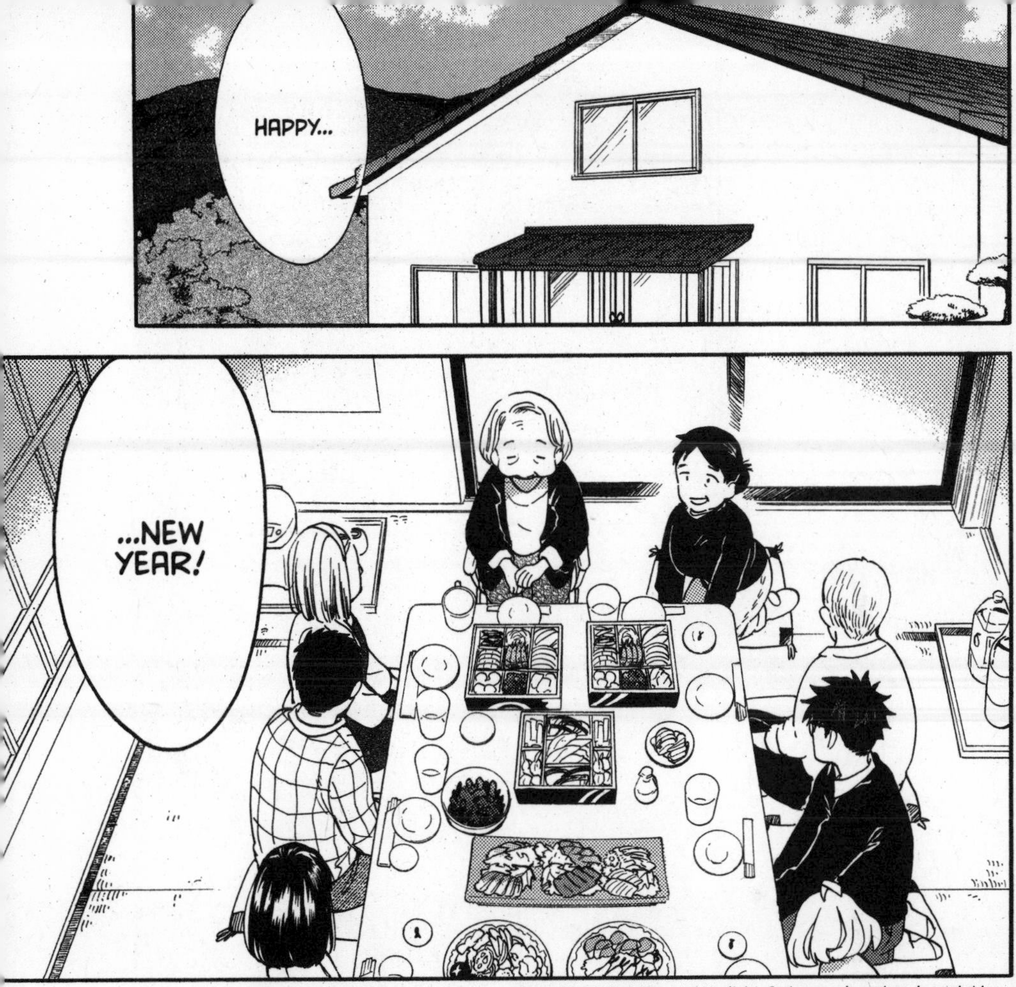
HAPPY...
...NEW YEAR!

"Onishime" is a New Year's dish of simmered meat and vegetables.

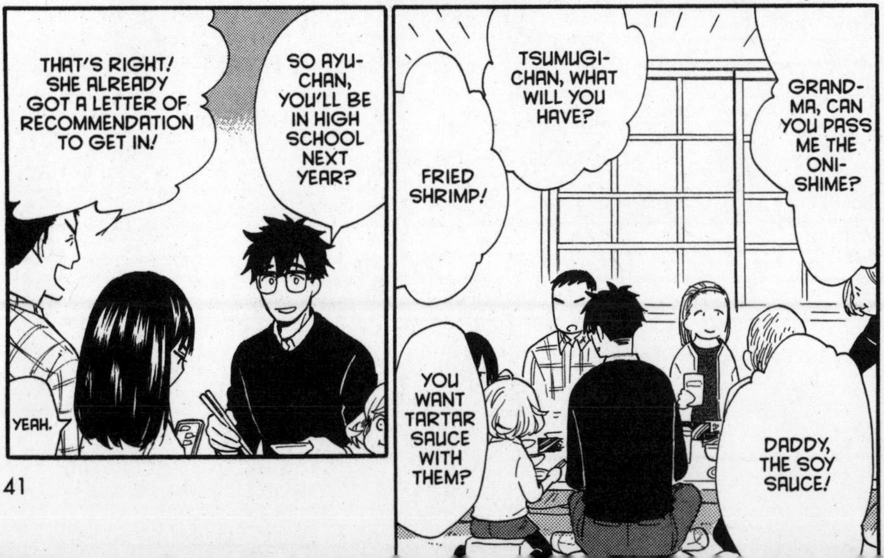
GRANDMA, CAN YOU PASS ME THE ONISHIME?
TSUMUGI-CHAN, WHAT WILL YOU HAVE?
FRIED SHRIMP!
DADDY, THE SOY SAUCE!
YOU WANT TARTAR SAUCE WITH THEM?
SO AYU-CHAN, YOU'LL BE IN HIGH SCHOOL NEXT YEAR?
THAT'S RIGHT! SHE ALREADY GOT A LETTER OF RECOMMENDATION TO GET IN!
YEAH.

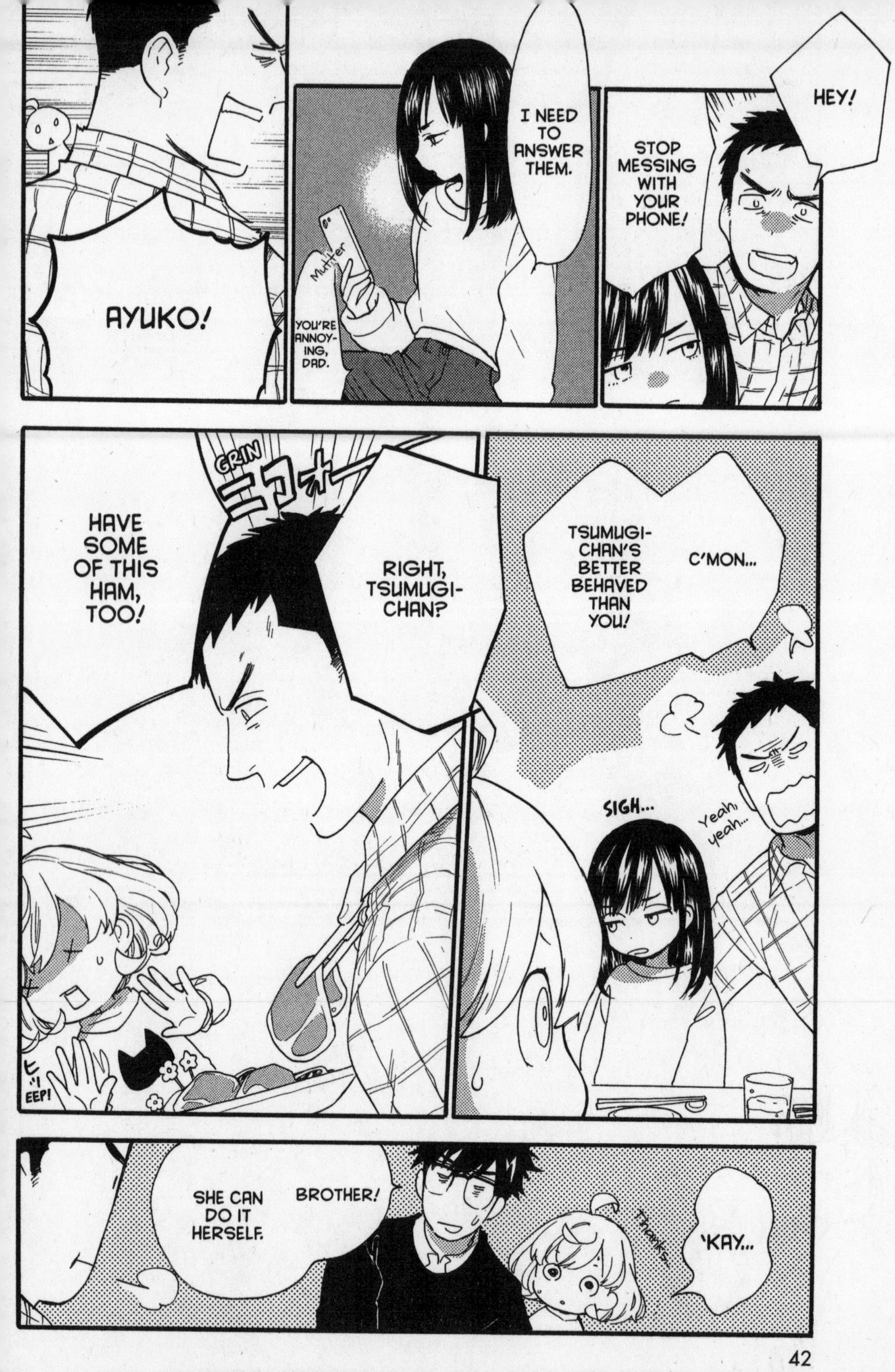
HEY!
STOP MESSING WITH YOUR PHONE!
I NEED TO ANSWER THEM.
Mutter
YOU'RE ANNOY-ING, DAD.
AYUKO!
C'MON...
TSUMUGI-CHAN'S BETTER BEHAVED THAN YOU!
SIGH...
Yeah, yeah...
GRIN
ニコォー
RIGHT, TSUMUGI-CHAN?
HAVE SOME OF THIS HAM, TOO!
ヒッ
EEP!
'KAY...
Thanks.
BROTHER!
SHE CAN DO IT HERSELF.

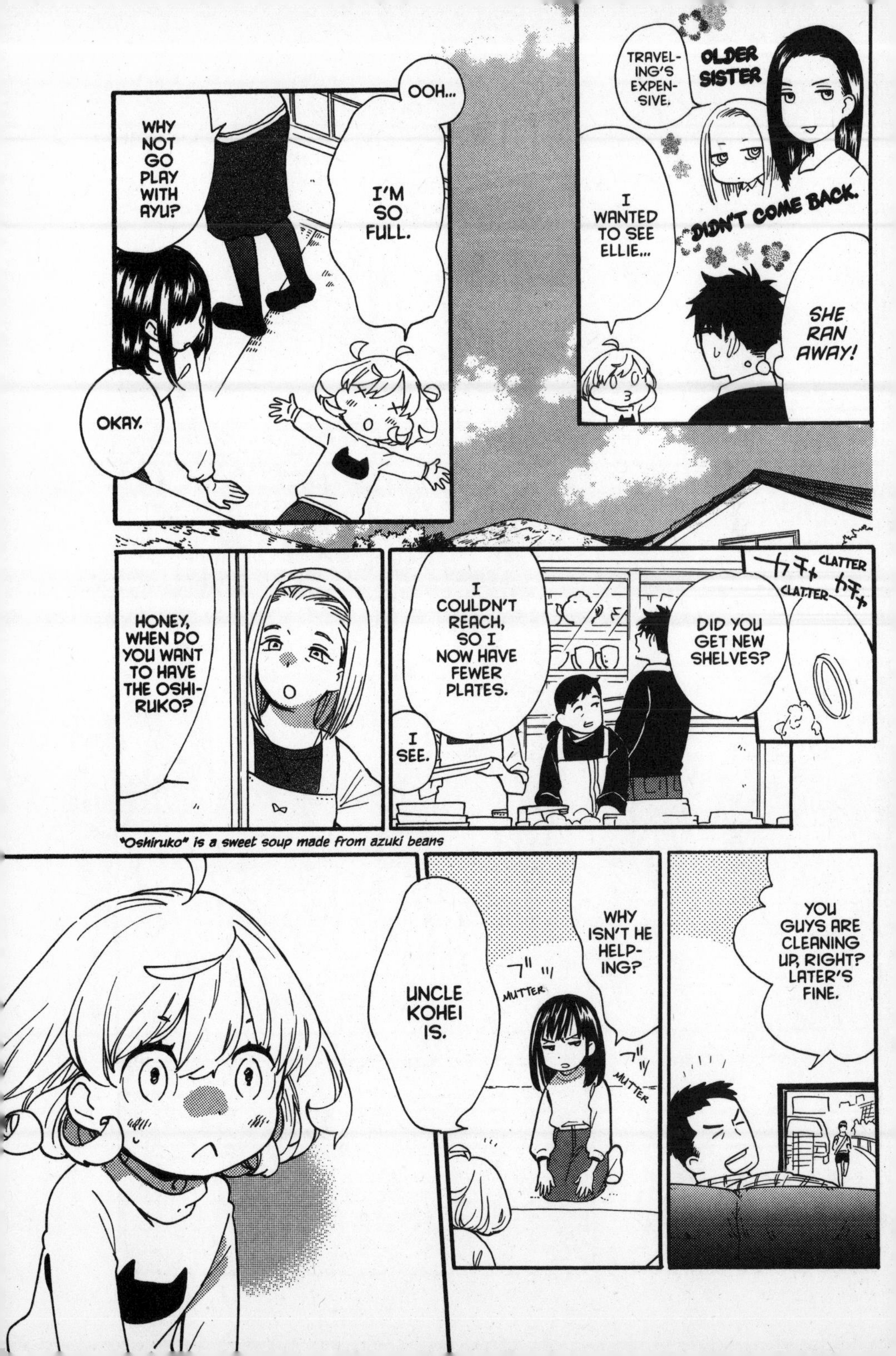
OLDER SISTER
TRAVEL-ING'S EXPEN-SIVE.
DIDN'T COME BACK.
SHE RAN AWAY!
I WANTED TO SEE ELLIE...
OOH...
I'M SO FULL.
WHY NOT GO PLAY WITH AYU?
OKAY.
CLATTER
CLATTER
DID YOU GET NEW SHELVES?
I COULDN'T REACH, SO I NOW HAVE FEWER PLATES.
I SEE.
HONEY, WHEN DO YOU WANT TO HAVE THE OSHI-RUKO?
YOU GUYS ARE CLEANING UP, RIGHT? LATER'S FINE.
WHY ISN'T HE HELP-ING?
MUTTER
MUTTER
UNCLE KOHEI IS.
"Oshiruko" is a sweet soup made from azuki beans

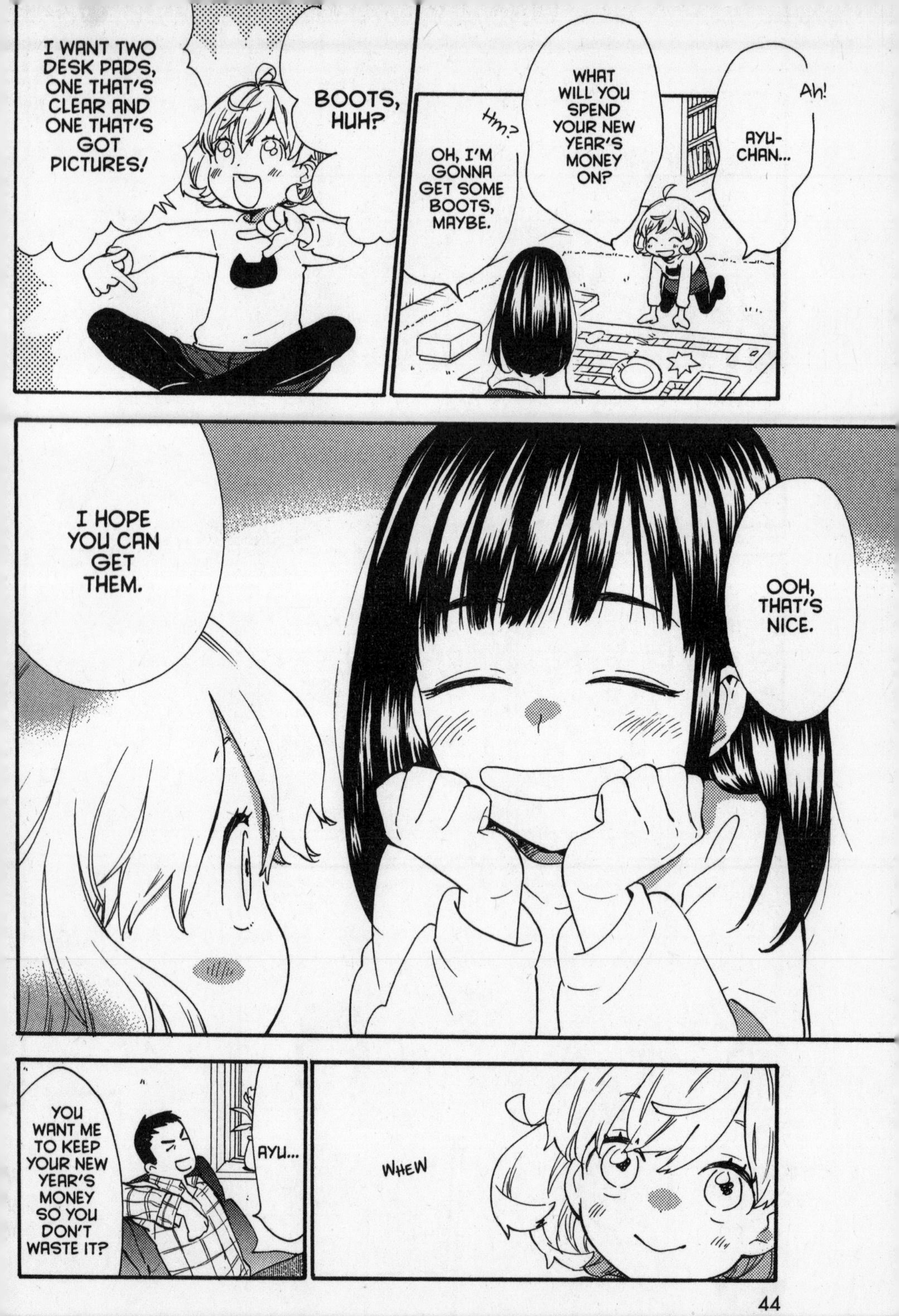
Ah!
AYU-CHAN...
WHAT WILL YOU SPEND YOUR NEW YEAR'S MONEY ON?
Hm?
OH, I'M GONNA GET SOME BOOTS, MAYBE.
BOOTS, HUH?
I WANT TWO DESK PADS, ONE THAT'S CLEAR AND ONE THAT'S GOT PICTURES!
OOH, THAT'S NICE.
I HOPE YOU CAN GET THEM.
WHEW
AYU...
YOU WANT ME TO KEEP YOUR NEW YEAR'S MONEY SO YOU DON'T WASTE IT?

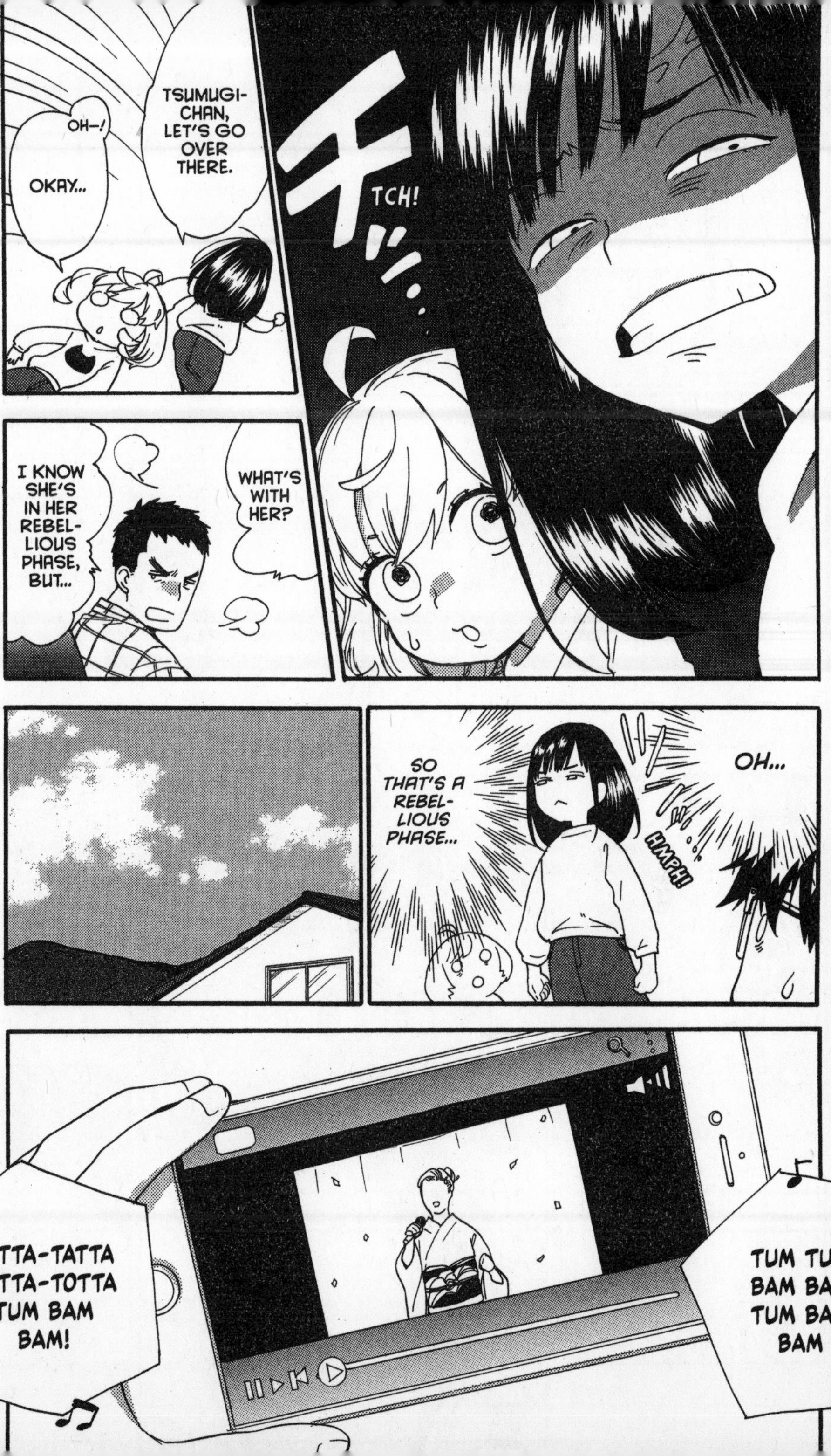
TCH!
TSUMUGI-CHAN, LET'S GO OVER THERE.
OH–!
OKAY...
WHAT'S WITH HER?
I KNOW SHE'S IN HER REBEL-LIOUS PHASE, BUT...
OH...
HMPH!
SO THAT'S A REBEL-LIOUS PHASE...
TUM TU
BAM BA
TUM BA
BAM
TATTA-TATTA TOTTA-TOTTA TUM BAM BAM!

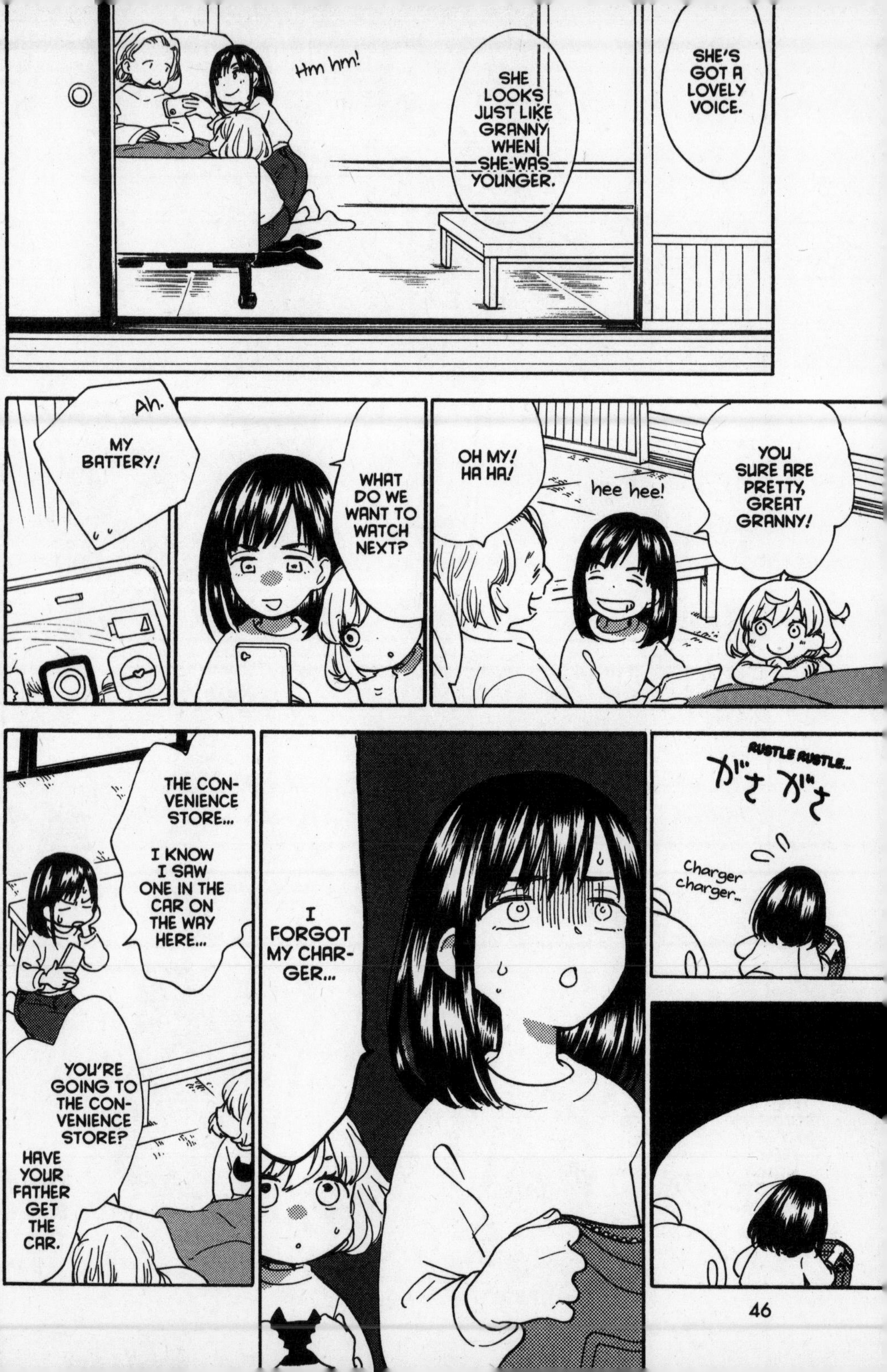
SHE'S GOT A LOVELY VOICE.
SHE LOOKS JUST LIKE GRANNY WHEN SHE WAS YOUNGER.
Hm hm!
YOU SURE ARE PRETTY, GREAT GRANNY!
hee hee!
OH MY! HA HA!
WHAT DO WE WANT TO WATCH NEXT?
Ah.
MY BATTERY!
RUSTLE RUSTLE...
がさがさ
Charger charger...
I FORGOT MY CHARGER...
THE CONVENIENCE STORE...
I KNOW I SAW ONE IN THE CAR ON THE WAY HERE...
YOU'RE GOING TO THE CONVENIENCE STORE?
HAVE YOUR FATHER GET THE CAR.

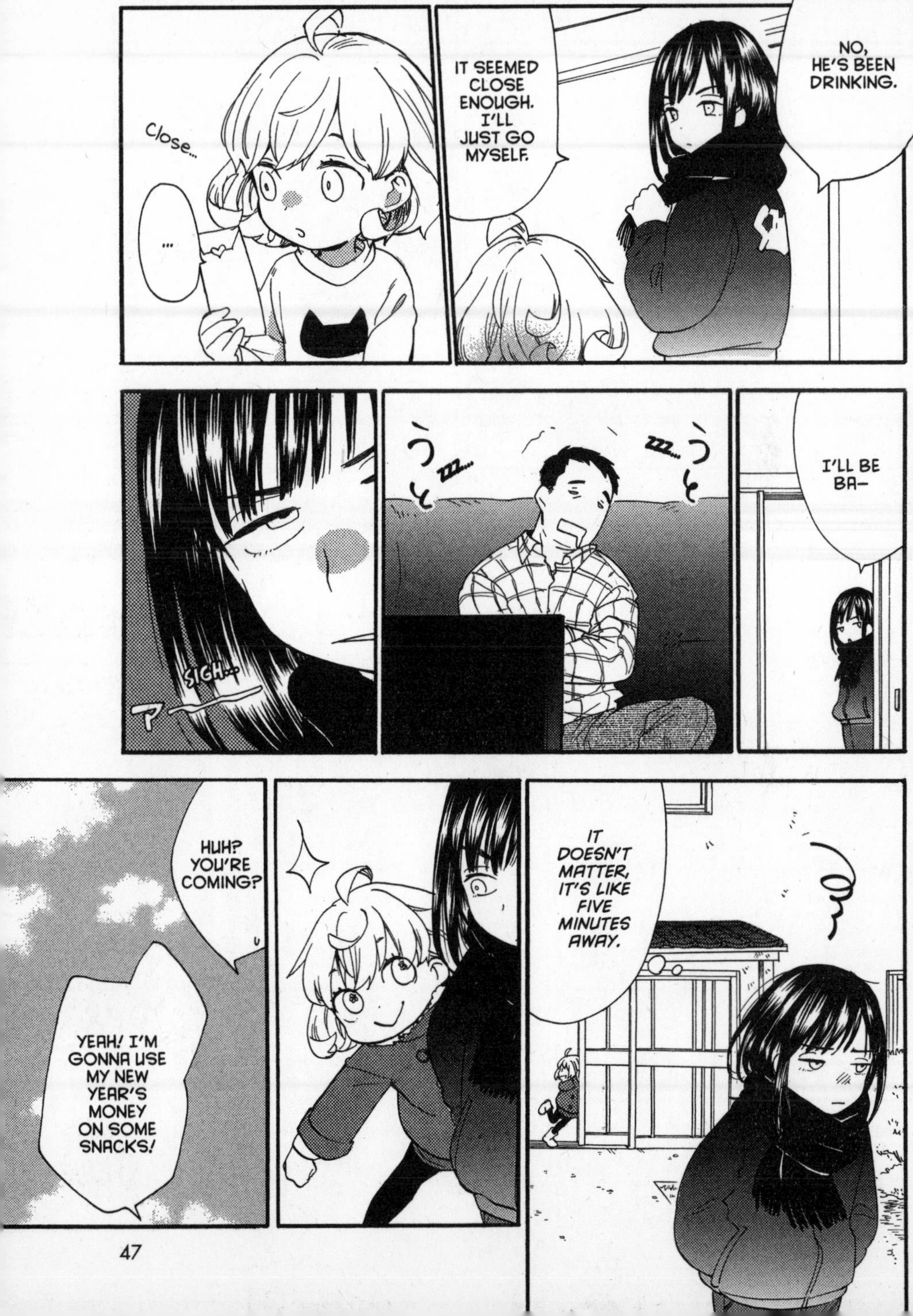
NO, HE'S BEEN DRINKING.
IT SEEMED CLOSE ENOUGH. I'LL JUST GO MYSELF.
Close...
...
I'LL BE BA-
ZZZ...
ZZZ...
SIGH...
HUH? YOU'RE COMING?
YEAH! I'M GONNA USE MY NEW YEAR'S MONEY ON SOME SNACKS!
IT DOESN'T MATTER, IT'S LIKE FIVE MINUTES AWAY.

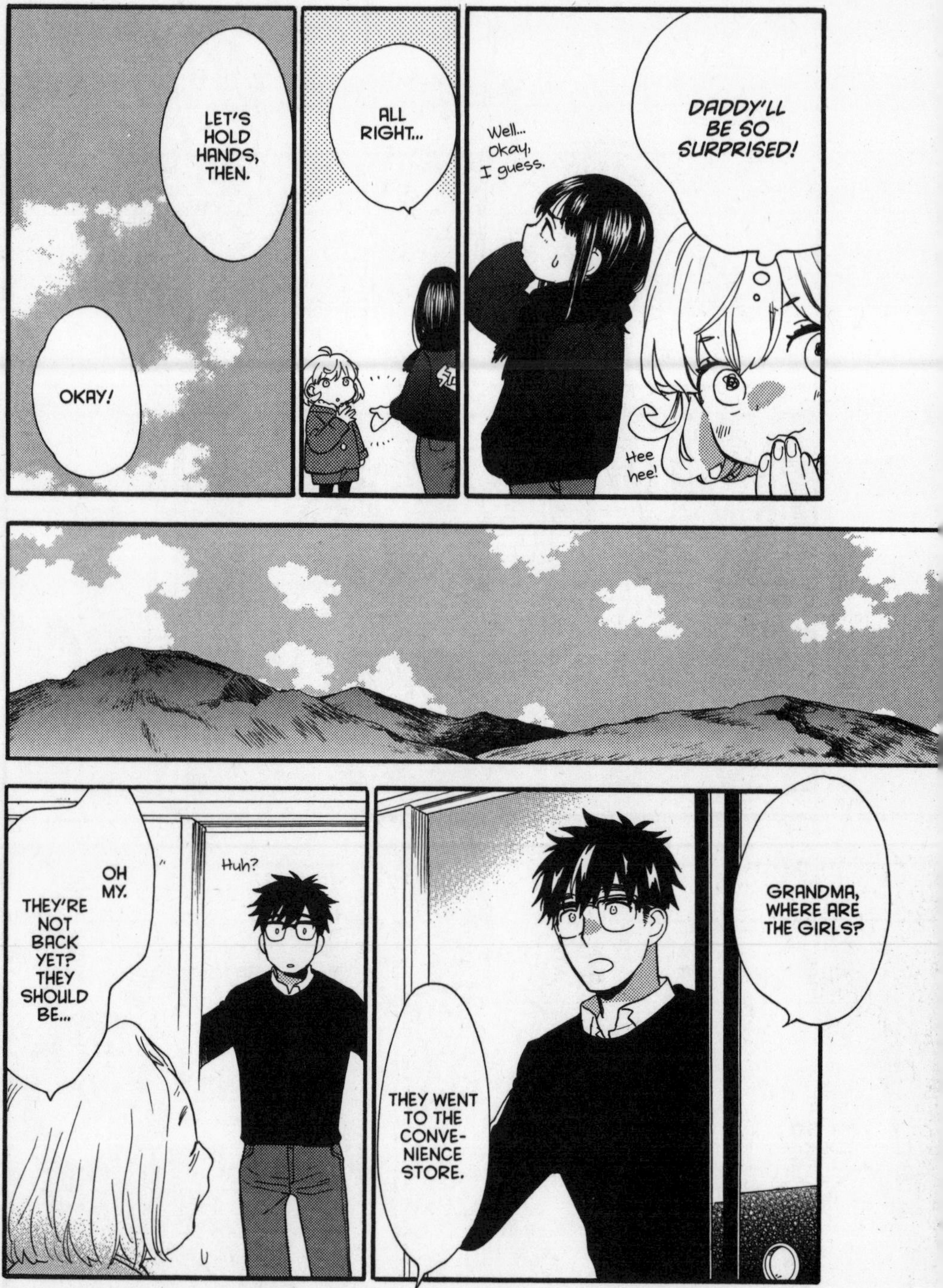
DADDY'LL BE SO SURPRISED!
Hee hee!
Well... Okay, I guess.
ALL RIGHT...
LET'S HOLD HANDS, THEN.
OKAY!
GRANDMA, WHERE ARE THE GIRLS?
THEY WENT TO THE CONVENIENCE STORE.
Huh?
OH MY.
THEY'RE NOT BACK YET? THEY SHOULD BE...

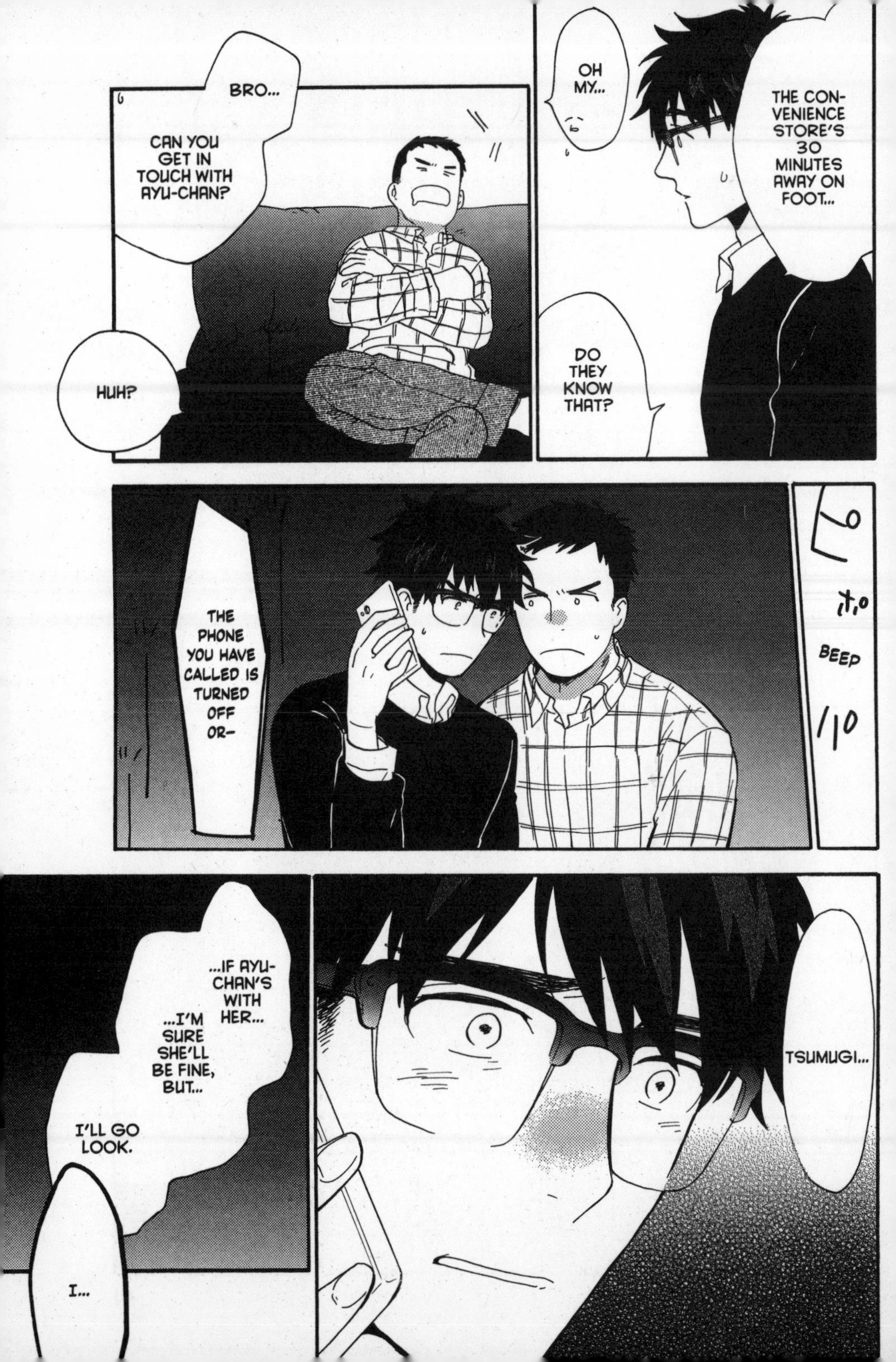
THE CON-VENIENCE STORE'S 30 MINUTES AWAY ON FOOT...
OH MY...
DO THEY KNOW THAT?
BRO...
CAN YOU GET IN TOUCH WITH AYU-CHAN?
HUH?
BEEP
THE PHONE YOU HAVE CALLED IS TURNED OFF OR-
TSUMUGI...
...IF AYU-CHAN'S WITH HER...
...I'M SURE SHE'LL BE FINE, BUT...
I'LL GO LOOK.
I...

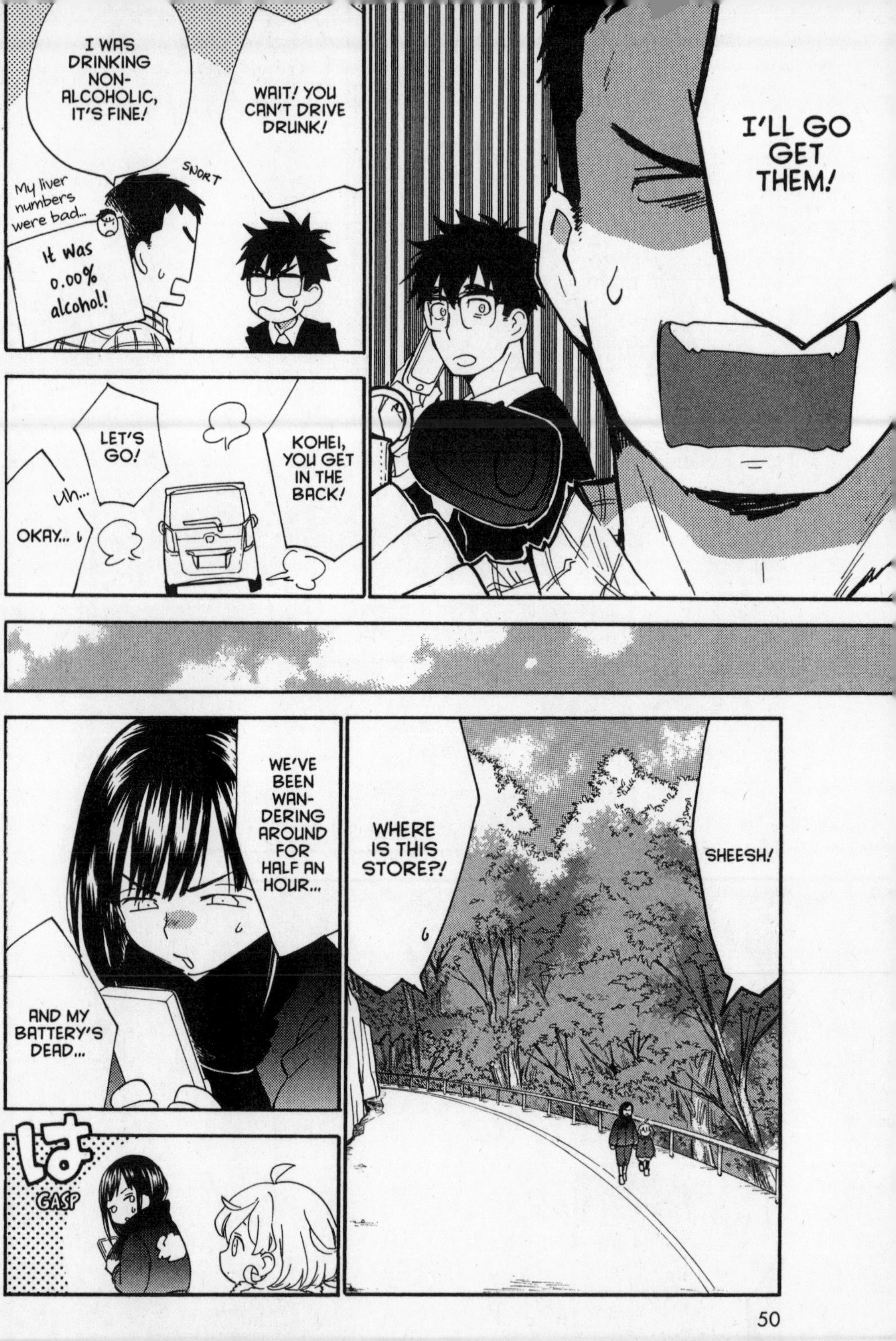
I'LL GO GET THEM!
WAIT! YOU CAN'T DRIVE DRUNK!
SNORT
I WAS DRINKING NON-ALCOHOLIC, IT'S FINE!
My liver numbers were bad...
It was 0.00% alcohol!
KOHEI, YOU GET IN THE BACK!
LET'S GO!
Uh...
OKAY...
SHEESH!
WHERE IS THIS STORE?!
WE'VE BEEN WAN-DERING AROUND FOR HALF AN HOUR...
AND MY BATTERY'S DEAD...
は
GASP

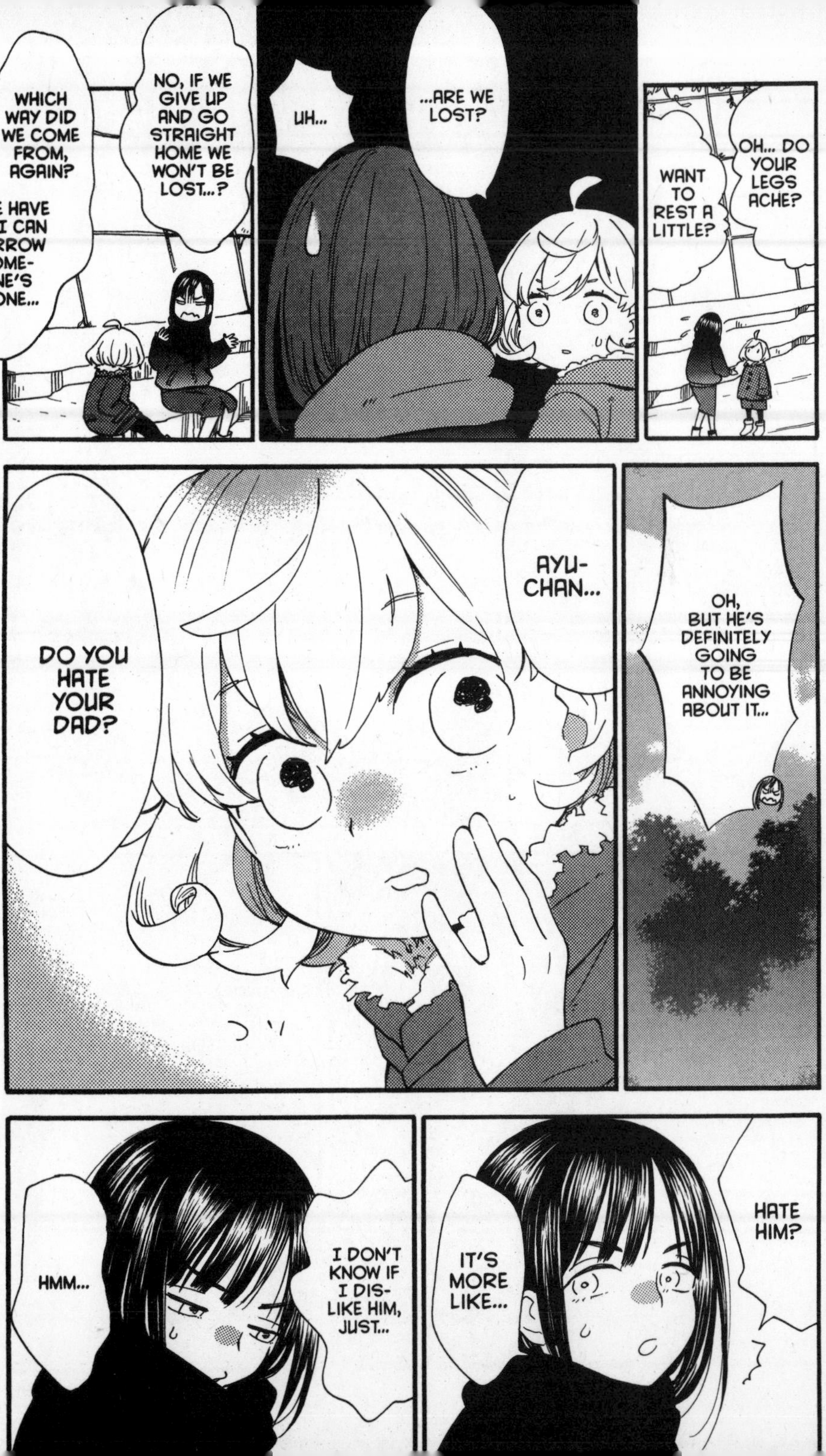
OH... DO YOUR LEGS ACHE?
WANT TO REST A LITTLE?
...ARE WE LOST?
UH...
NO, IF WE GIVE UP AND GO STRAIGHT HOME WE WON'T BE LOST...?
WHICH WAY DID WE COME FROM, AGAIN?
IF WE HAVE TO, I CAN BORROW SOME-ONE'S PHONE...
OH, BUT HE'S DEFINITELY GOING TO BE ANNOYING ABOUT IT...
AYU-CHAN...
DO YOU HATE YOUR DAD?
HATE HIM?
IT'S MORE LIKE...
I DON'T KNOW IF I DIS-LIKE HIM, JUST...
HMM...

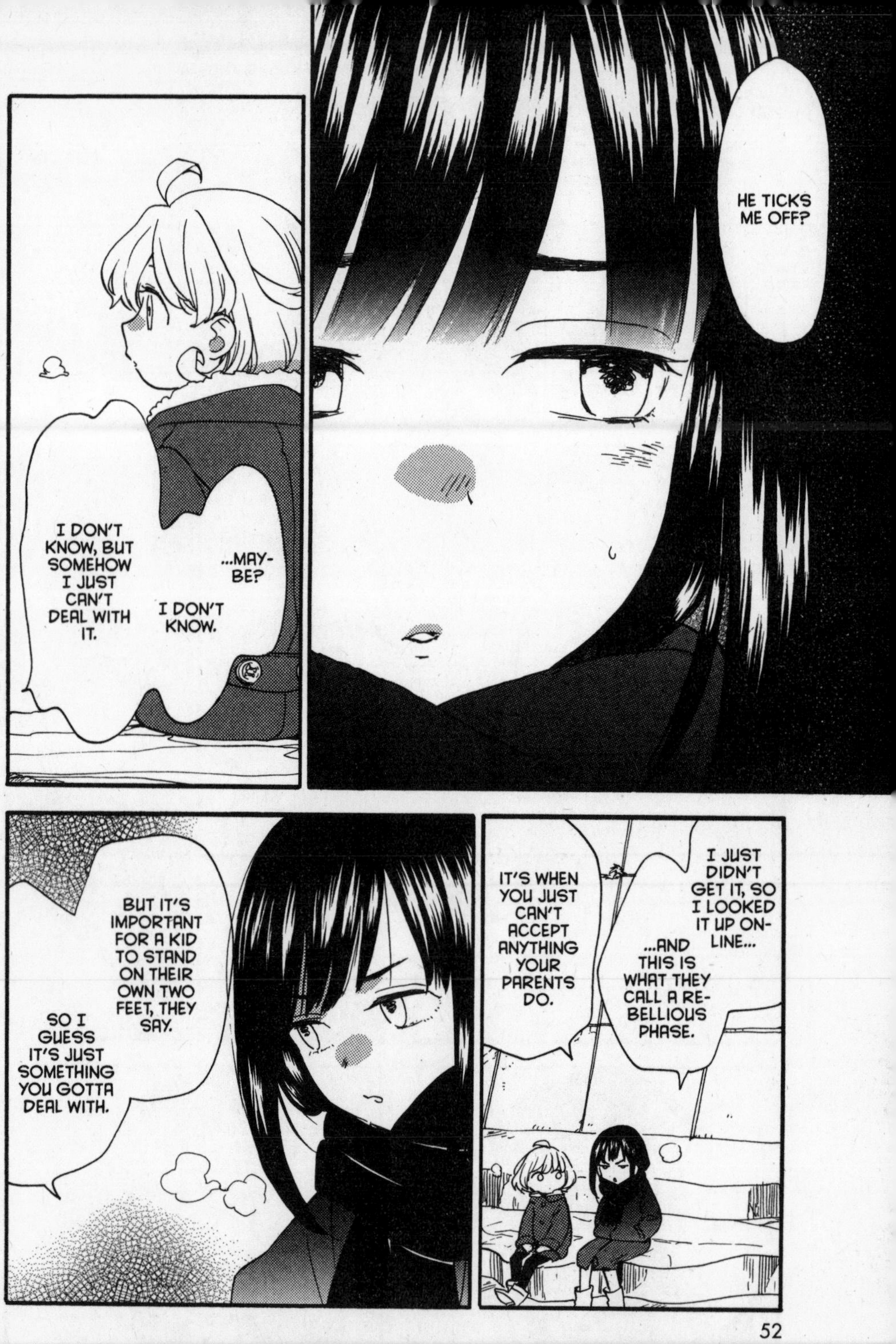
HE TICKS ME OFF?
...MAY-BE?
I DON'T KNOW.
I DON'T KNOW, BUT SOMEHOW I JUST CAN'T DEAL WITH IT.
I JUST DIDN'T GET IT, SO I LOOKED IT UP ON-LINE...
...AND THIS IS WHAT THEY CALL A RE-BELLIOUS PHASE.
IT'S WHEN YOU JUST CAN'T ACCEPT ANYTHING YOUR PARENTS DO.
BUT IT'S IMPORTANT FOR A KID TO STAND ON THEIR OWN TWO FEET, THEY SAY.
SO I GUESS IT'S JUST SOMETHING YOU GOTTA DEAL WITH.

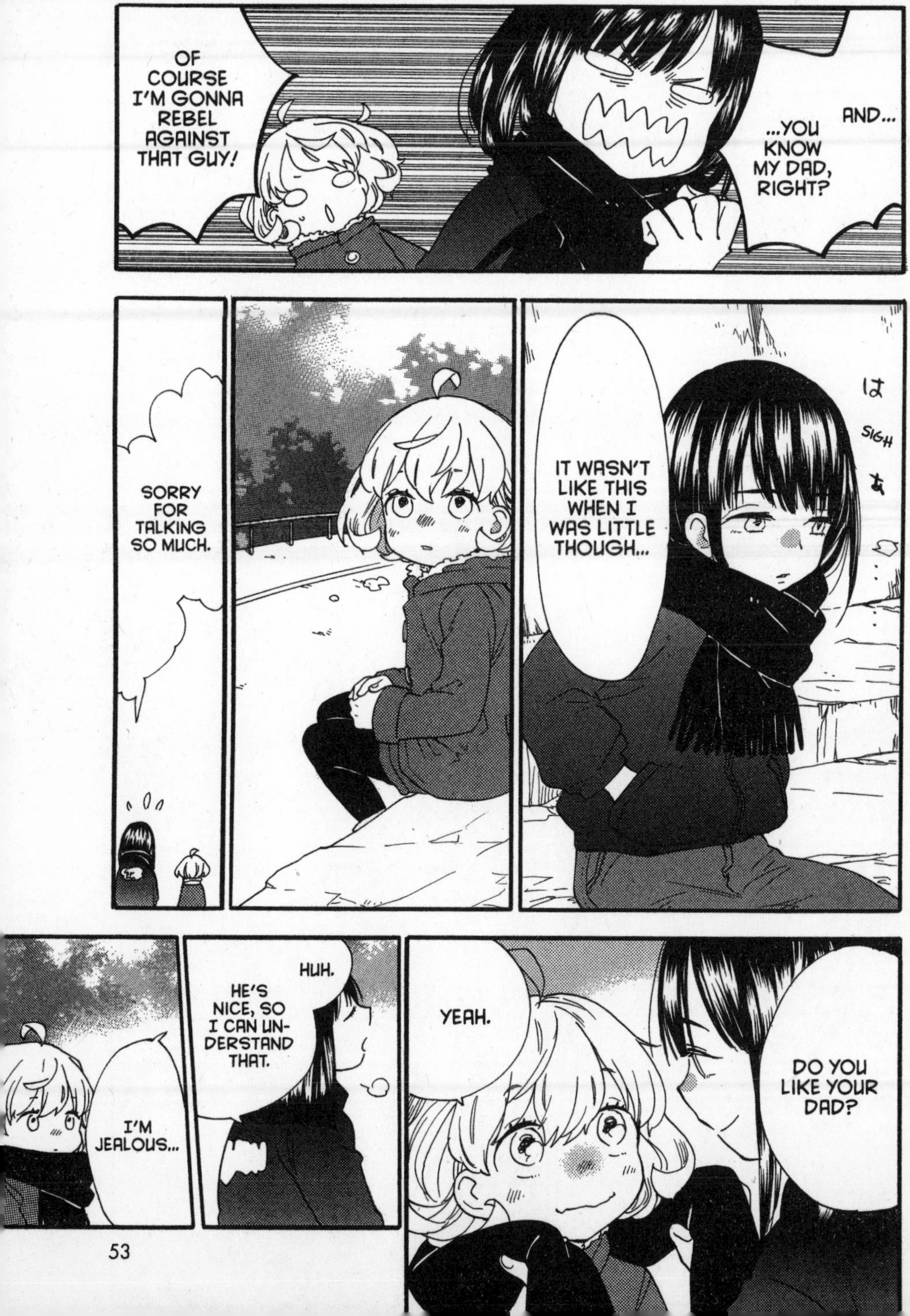
AND...
...YOU KNOW MY DAD, RIGHT?
OF COURSE I'M GONNA REBEL AGAINST THAT GUY!
はぁ SIGH
IT WASN'T LIKE THIS WHEN I WAS LITTLE THOUGH...
SORRY FOR TALKING SO MUCH.
DO YOU LIKE YOUR DAD?
YEAH.
HUH.
HE'S NICE, SO I CAN UNDERSTAND THAT.
I'M JEALOUS...

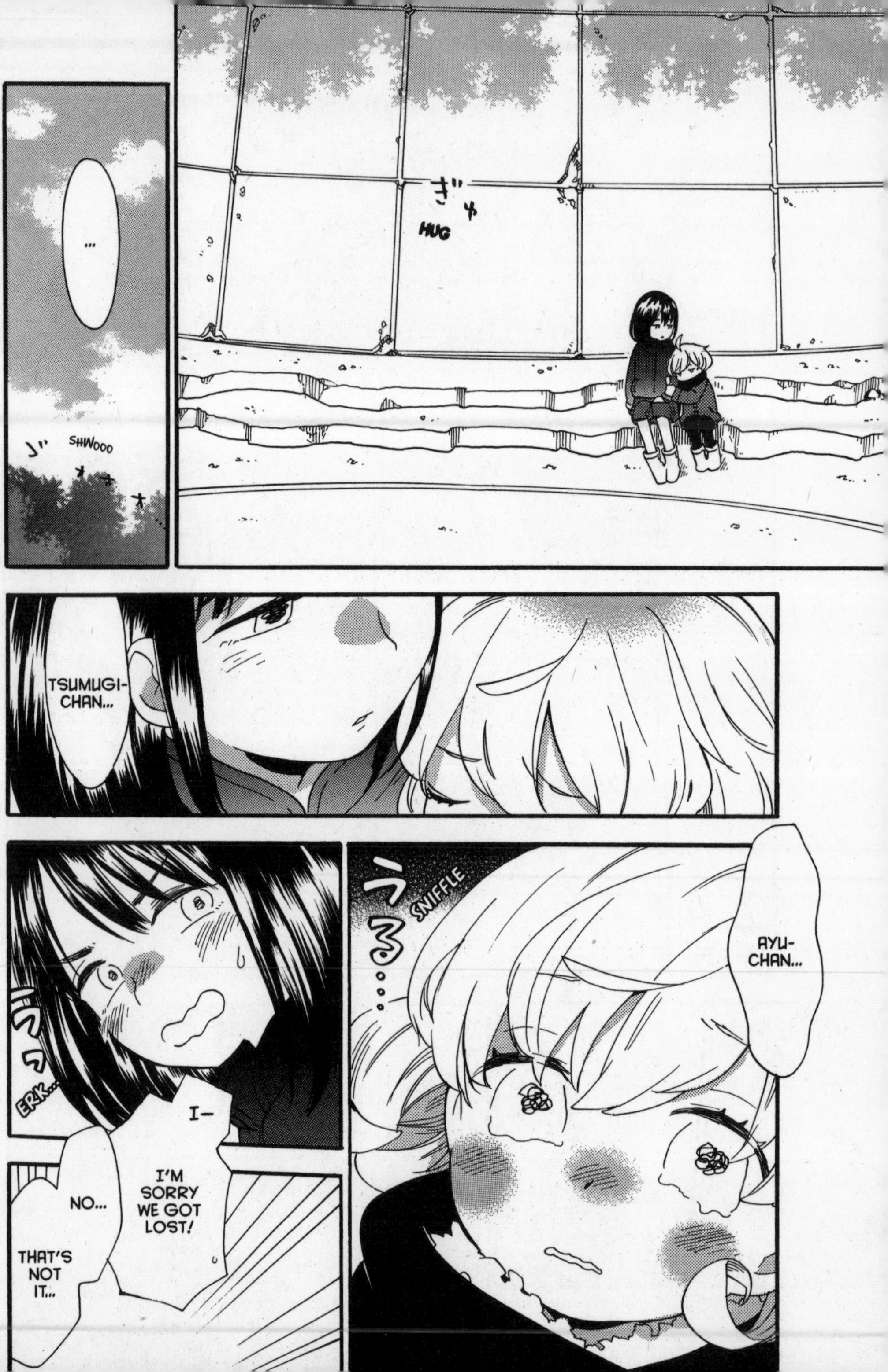
ぎゅ
HUG
...
SHWOOO
TSUMUGI-CHAN...
うる…
SNIFFLE
AYU-CHAN...
ERK...
I—
I'M SORRY WE GOT LOST!
NO...
THAT'S NOT IT...

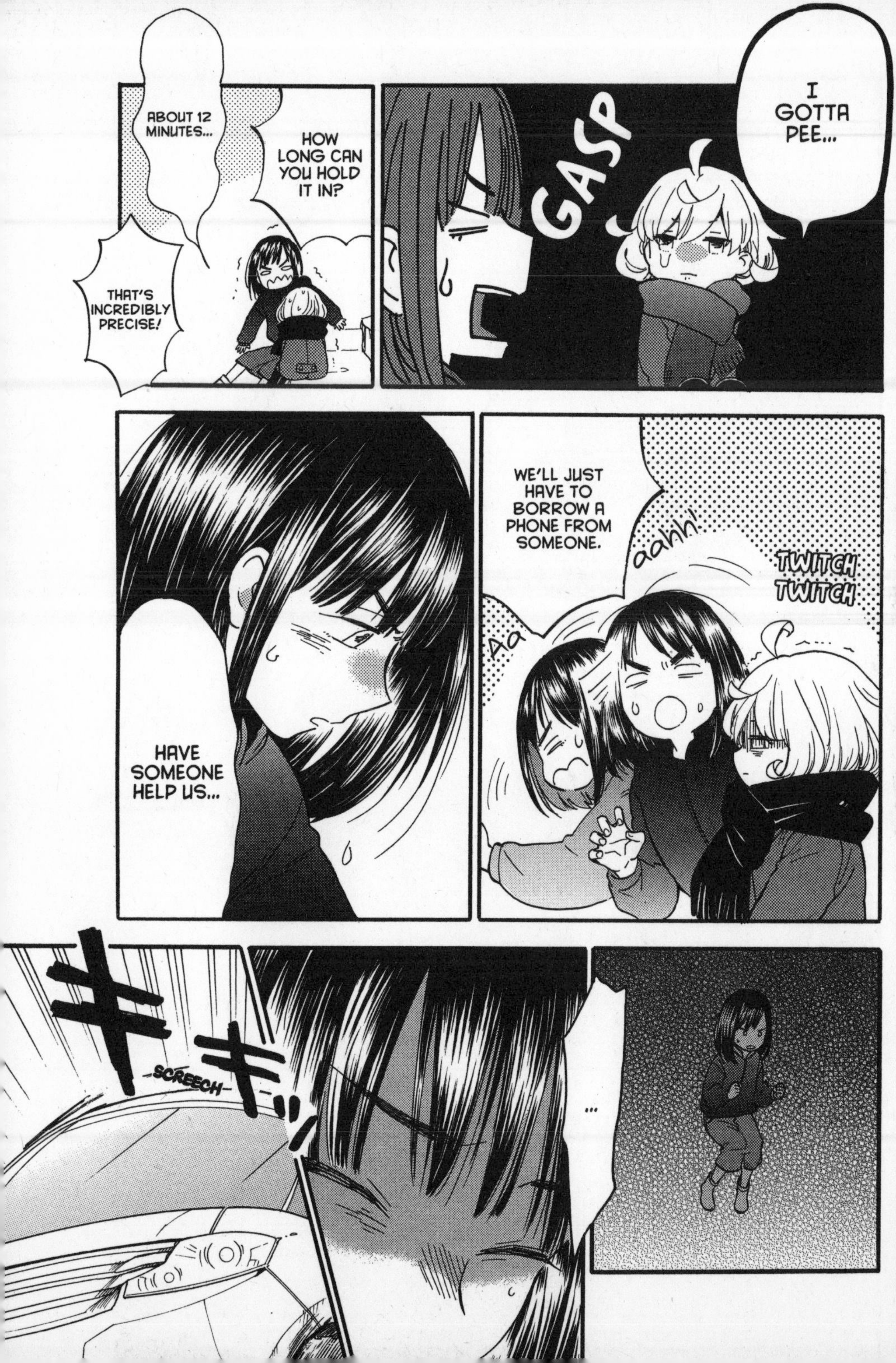
I GOTTA PEE...
GASP
HOW LONG CAN YOU HOLD IT IN?
ABOUT 12 MINUTES...
THAT'S INCREDIBLY PRECISE!
WE'LL JUST HAVE TO BORROW A PHONE FROM SOMEONE.
aahh!
TWITCH TWITCH
Aa
HAVE SOMEONE HELP US...
...
SCREECH

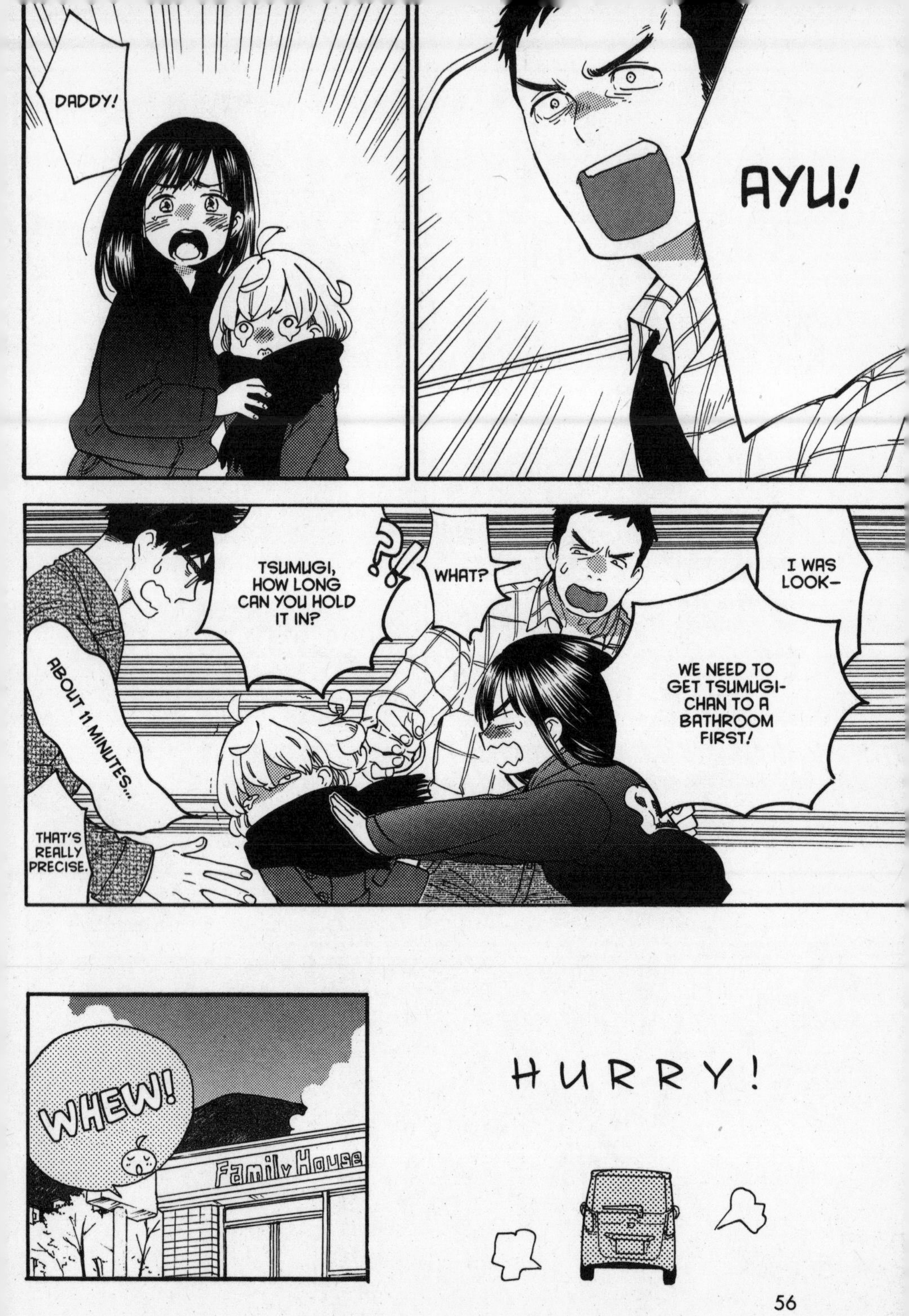
AYU!
DADDY!
I WAS LOOK—
WE NEED TO GET TSUMUGI-CHAN TO A BATHROOM FIRST!
WHAT?
TSUMUGI, HOW LONG CAN YOU HOLD IT IN?
?!
ABOUT 11 MINUTES...
THAT'S REALLY PRECISE.
HURRY!
WHEW!
Family House

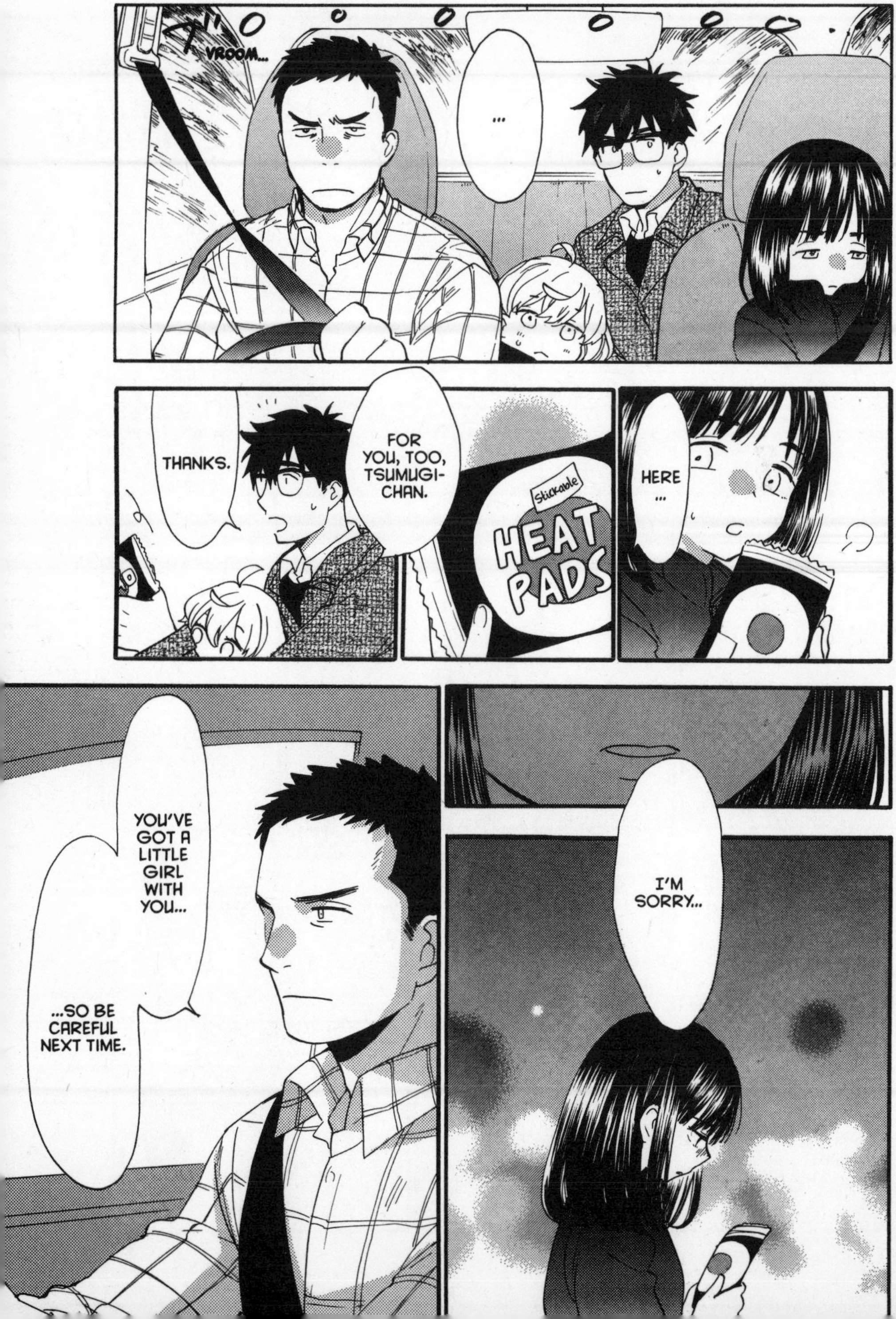
VROOM...
...
HERE ...
Stickable
HEAT PADS
FOR YOU, TOO, TSUMUGI-CHAN.
THANKS.
I'M SORRY...
YOU'VE GOT A LITTLE GIRL WITH YOU...
...SO BE CAREFUL NEXT TIME.

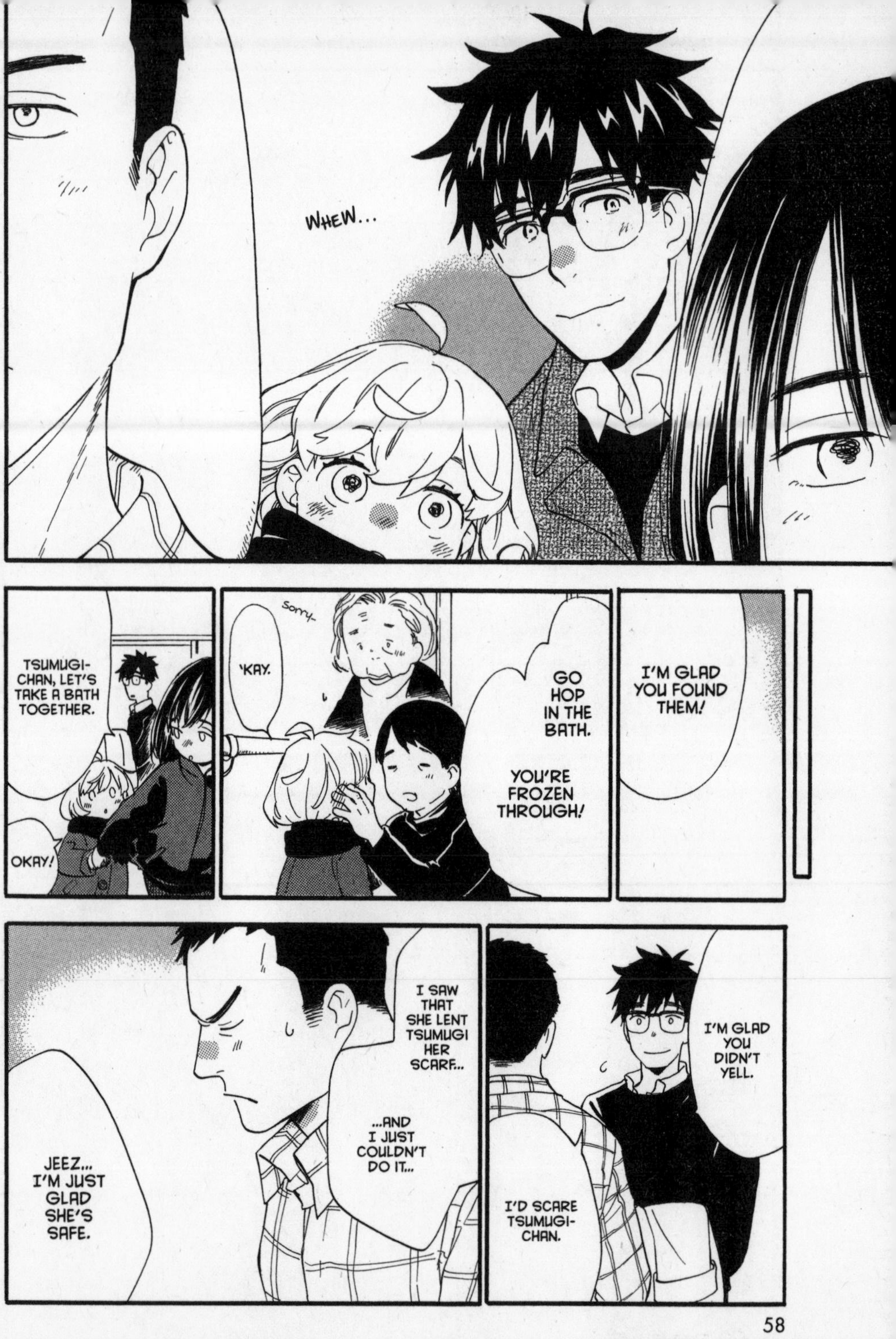
WHEW...
I'M GLAD YOU FOUND THEM!
GO HOP IN THE BATH.
YOU'RE FROZEN THROUGH!
Sorry...
'KAY.
TSUMUGI-CHAN, LET'S TAKE A BATH TOGETHER.
OKAY!
I'M GLAD YOU DIDN'T YELL.
I'D SCARE TSUMUGI-CHAN.
I SAW THAT SHE LENT TSUMUGI HER SCARF...
...AND I JUST COULDN'T DO IT...
JEEZ... I'M JUST GLAD SHE'S SAFE.

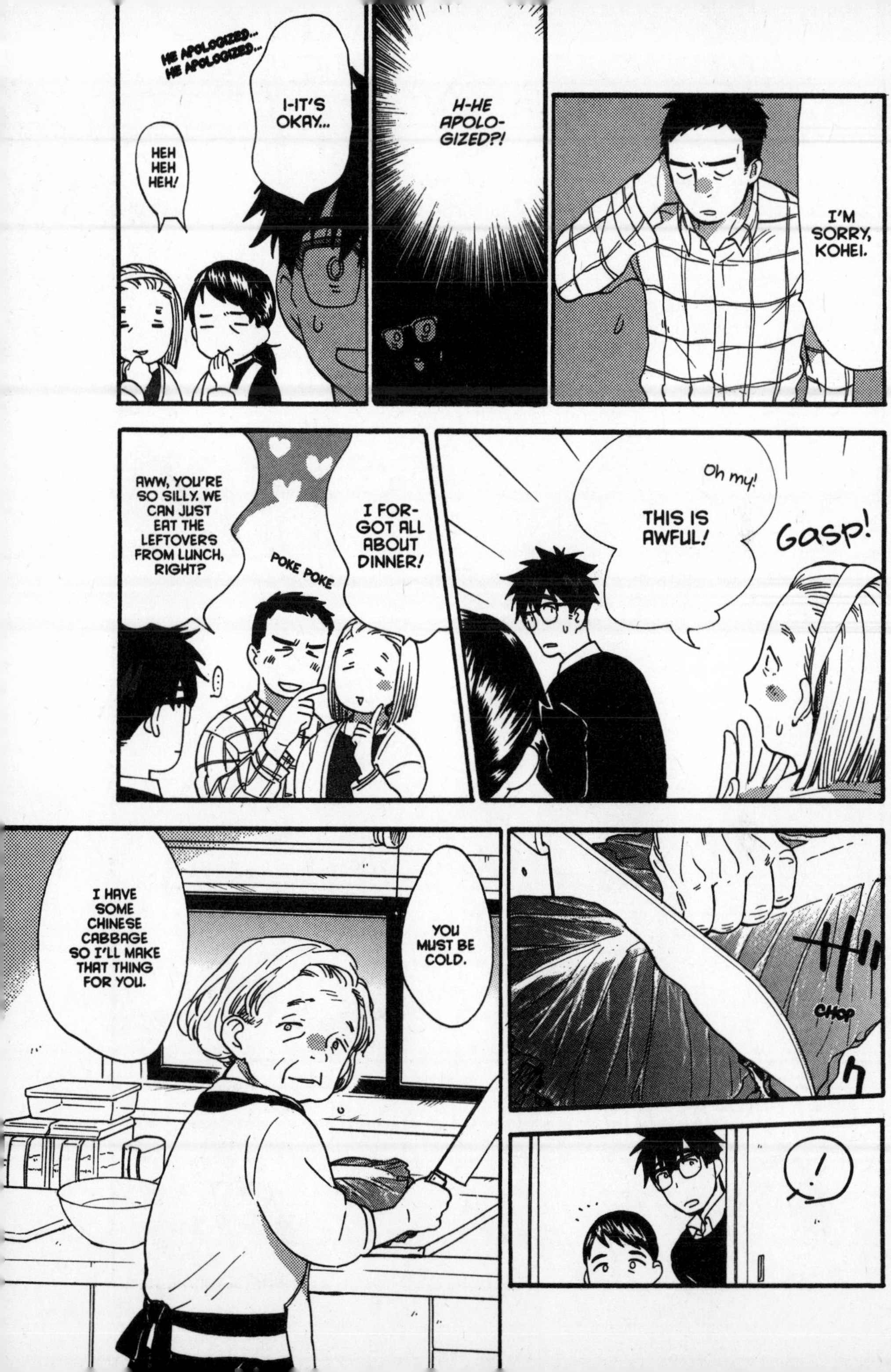
I'M SORRY, KOHEI.
H-HE APOLO-GIZED?!
I-IT'S OKAY...
HE APOLOGIZED... HE APOLOGIZED...
HEH HEH HEH!
Gasp!
Oh my!
THIS IS AWFUL!
I FOR-GOT ALL ABOUT DINNER!
POKE POKE
AWW, YOU'RE SO SILLY. WE CAN JUST EAT THE LEFTOVERS FROM LUNCH, RIGHT?
CHOP
!
YOU MUST BE COLD.
I HAVE SOME CHINESE CABBAGE SO I'LL MAKE THAT THING FOR YOU.

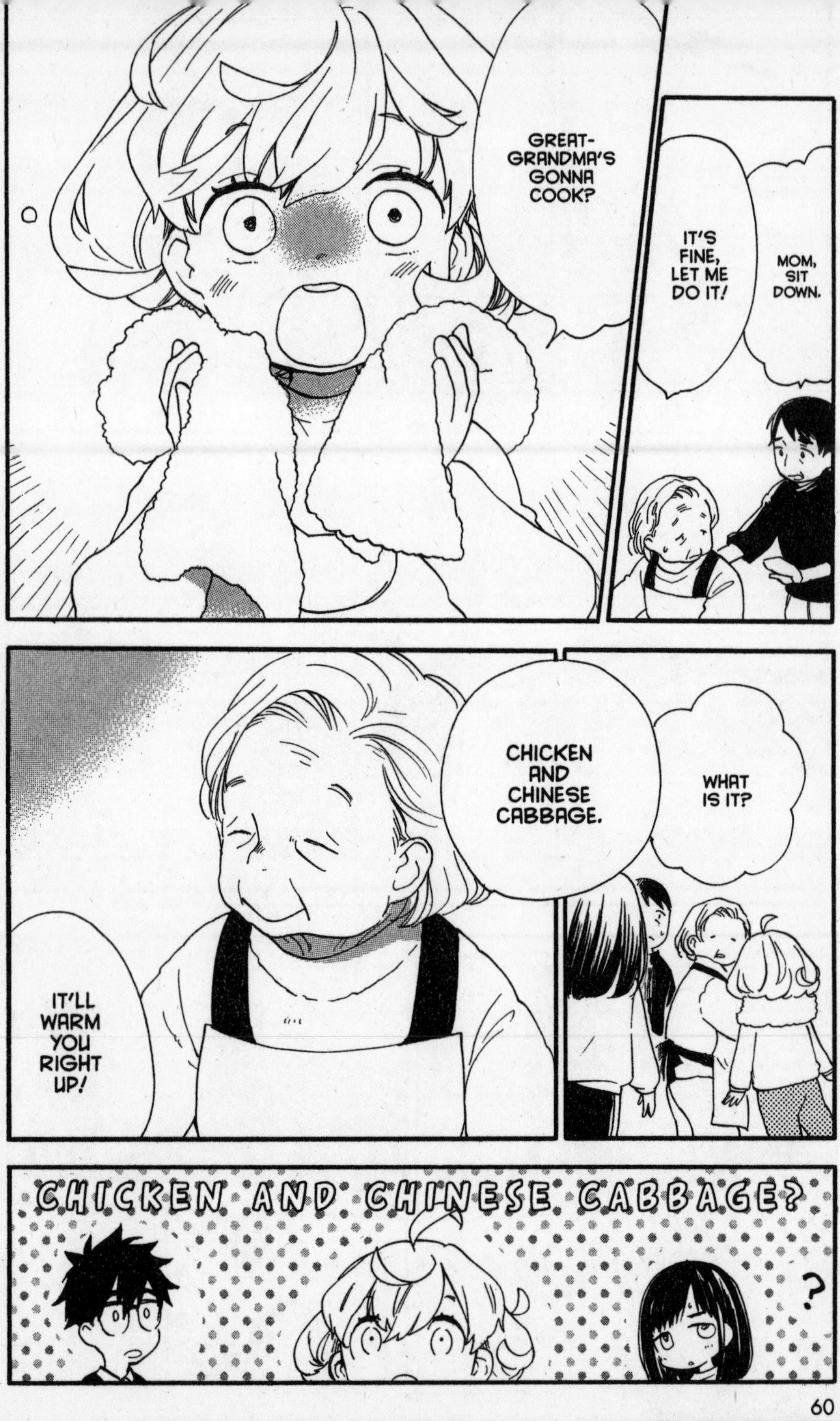
MOM, SIT DOWN.
IT'S FINE, LET ME DO IT!
GREAT-GRANDMA'S GONNA COOK?
WHAT IS IT?
CHICKEN AND CHINESE CABBAGE.
IT'LL WARM YOU RIGHT UP!
CHICKEN AND CHINESE CABBAGE?
?

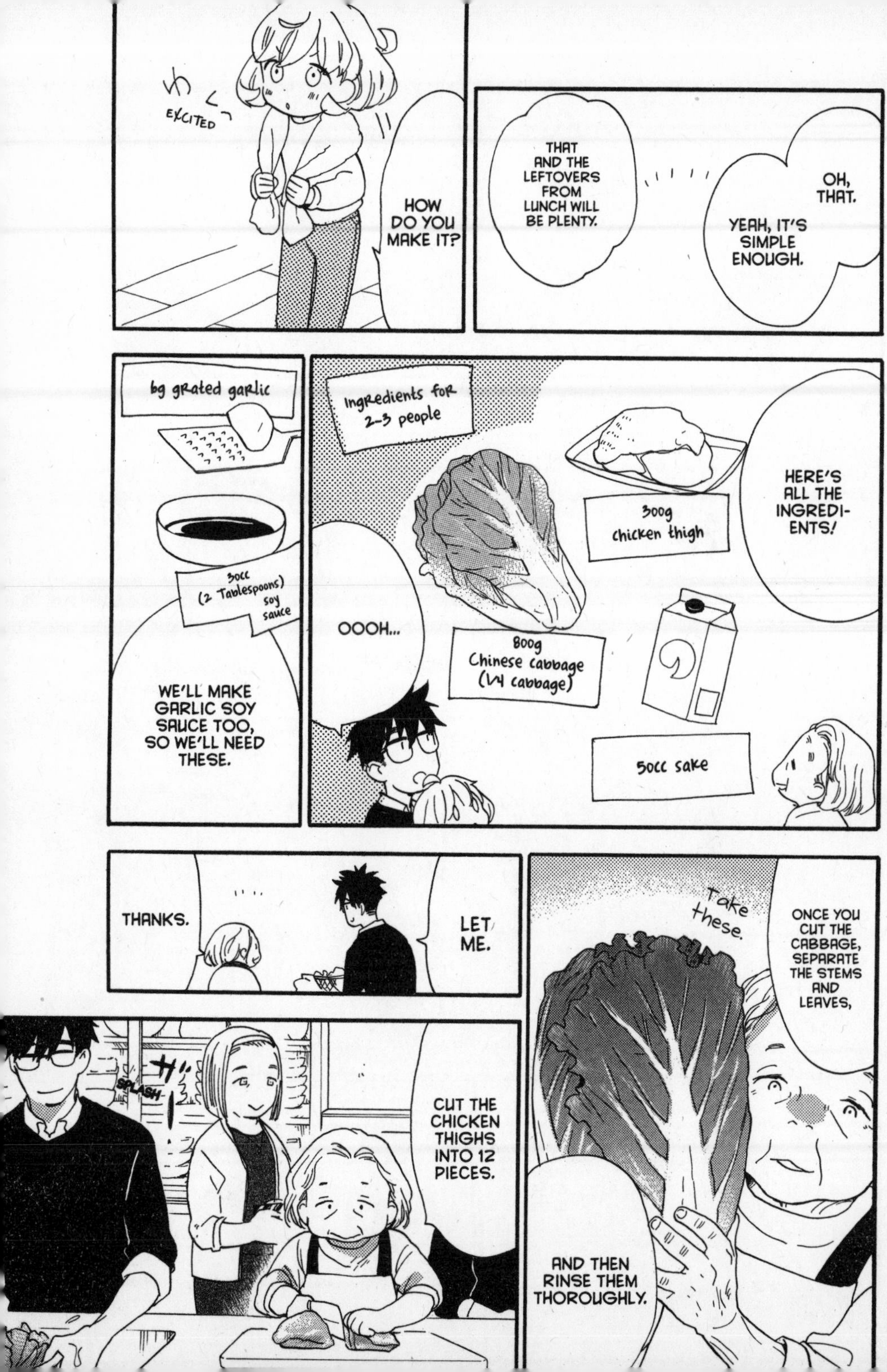
OH, THAT.
YEAH, IT'S SIMPLE ENOUGH.
THAT AND THE LEFTOVERS FROM LUNCH WILL BE PLENTY.
EXCITED
HOW DO YOU MAKE IT?
HERE'S ALL THE INGREDI-ENTS!
Ingredients for 2-3 people
300g chicken thigh
800g Chinese cabbage (1/4 cabbage)
OOOH...
50cc sake
6g grated garlic
30cc (2 Tablespoons) soy sauce
WE'LL MAKE GARLIC SOY SAUCE TOO, SO WE'LL NEED THESE.
ONCE YOU CUT THE CABBAGE, SEPARATE THE STEMS AND LEAVES,
Take these.
AND THEN RINSE THEM THOROUGHLY.
LET ME.
THANKS.
CUT THE CHICKEN THIGHS INTO 12 PIECES.
SPLASH

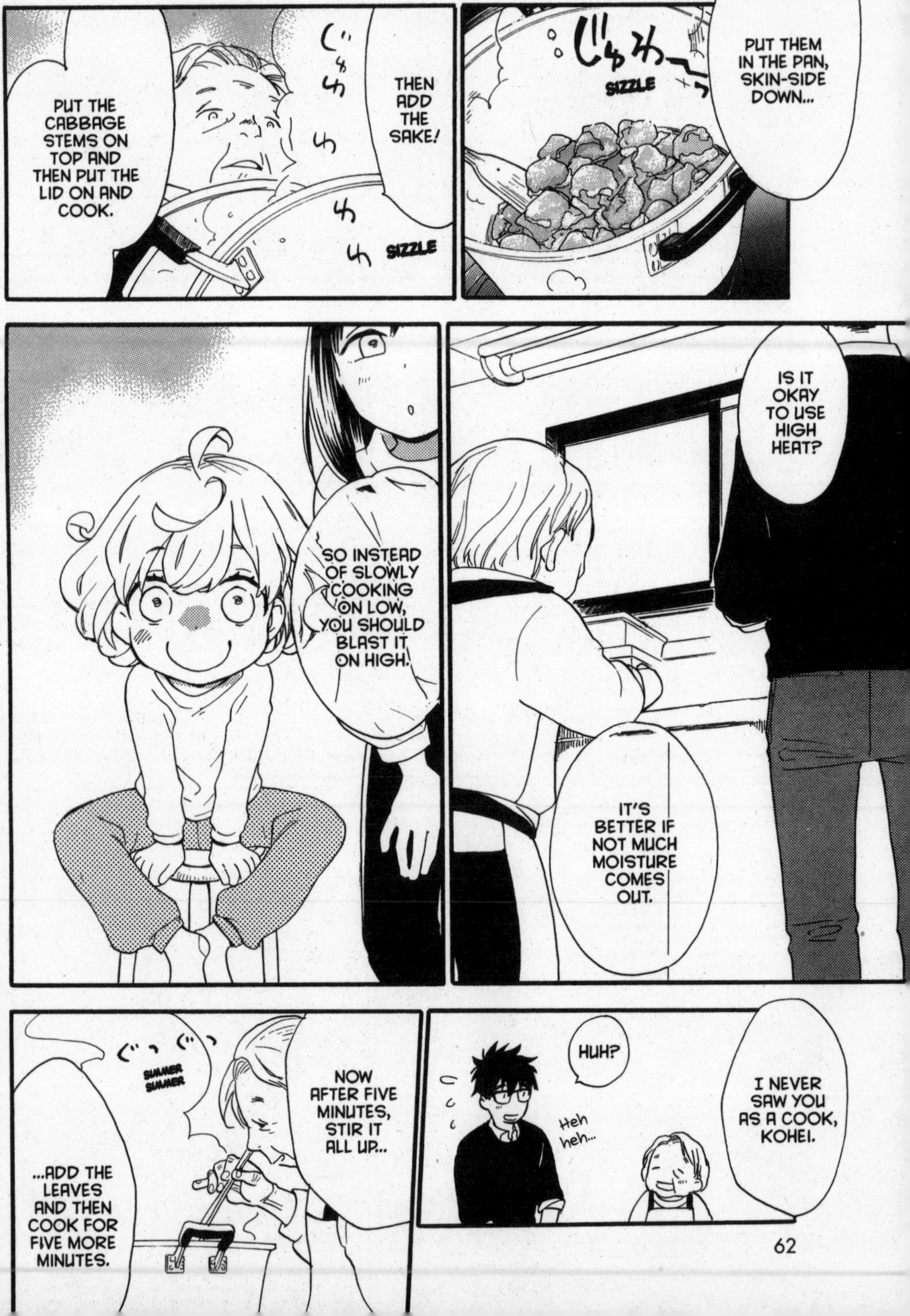
PUT THEM IN THE PAN, SKIN-SIDE DOWN...
じゅわ~
SIZZLE
THEN ADD THE SAKE!
PUT THE CABBAGE STEMS ON TOP AND THEN PUT THE LID ON AND COOK.
SIZZLE
IS IT OKAY TO USE HIGH HEAT?
IT'S BETTER IF NOT MUCH MOISTURE COMES OUT.
SO INSTEAD OF SLOWLY COOKING ON LOW, YOU SHOULD BLAST IT ON HIGH.
I NEVER SAW YOU AS A COOK, KOHEI.
HUH?
Heh heh...
NOW AFTER FIVE MINUTES, STIR IT ALL UP...
ぐつぐつ
SIMMER SIMMER
...ADD THE LEAVES AND THEN COOK FOR FIVE MORE MINUTES.

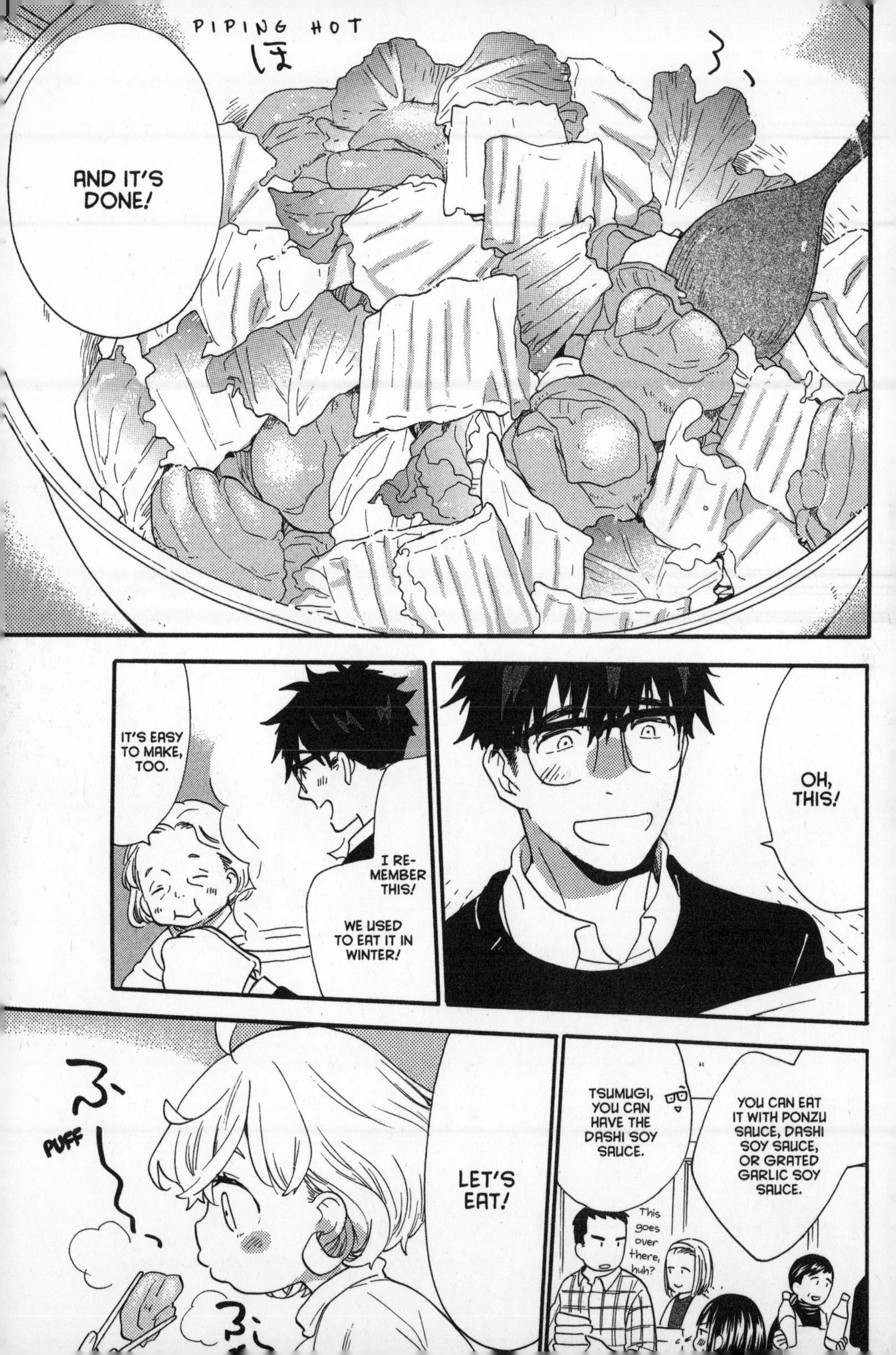

PIPING HOT
ほ
ふ、
AND IT'S DONE!
OH, THIS!
I RE-MEMBER THIS!
WE USED TO EAT IT IN WINTER!
IT'S EASY TO MAKE, TOO.
YOU CAN EAT IT WITH PONZU SAUCE, DASHI SOY SAUCE, OR GRATED GARLIC SOY SAUCE.
TSUMUGI, YOU CAN HAVE THE DASHI SOY SAUCE.
This goes over there, huh?
LET'S EAT!
ふ〜
PUFF
ふ

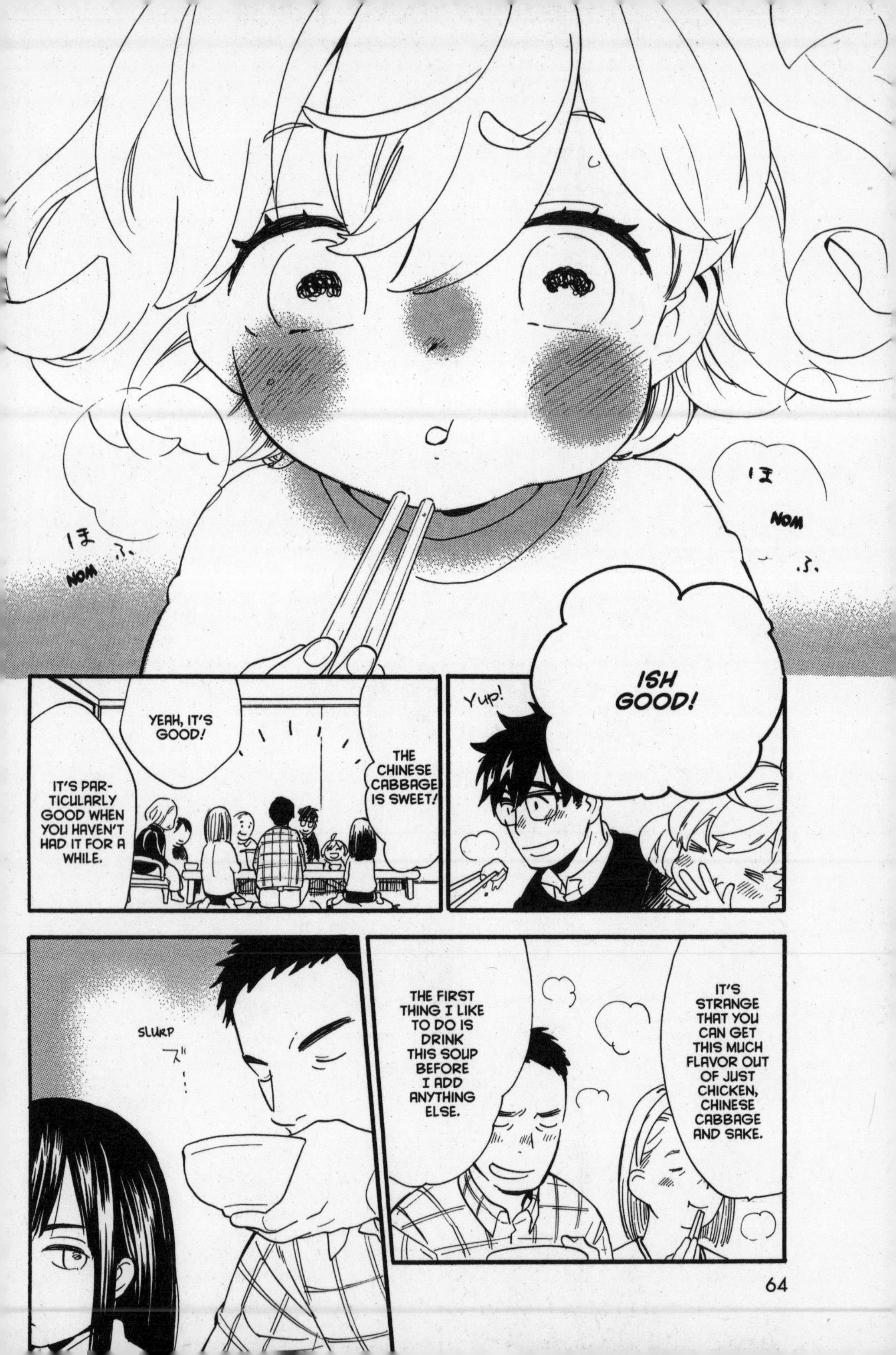
ほ NOM ふ
ほ ふ NOM
ISH GOOD!
Yup!
THE CHINESE CABBAGE IS SWEET!
YEAH, IT'S GOOD!
IT'S PARTICULARLY GOOD WHEN YOU HAVEN'T HAD IT FOR A WHILE.
IT'S STRANGE THAT YOU CAN GET THIS MUCH FLAVOR OUT OF JUST CHICKEN, CHINESE CABBAGE AND SAKE.
THE FIRST THING I LIKE TO DO IS DRINK THIS SOUP BEFORE I ADD ANYTHING ELSE.
SLURP
ズ…

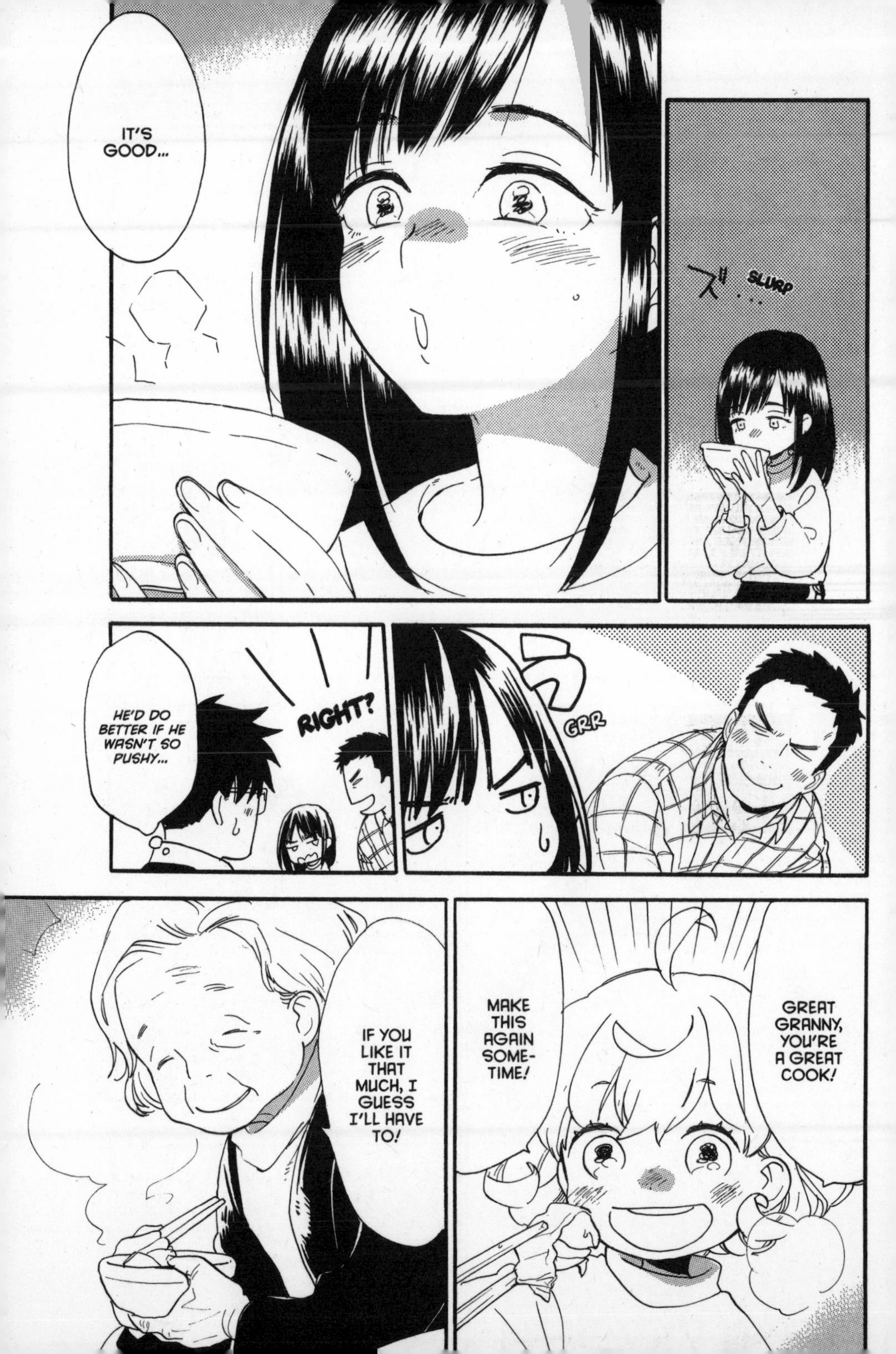
ズ
SLURP
IT'S GOOD...
GRR
RIGHT?
HE'D DO BETTER IF HE WASN'T SO PUSHY...
GREAT GRANNY, YOU'RE A GREAT COOK!
MAKE THIS AGAIN SOME-TIME!
IF YOU LIKE IT THAT MUCH, I GUESS I'LL HAVE TO!

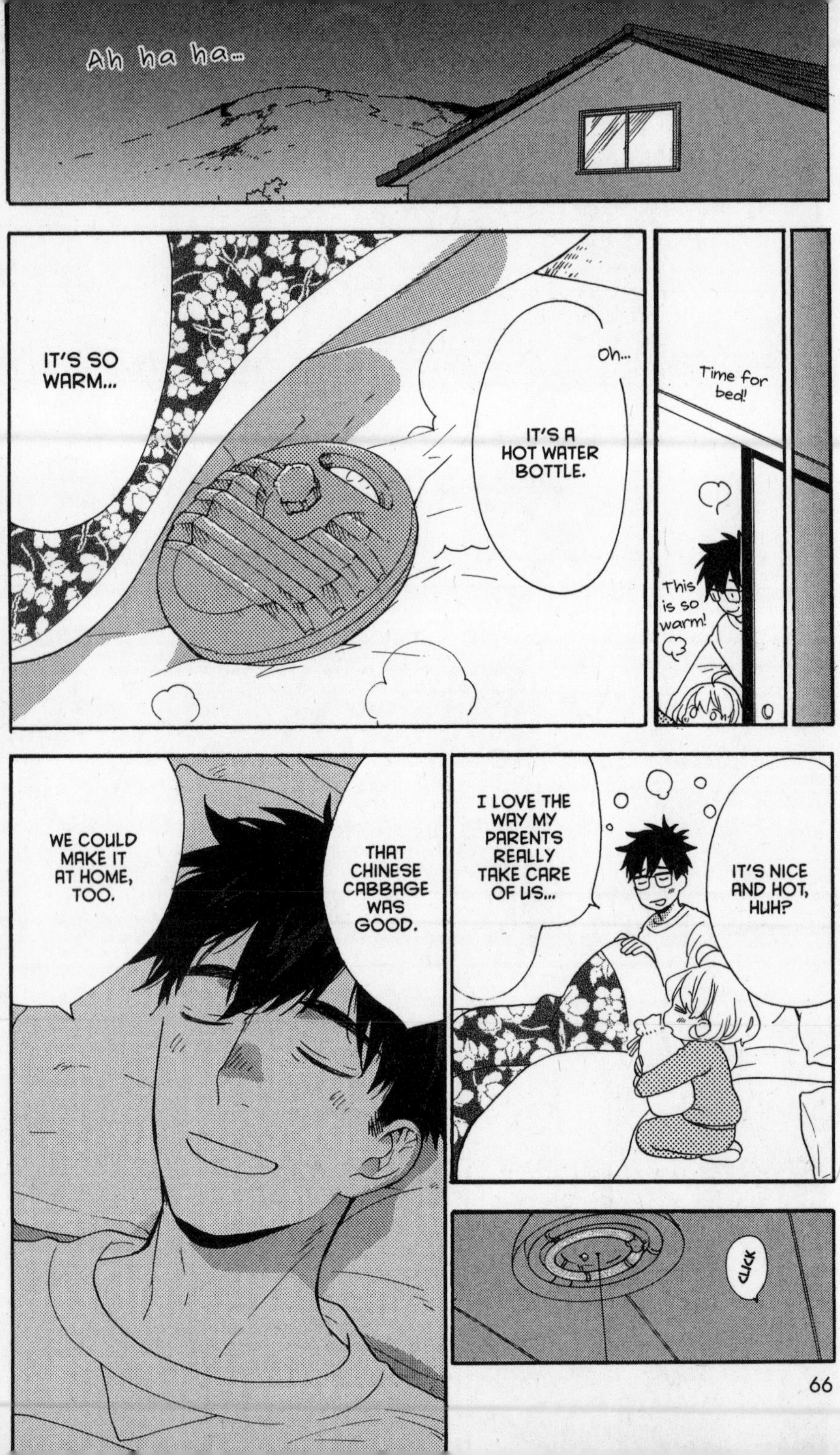
Ah ha ha...
Time for bed!
This is so warm!
Oh...
IT'S A HOT WATER BOTTLE.
IT'S SO WARM...
IT'S NICE AND HOT, HUH?
I LOVE THE WAY MY PARENTS REALLY TAKE CARE OF US...
CLICK
THAT CHINESE CABBAGE WAS GOOD.
WE COULD MAKE IT AT HOME, TOO.

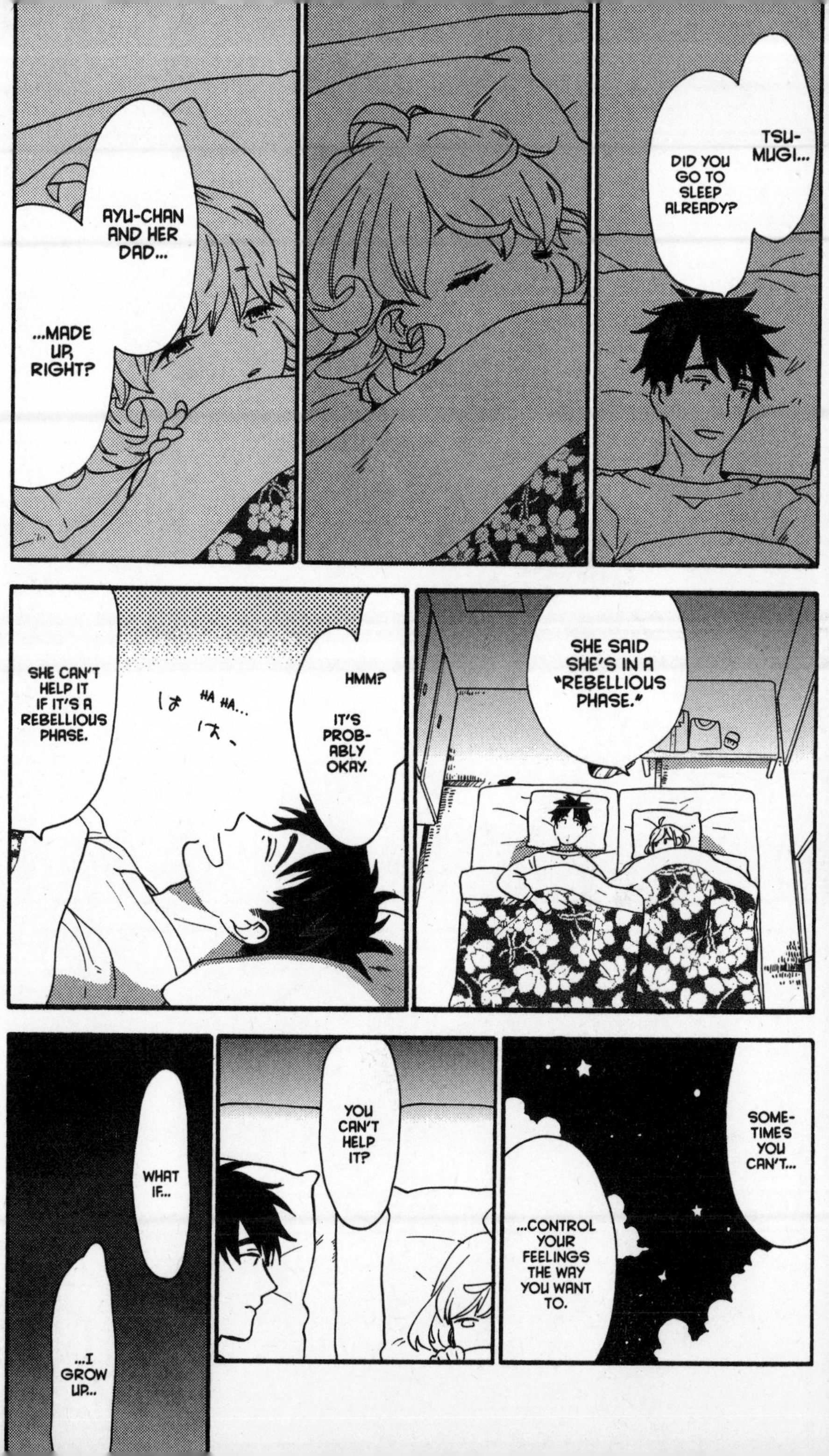
TSU-MUGI...
DID YOU GO TO SLEEP ALREADY?
AYU-CHAN AND HER DAD...
...MADE UP, RIGHT?
SHE SAID SHE'S IN A "REBELLIOUS PHASE."
HMM?
IT'S PROB-ABLY OKAY.
はは、
HA HA...
SHE CAN'T HELP IT IF IT'S A REBELLIOUS PHASE.
SOME-TIMES YOU CAN'T...
...CONTROL YOUR FEELINGS THE WAY YOU WANT TO.
YOU CAN'T HELP IT?
WHAT IF...
...I GROW UP...

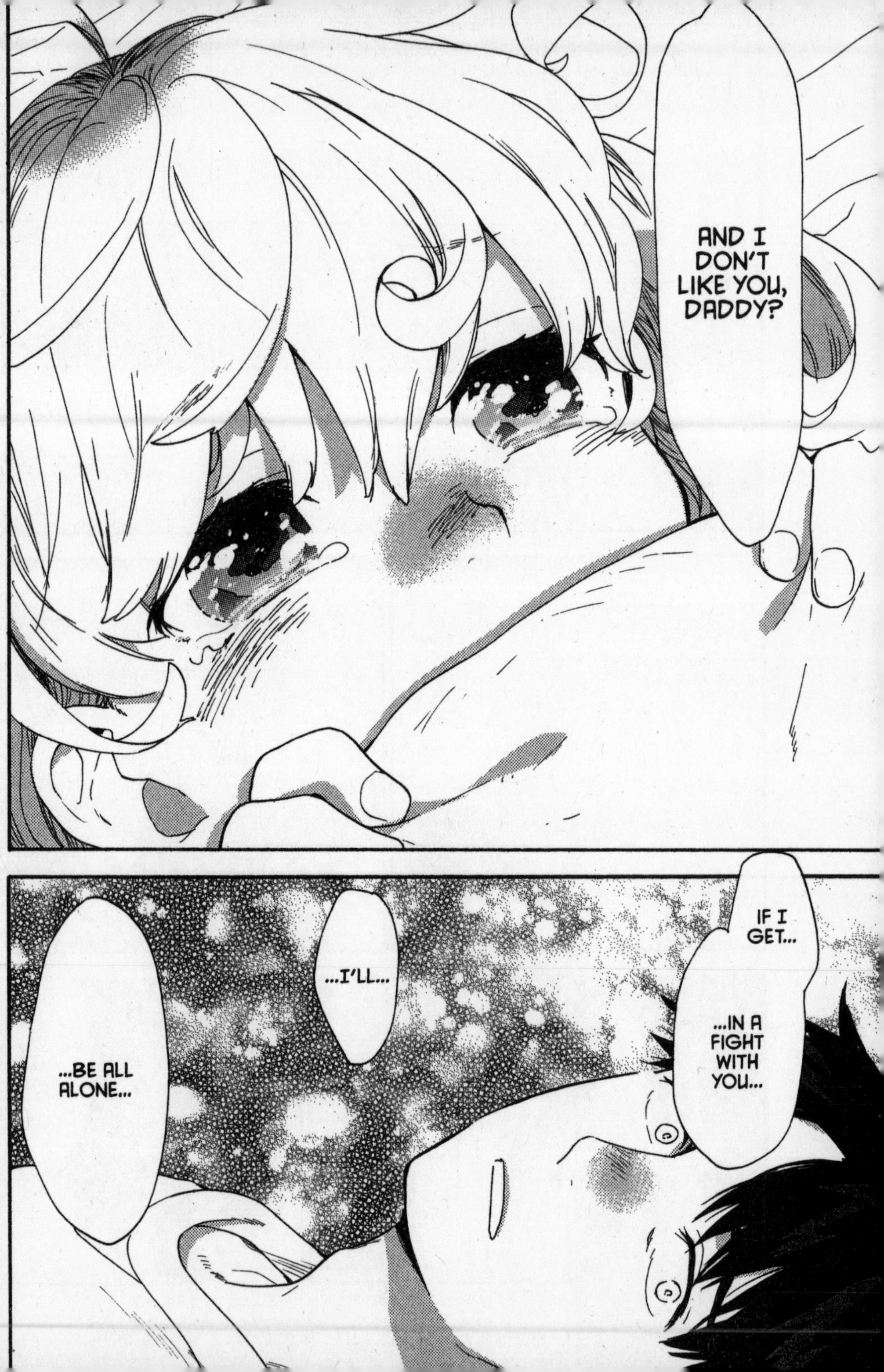
AND I DON'T LIKE YOU, DADDY?
IF I GET...
...IN A FIGHT WITH YOU...
...I'LL...
...BE ALL ALONE...

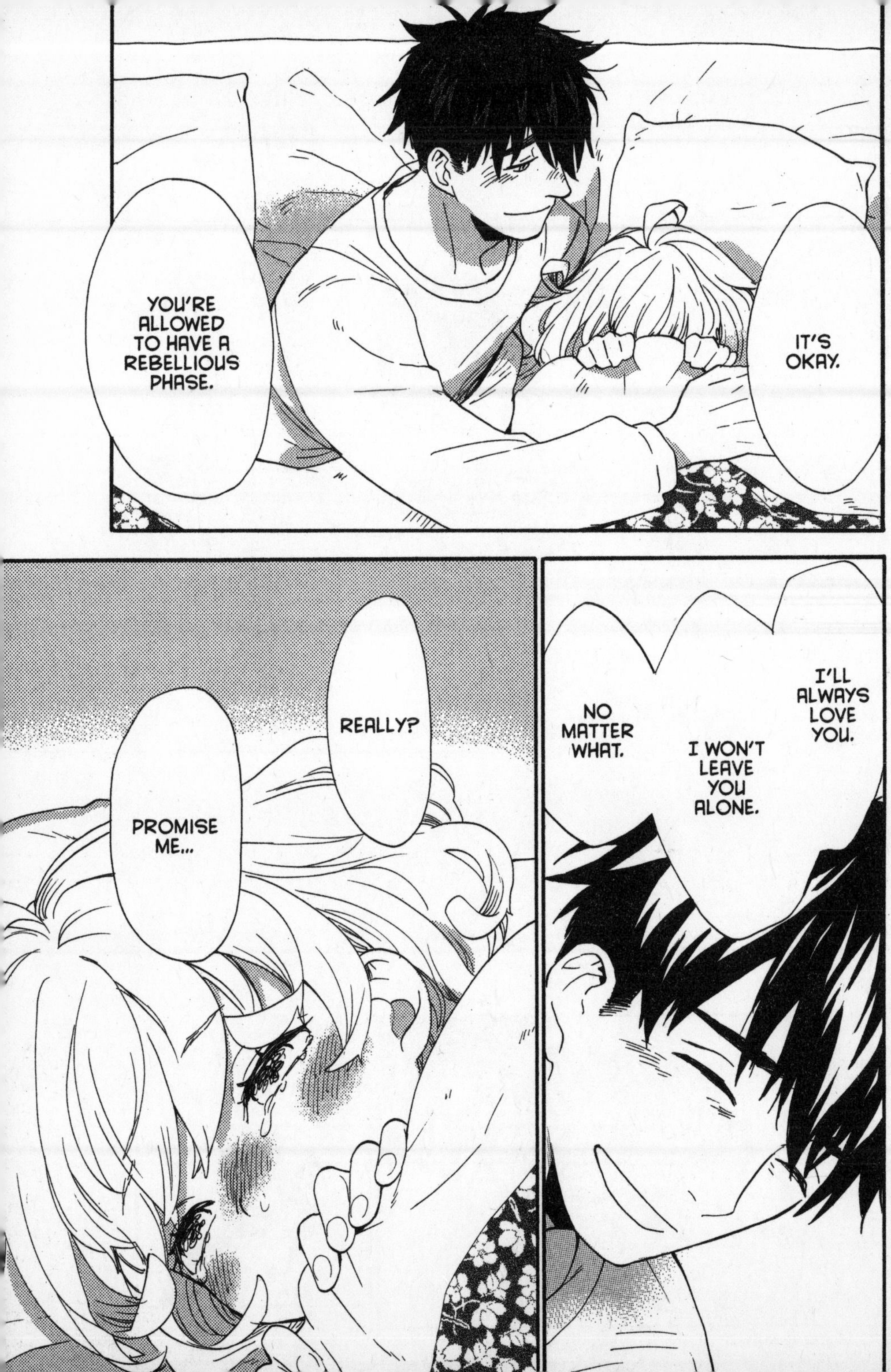
IT'S OKAY.
YOU'RE ALLOWED TO HAVE A REBELLIOUS PHASE.
I'LL ALWAYS LOVE YOU.
I WON'T LEAVE YOU ALONE.
NO MATTER WHAT.
REALLY?
PROMISE ME...

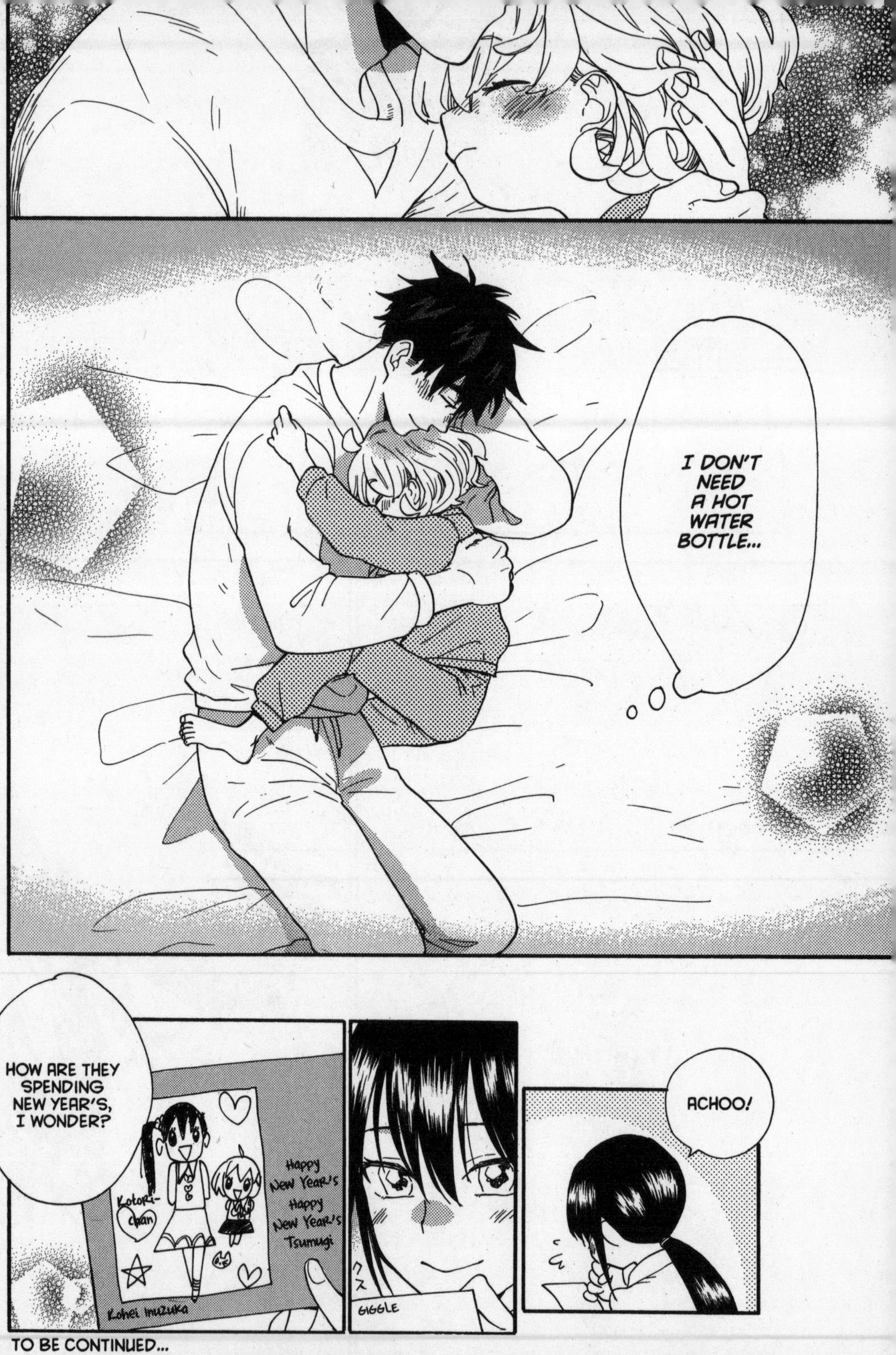
I DON'T NEED A HOT WATER BOTTLE...
ACHOO!
GIGGLE
HOW ARE THEY SPENDING NEW YEAR'S, I WONDER?
Happy New Year's Happy New Year's Tsumugi
Kotori-chan
Kohei Inuzuka

TO BE CONTINUED...

CHICKEN AND CABBAGE

☆ Ingredients ☆ (Serves 2-3)

★ 800g cabbage (1/4 of 1 large head)
★ 300g chicken thighs   ★ 50cc sake
Ⓐ 6g grated garlic   2 tbsp (30cc) soy sauce

1. Cut the cabbage into 3-4cm chunks. Separate the leaves from the core. Cut the thicker parts in half. Remove moisture.

2. Slice the chicken into 12 equal pieces.

3. Lay the chicken skin side down in a pan and pour sake over the top. Add the cabbage core pieces, cover with a lid and cook.

4. Cook over a high heat for 5 minutes. Stir once then add the remaining leaves.

> During step 4 the chicken should turn white

5. Cook for another five minutes and you're done! Cover in Ⓐ and enjoy.

// Garlic soy sauce is spicy, try a mild sauce for children.

> See udon recipe.

> I like to add a blend of green chili and yuzu citrus!

✦ POINT ✦ Only using a little sauce exemplifies the umami. When simmering make sure it doesn't burn and lose all its moisture over the high heat!

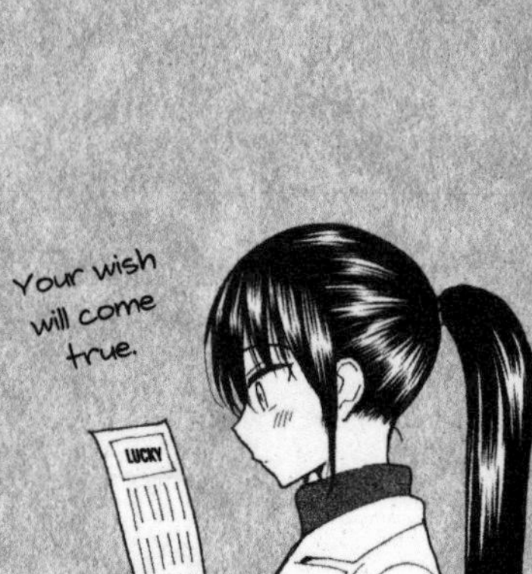
Your wish will come true.
LUCKY

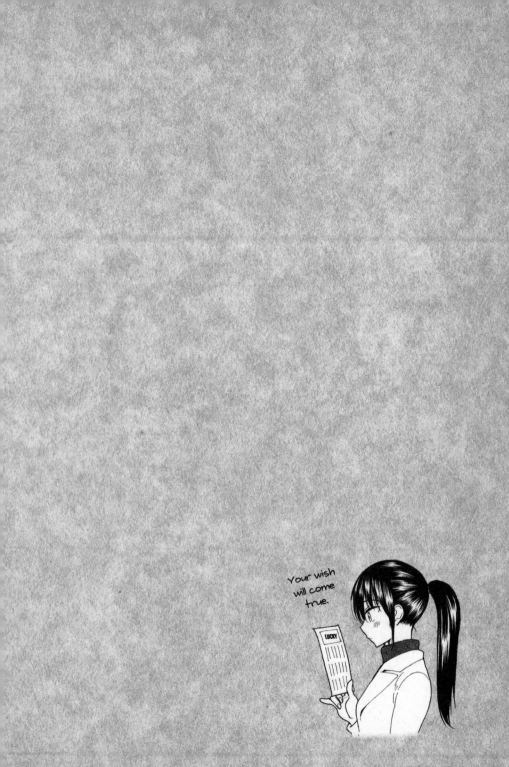

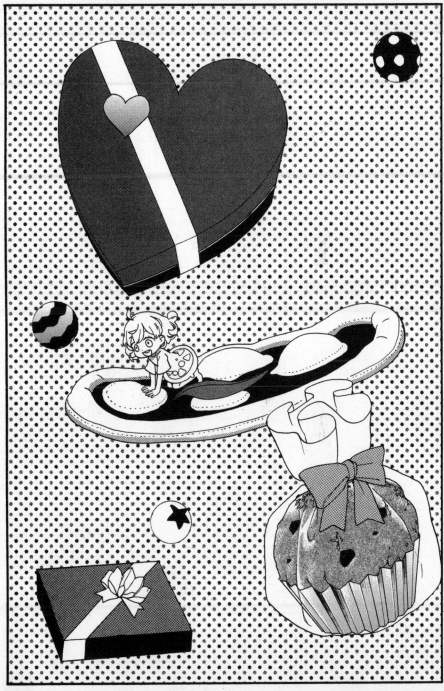

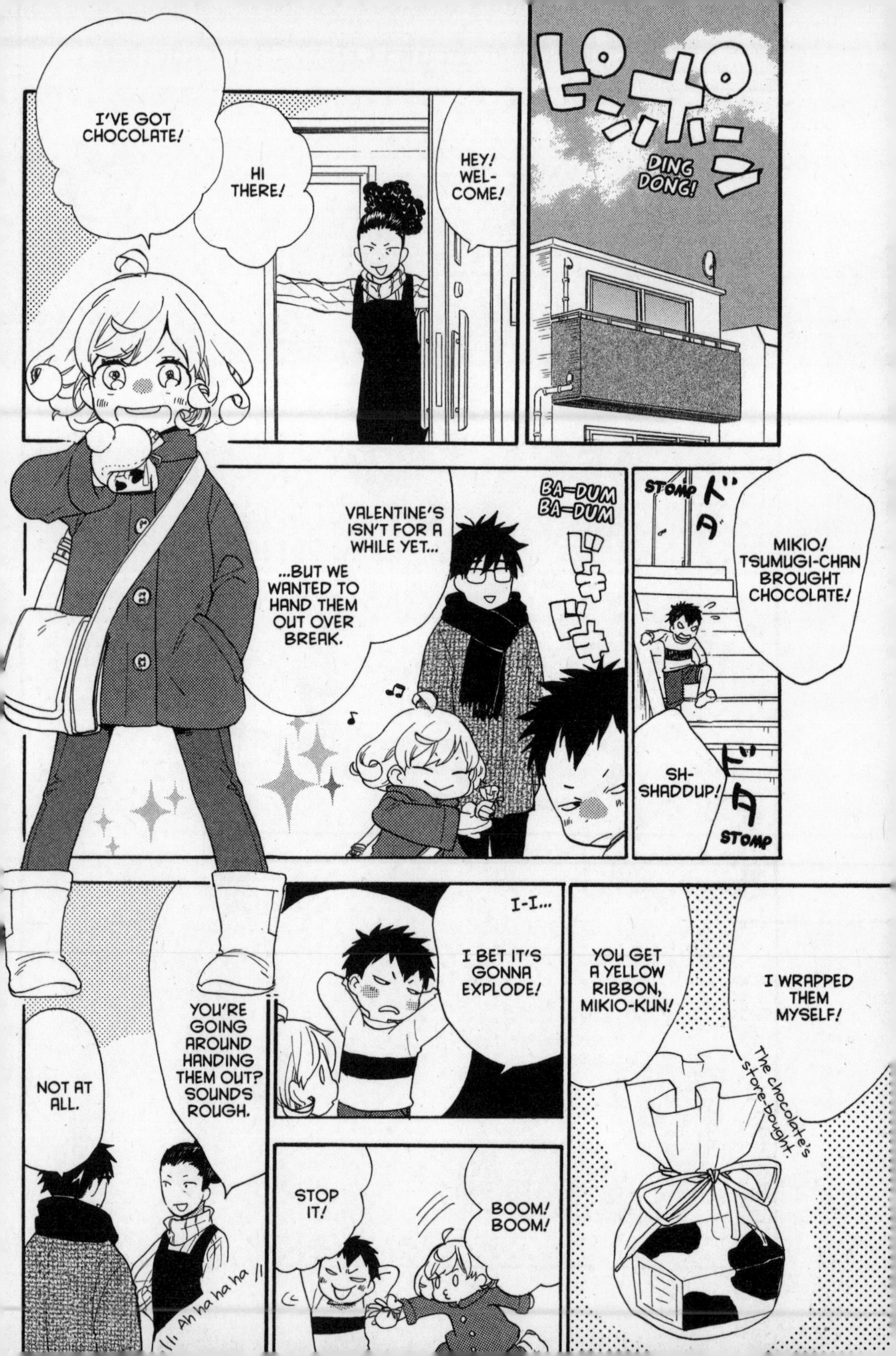

ピンポーン
DING DONG!
HEY! WEL-COME!
HI THERE!
I'VE GOT CHOCOLATE!
STOMP
MIKIO! TSUMUGI-CHAN BROUGHT CHOCOLATE!
SH-SHADDUP!
STOMP
BA-DUM BA-DUM
VALENTINE'S ISN'T FOR A WHILE YET...
...BUT WE WANTED TO HAND THEM OUT OVER BREAK.
I WRAPPED THEM MYSELF!
The chocolate's store-bought.
YOU GET A YELLOW RIBBON, MIKIO-KUN!
I-I...
I BET IT'S GONNA EXPLODE!
BOOM! BOOM!
STOP IT!
YOU'RE GOING AROUND HANDING THEM OUT? SOUNDS ROUGH.
NOT AT ALL.
Ah ha ha ha

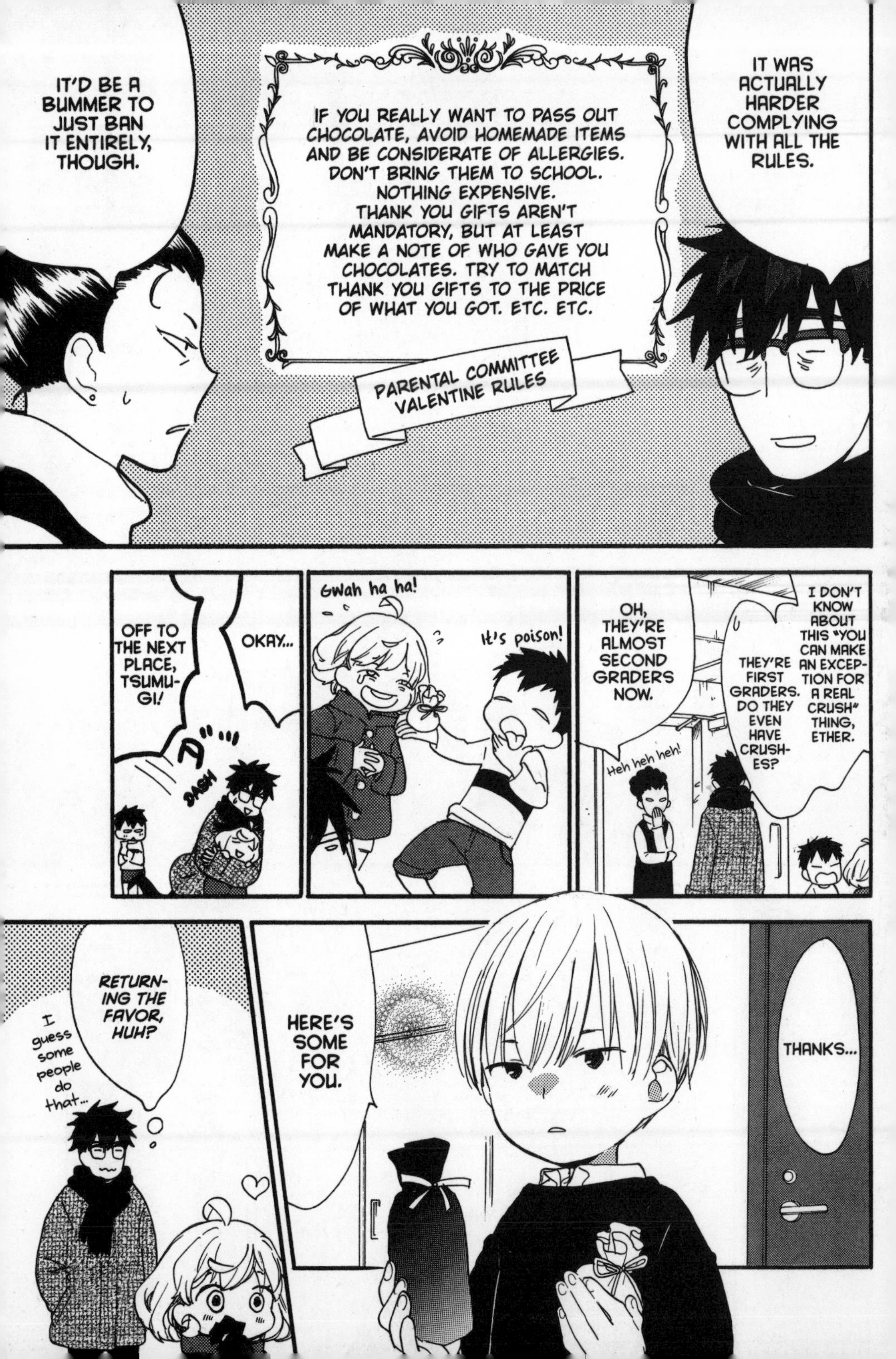
IT WAS ACTUALLY HARDER COMPLYING WITH ALL THE RULES.
IF YOU REALLY WANT TO PASS OUT CHOCOLATE, AVOID HOMEMADE ITEMS AND BE CONSIDERATE OF ALLERGIES. DON'T BRING THEM TO SCHOOL. NOTHING EXPENSIVE. THANK YOU GIFTS AREN'T MANDATORY, BUT AT LEAST MAKE A NOTE OF WHO GAVE YOU CHOCOLATES. TRY TO MATCH THANK YOU GIFTS TO THE PRICE OF WHAT YOU GOT. ETC. ETC.
PARENTAL COMMITTEE VALENTINE RULES
IT'D BE A BUMMER TO JUST BAN IT ENTIRELY, THOUGH.
I DON'T KNOW ABOUT THIS "YOU CAN MAKE AN EXCEPTION FOR A REAL CRUSH" THING, ETHER.
THEY'RE FIRST GRADERS. DO THEY EVEN HAVE CRUSHES?
OH, THEY'RE ALMOST SECOND GRADERS NOW.
Heh heh heh!
Gwah ha ha!
It's poison!
OKAY...
OFF TO THE NEXT PLACE, TSUMUGI!
DASH
THANKS...
HERE'S SOME FOR YOU.
RETURNING THE FAVOR, HUH?
I guess some people do that...

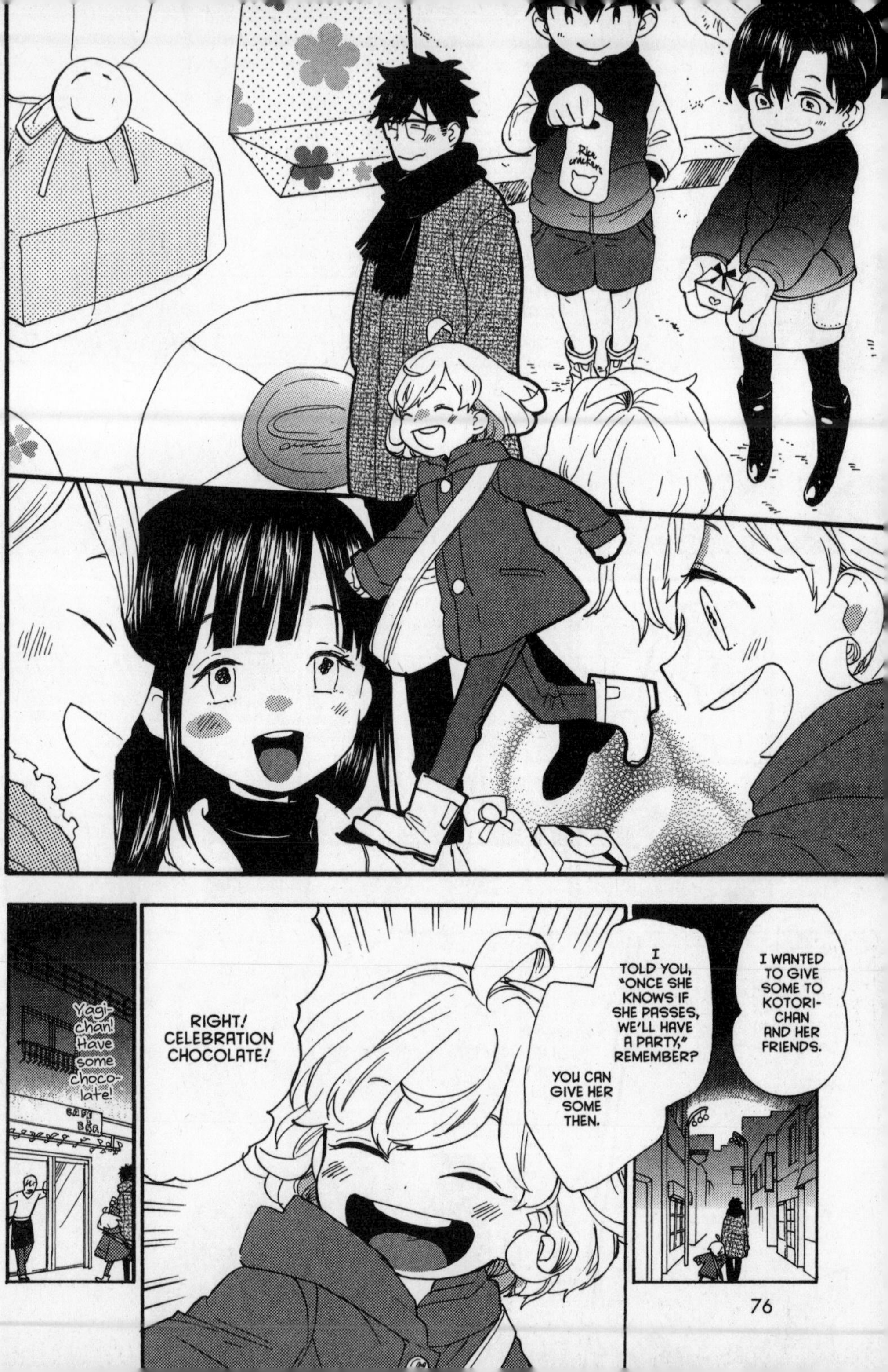
Rice crackers
I WANTED TO GIVE SOME TO KOTORI-CHAN AND HER FRIENDS.
I TOLD YOU, "ONCE SHE KNOWS IF SHE PASSES, WE'LL HAVE A PARTY," REMEMBER?
YOU CAN GIVE HER SOME THEN.
RIGHT! CELEBRATION CHOCOLATE!
Yagi-chan! Have some choco-late!
CAFE & BAR

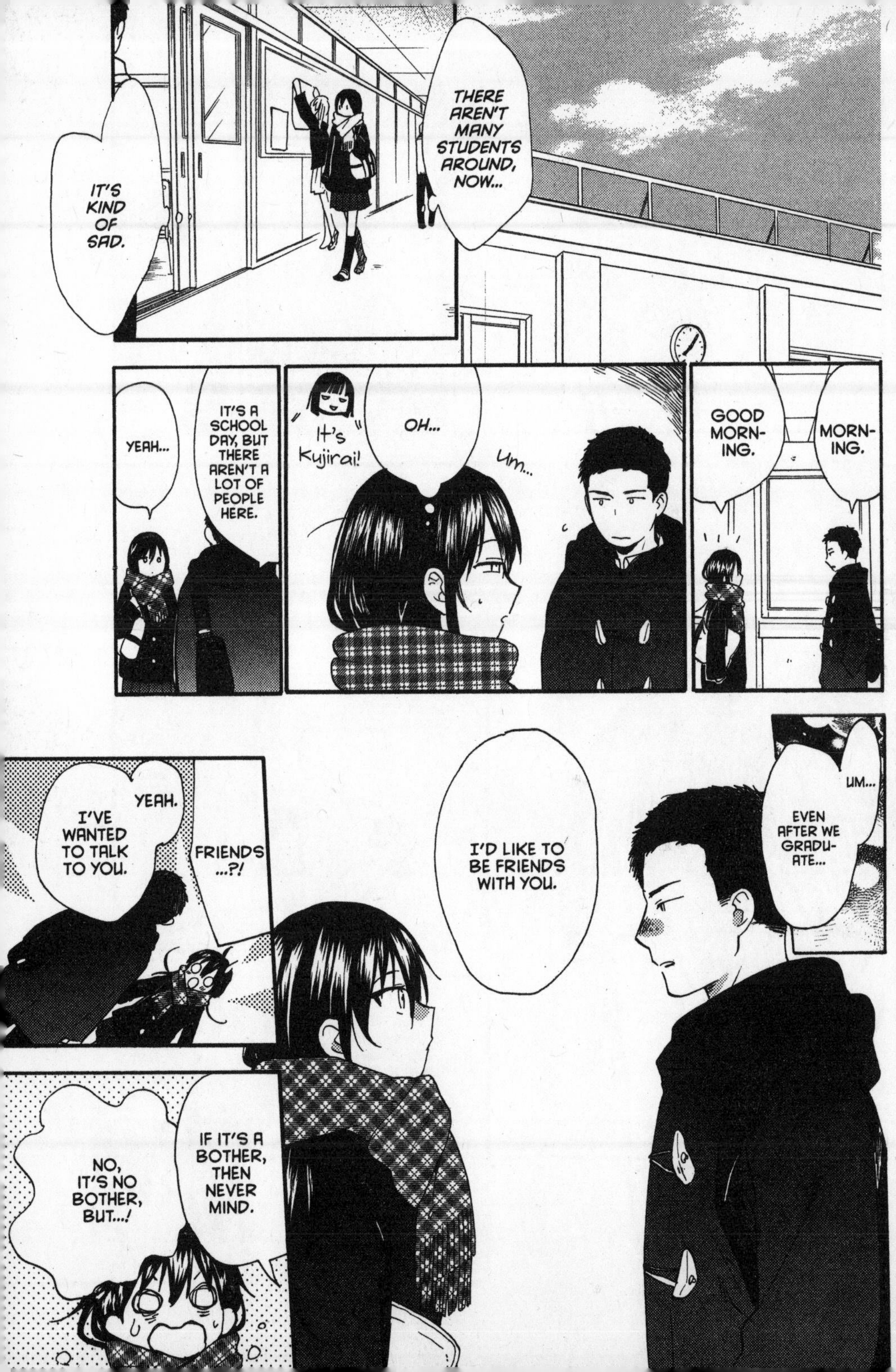

THERE AREN'T MANY STUDENTS AROUND, NOW...
IT'S KIND OF SAD.
MORNING.
GOOD MORNING.
OH...
Um...
It's Kujirai!
IT'S A SCHOOL DAY, BUT THERE AREN'T A LOT OF PEOPLE HERE.
YEAH...
UM...
EVEN AFTER WE GRADUATE...
I'D LIKE TO BE FRIENDS WITH YOU.
FRIENDS ...?!
YEAH.
I'VE WANTED TO TALK TO YOU.
IF IT'S A BOTHER, THEN NEVER MIND.
NO, IT'S NO BOTHER, BUT...!

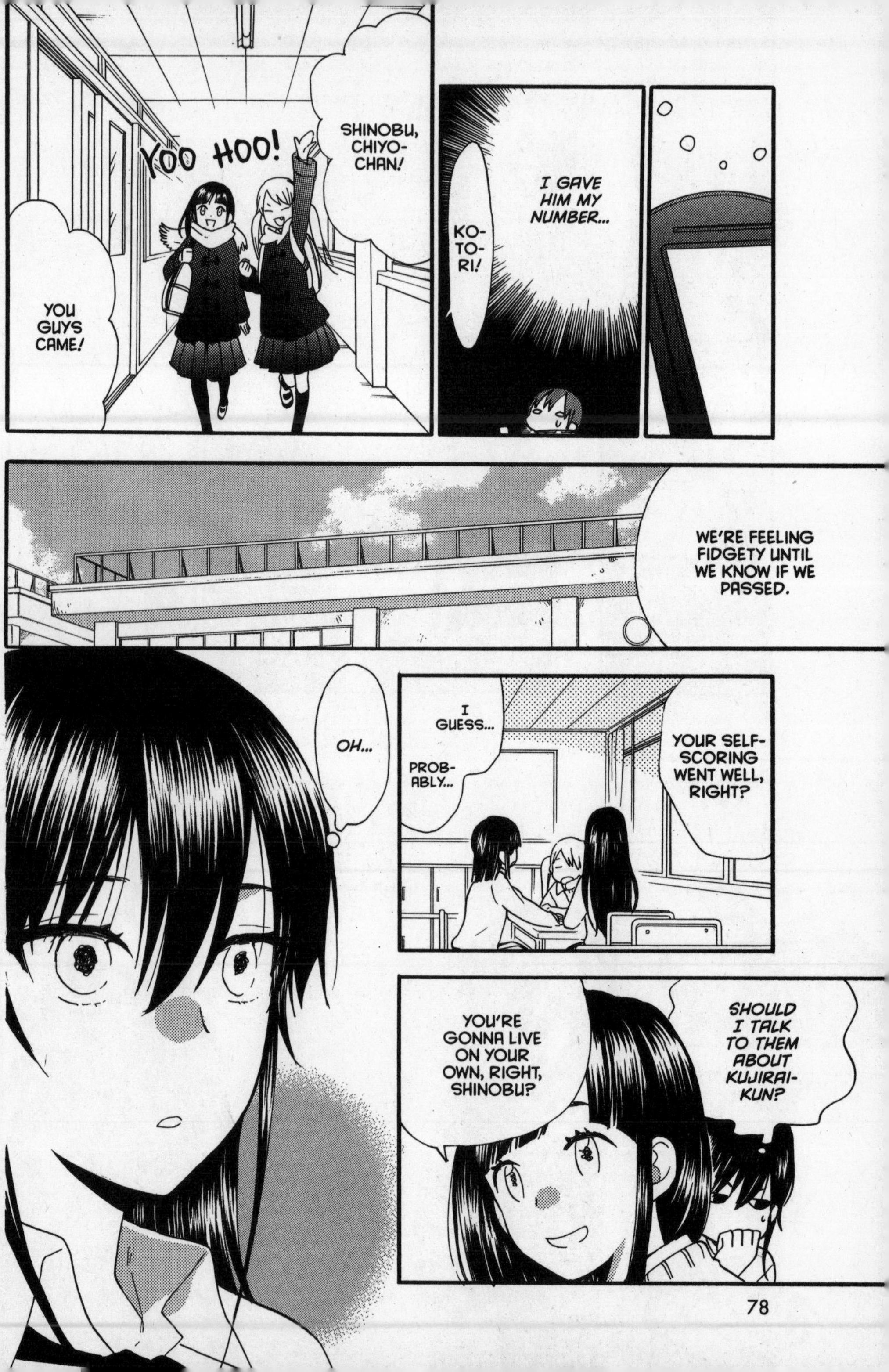
I GAVE HIM MY NUMBER...
KO-TO-RI!
SHINOBU, CHIYO-CHAN!
YOO HOO!
YOU GUYS CAME!
WE'RE FEELING FIDGETY UNTIL WE KNOW IF WE PASSED.
YOUR SELF-SCORING WENT WELL, RIGHT?
I GUESS...
PROB-ABLY...
SHOULD I TALK TO THEM ABOUT KUJIRAI-KUN?
YOU'RE GONNA LIVE ON YOUR OWN, RIGHT, SHINOBU?
OH...

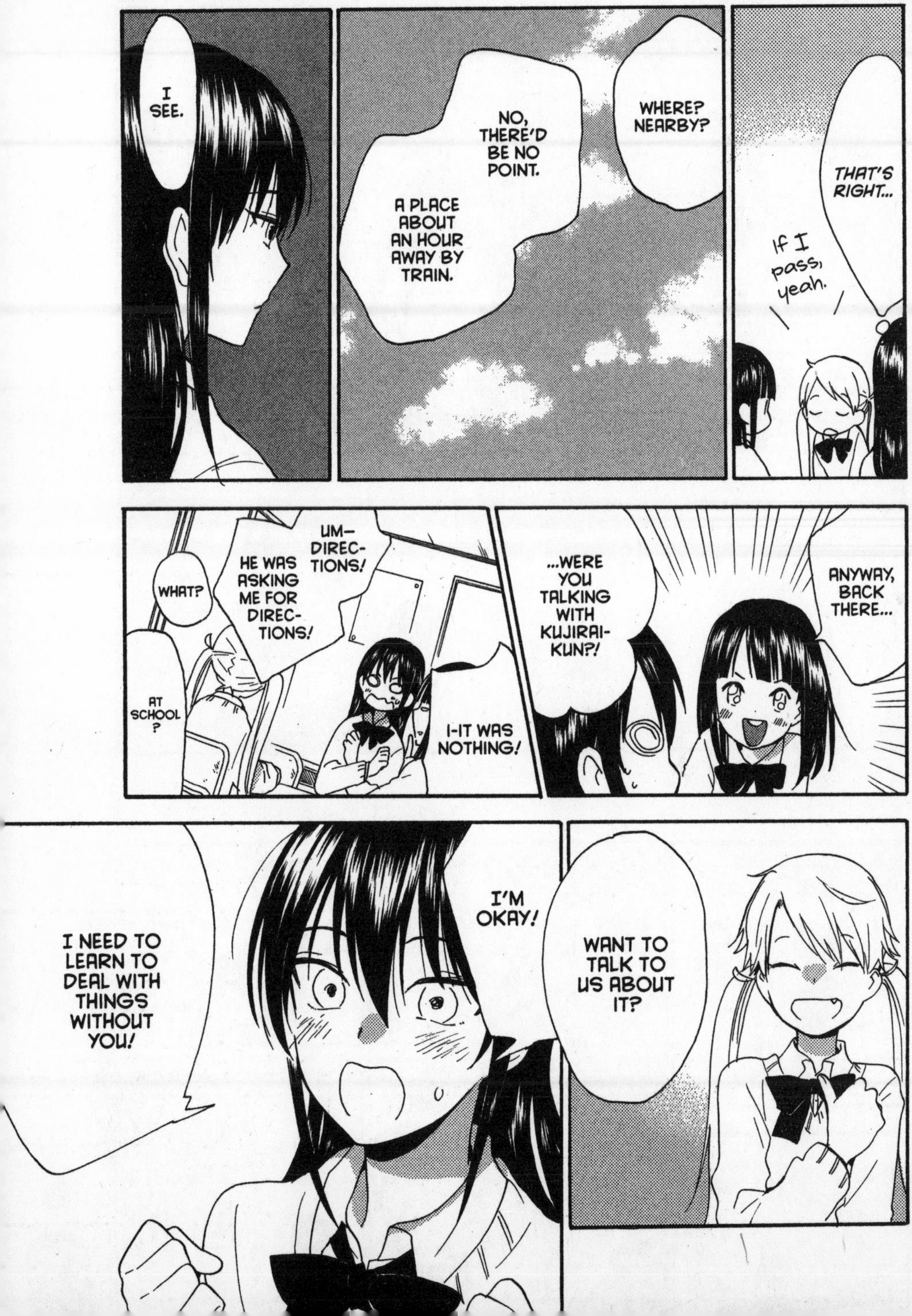
THAT'S RIGHT...
If I pass, yeah.
WHERE? NEARBY?
NO, THERE'D BE NO POINT.
A PLACE ABOUT AN HOUR AWAY BY TRAIN.
I SEE.
ANYWAY, BACK THERE...
...WERE YOU TALKING WITH KUJIRAI-KUN?!
I-IT WAS NOTHING!
UM— DIRECTIONS!
HE WAS ASKING ME FOR DIRECTIONS!
WHAT?
AT SCHOOL?
WANT TO TALK TO US ABOUT IT?
I'M OKAY!
I NEED TO LEARN TO DEAL WITH THINGS WITHOUT YOU!

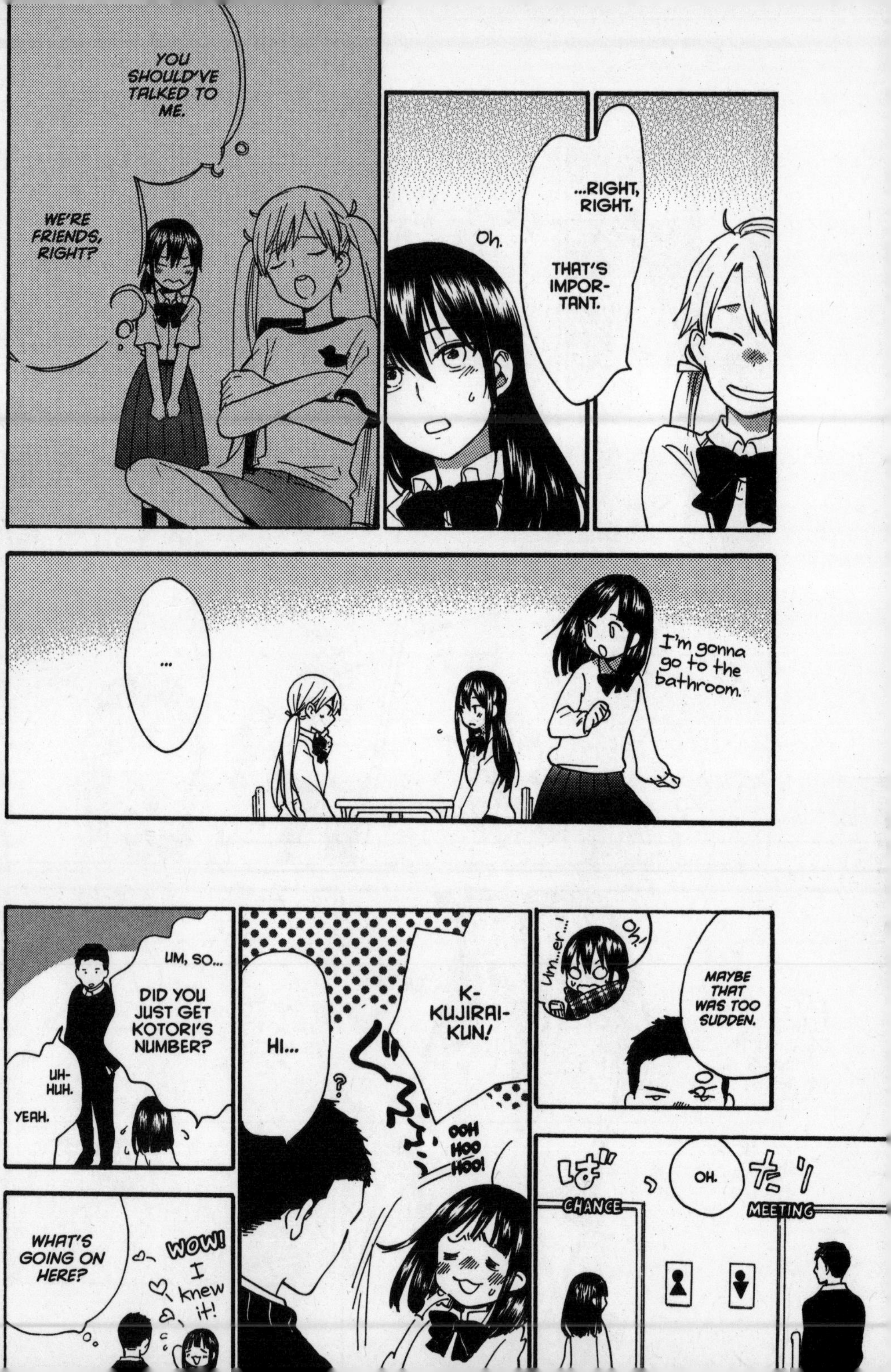
...RIGHT, RIGHT.
THAT'S IMPORTANT.
Oh.
YOU SHOULD'VE TALKED TO ME.
WE'RE FRIENDS, RIGHT?
I'm gonna go to the bathroom.
...
Oh!
Um...er...!
MAYBE THAT WAS TOO SUDDEN.
ばったり
OH.
CHANCE MEETING
K-KUJIRAI-KUN!
HI...
OOH HOO HOO!
UM, SO...
DID YOU JUST GET KOTORI'S NUMBER?
UH-HUH.
YEAH.
WHAT'S GOING ON HERE?
WOW! I knew it!

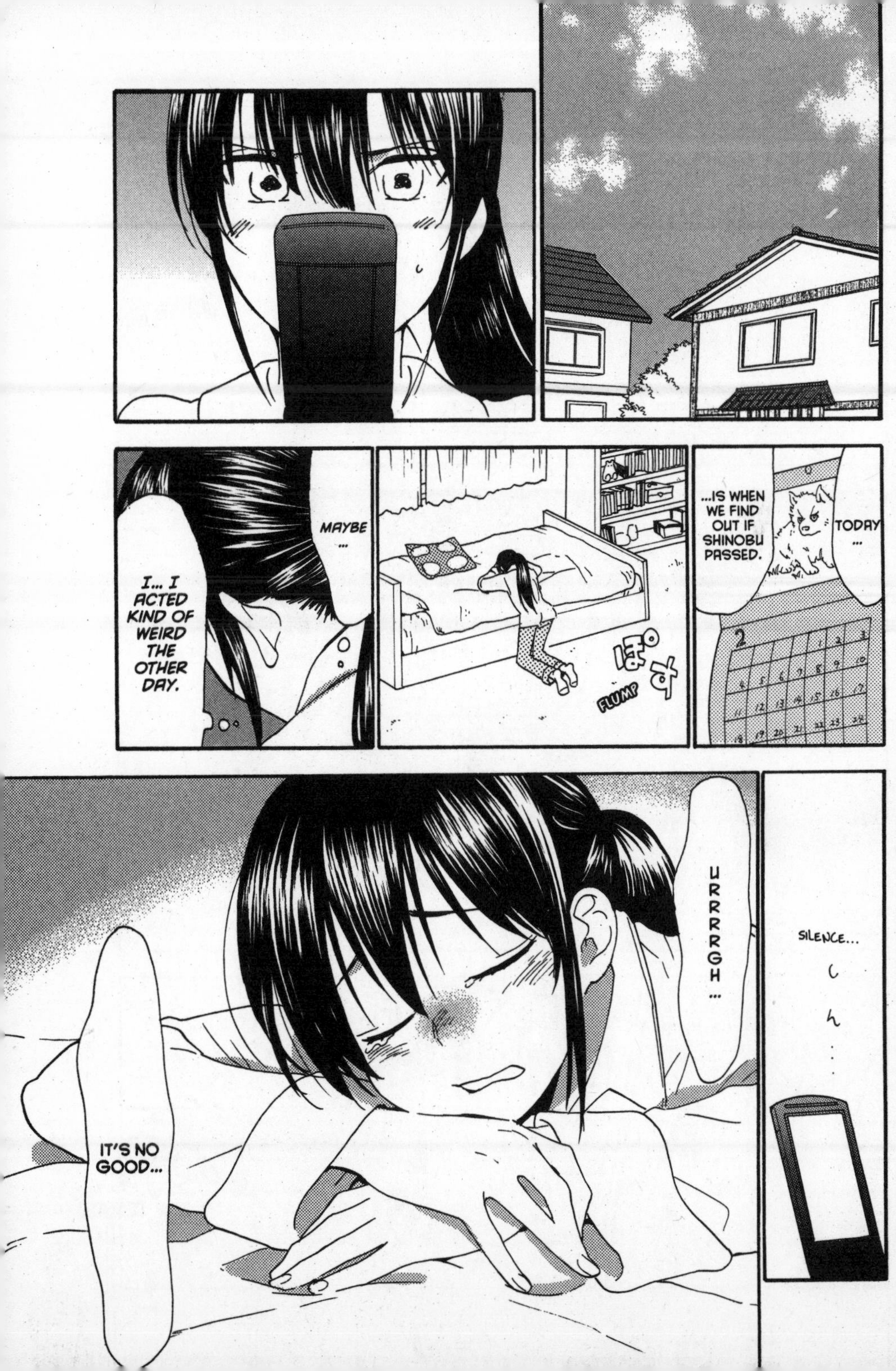
TODAY ...
...IS WHEN WE FIND OUT IF SHINOBU PASSED.
ぽす
FLUMP
MAYBE ...
I... I ACTED KIND OF WEIRD THE OTHER DAY.
SILENCE...
しん・・・
URRRRGH ...
IT'S NO GOOD...

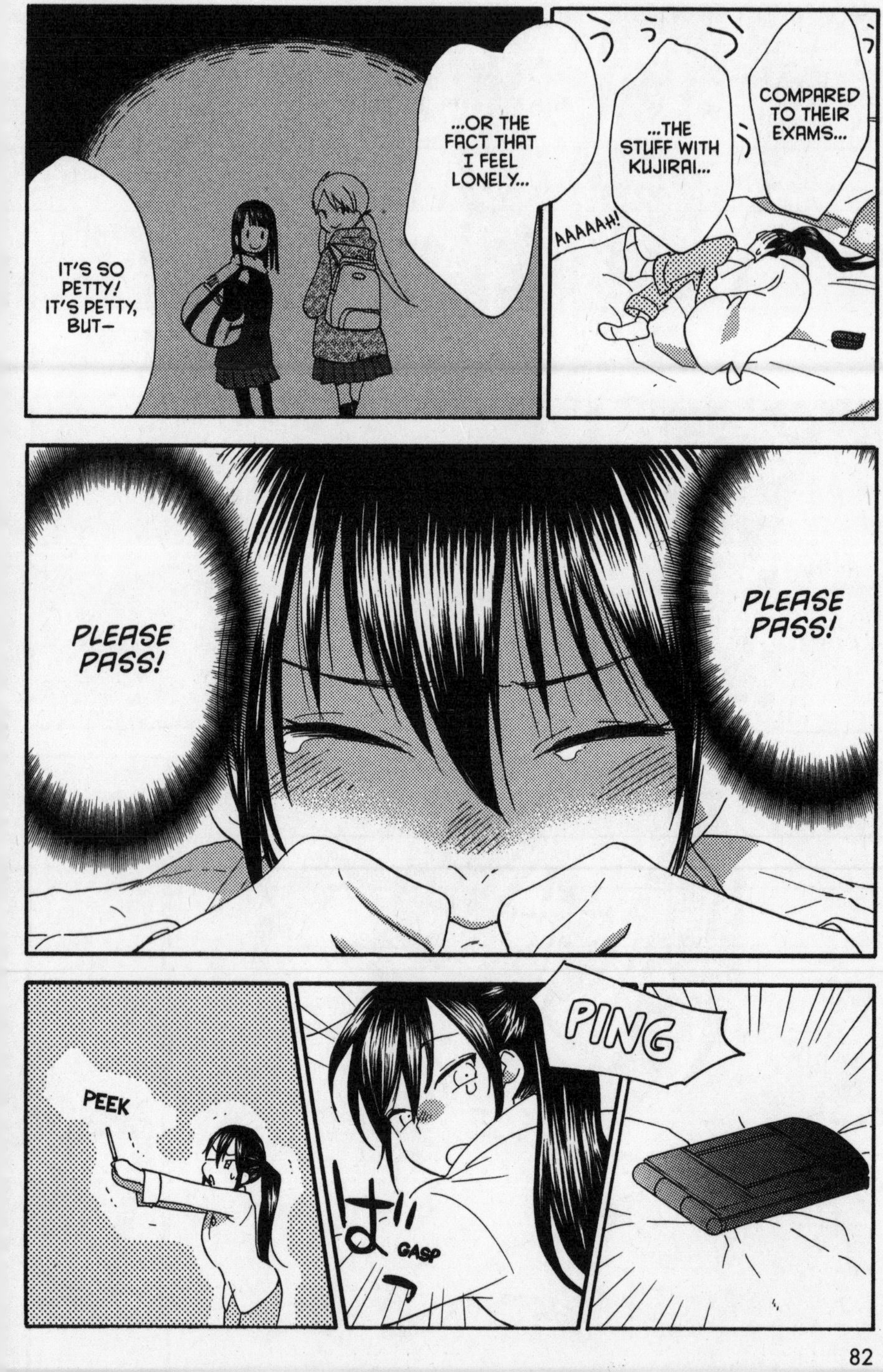
COMPARED TO THEIR EXAMS...
...THE STUFF WITH KUJIRAI...
AAAAAH!
...OR THE FACT THAT I FEEL LONELY...
IT'S SO PETTY! IT'S PETTY, BUT—
PLEASE PASS!
PLEASE PASS!
PING
は
GASP
PEEK

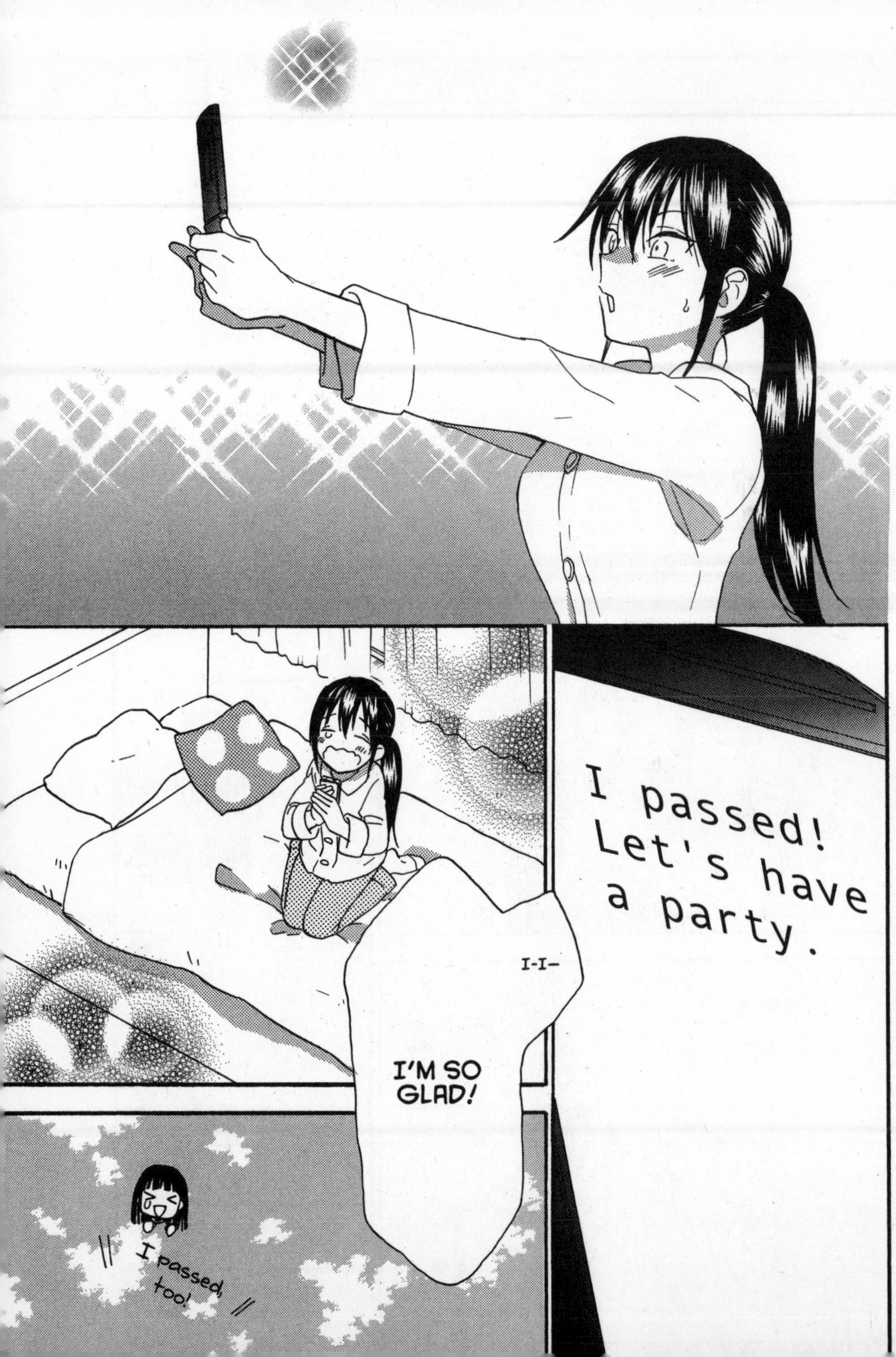
I passed! Let's have a party.
I-I—
I'M SO GLAD!
I passed, too!

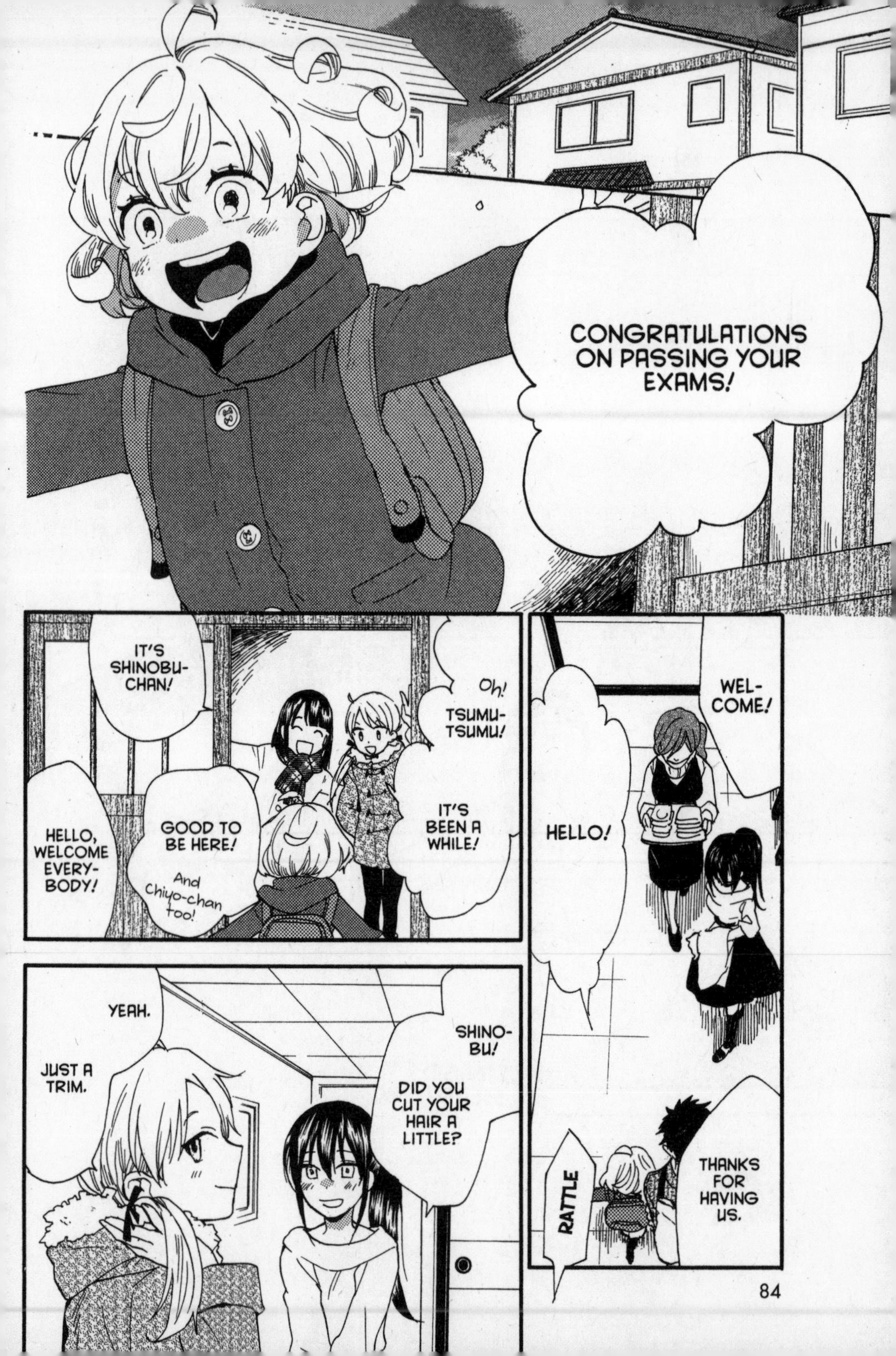
CONGRATULATIONS ON PASSING YOUR EXAMS!
WEL-COME!
HELLO!
THANKS FOR HAVING US.
RATTLE
Oh! TSUMU-TSUMU!
IT'S SHINOBU-CHAN!
IT'S BEEN A WHILE!
GOOD TO BE HERE!
And Chiyo-chan too!
HELLO, WELCOME EVERY-BODY!
SHINO-BU!
DID YOU CUT YOUR HAIR A LITTLE?
YEAH.
JUST A TRIM.

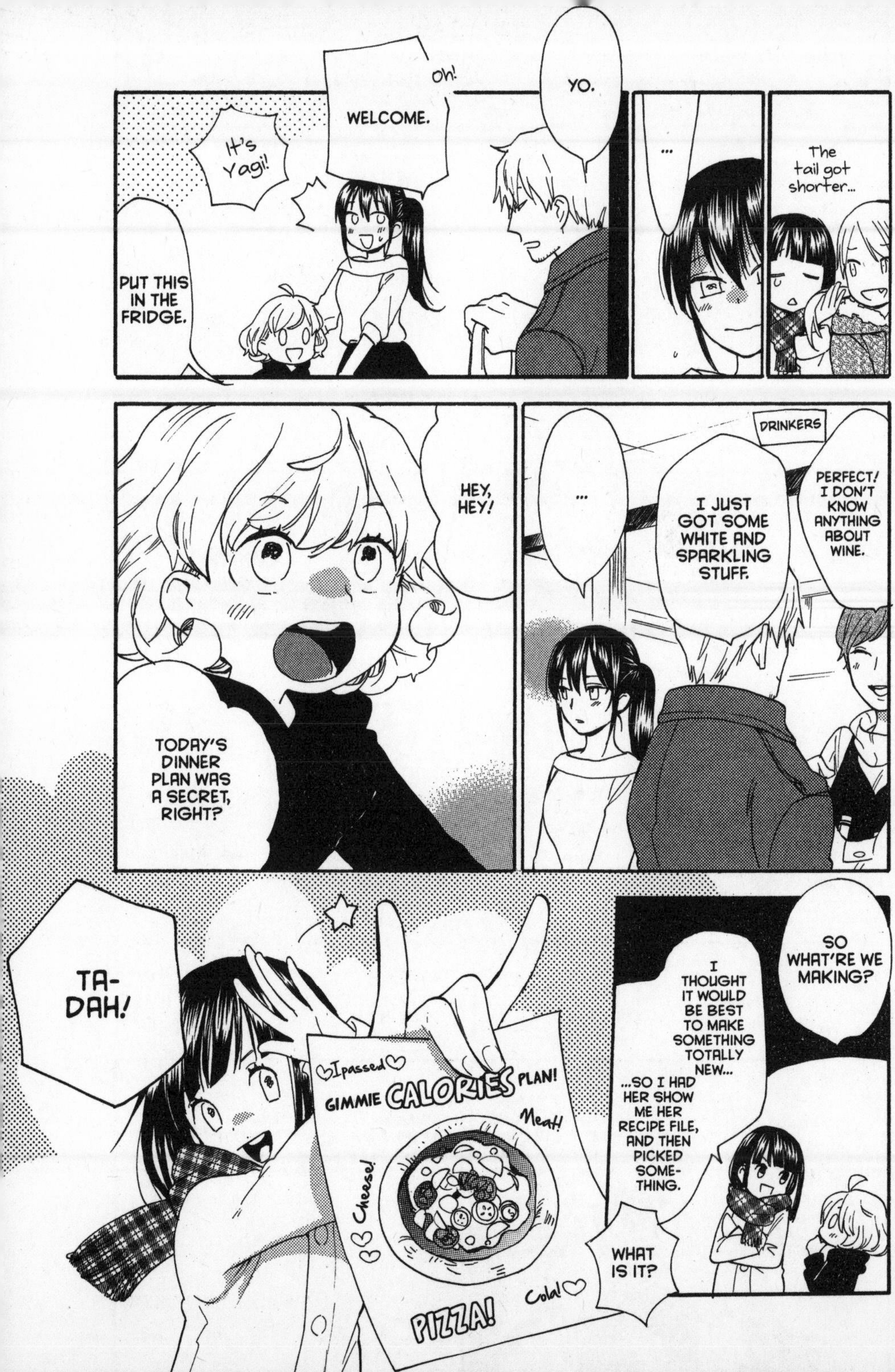

The tail got shorter...
...
YO.
Oh!
WELCOME.
It's Yagi!
PUT THIS IN THE FRIDGE.
PERFECT! I DON'T KNOW ANYTHING ABOUT WINE.
DRINKERS
I JUST GOT SOME WHITE AND SPARKLING STUFF.
...
HEY, HEY!
TODAY'S DINNER PLAN WAS A SECRET, RIGHT?
SO WHAT'RE WE MAKING?
I THOUGHT IT WOULD BE BEST TO MAKE SOMETHING TOTALLY NEW...
...SO I HAD HER SHOW ME HER RECIPE FILE, AND THEN PICKED SOME-THING.
WHAT IS IT?
TA-DAH!
I passed
GIMMIE CALORIES PLAN!
Meat!
Cheese!
Cola!
PIZZA!

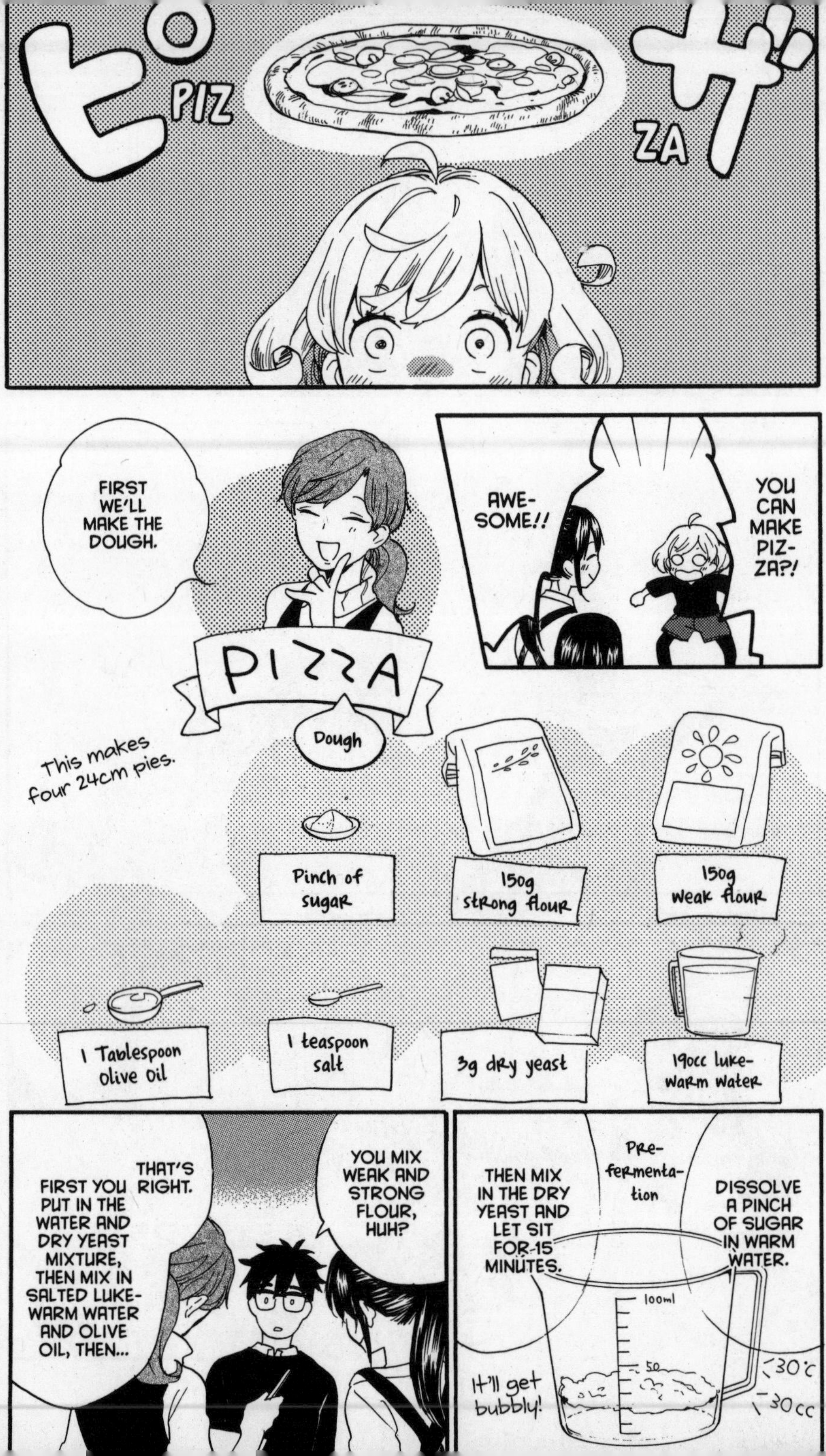
ピ PIZ
ザ ZA
YOU CAN MAKE PIZ-ZA?!
AWE-SOME!!
FIRST WE'LL MAKE THE DOUGH.
PIZZA
Dough
This makes four 24cm pies.
150g weak flour
150g strong flour
Pinch of sugar
190cc luke-warm water
3g dry yeast
1 teaspoon salt
1 Tablespoon olive oil
DISSOLVE A PINCH OF SUGAR IN WARM WATER.
Pre-fermentation
THEN MIX IN THE DRY YEAST AND LET SIT FOR 15 MINUTES.
100ml
50
<30°C
30cc
It'll get bubbly!
YOU MIX WEAK AND STRONG FLOUR, HUH?
THAT'S RIGHT.
FIRST YOU PUT IN THE WATER AND DRY YEAST MIXTURE, THEN MIX IN SALTED LUKE-WARM WATER AND OLIVE OIL, THEN...

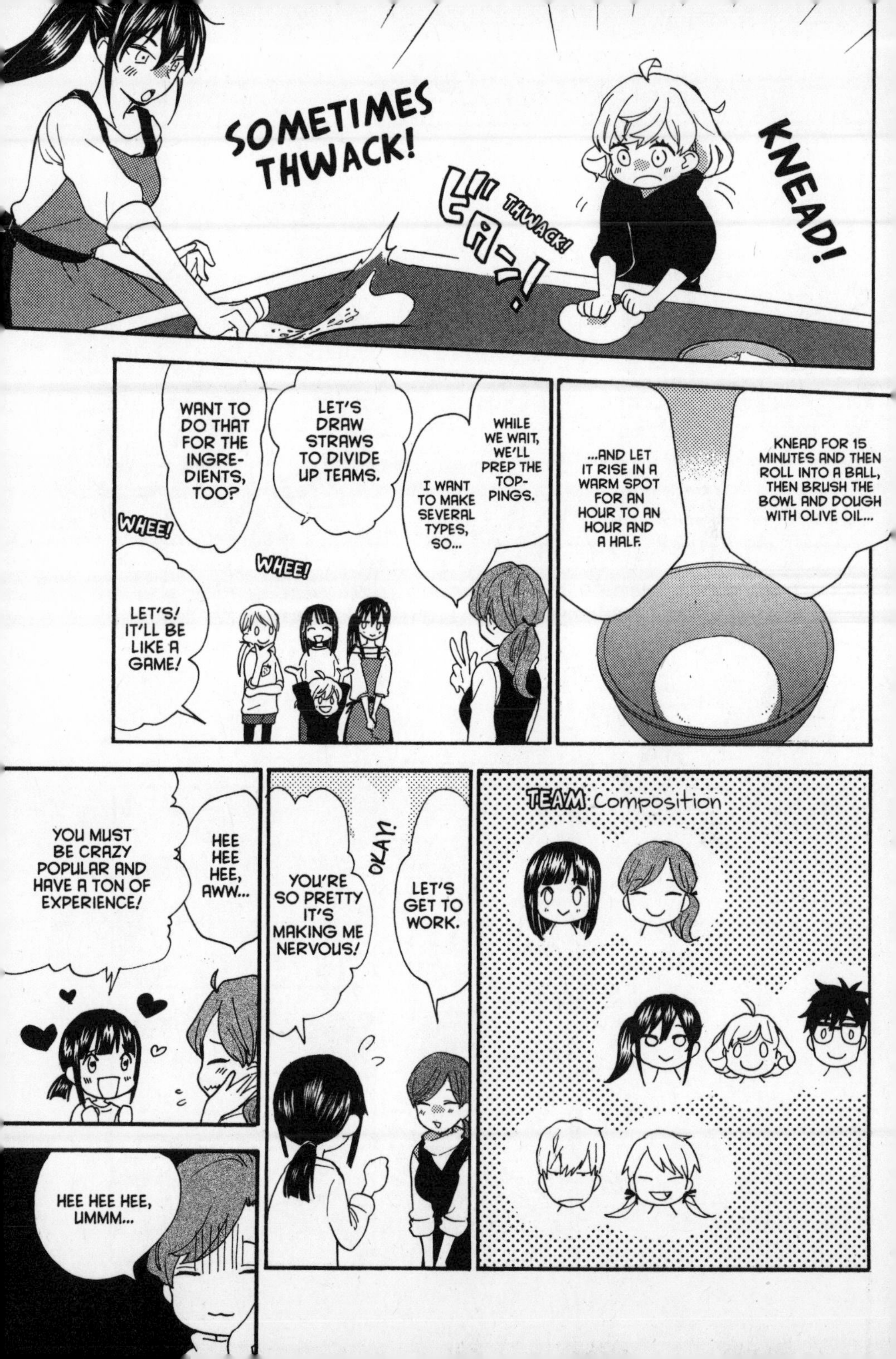
KNEAD!
THWACK!
SOMETIMES THWACK!
KNEAD FOR 15 MINUTES AND THEN ROLL INTO A BALL, THEN BRUSH THE BOWL AND DOUGH WITH OLIVE OIL...
...AND LET IT RISE IN A WARM SPOT FOR AN HOUR TO AN HOUR AND A HALF.
WHILE WE WAIT, WE'LL PREP THE TOP-PINGS.
I WANT TO MAKE SEVERAL TYPES, SO...
LET'S DRAW STRAWS TO DIVIDE UP TEAMS.
WANT TO DO THAT FOR THE INGRE-DIENTS, TOO?
WHEE!
WHEE!
LET'S! IT'LL BE LIKE A GAME!
TEAM Composition
LET'S GET TO WORK.
OKAY!
YOU'RE SO PRETTY IT'S MAKING ME NERVOUS!
HEE HEE HEE, AWW...
YOU MUST BE CRAZY POPULAR AND HAVE A TON OF EXPERIENCE!
HEE HEE HEE, UMMM...

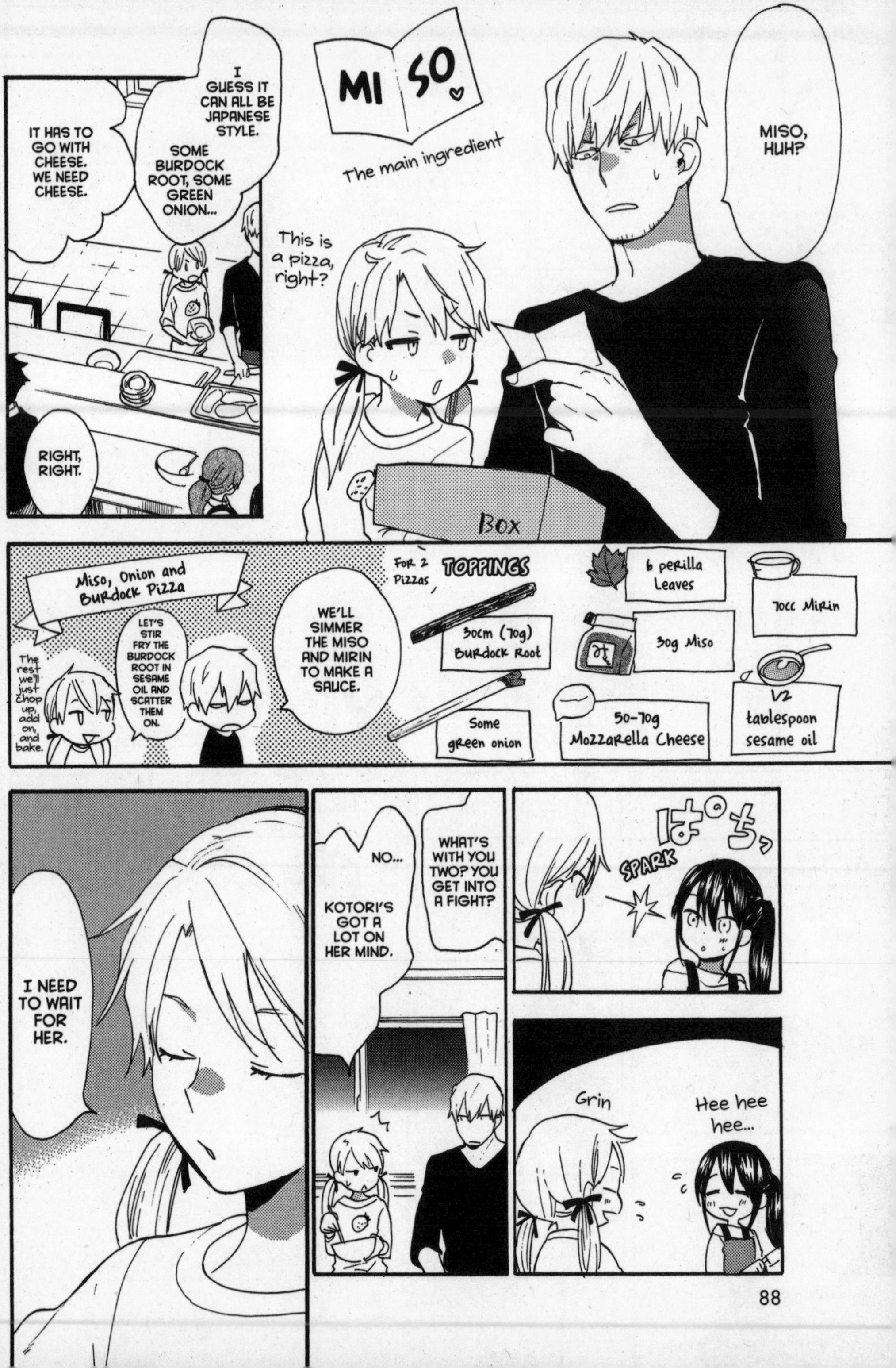
MISO, HUH?
MI SO
The main ingredient
This is a pizza, right?
Box
I GUESS IT CAN ALL BE JAPANESE STYLE.
SOME BURDOCK ROOT, SOME GREEN ONION...
IT HAS TO GO WITH CHEESE. WE NEED CHEESE.
RIGHT, RIGHT.
Miso, Onion and Burdock Pizza
WE'LL SIMMER THE MISO AND MIRIN TO MAKE A SAUCE.
LET'S STIR FRY THE BURDOCK ROOT IN SESAME OIL AND SCATTER THEM ON.
The rest we'll just chop up, add on, and bake.
For 2 Pizzas
TOPPINGS
6 perilla Leaves
70cc Mirin
30cm (70g) Burdock Root
30g Miso
Some green onion
50-70g Mozzarella Cheese
1/2 tablespoon sesame oil
ぱちっ
SPARK
Grin
Hee hee hee...
WHAT'S WITH YOU TWO? YOU GET INTO A FIGHT?
NO...
KOTORI'S GOT A LOT ON HER MIND.
I NEED TO WAIT FOR HER.

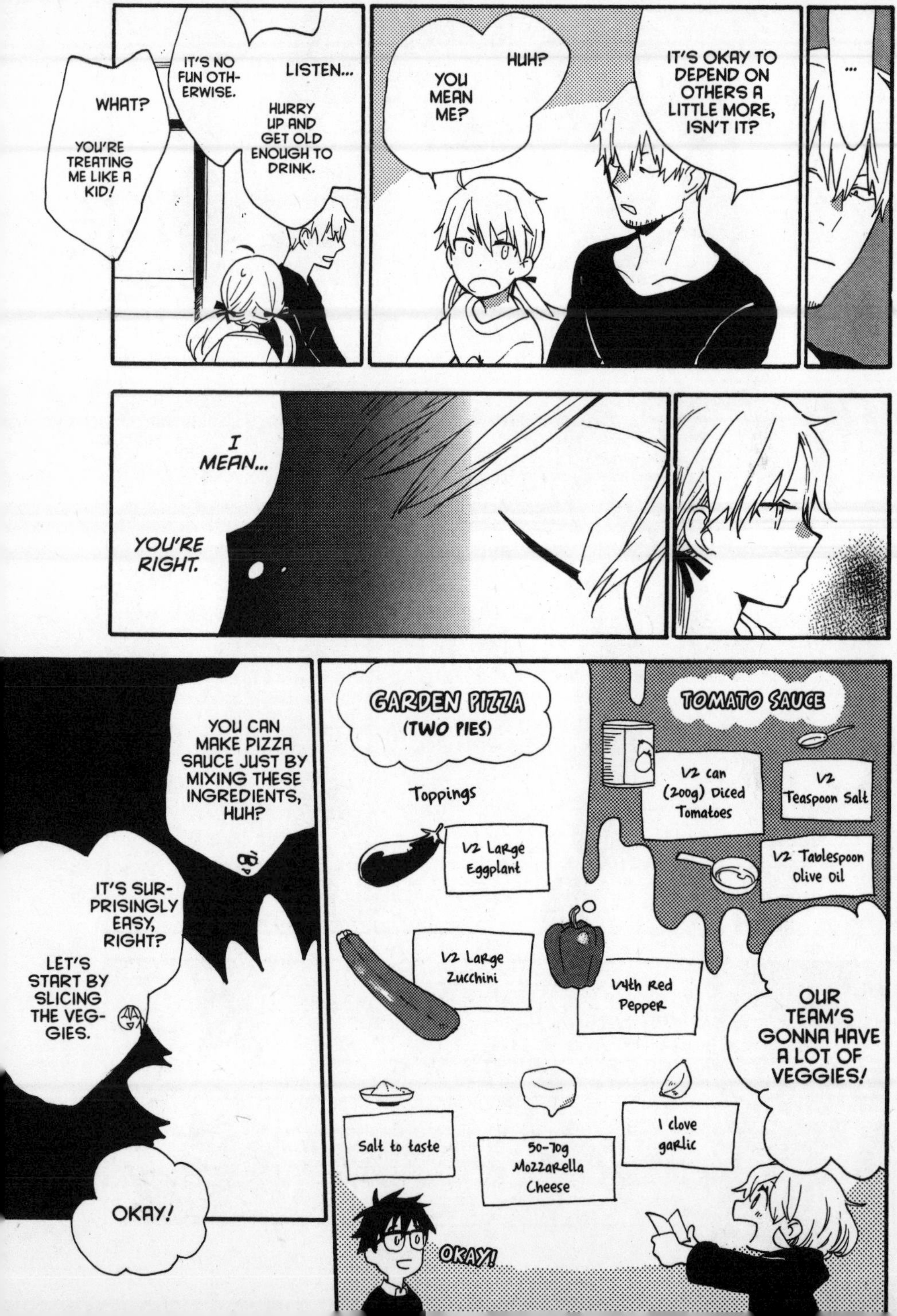
...
IT'S OKAY TO DEPEND ON OTHERS A LITTLE MORE, ISN'T IT?
HUH?
YOU MEAN ME?
LISTEN...
HURRY UP AND GET OLD ENOUGH TO DRINK.
IT'S NO FUN OTH-ERWISE.
WHAT?
YOU'RE TREATING ME LIKE A KID!
I MEAN...
YOU'RE RIGHT.
TOMATO SAUCE
1/2 can (200g) Diced Tomatoes
1/2 Teaspoon Salt
1/2 Tablespoon Olive Oil
GARDEN PIZZA
(TWO PIES)
Toppings
1/2 Large Eggplant
1/2 Large Zucchini
1/4th Red Pepper
OUR TEAM'S GONNA HAVE A LOT OF VEGGIES!
1 clove garlic
50-70g Mozzarella Cheese
Salt to taste
OKAY!
YOU CAN MAKE PIZZA SAUCE JUST BY MIXING THESE INGREDIENTS, HUH?
IT'S SUR-PRISINGLY EASY, RIGHT?
LET'S START BY SLICING THE VEG-GIES.
OKAY!

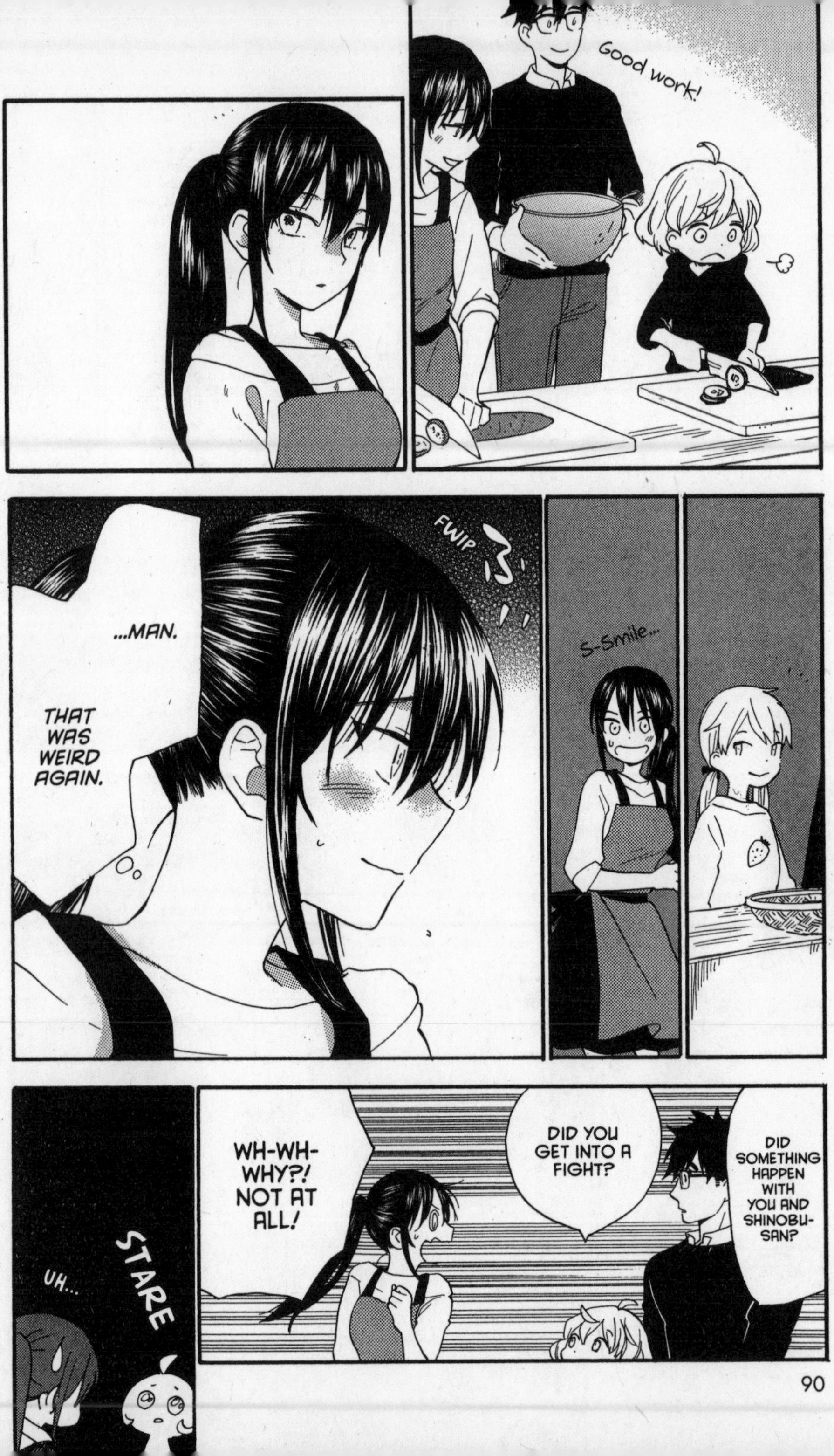
Good work!
...
S-Smile...
FWIP
...MAN.
THAT WAS WEIRD AGAIN.
DID SOMETHING HAPPEN WITH YOU AND SHINOBU-SAN?
DID YOU GET INTO A FIGHT?
WH-WH-WHY?! NOT AT ALL!
STARE
UH...

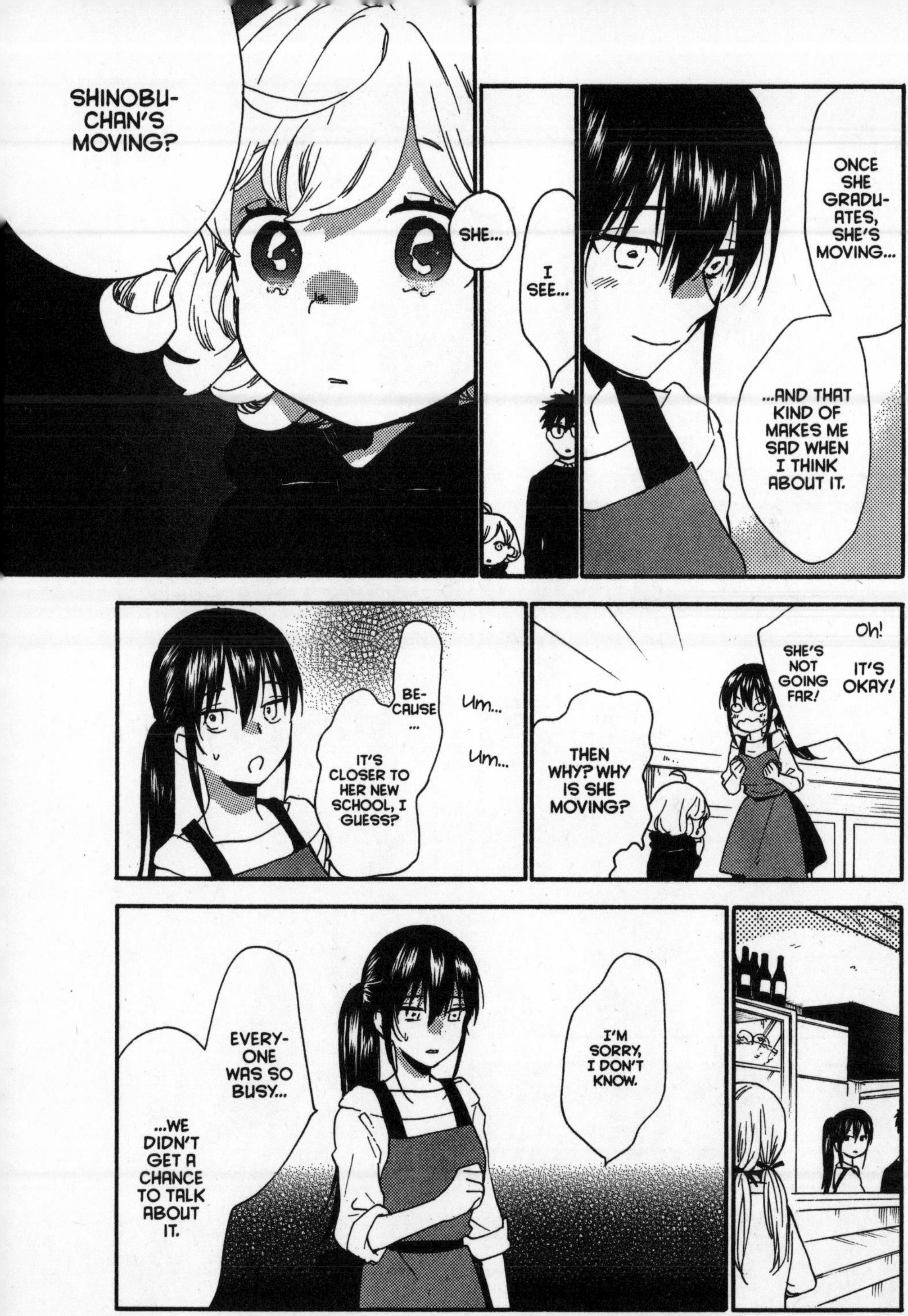
ONCE SHE GRADUATES, SHE'S MOVING...
...AND THAT KIND OF MAKES ME SAD WHEN I THINK ABOUT IT.
I SEE...
SHE...
SHINOBU-CHAN'S MOVING?
Oh!
IT'S OKAY!
SHE'S NOT GOING FAR!
THEN WHY? WHY IS SHE MOVING?
Um...
Um...
BE-CAUSE...
IT'S CLOSER TO HER NEW SCHOOL, I GUESS?
I'M SORRY, I DON'T KNOW.
EVERY-ONE WAS SO BUSY...
...WE DIDN'T GET A CHANCE TO TALK ABOUT IT.

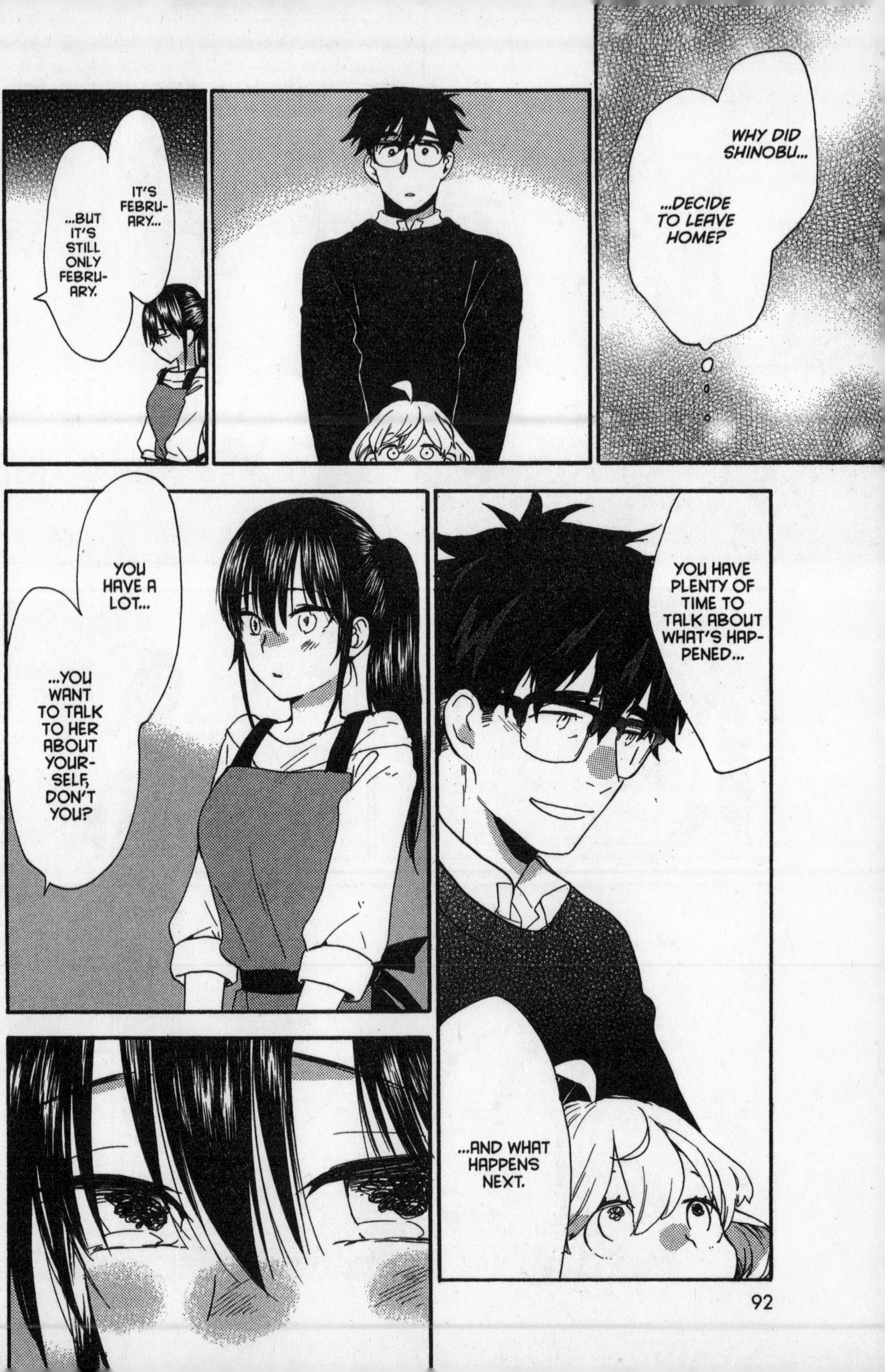
WHY DID SHINOBU...
...DECIDE TO LEAVE HOME?
IT'S FEBRU-ARY...
...BUT IT'S STILL ONLY FEBRU-ARY.
YOU HAVE PLENTY OF TIME TO TALK ABOUT WHAT'S HAP-PENED...
...AND WHAT HAPPENS NEXT.
YOU HAVE A LOT...
...YOU WANT TO TALK TO HER ABOUT YOUR-SELF, DON'T YOU?

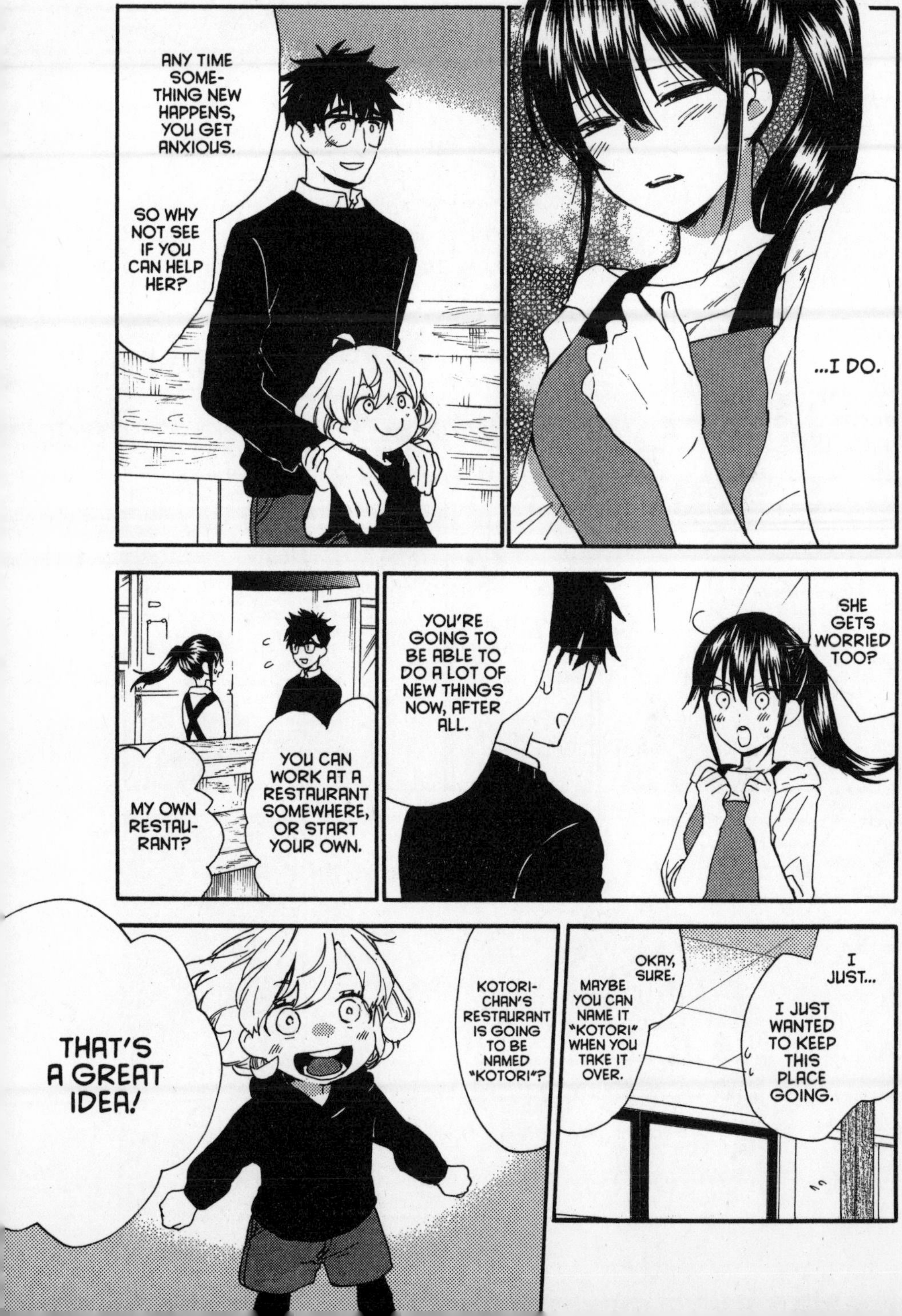
...I DO.
ANY TIME SOME-THING NEW HAPPENS, YOU GET ANXIOUS.
SO WHY NOT SEE IF YOU CAN HELP HER?
SHE GETS WORRIED TOO?
YOU'RE GOING TO BE ABLE TO DO A LOT OF NEW THINGS NOW, AFTER ALL.
YOU CAN WORK AT A RESTAURANT SOMEWHERE, OR START YOUR OWN.
MY OWN RESTAU-RANT?
I JUST...
I JUST WANTED TO KEEP THIS PLACE GOING.
OKAY, SURE.
MAYBE YOU CAN NAME IT "KOTORI" WHEN YOU TAKE IT OVER.
KOTORI-CHAN'S RESTAURANT IS GOING TO BE NAMED "KOTORI"?
THAT'S A GREAT IDEA!

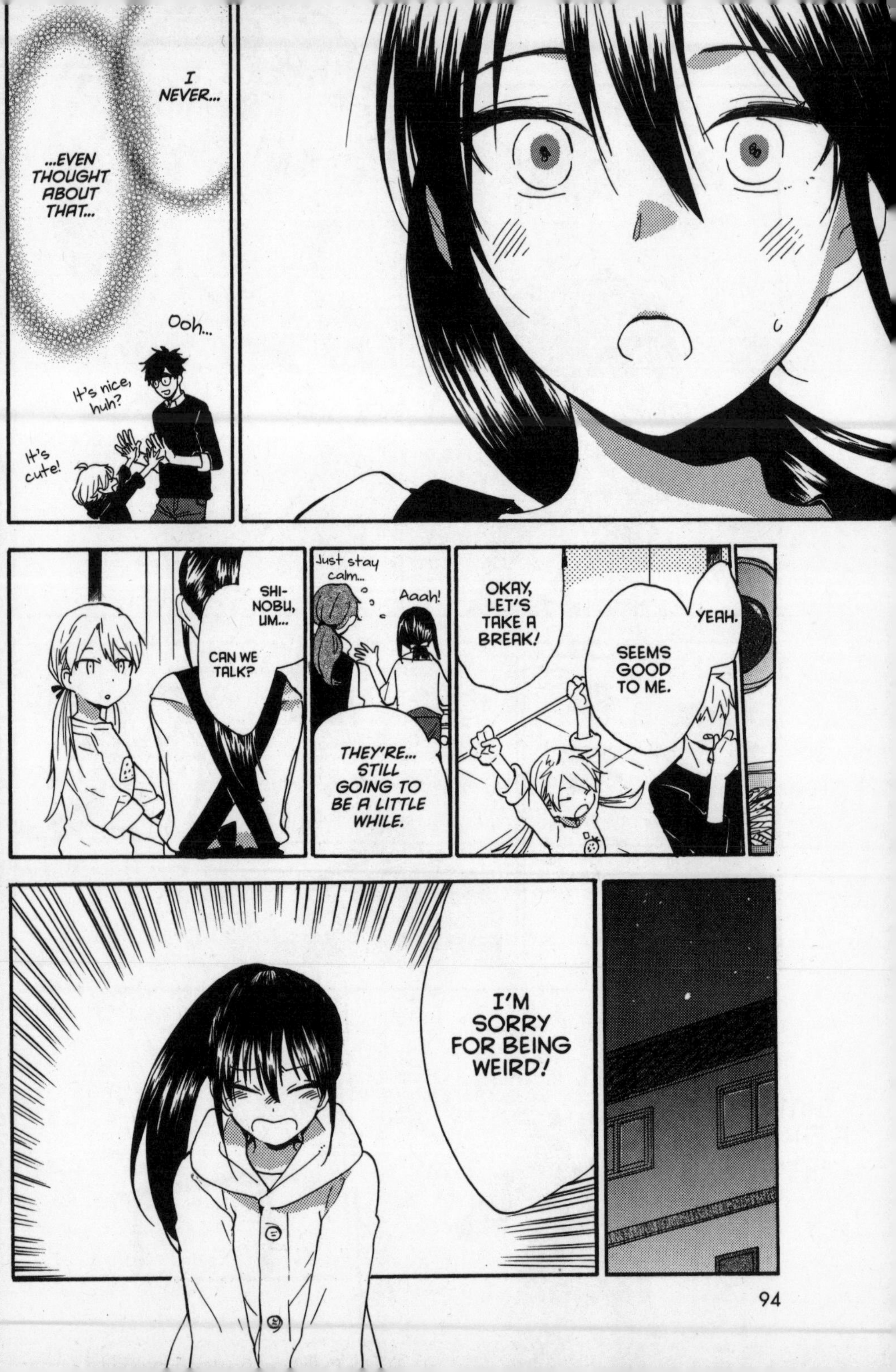
I NEVER...
...EVEN THOUGHT ABOUT THAT...
Ooh...
It's nice, huh?
It's cute!
YEAH.
SEEMS GOOD TO ME.
OKAY, LET'S TAKE A BREAK!
Aaah!
Just stay calm...
THEY'RE... STILL GOING TO BE A LITTLE WHILE.
SHI-NOBU, UM...
CAN WE TALK?
I'M SORRY FOR BEING WEIRD!

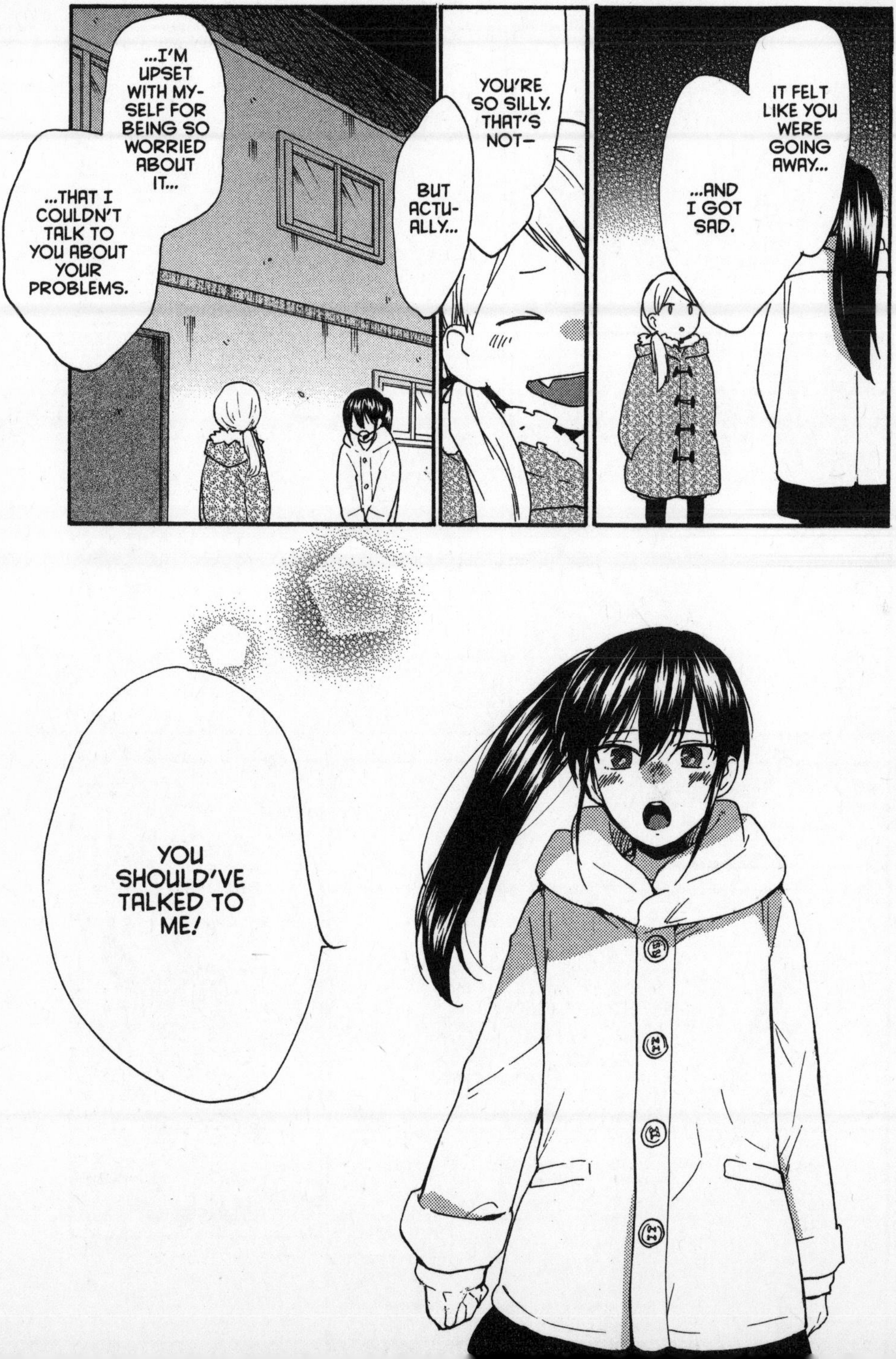
IT FELT LIKE YOU WERE GOING AWAY...
...AND I GOT SAD.
YOU'RE SO SILLY. THAT'S NOT—
BUT ACTU-ALLY...
...I'M UPSET WITH MY-SELF FOR BEING SO WORRIED ABOUT IT...
...THAT I COULDN'T TALK TO YOU ABOUT YOUR PROBLEMS.
YOU SHOULD'VE TALKED TO ME!

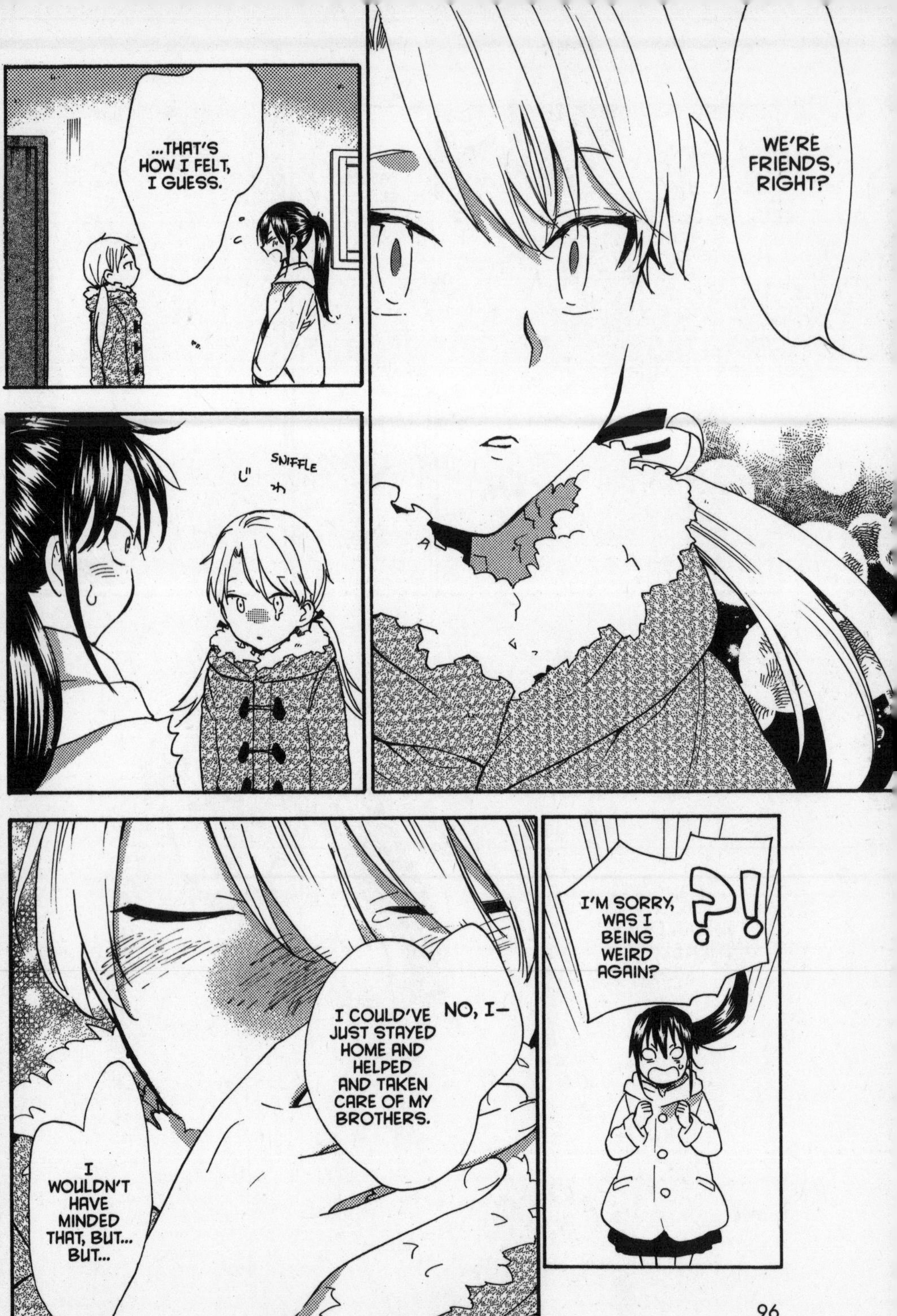
WE'RE FRIENDS, RIGHT?
...THAT'S HOW I FELT, I GUESS.
SNIFFLE
I'M SORRY, WAS I BEING WEIRD AGAIN?
NO, I—
I COULD'VE JUST STAYED HOME AND HELPED AND TAKEN CARE OF MY BROTHERS.
I WOULDN'T HAVE MINDED THAT, BUT... BUT...

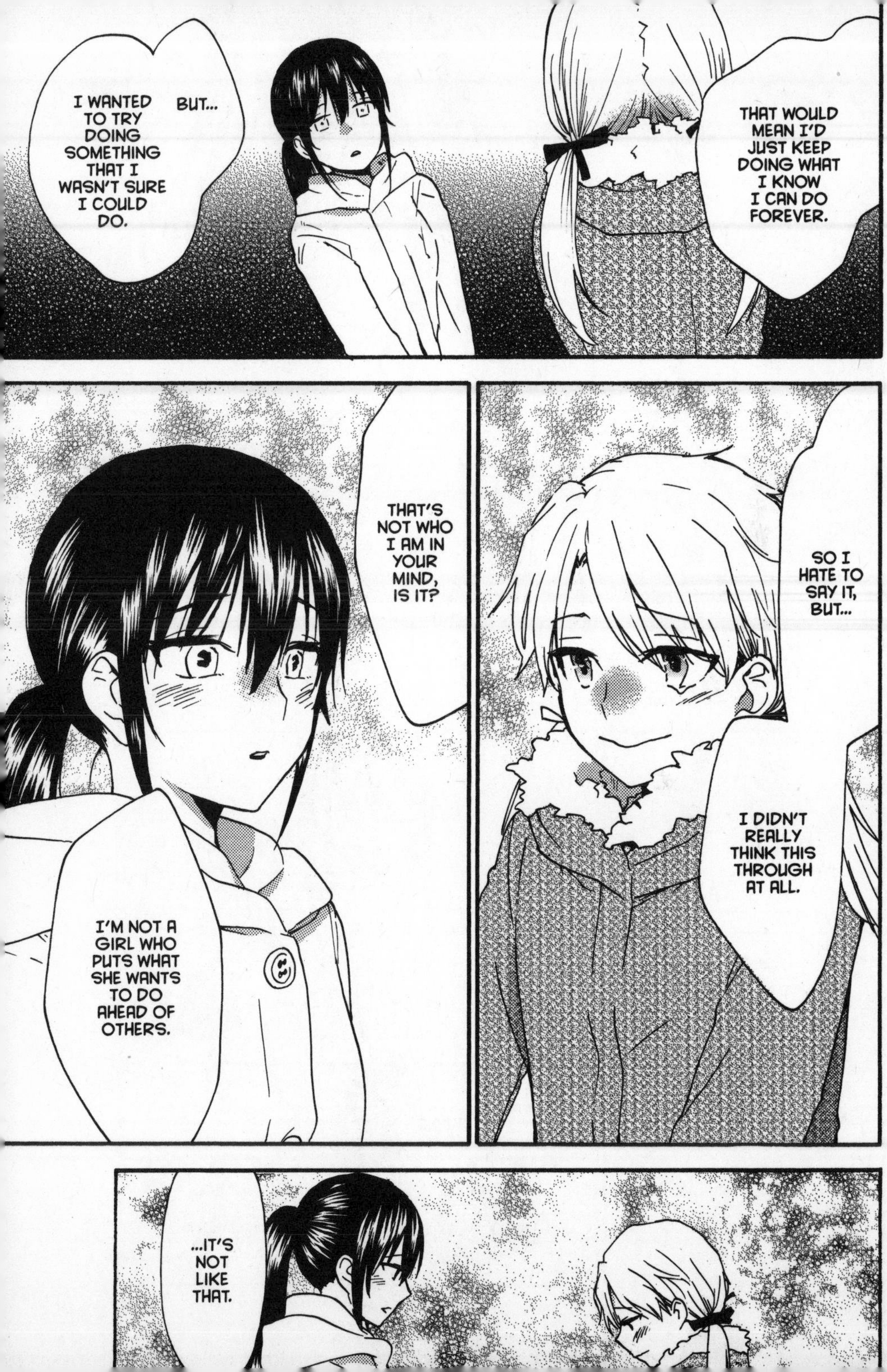
THAT WOULD MEAN I'D JUST KEEP DOING WHAT I KNOW I CAN DO FOREVER.
BUT...
I WANTED TO TRY DOING SOMETHING THAT I WASN'T SURE I COULD DO.
SO I HATE TO SAY IT, BUT...
I DIDN'T REALLY THINK THIS THROUGH AT ALL.
THAT'S NOT WHO I AM IN YOUR MIND, IS IT?
I'M NOT A GIRL WHO PUTS WHAT SHE WANTS TO DO AHEAD OF OTHERS.
...IT'S NOT LIKE THAT.

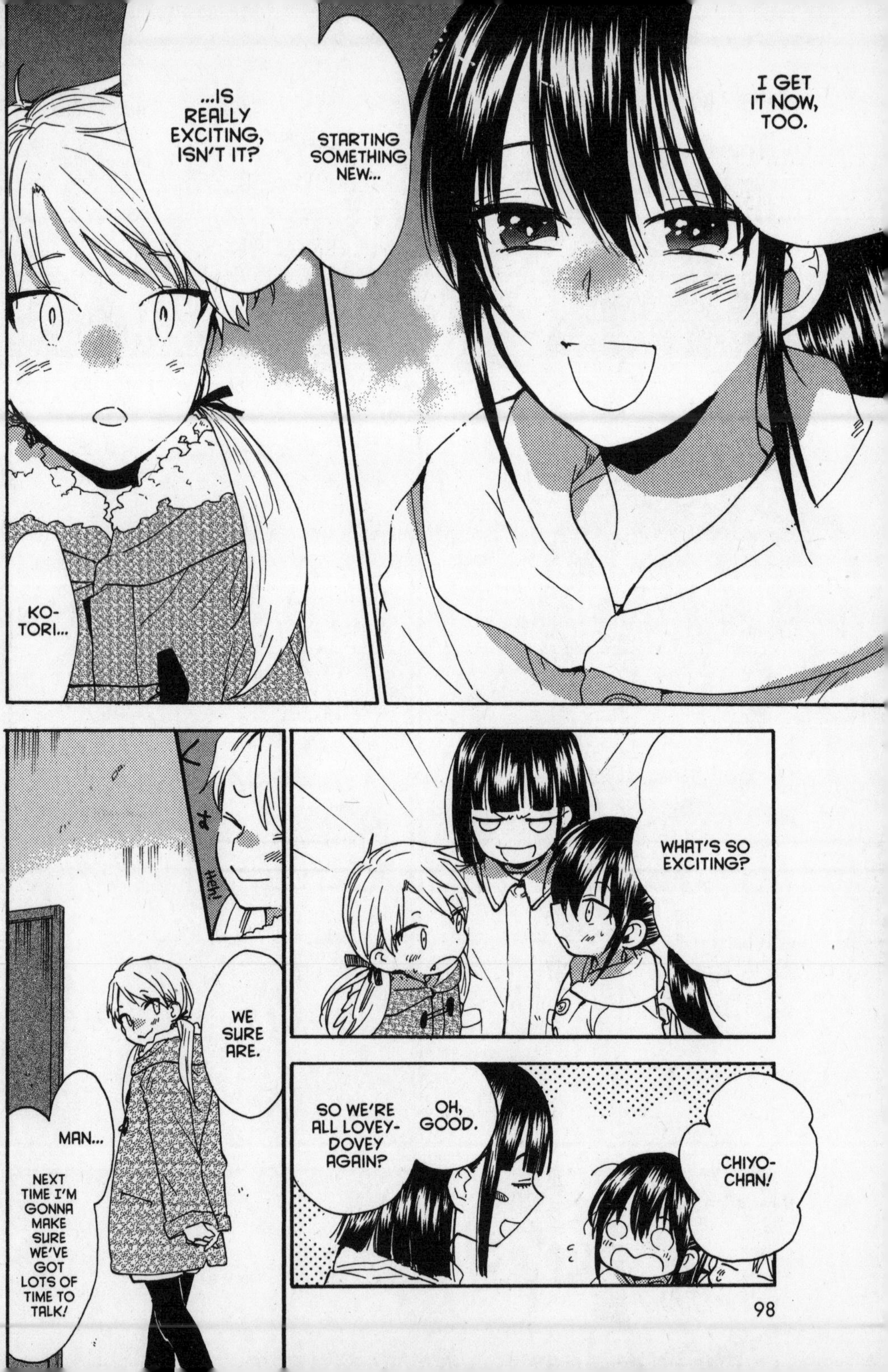
I GET IT NOW, TOO.
STARTING SOMETHING NEW...
...IS REALLY EXCITING, ISN'T IT?
KO-TORI...
WHAT'S SO EXCITING?
CHIYO-CHAN!
OH, GOOD.
SO WE'RE ALL LOVEY-DOVEY AGAIN?
WE SURE ARE.
MAN...
NEXT TIME I'M GONNA MAKE SURE WE'VE GOT LOTS OF TIME TO TALK!

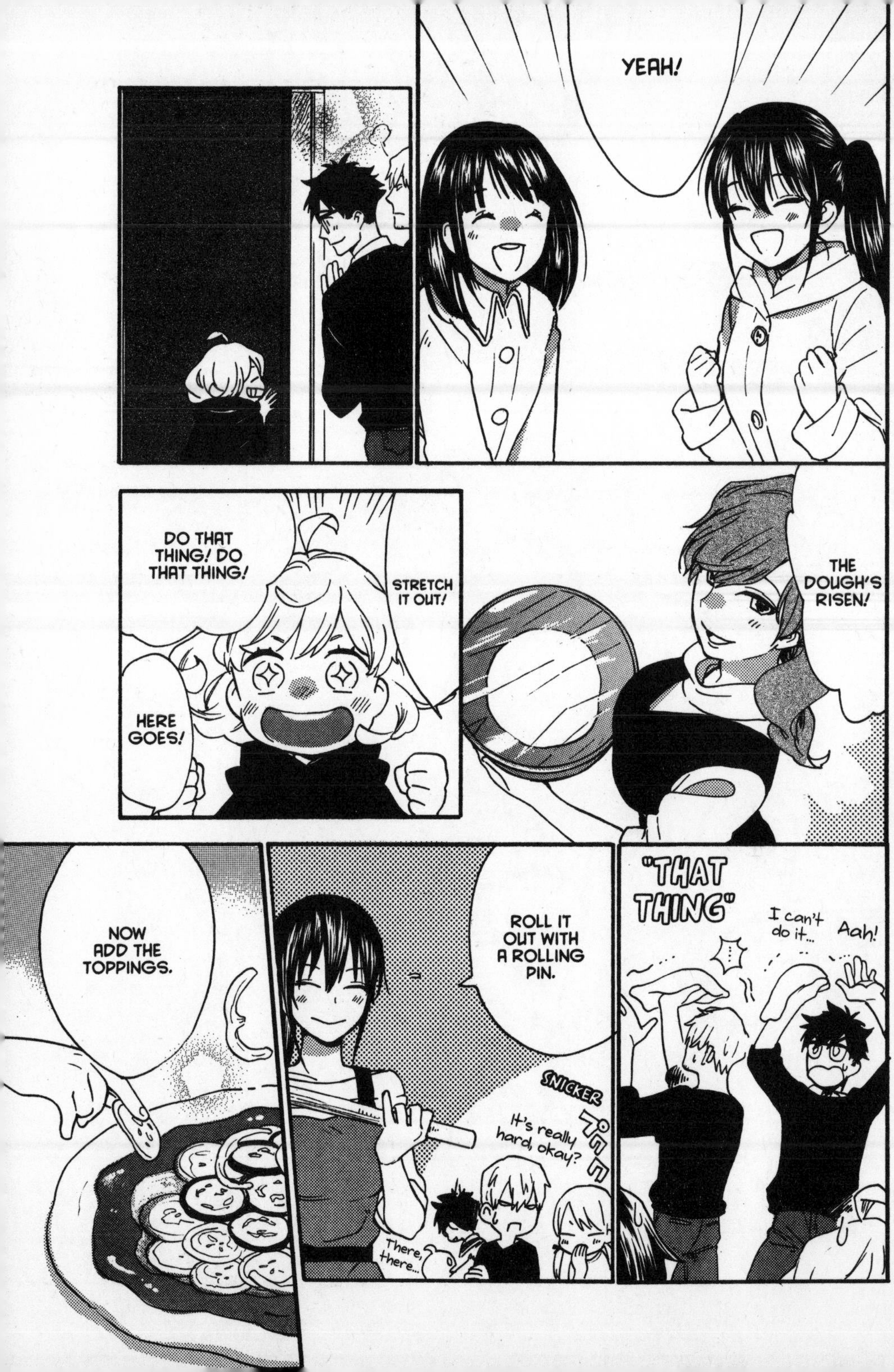
YEAH!
THE DOUGH'S RISEN!
STRETCH IT OUT!
DO THAT THING! DO THAT THING!
HERE GOES!
"THAT THING"
Aah!
I can't do it...
ROLL IT OUT WITH A ROLLING PIN.
SNICKER
It's really hard, okay?
There, there...
NOW ADD THE TOPPINGS.

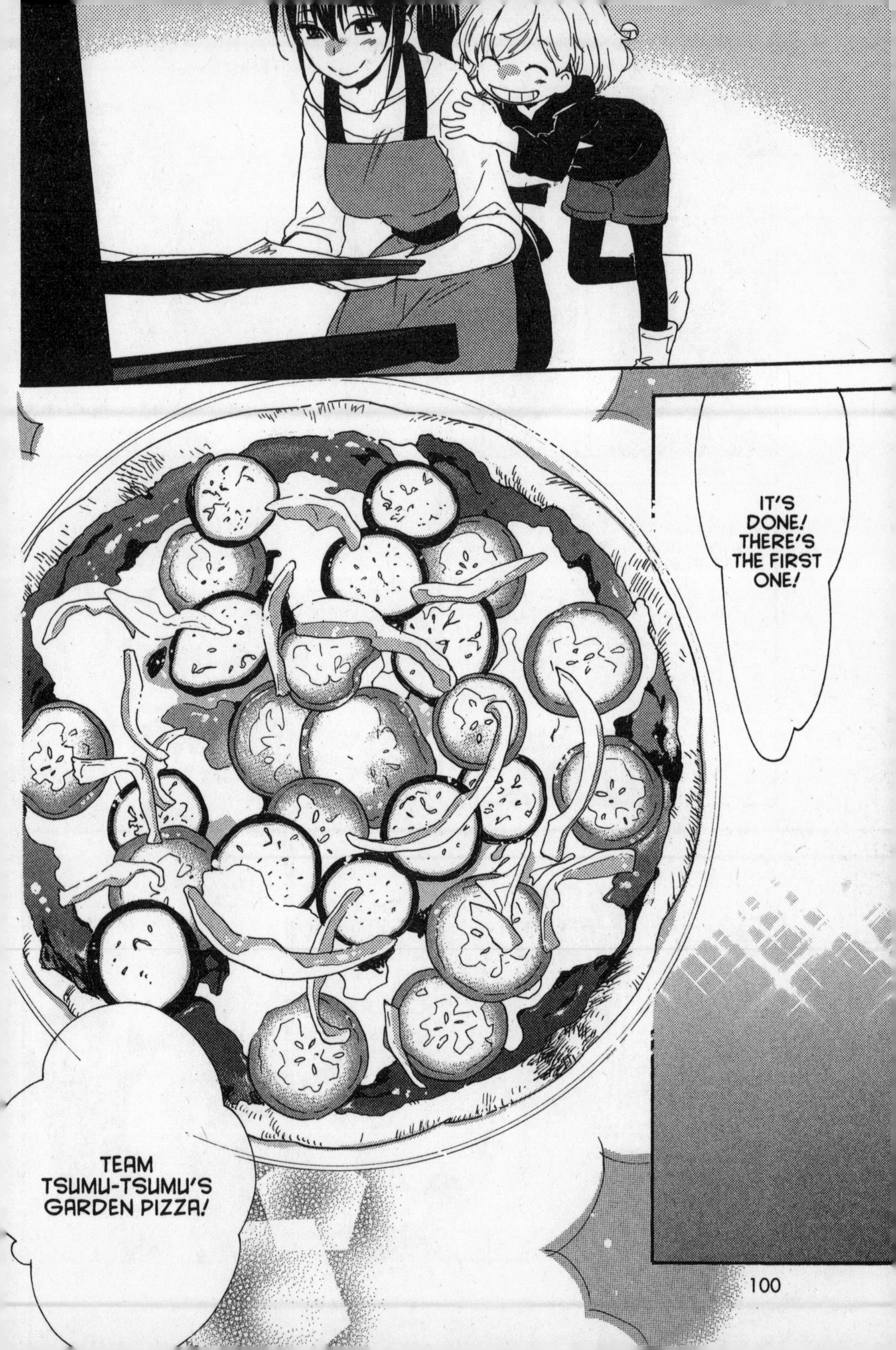
IT'S DONE! THERE'S THE FIRST ONE!
TEAM TSUMU-TSUMU'S GARDEN PIZZA!

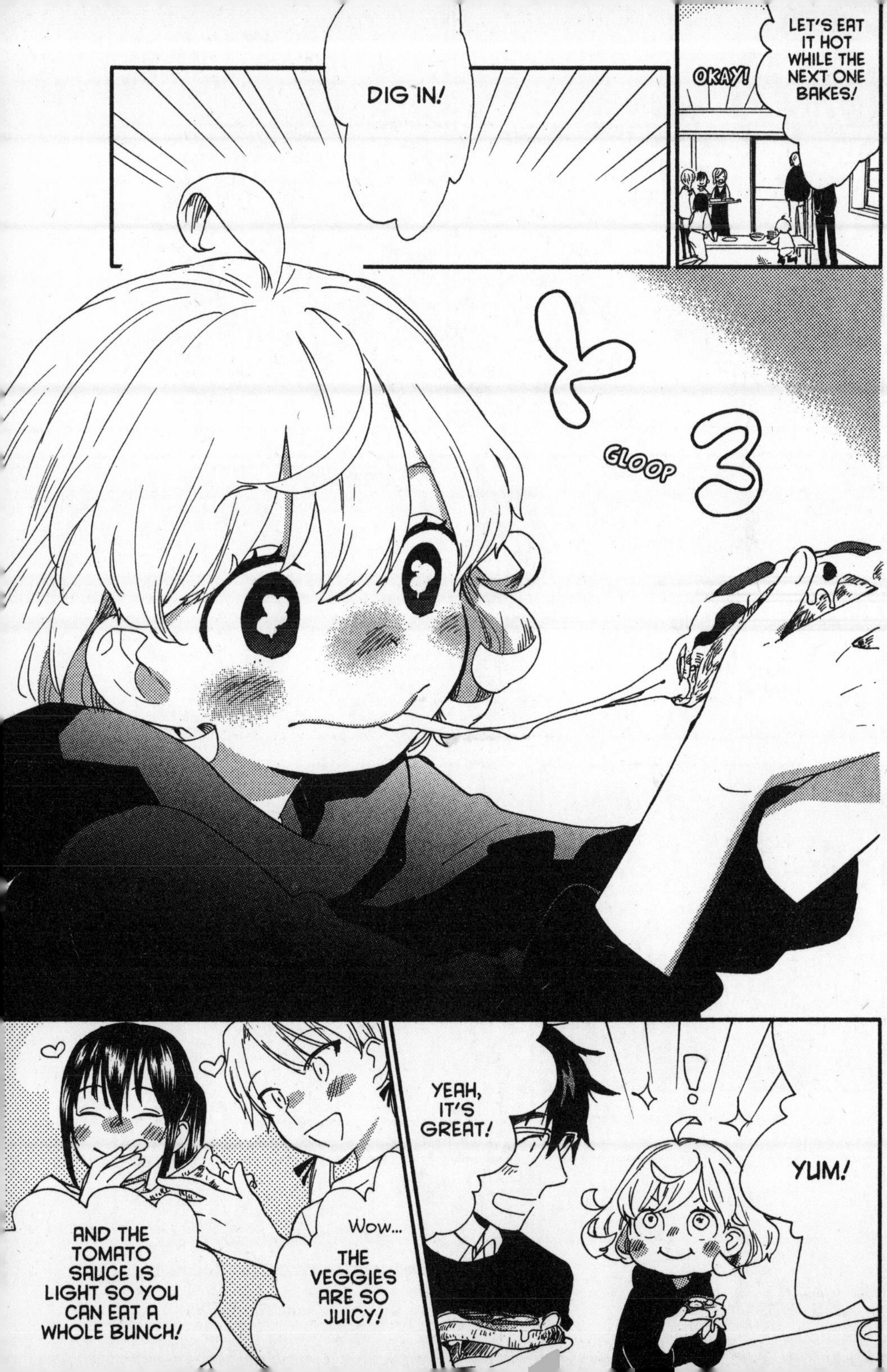
LET'S EAT IT HOT WHILE THE NEXT ONE BAKES!
OKAY!
DIG IN!
GLOOP
YUM!
YEAH, IT'S GREAT!
Wow...
THE VEGGIES ARE SO JUICY!
AND THE TOMATO SAUCE IS LIGHT SO YOU CAN EAT A WHOLE BUNCH!

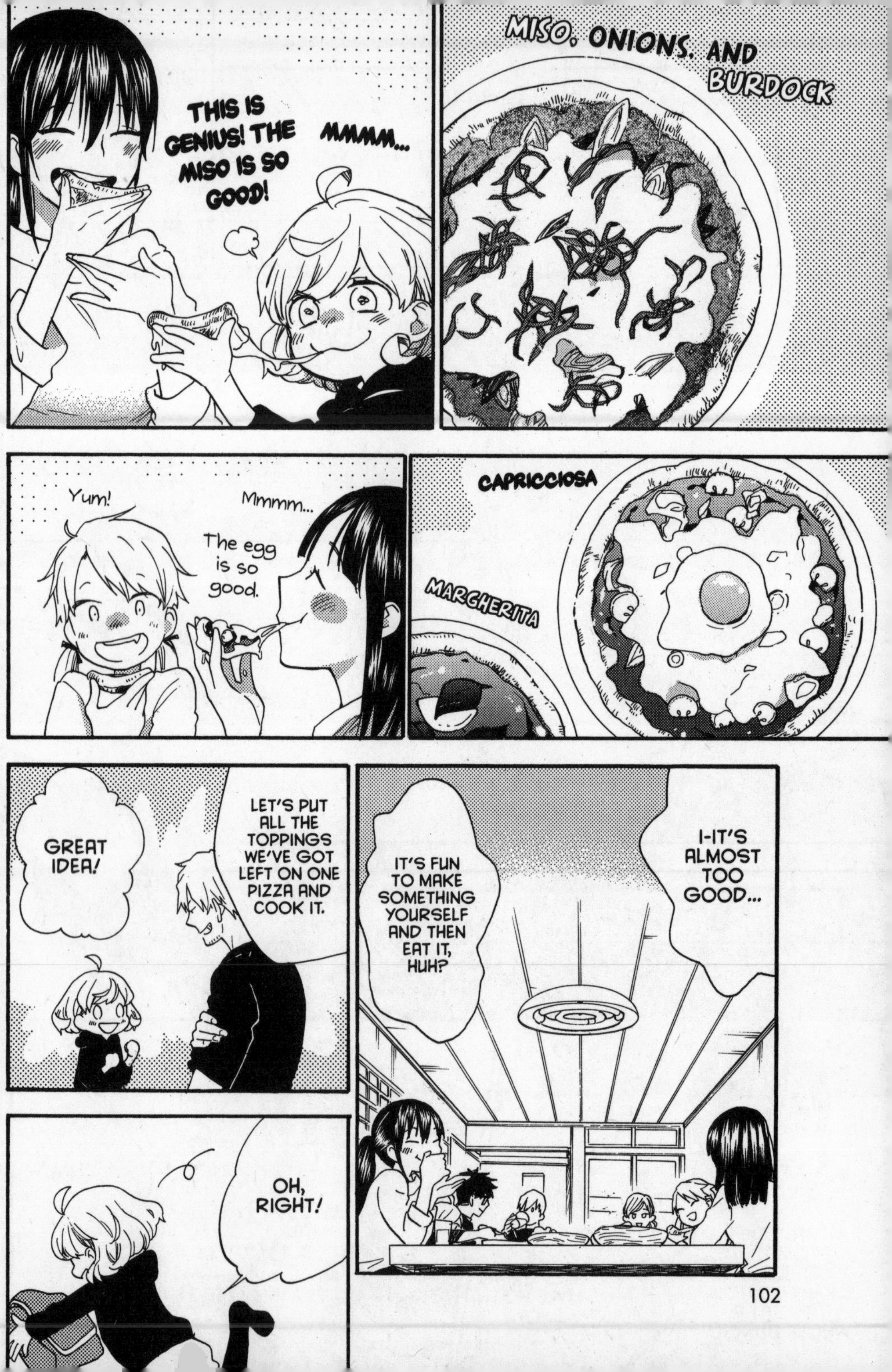
MISO, ONIONS, AND BURDOCK
MMMM...
THIS IS GENIUS! THE MISO IS SO GOOD!
CAPRICCIOSA
MARGHERITA
Mmmm...
The egg is so good.
Yum!
I-IT'S ALMOST TOO GOOD...
IT'S FUN TO MAKE SOMETHING YOURSELF AND THEN EAT IT, HUH?
LET'S PUT ALL THE TOPPINGS WE'VE GOT LEFT ON ONE PIZZA AND COOK IT.
GREAT IDEA!
OH, RIGHT!

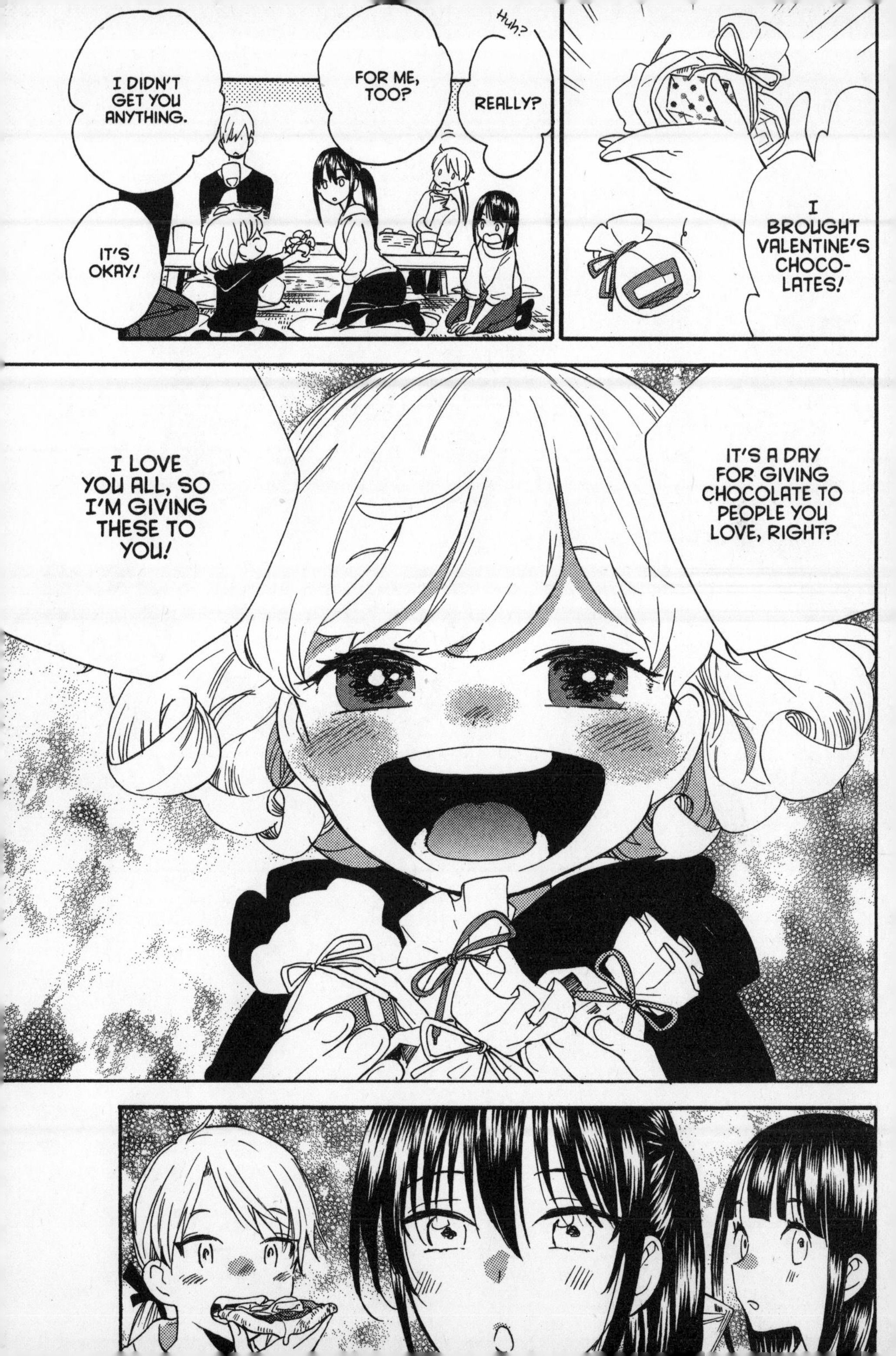
I BROUGHT VALENTINE'S CHOCO-LATES!
Huh?
REALLY?
FOR ME, TOO?
I DIDN'T GET YOU ANYTHING.
IT'S OKAY!
IT'S A DAY FOR GIVING CHOCOLATE TO PEOPLE YOU LOVE, RIGHT?
I LOVE YOU ALL, SO I'M GIVING THESE TO YOU!

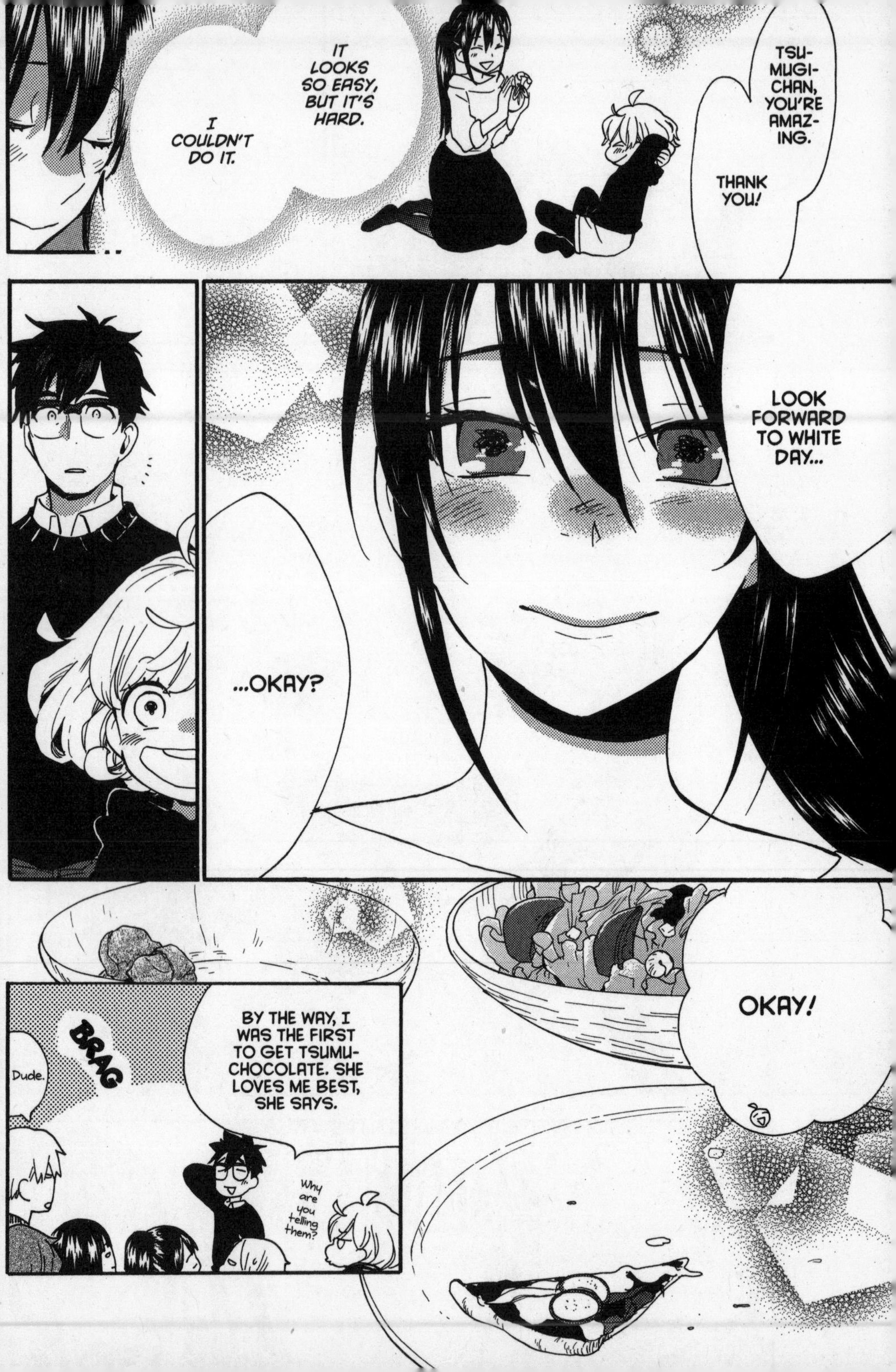
TSU-MUGI-CHAN, YOU'RE AMAZ-ING.
THANK YOU!
IT LOOKS SO EASY, BUT IT'S HARD.
I COULDN'T DO IT.
LOOK FORWARD TO WHITE DAY...
...OKAY?
OKAY!
BY THE WAY, I WAS THE FIRST TO GET TSUMU-CHOCOLATE. SHE LOVES ME BEST, SHE SAYS.
BRAG
Dude.
Why are you telling them?

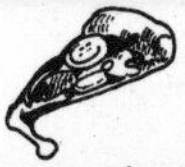

PIZZA

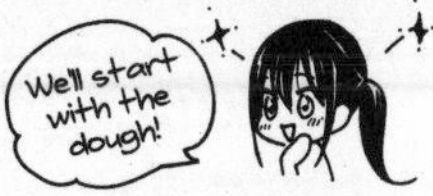
We'll start with the dough!

☆ Ingredients ☆ (24cm pizzas x4)

- Ⓐ 150g flour · 150g strong flour
- ★ 190cc warm water (30ºC)
- ★ 3g dry yeast
- ★ 1 tsp salt
- ★ pinch of sugar
- ★ 1 tbsp olive oil

Directions

1. Dissolve the sugar in 30cc of the warm water, add yeast, leave for 15 mins. (To ferment.)
2. Combine A in a large bowl. Dissolve the salt in the remaining water.
3. Hollow out the center of the flour. Add (1), (2) and the olive oil. Gradually incorporate the flour in the bowl.
4. Move the dough to a clean counter and knead.
   !POINT! As you knead hit the dough now and then!
5. Knead for about 15 minutes, fold edges into center until the dough is a ball. Pinch it closed.
6. Lightly grease a large bowl with olive oil. Place dough in bowl pinched side down. Leave for 1 to 1.5 hours in a warm place to rise.
7. When the dough has risen to about twice the size, place on floured surface. Use hands to push out excess gas, then divide into 4 pieces.
8. Fold the edges of each piece into the center and pinch closed. Place on a tray and cover in a damp cloth. Leave for 15 mins.
9. Once toppings are prepared place dough on floured surface. Push down with hands. Use rolling pin to roll out dough into 24cm base.

"Pizza base is done"

MISO ONION BURDOCK PIZZA

☆ Ingredients ☆ (for 2 pizzas)

- ★ 30cm (70g) burdock
- ★ 20cm (60g) green onion
- ★ 100g mozzarella cheese
- ★ 6 beefsteak leaves
- ★ ½ tbsp sesame oil
- Ⓐ 30g miso 70cc mirin

Directions

1. Slice the burdock into thin slices, add sesame oil and fry for 3-4 minutes. Slice onion into thin slices.
2. Combine Ⓐ in small pan and simmer until everything is dissolved.
3. Pre-heat an empty baking tray in oven at 250 ºC. Place a pizza base on a piece of baking paper. Sprinkle (2) on top, then arrange burdock and onion from (1) with the mozzarella cheese.
4. Take the tray out of the oven and place the baking sheet with pizza on top. Bake at 250 ºC for 7 minutes. Remove from oven, add the leaves and serve!

★POINT★ Don't spread the sauce right to the edge to allow it to rise!

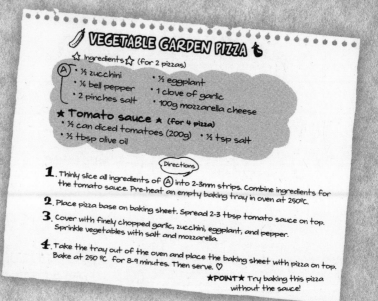

🥒 VEGETABLE GARDEN PIZZA 🍆

☆ Ingredients ☆ (for 2 pizzas)

Ⓐ
- ½ zucchini
- ¼ bell pepper
- 2 pinches salt
- ½ eggplant
- 1 clove of garlic
- 100g mozzarella cheese

★ **Tomato sauce** ★ (for 4 pizza)
- ½ can diced tomatoes (200g)   • ½ tsp salt
- ½ tbsp olive oil

Directions

1. Thinly slice all ingredients of Ⓐ into 2-3mm strips. Combine ingredients for the tomato sauce. Pre-heat an empty baking tray in oven at 250°C.

2. Place pizza base on baking sheet. Spread 2-3 tbsp tomato sauce on top.

3. Cover with finely chopped garlic, zucchini, eggplant, and pepper. Sprinkle vegetables with salt and mozzarella.

4. Take the tray out of the oven and place the baking sheet with pizza on top. Bake at 250°C for 8-9 minutes. Then serve. ♡

★POINT★ Try baking this pizza without the sauce!

Chapter 53 | Parent and Child Cookies to Thank You

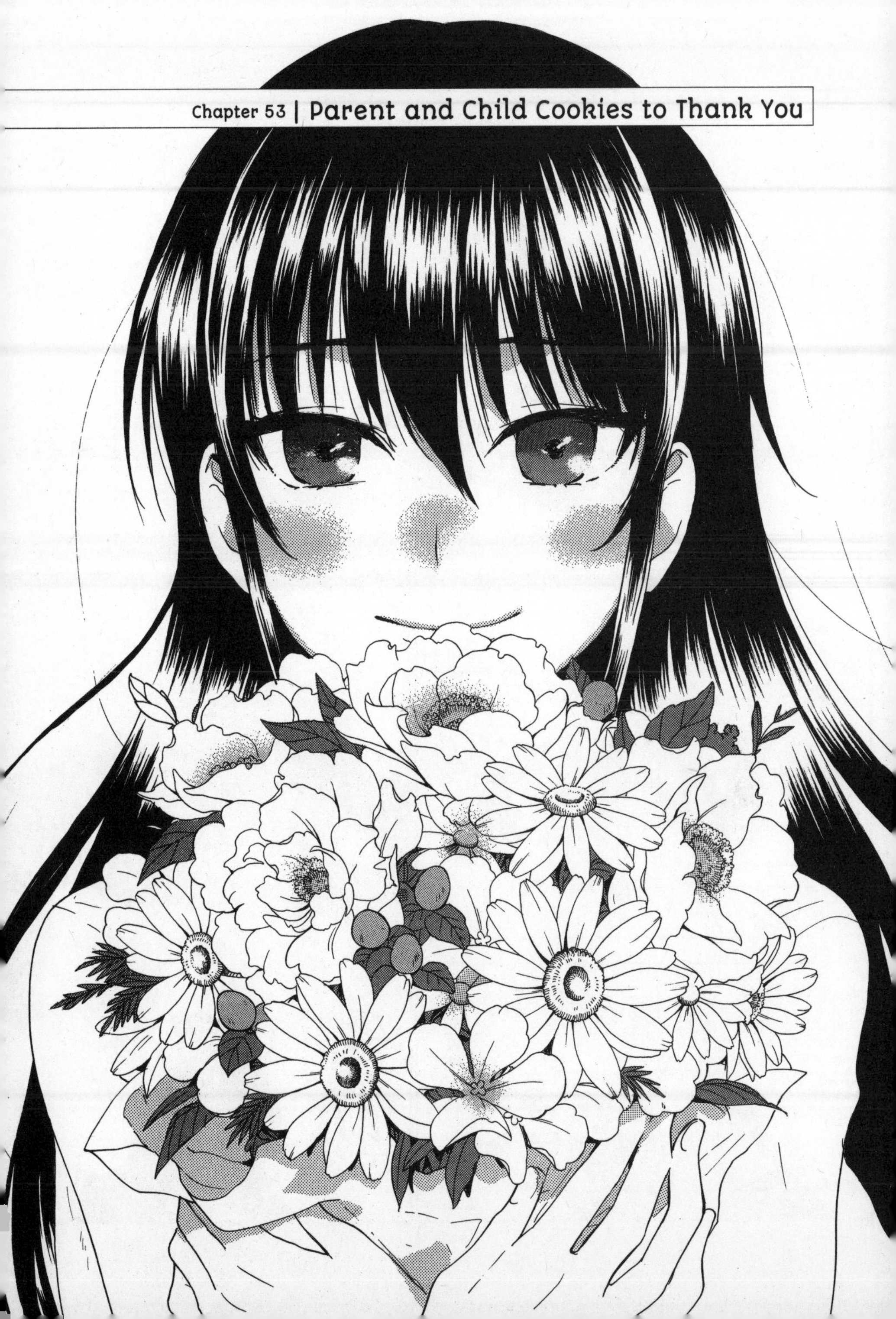

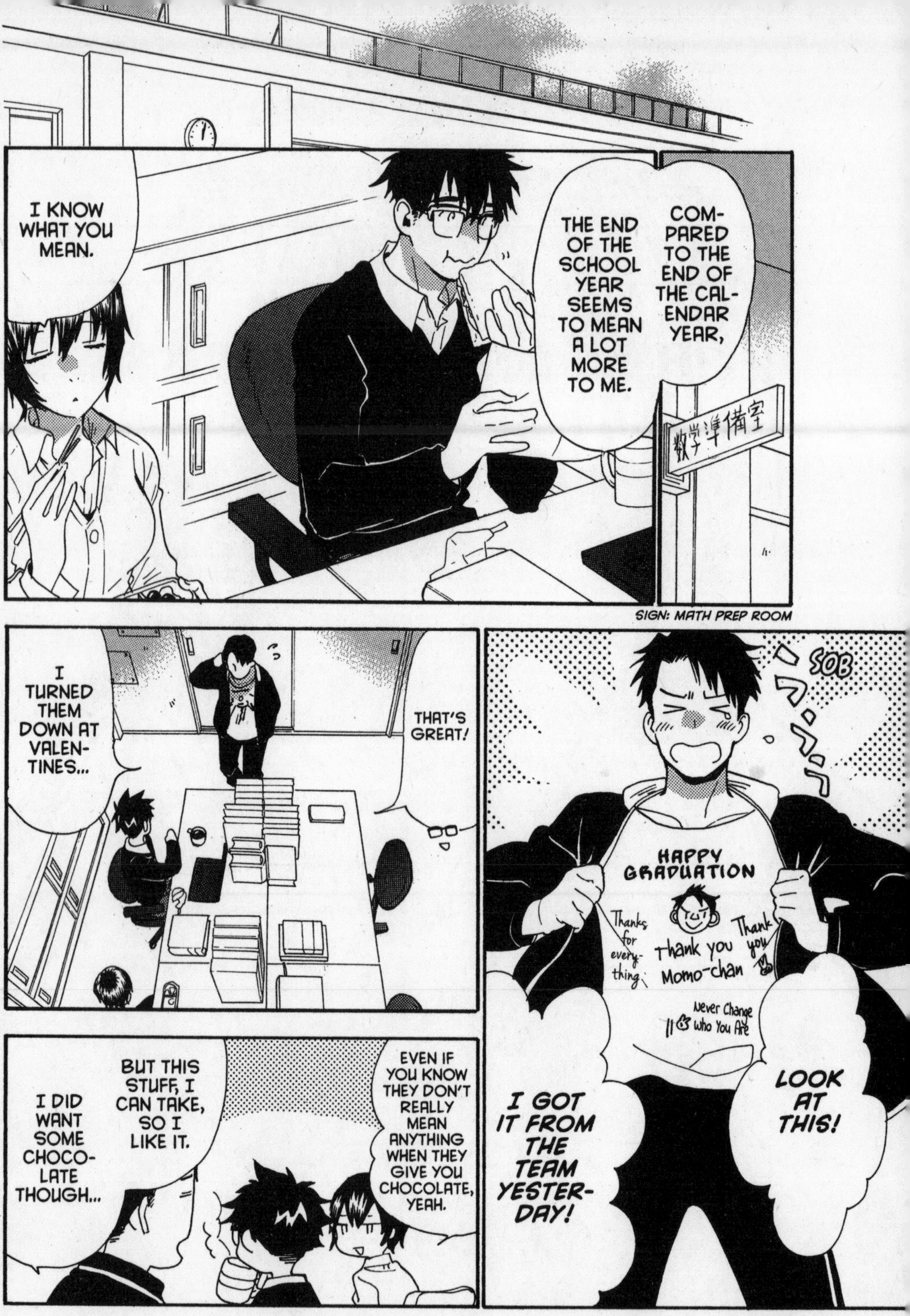
COMPARED TO THE END OF THE CALENDAR YEAR,
THE END OF THE SCHOOL YEAR SEEMS TO MEAN A LOT MORE TO ME.
I KNOW WHAT YOU MEAN.
数学準備室
SIGN: MATH PREP ROOM
SOB
LOOK AT THIS!
HAPPY GRADUATION
Thank you
Thank you Momo-chan
Thanks for everything
Never Change Who You Are
I GOT IT FROM THE TEAM YESTERDAY!
THAT'S GREAT!
I TURNED THEM DOWN AT VALENTINES...
EVEN IF YOU KNOW THEY DON'T REALLY MEAN ANYTHING WHEN THEY GIVE YOU CHOCOLATE, YEAH.
BUT THIS STUFF, I CAN TAKE, SO I LIKE IT.
I DID WANT SOME CHOCOLATE THOUGH...

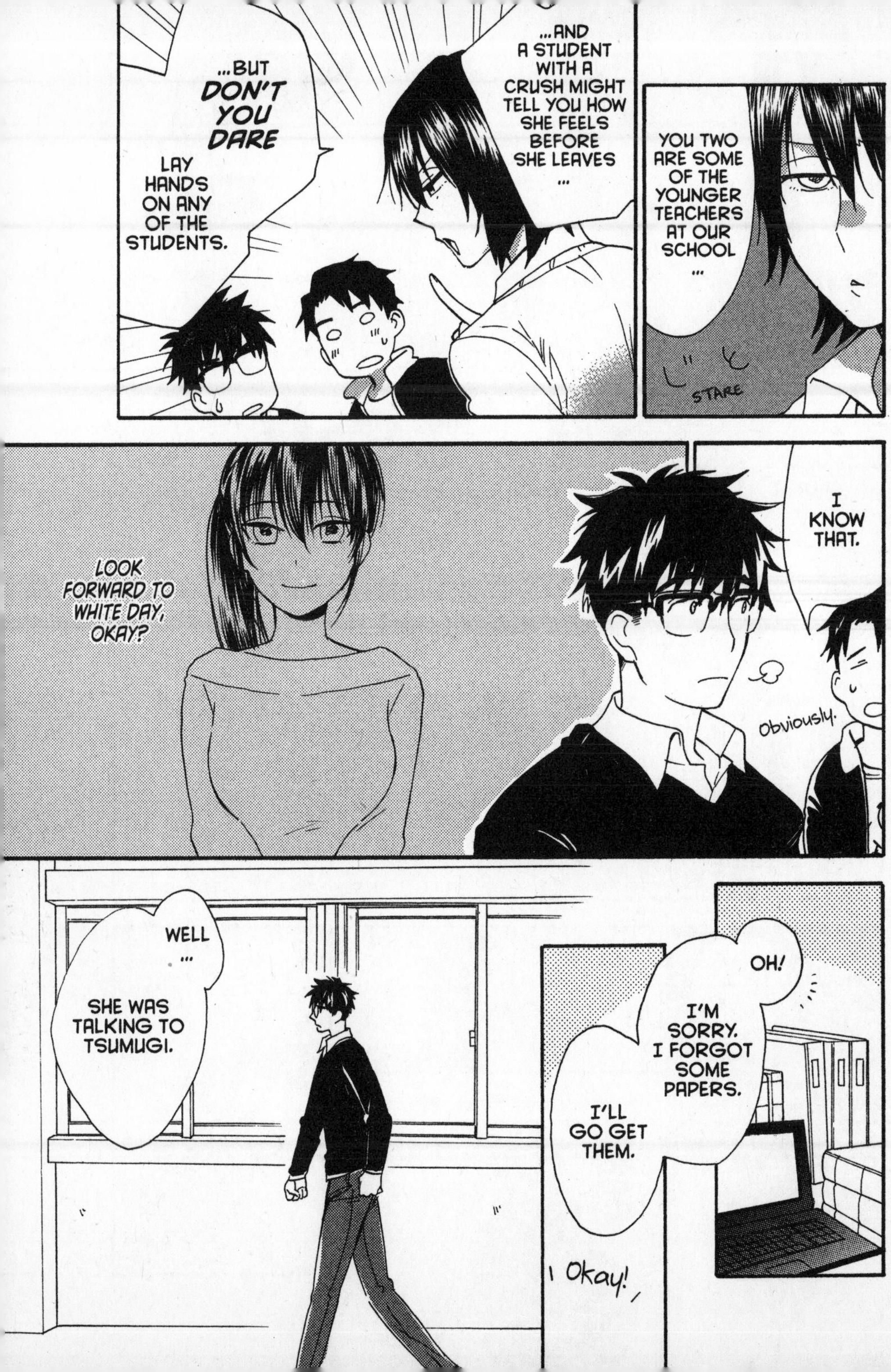
YOU TWO ARE SOME OF THE YOUNGER TEACHERS AT OUR SCHOOL ...
STARE
...AND A STUDENT WITH A CRUSH MIGHT TELL YOU HOW SHE FEELS BEFORE SHE LEAVES ...
...BUT DON'T YOU DARE
LAY HANDS ON ANY OF THE STUDENTS.
I KNOW THAT.
Obviously.
LOOK FORWARD TO WHITE DAY, OKAY?
OH!
I'M SORRY. I FORGOT SOME PAPERS.
I'LL GO GET THEM.
Okay!
WELL ...
SHE WAS TALKING TO TSUMUGI.

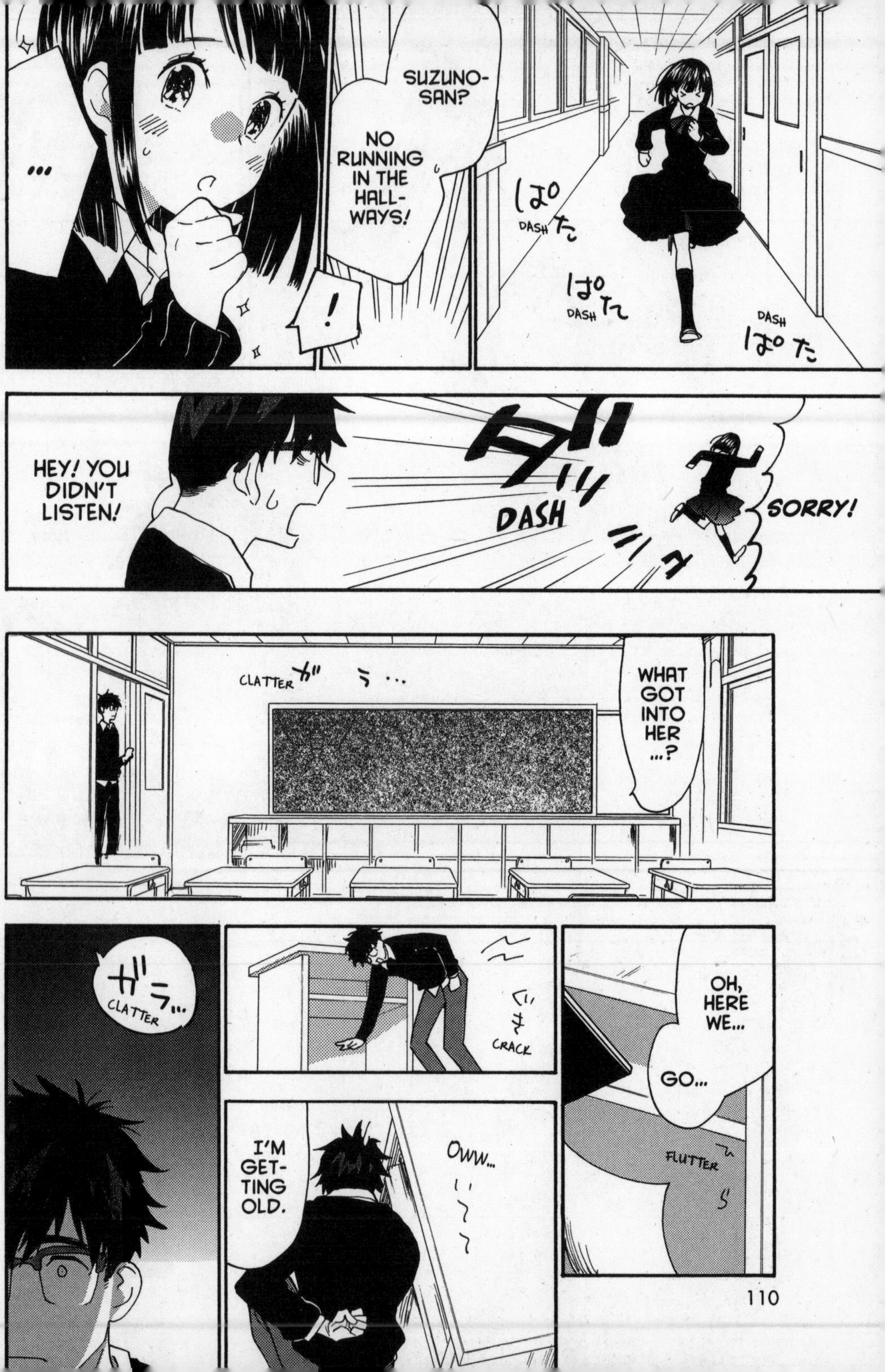

DASH ぱた
DASH ぱた
DASH ぱた
SUZUNO-SAN?
NO RUNNING IN THE HALL-WAYS!
!
...
SORRY!
ダッ
DASH
HEY! YOU DIDN'T LISTEN!
WHAT GOT INTO HER ...?
CLATTER ガラ…
OH, HERE WE...
GO...
FLUTTER
ぐき
CRACK
Oww...
いてて
I'M GET-TING OLD.
ガラ..
CLATTER

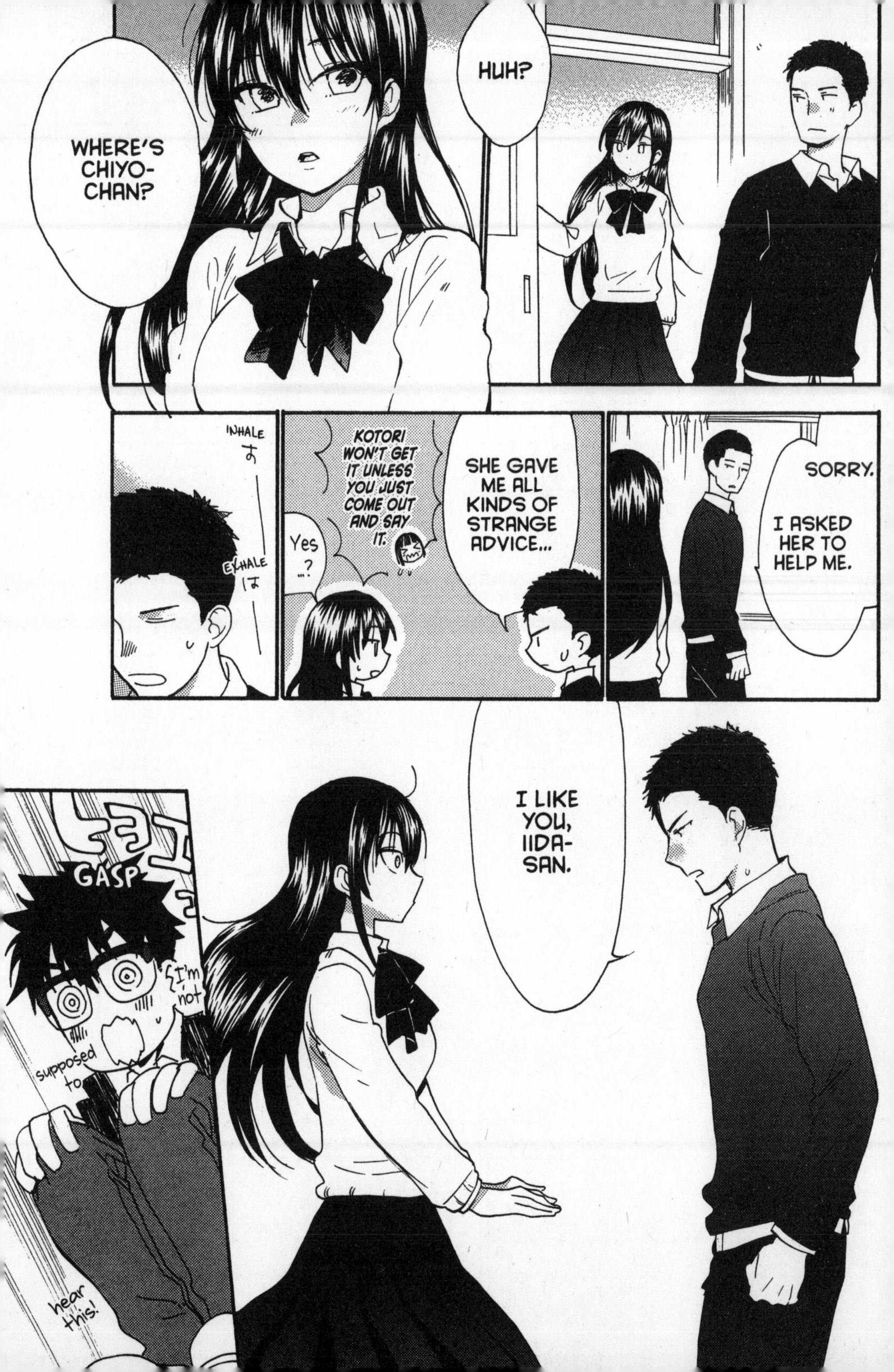
HUH?
WHERE'S CHIYO-CHAN?
SORRY.
I ASKED HER TO HELP ME.
SHE GAVE ME ALL KINDS OF STRANGE ADVICE...
KOTORI WON'T GET IT UNLESS YOU JUST COME OUT AND SAY IT.
Yes ...?
INHALE お
EXHALE は
I LIKE YOU, IIDA-SAN.
GASP
I'm not supposed to hear this!

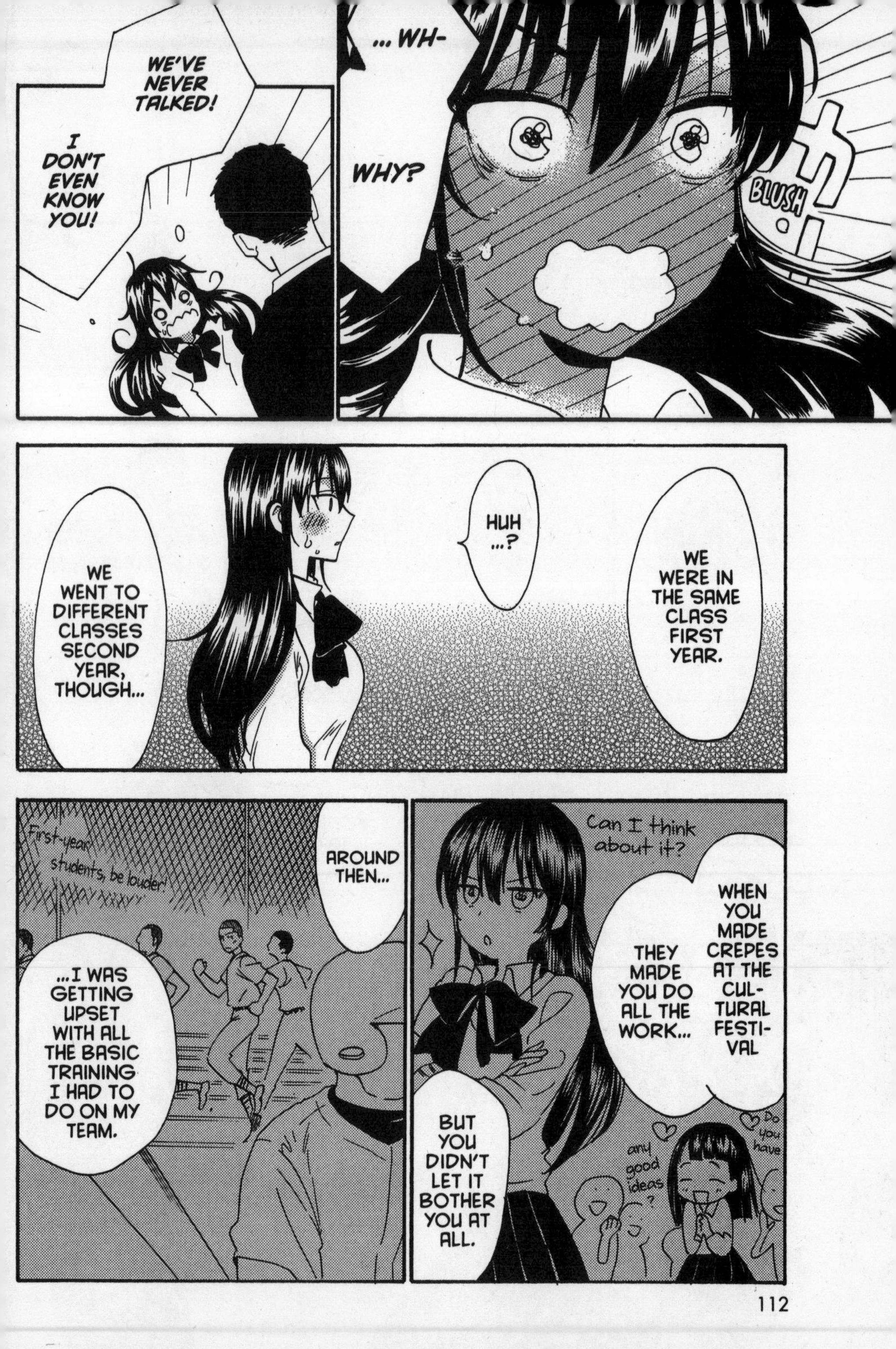
...WH-
WHY?
BLUSH
WE'VE NEVER TALKED!
I DON'T EVEN KNOW YOU!
WE WERE IN THE SAME CLASS FIRST YEAR.
HUH ...?
WE WENT TO DIFFERENT CLASSES SECOND YEAR, THOUGH...
Can I think about it?
WHEN YOU MADE CREPES AT THE CUL-TURAL FESTI-VAL
THEY MADE YOU DO ALL THE WORK...
Do you have any good ideas?
BUT YOU DIDN'T LET IT BOTHER YOU AT ALL.
AROUND THEN...
First-year students, be louder!
...I WAS GETTING UPSET WITH ALL THE BASIC TRAINING I HAD TO DO ON MY TEAM.

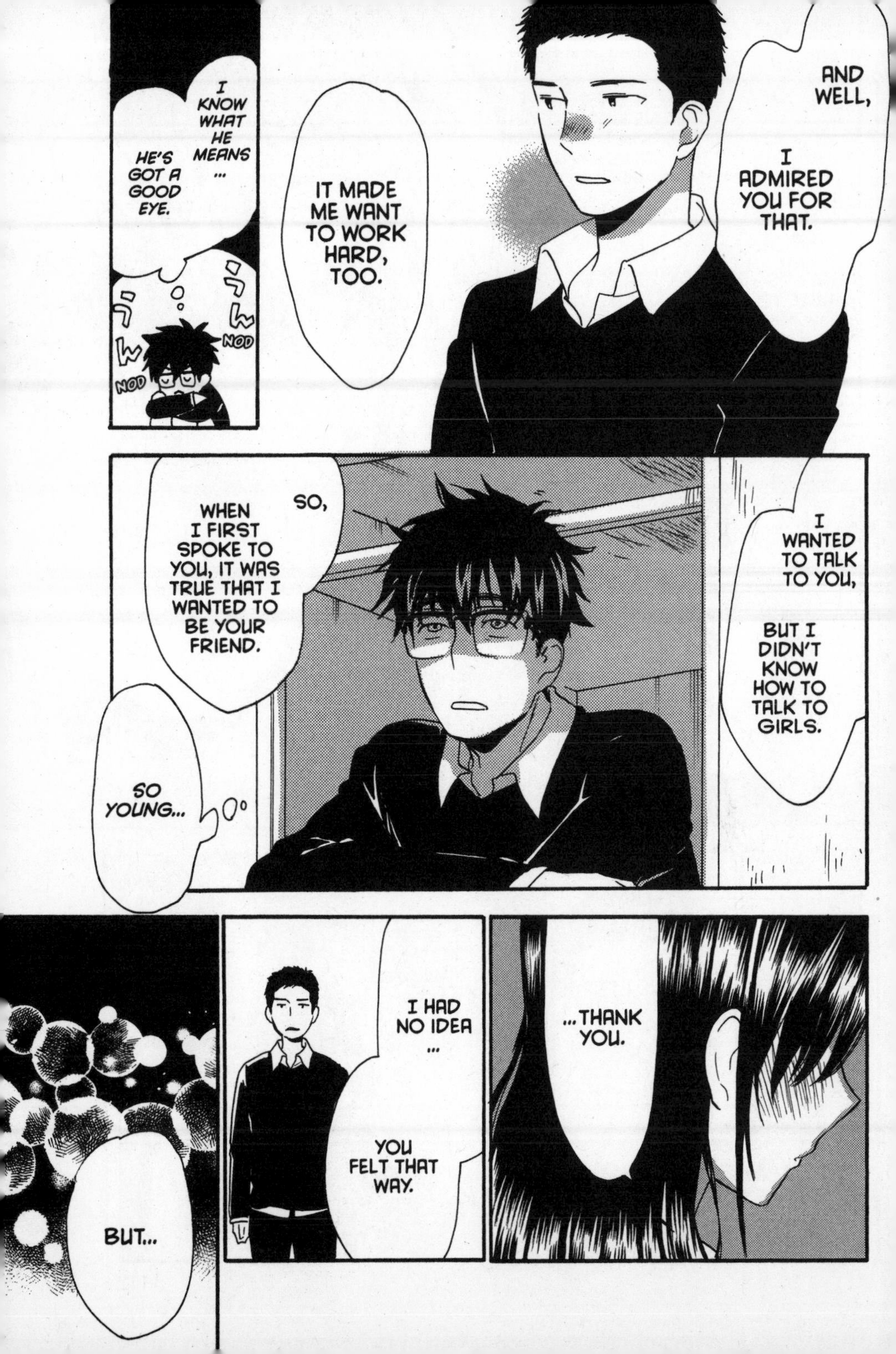
AND WELL,
I ADMIRED YOU FOR THAT.
IT MADE ME WANT TO WORK HARD, TOO.
I KNOW WHAT HE MEANS...
HE'S GOT A GOOD EYE.
NOD
NOD
I WANTED TO TALK TO YOU,
BUT I DIDN'T KNOW HOW TO TALK TO GIRLS.
SO,
WHEN I FIRST SPOKE TO YOU, IT WAS TRUE THAT I WANTED TO BE YOUR FRIEND.
SO YOUNG...
...THANK YOU.
I HAD NO IDEA...
YOU FELT THAT WAY.
BUT...

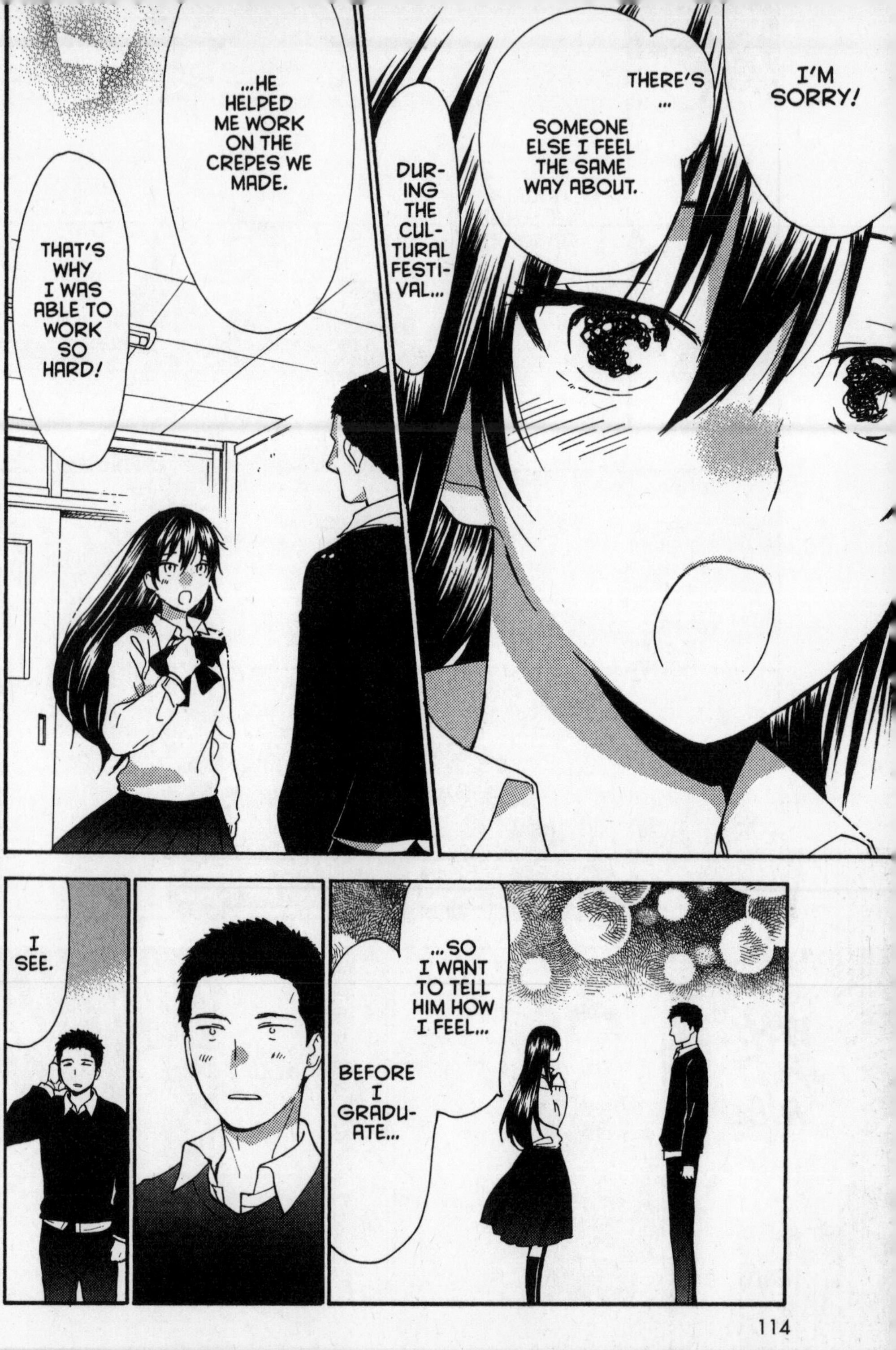
I'M SORRY!
THERE'S ... SOMEONE ELSE I FEEL THE SAME WAY ABOUT.
DURING THE CULTURAL FESTIVAL...
...HE HELPED ME WORK ON THE CREPES WE MADE.
THAT'S WHY I WAS ABLE TO WORK SO HARD!
...SO I WANT TO TELL HIM HOW I FEEL...
BEFORE I GRADUATE...
I SEE.

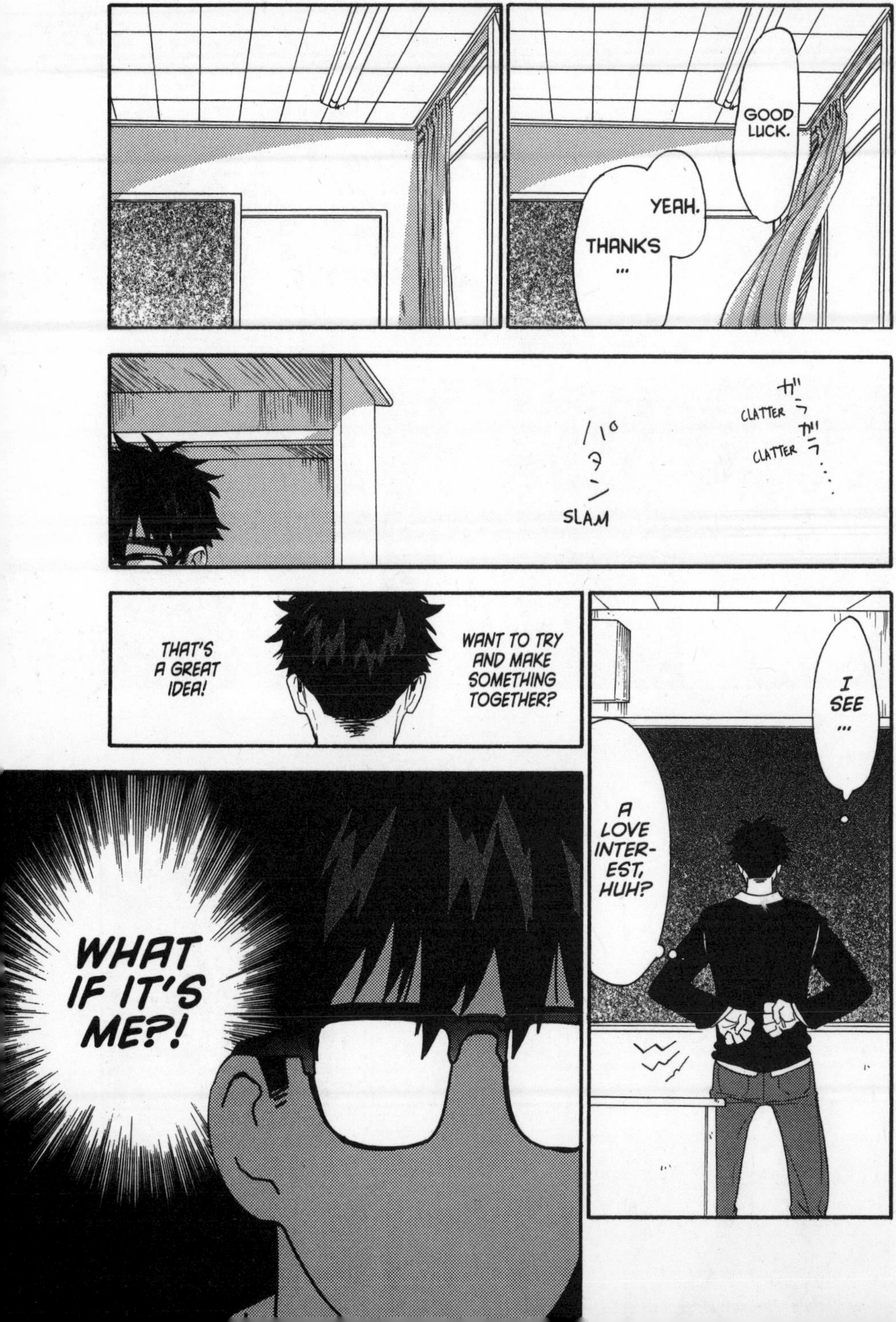
GOOD LUCK.
YEAH. THANKS ...
CLATTER
CLATTER
SLAM
I SEE ...
A LOVE INTER-EST, HUH?
WANT TO TRY AND MAKE SOMETHING TOGETHER?
THAT'S A GREAT IDEA!
WHAT IF IT'S ME?!

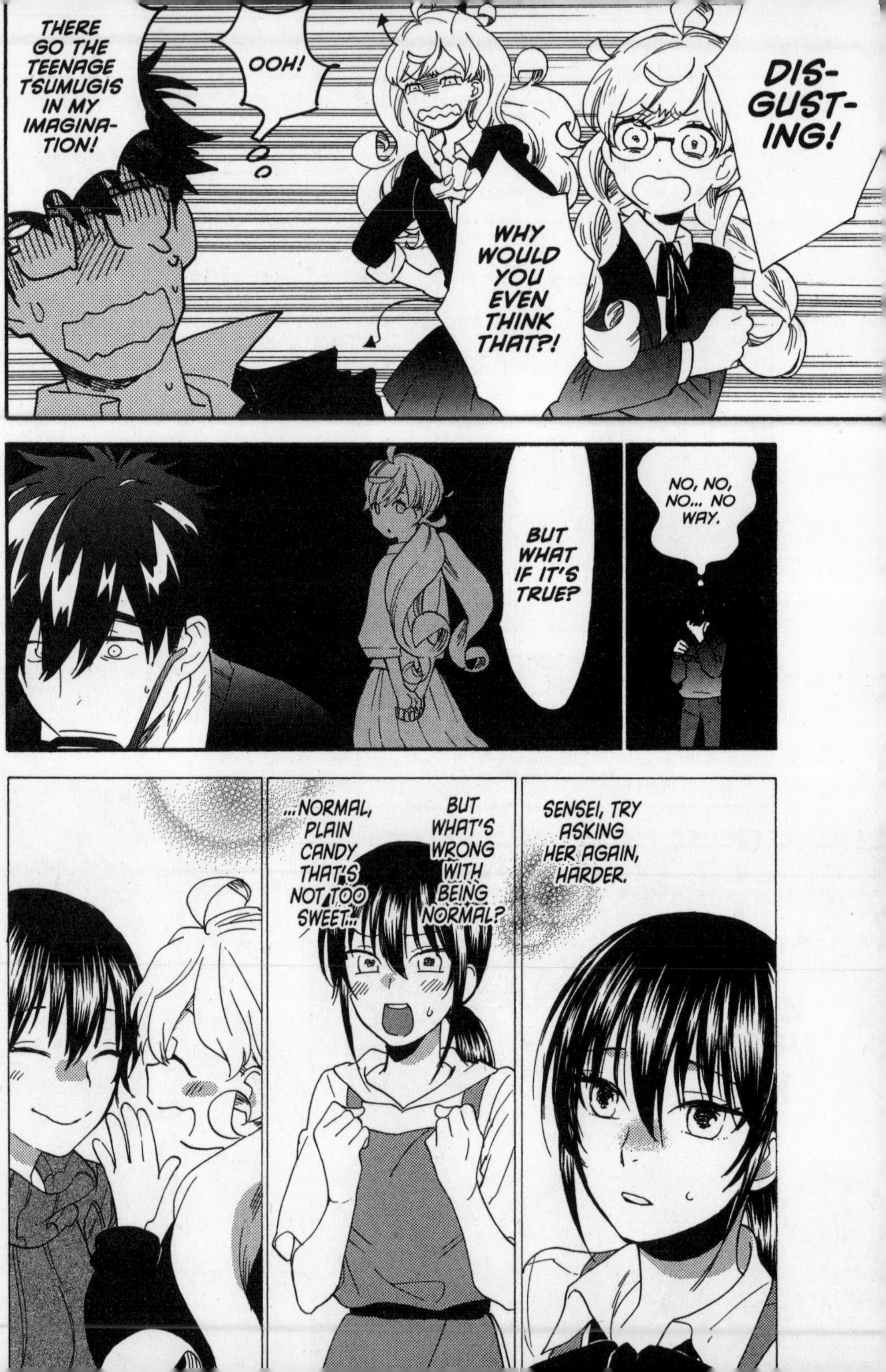
DIS-GUST-ING!
WHY WOULD YOU EVEN THINK THAT?!
OOH!
THERE GO THE TEENAGE TSUMUGIS IN MY IMAGINA-TION!
NO, NO, NO... NO WAY.
BUT WHAT IF IT'S TRUE?
SENSEI, TRY ASKING HER AGAIN, HARDER.
BUT WHAT'S WRONG WITH BEING NORMAL?
...NORMAL, PLAIN CANDY THAT'S NOT TOO SWEET...

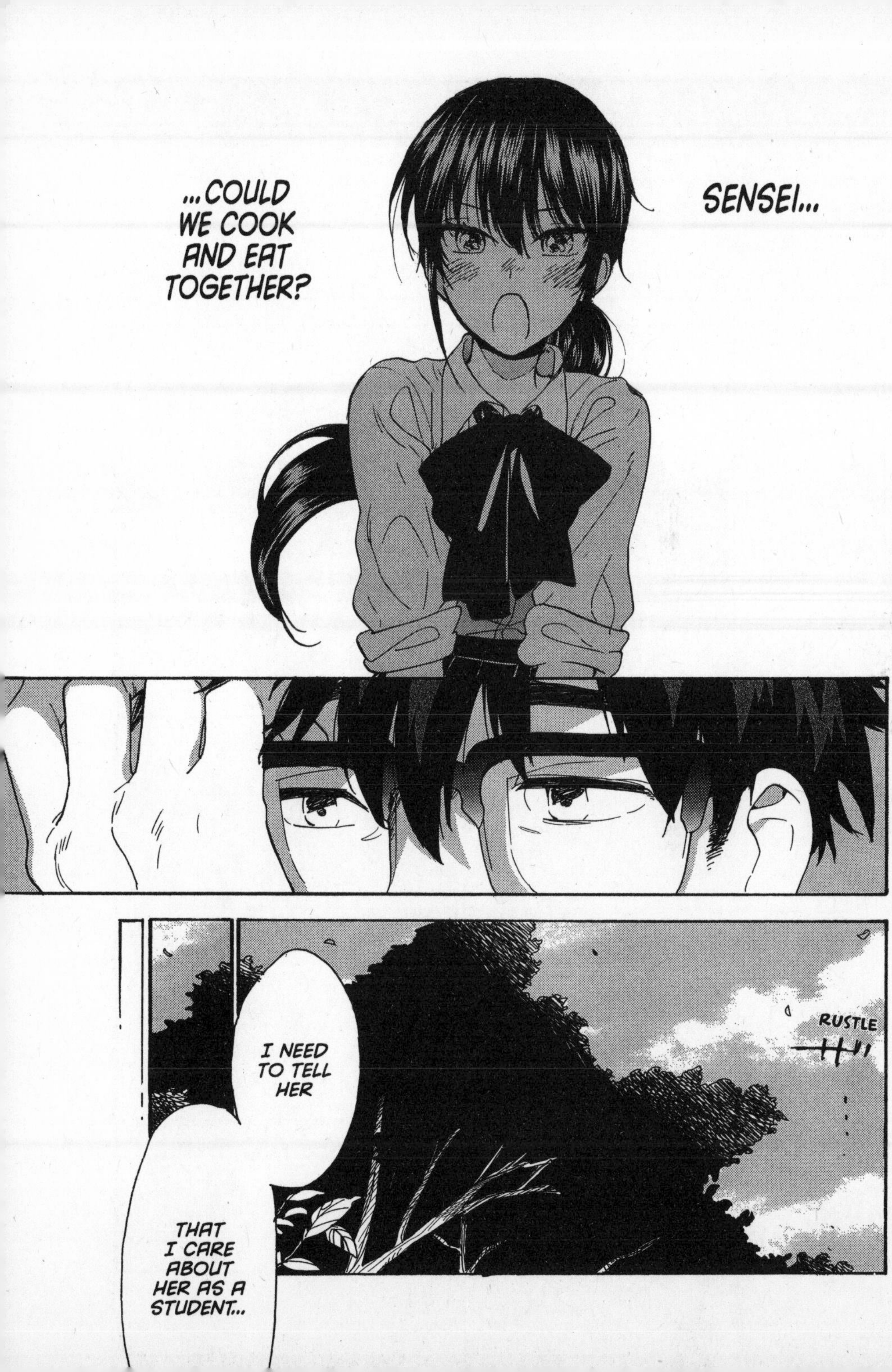
SENSEI...
...COULD WE COOK AND EAT TOGETHER?
RUSTLE
I NEED TO TELL HER
THAT I CARE ABOUT HER AS A STUDENT...

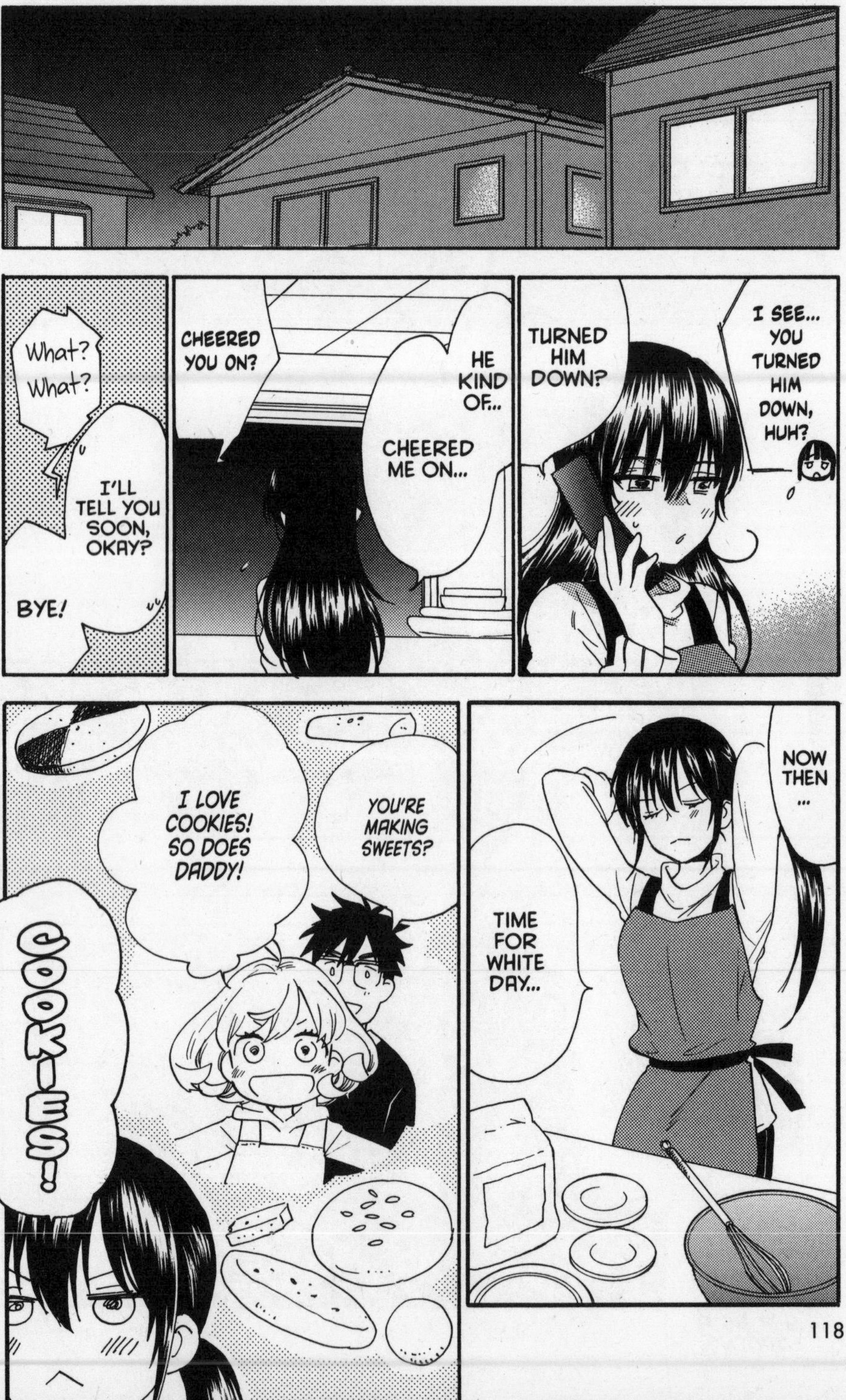
I SEE... YOU TURNED HIM DOWN, HUH?
TURNED HIM DOWN?
HE KIND OF...
CHEERED ME ON...
CHEERED YOU ON?
What? What?
I'LL TELL YOU SOON, OKAY?
BYE!
NOW THEN ...
TIME FOR WHITE DAY...
YOU'RE MAKING SWEETS?
I LOVE COOKIES! SO DOES DADDY!
COOKIES!

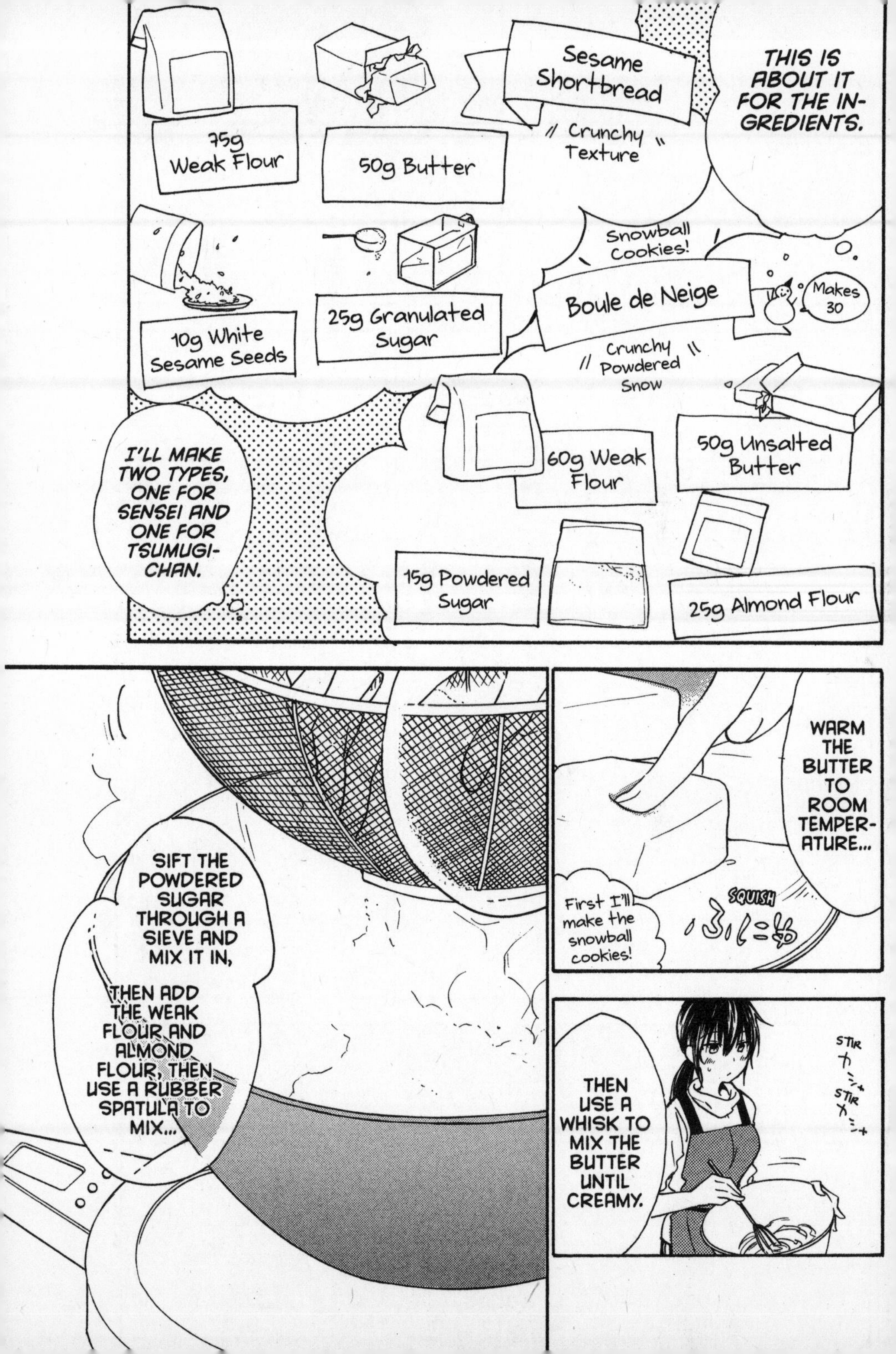
THIS IS ABOUT IT FOR THE INGREDIENTS.
Sesame Shortbread
Crunchy Texture
75g Weak Flour
50g Butter
10g White Sesame Seeds
25g Granulated Sugar
Snowball Cookies!
Boule de Neige
Makes 30
Crunchy Powdered Snow
50g Unsalted Butter
60g Weak Flour
25g Almond Flour
15g Powdered Sugar
I'LL MAKE TWO TYPES, ONE FOR SENSEI AND ONE FOR TSUMUGI-CHAN.
WARM THE BUTTER TO ROOM TEMPERATURE...
SQUISH
First I'll make the snowball cookies!
THEN USE A WHISK TO MIX THE BUTTER UNTIL CREAMY.
STIR
STIR
SIFT THE POWDERED SUGAR THROUGH A SIEVE AND MIX IT IN,
THEN ADD THE WEAK FLOUR AND ALMOND FLOUR, THEN USE A RUBBER SPATULA TO MIX...

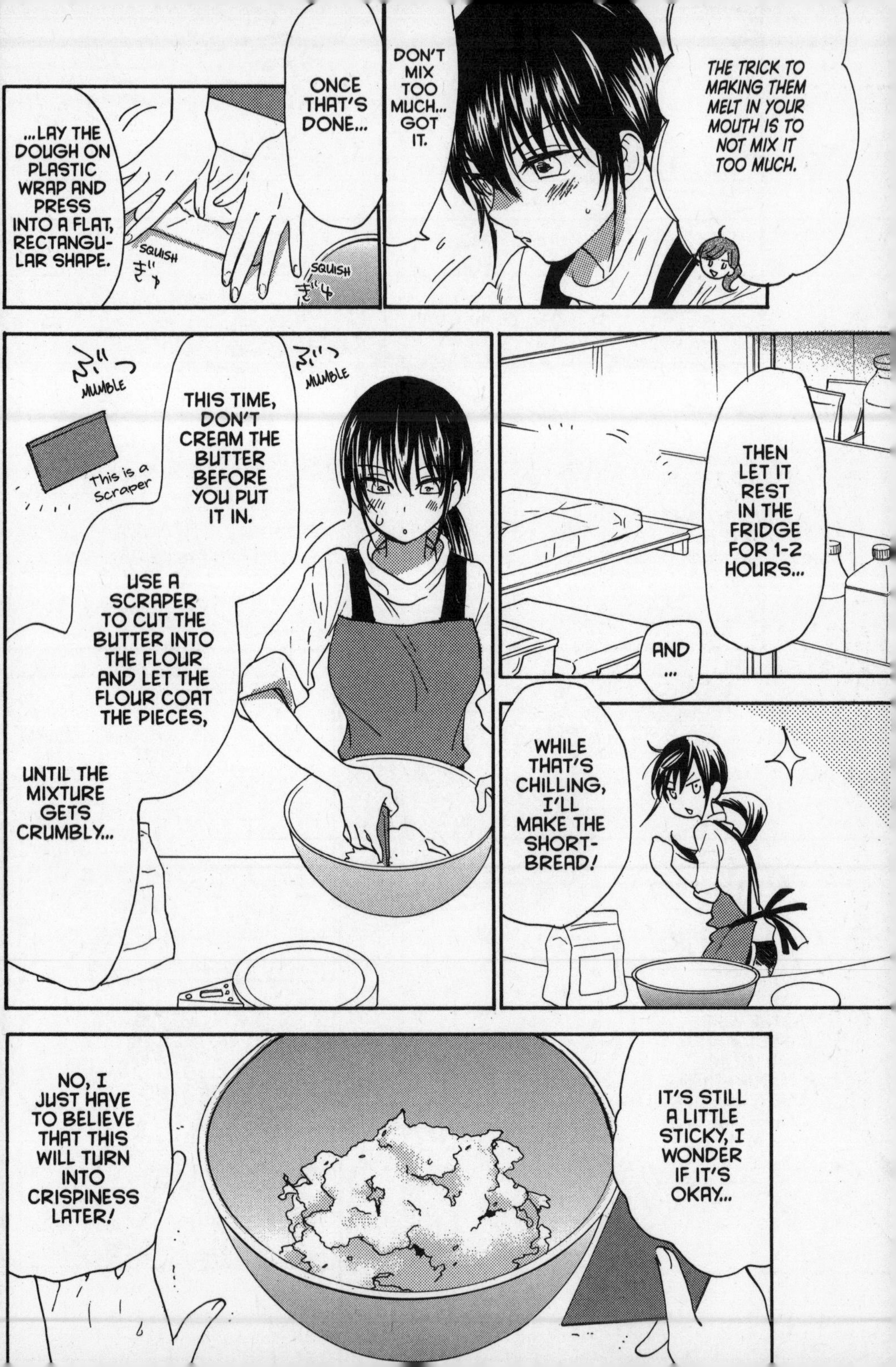
THE TRICK TO MAKING THEM MELT IN YOUR MOUTH IS TO NOT MIX IT TOO MUCH.
DON'T MIX TOO MUCH... GOT IT.
ONCE THAT'S DONE...
...LAY THE DOUGH ON PLASTIC WRAP AND PRESS INTO A FLAT, RECTANGULAR SHAPE.
SQUISH
ぎゅ
SQUISH
ぎゅ
THEN LET IT REST IN THE FRIDGE FOR 1-2 HOURS...
AND ...
WHILE THAT'S CHILLING, I'LL MAKE THE SHORTBREAD!
ぶつ
MUMBLE
THIS TIME, DON'T CREAM THE BUTTER BEFORE YOU PUT IT IN.
ぶつ
MUMBLE
This is a Scraper
USE A SCRAPER TO CUT THE BUTTER INTO THE FLOUR AND LET THE FLOUR COAT THE PIECES,
UNTIL THE MIXTURE GETS CRUMBLY...
IT'S STILL A LITTLE STICKY, I WONDER IF IT'S OKAY...
NO, I JUST HAVE TO BELIEVE THAT THIS WILL TURN INTO CRISPINESS LATER!

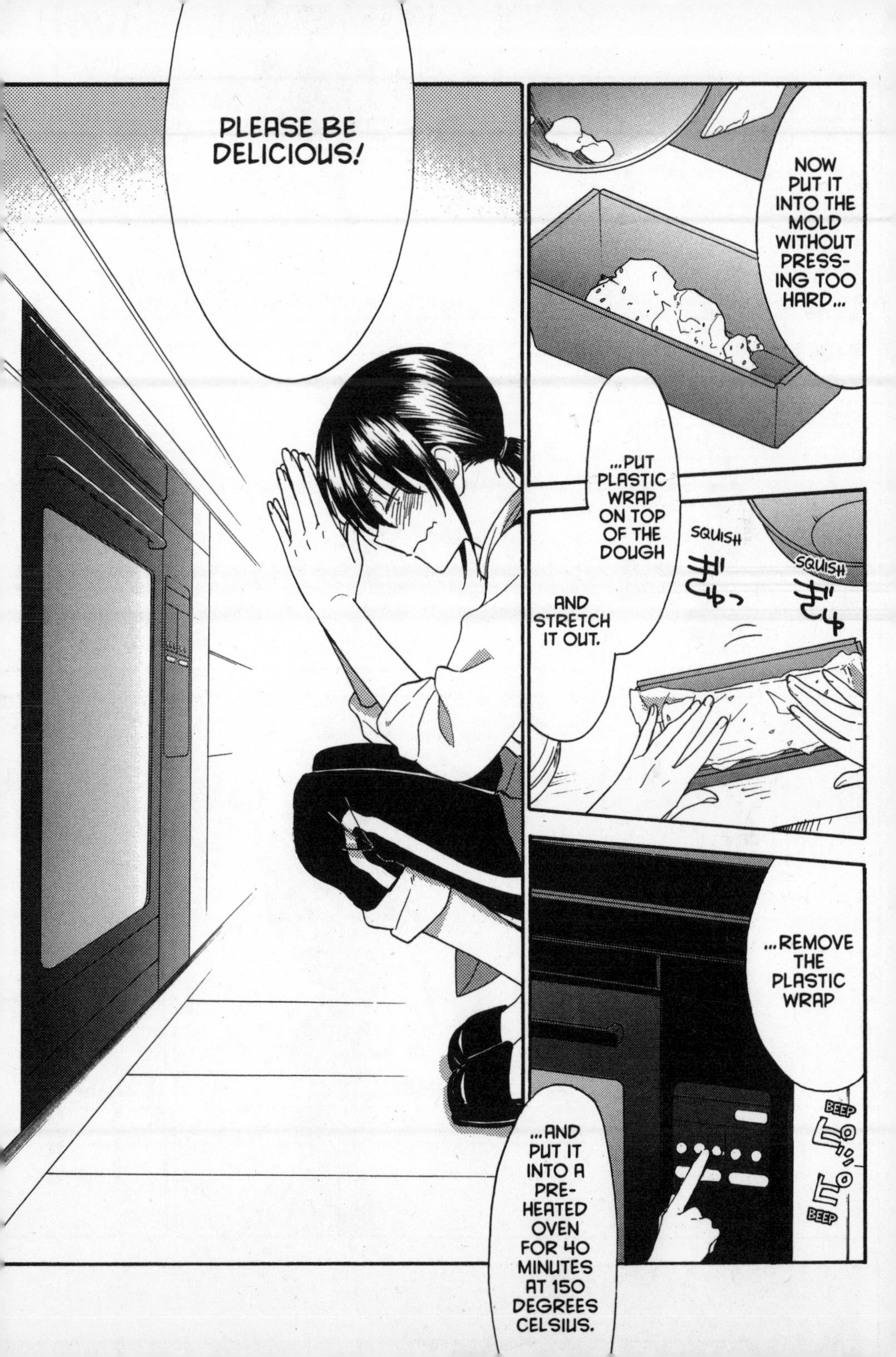
NOW PUT IT INTO THE MOLD WITHOUT PRESS-ING TOO HARD...
...PUT PLASTIC WRAP ON TOP OF THE DOUGH AND STRETCH IT OUT.
SQUISH
SQUISH
...REMOVE THE PLASTIC WRAP
...AND PUT IT INTO A PRE-HEATED OVEN FOR 40 MINUTES AT 150 DEGREES CELSIUS.
BEEP
BEEP
PLEASE BE DELICIOUS!

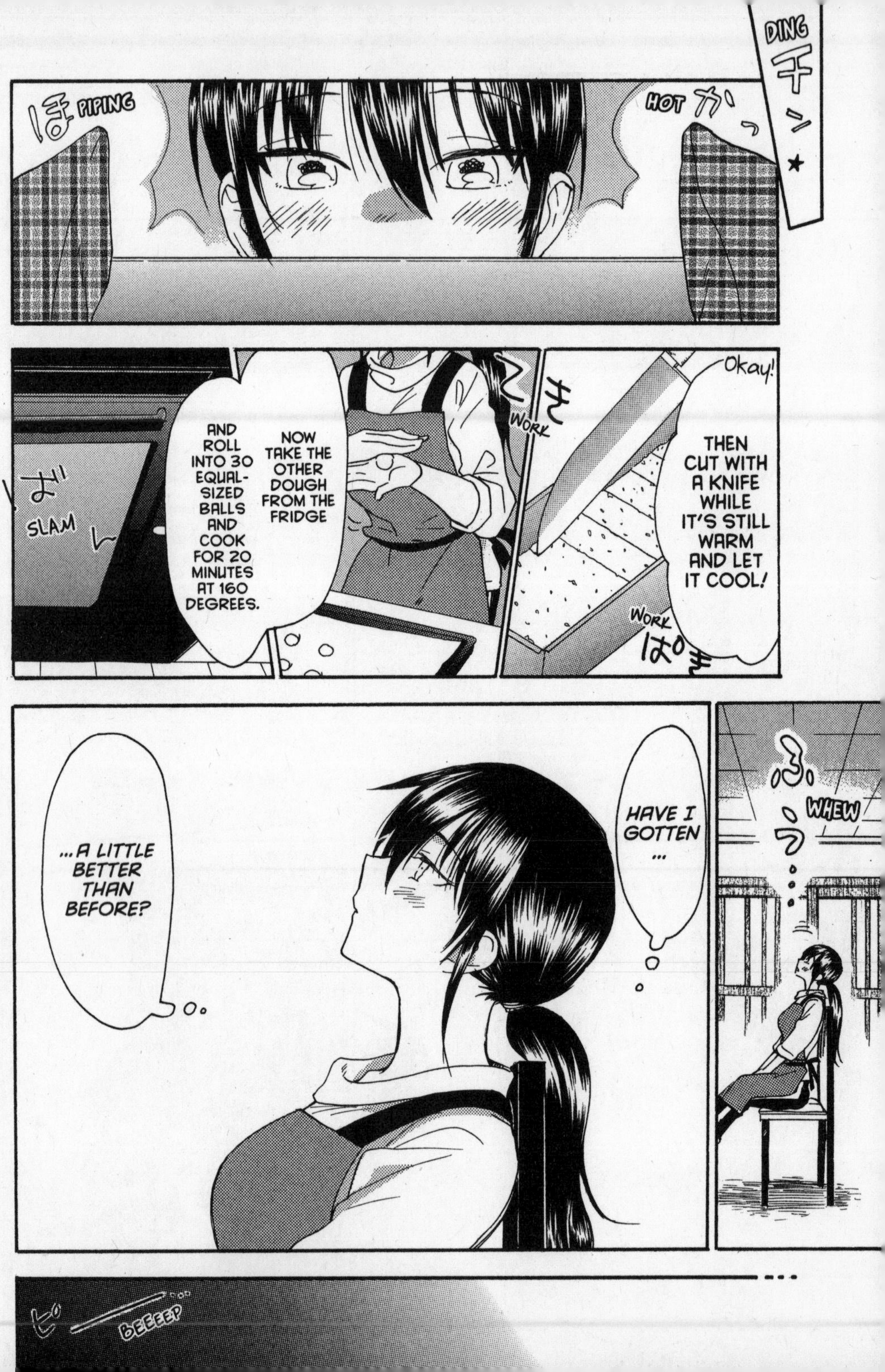
DING
HOT
PIPING
Okay!
THEN CUT WITH A KNIFE WHILE IT'S STILL WARM AND LET IT COOL!
WORK
WORK
NOW TAKE THE OTHER DOUGH FROM THE FRIDGE
AND ROLL INTO 30 EQUAL-SIZED BALLS AND COOK FOR 20 MINUTES AT 160 DEGREES.
SLAM
WHEW
HAVE I GOTTEN ...
...A LITTLE BETTER THAN BEFORE?
BEEEEP

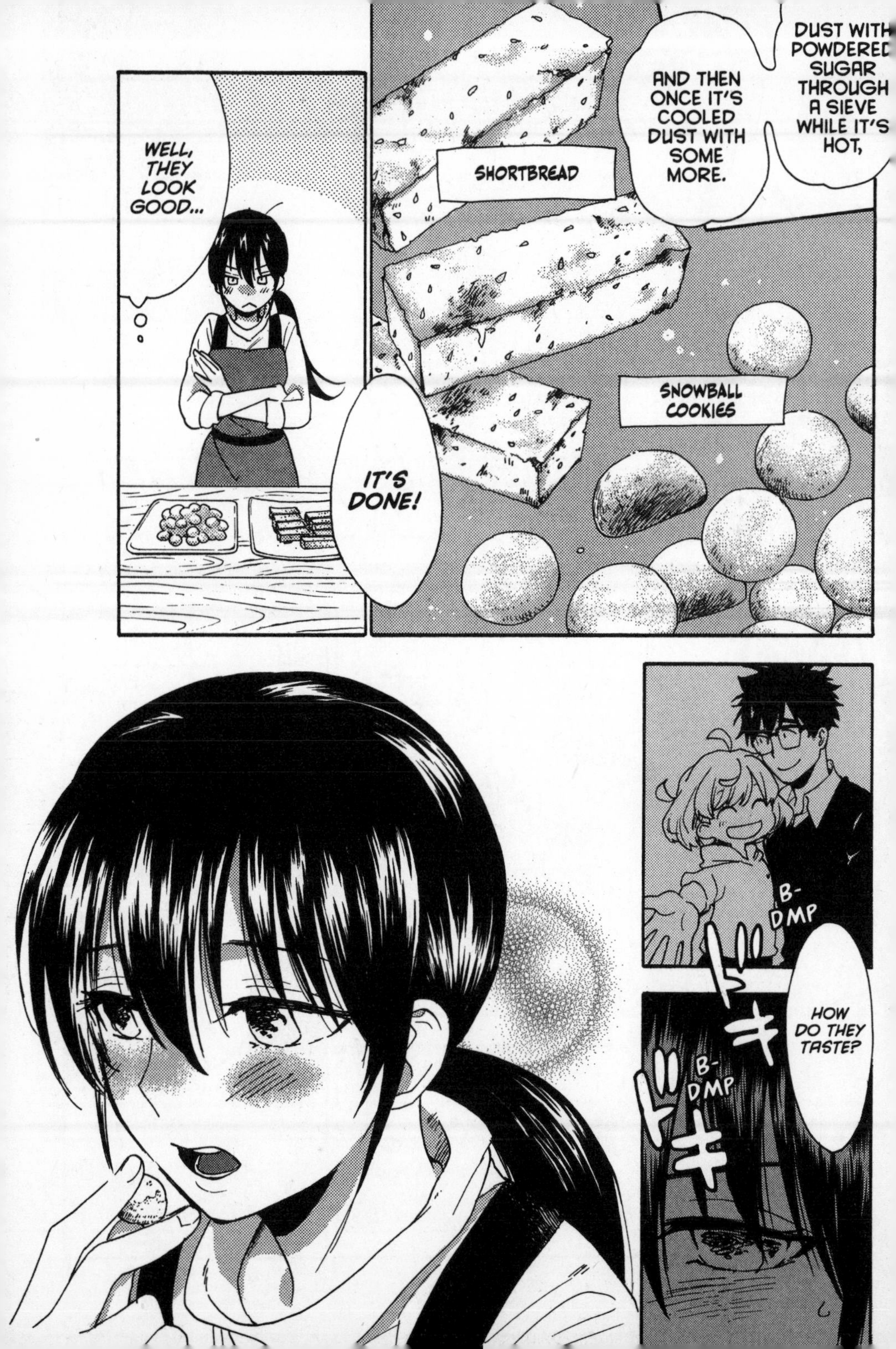
DUST WITH POWDERED SUGAR THROUGH A SIEVE WHILE IT'S HOT,
AND THEN ONCE IT'S COOLED DUST WITH SOME MORE.
SHORTBREAD
SNOWBALL COOKIES
IT'S DONE!
WELL, THEY LOOK GOOD...
B-DMP
ドキ
HOW DO THEY TASTE?
B-DMP
ドキ

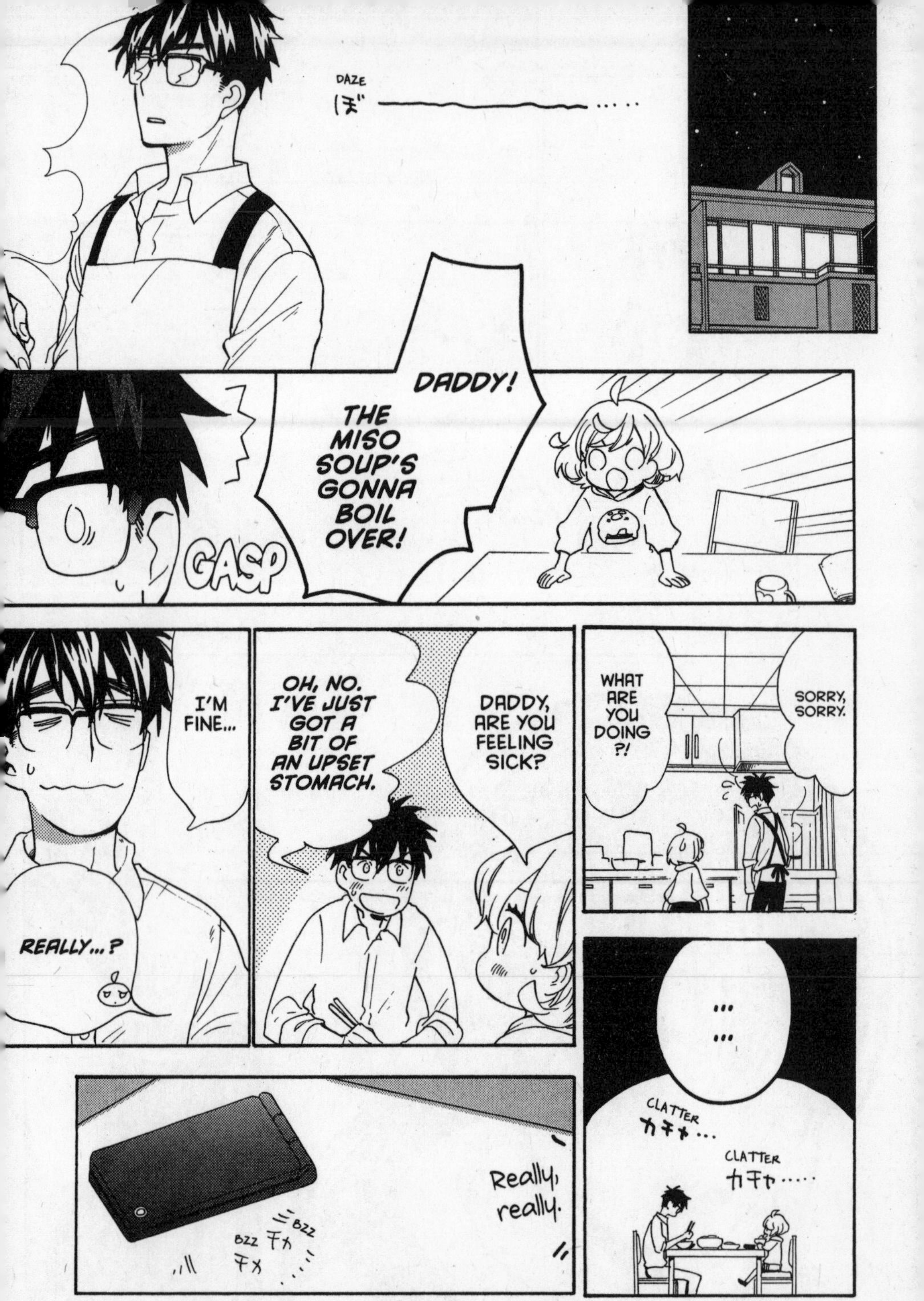
DAZE
ぼ——……
DADDY! THE MISO SOUP'S GONNA BOIL OVER!
GASP
WHAT ARE YOU DOING?!
SORRY, SORRY.
DADDY, ARE YOU FEELING SICK?
OH, NO. I'VE JUST GOT A BIT OF AN UPSET STOMACH.
I'M FINE...
REALLY...?
...
...
CLATTER
カチャ…
CLATTER
カチャ……
Really, really.
BZZ
チカ
BZZ
チカ

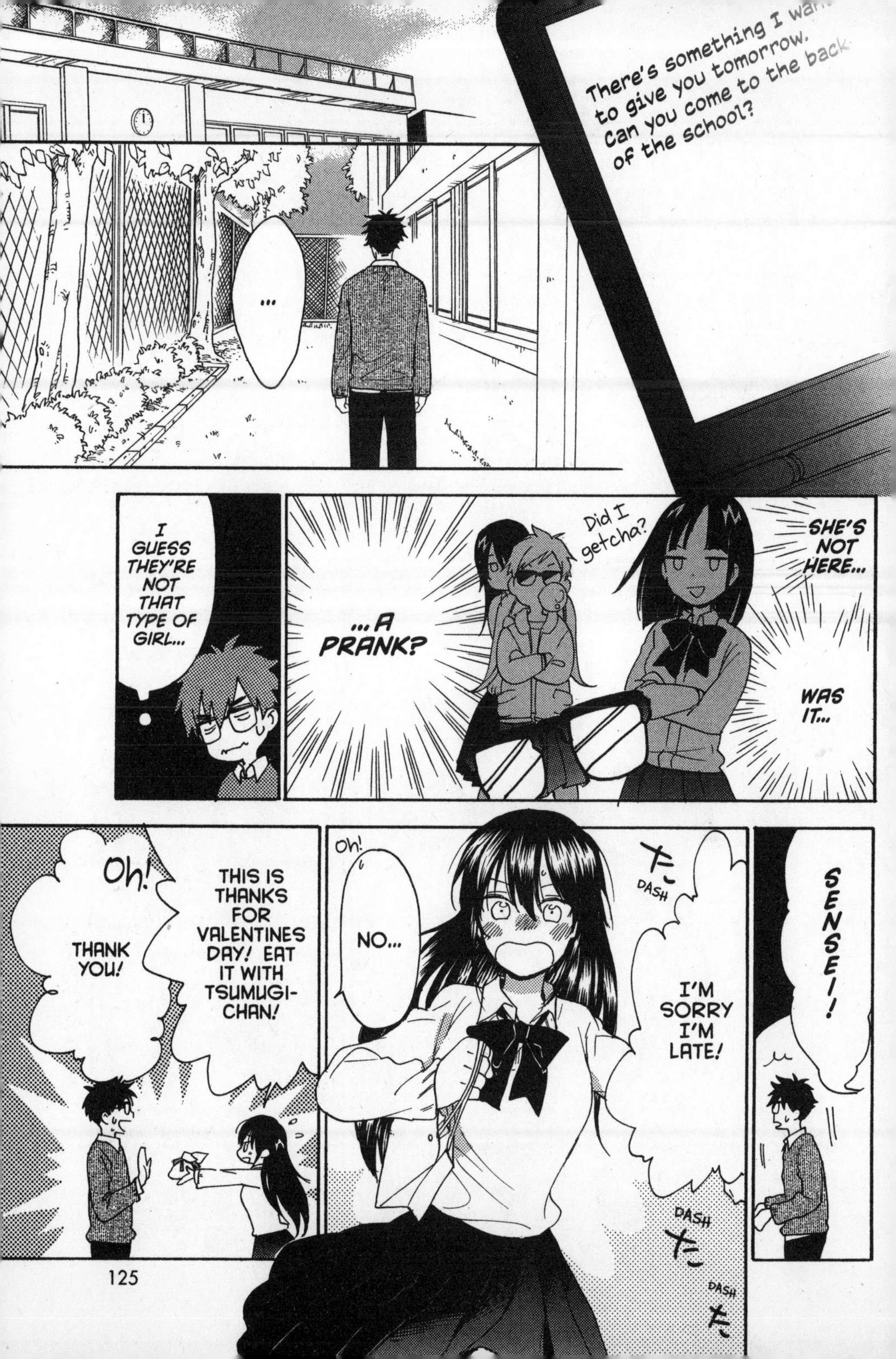
There's something I want to give you tomorrow. Can you come to the back of the school?
...
Did I getcha?
SHE'S NOT HERE...
WAS IT...
...A PRANK?
I GUESS THEY'RE NOT THAT TYPE OF GIRL...
SENSEI!
DASH
I'M SORRY I'M LATE!
Oh!
NO...
DASH
DASH
THIS IS THANKS FOR VALENTINES DAY! EAT IT WITH TSUMUGI-CHAN!
Oh!
THANK YOU!

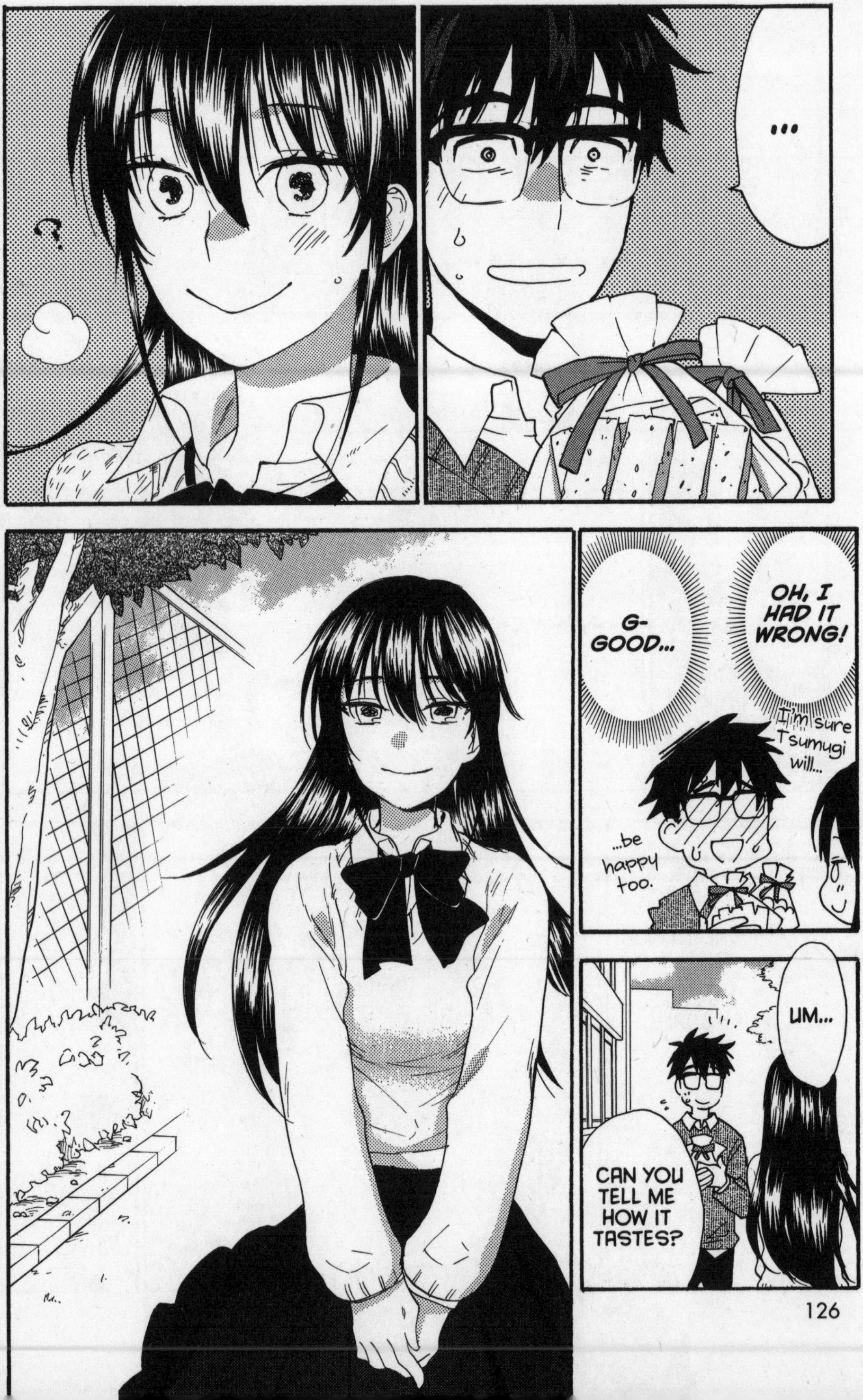
...
?
OH, I HAD IT WRONG!
G-GOOD...
I'm sure Tsumugi will...
...be happy too.
UM...
CAN YOU TELL ME HOW IT TASTES?

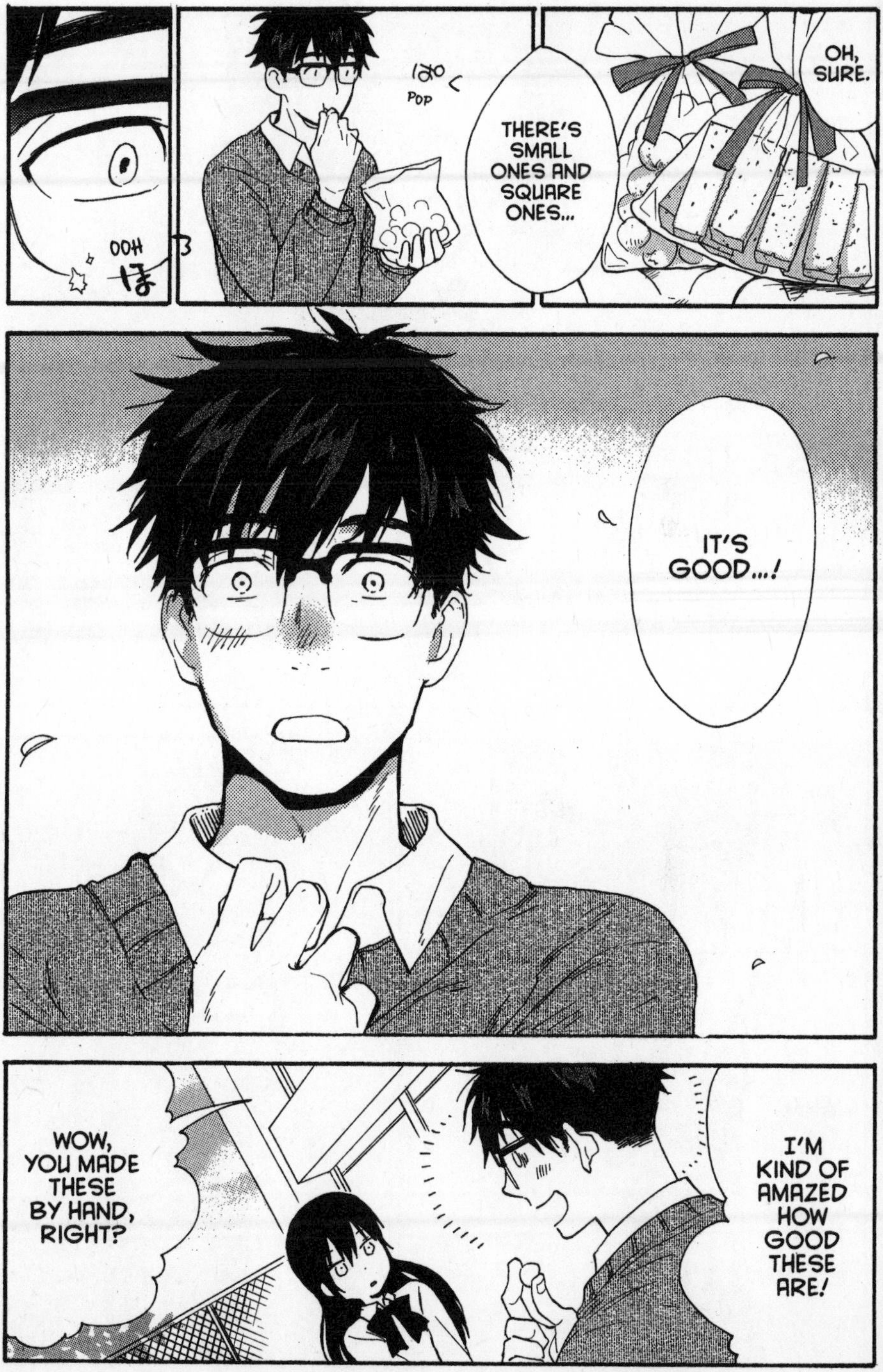
OH, SURE.
THERE'S SMALL ONES AND SQUARE ONES...
ぱく
POP
ほっ
OOH
IT'S GOOD...!
I'M KIND OF AMAZED HOW GOOD THESE ARE!
WOW, YOU MADE THESE BY HAND, RIGHT?

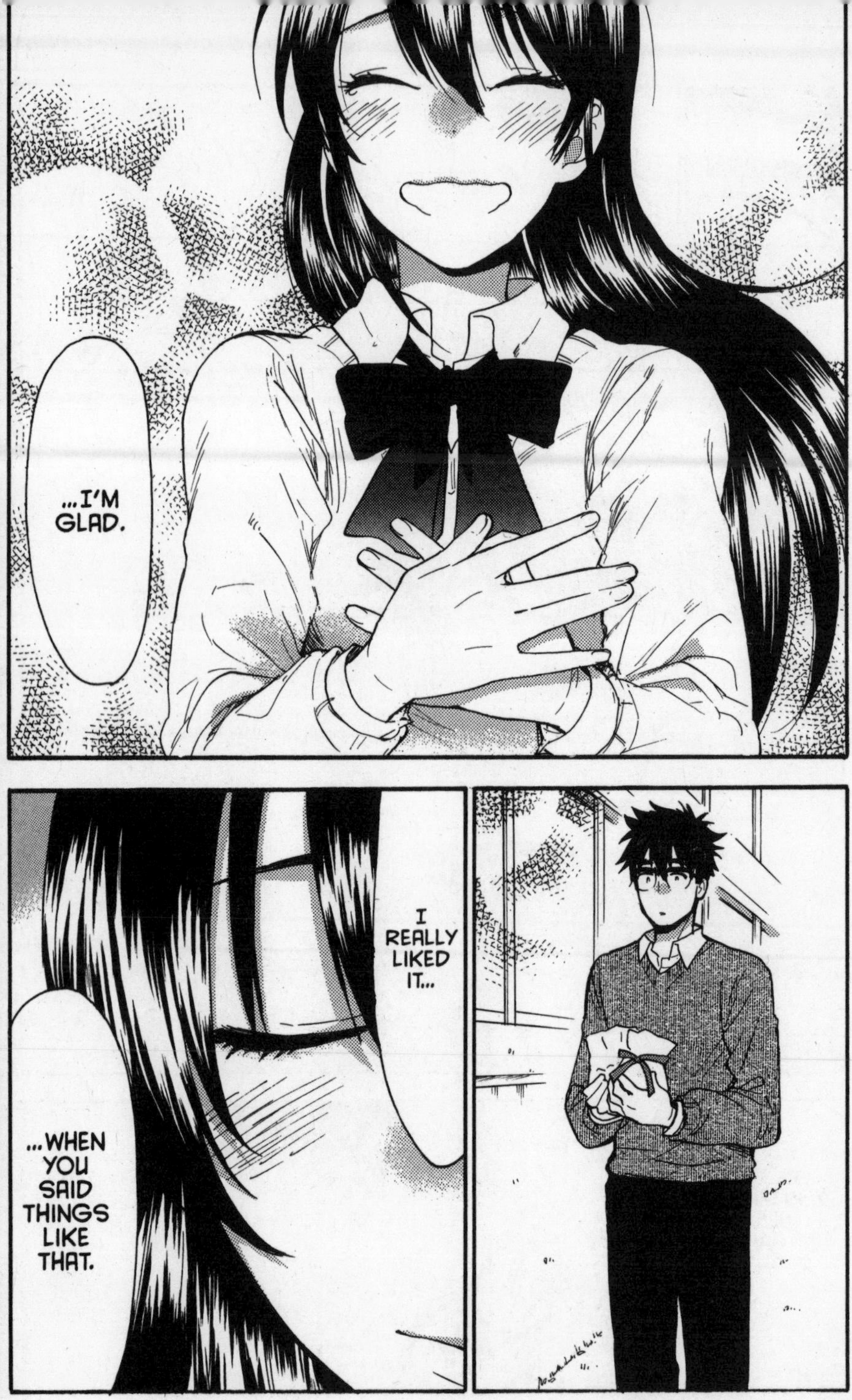
...I'M GLAD.
I REALLY LIKED IT...
...WHEN YOU SAID THINGS LIKE THAT.

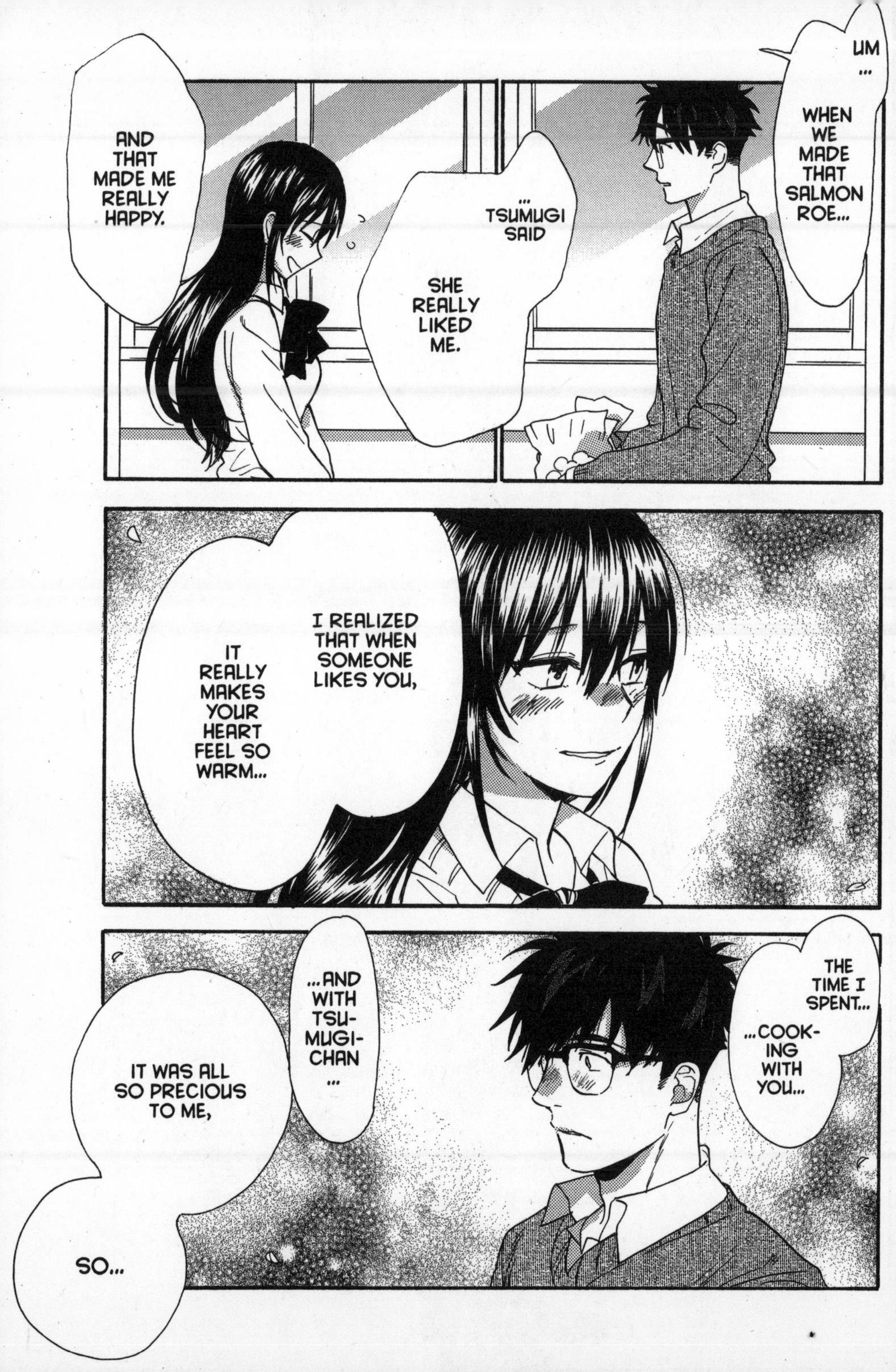
UM ...
WHEN WE MADE THAT SALMON ROE...
... TSUMUGI SAID
SHE REALLY LIKED ME.
AND THAT MADE ME REALLY HAPPY.
I REALIZED THAT WHEN SOMEONE LIKES YOU,
IT REALLY MAKES YOUR HEART FEEL SO WARM...
THE TIME I SPENT...
...COOKING WITH YOU...
...AND WITH TSUMUGI-CHAN ...
IT WAS ALL SO PRECIOUS TO ME,
SO...

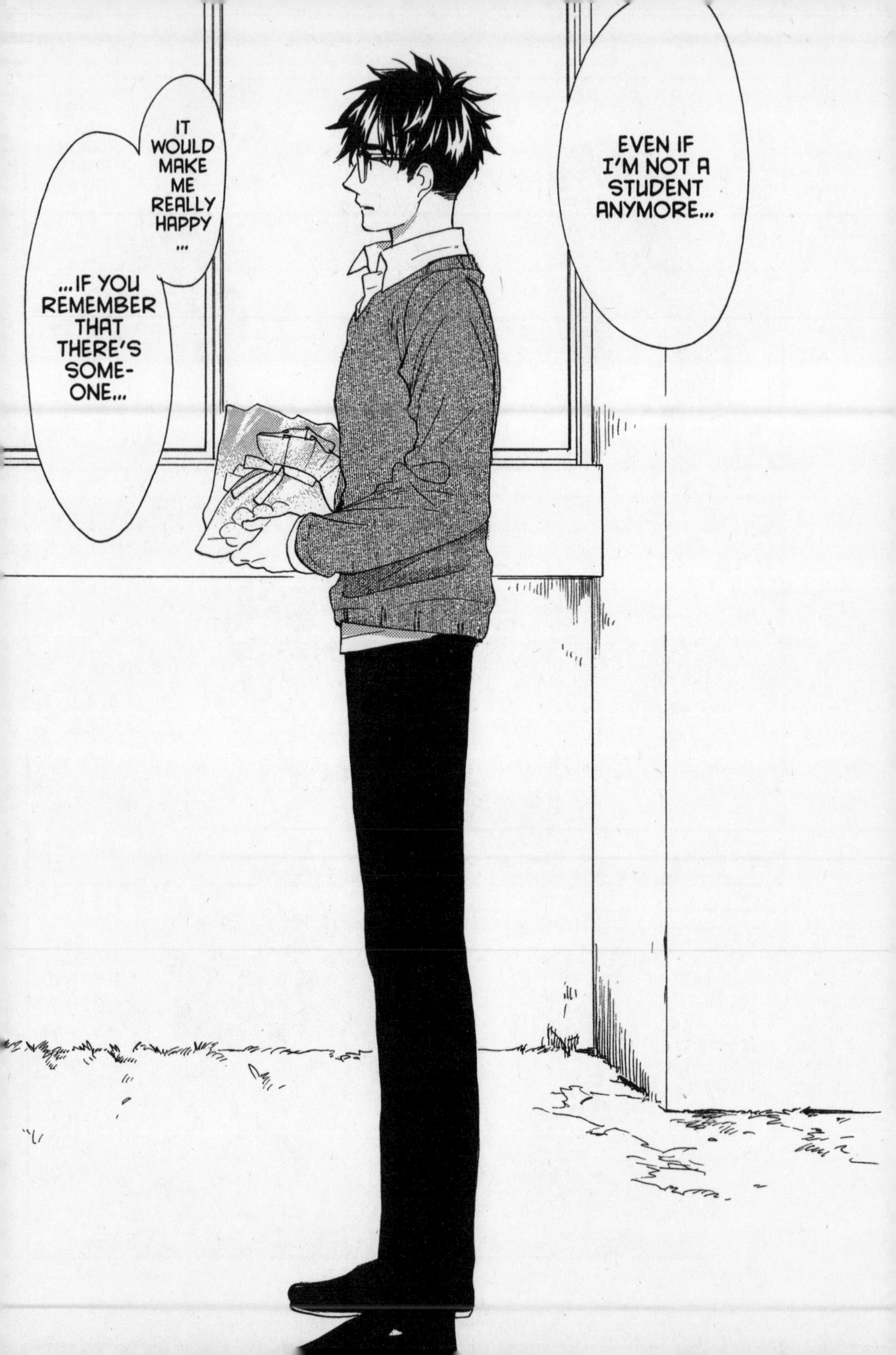
EVEN IF I'M NOT A STUDENT ANYMORE...
IT WOULD MAKE ME REALLY HAPPY ...
...IF YOU REMEMBER THAT THERE'S SOME-ONE...

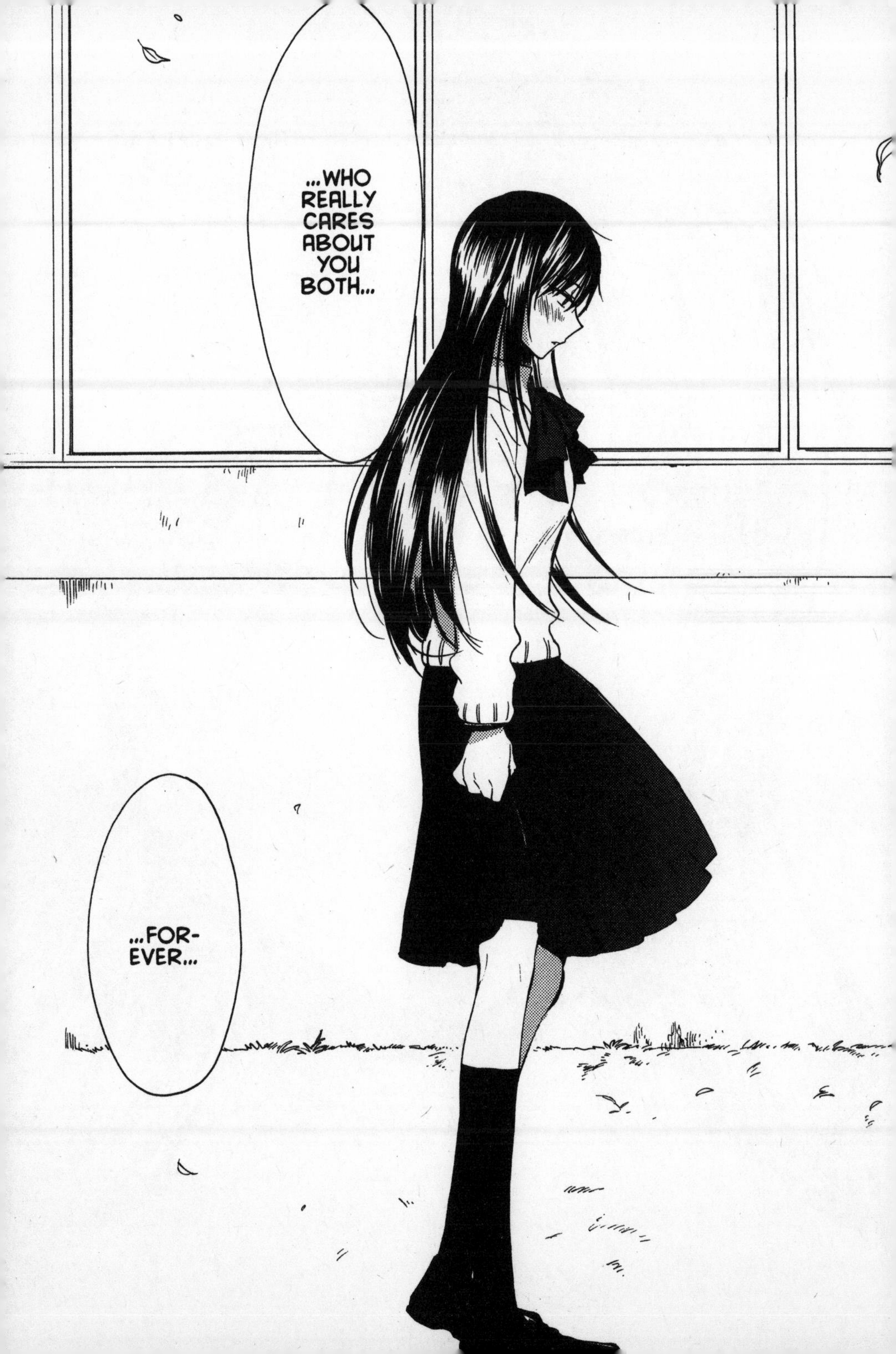
...WHO REALLY CARES ABOUT YOU BOTH...
...FOR-EVER...

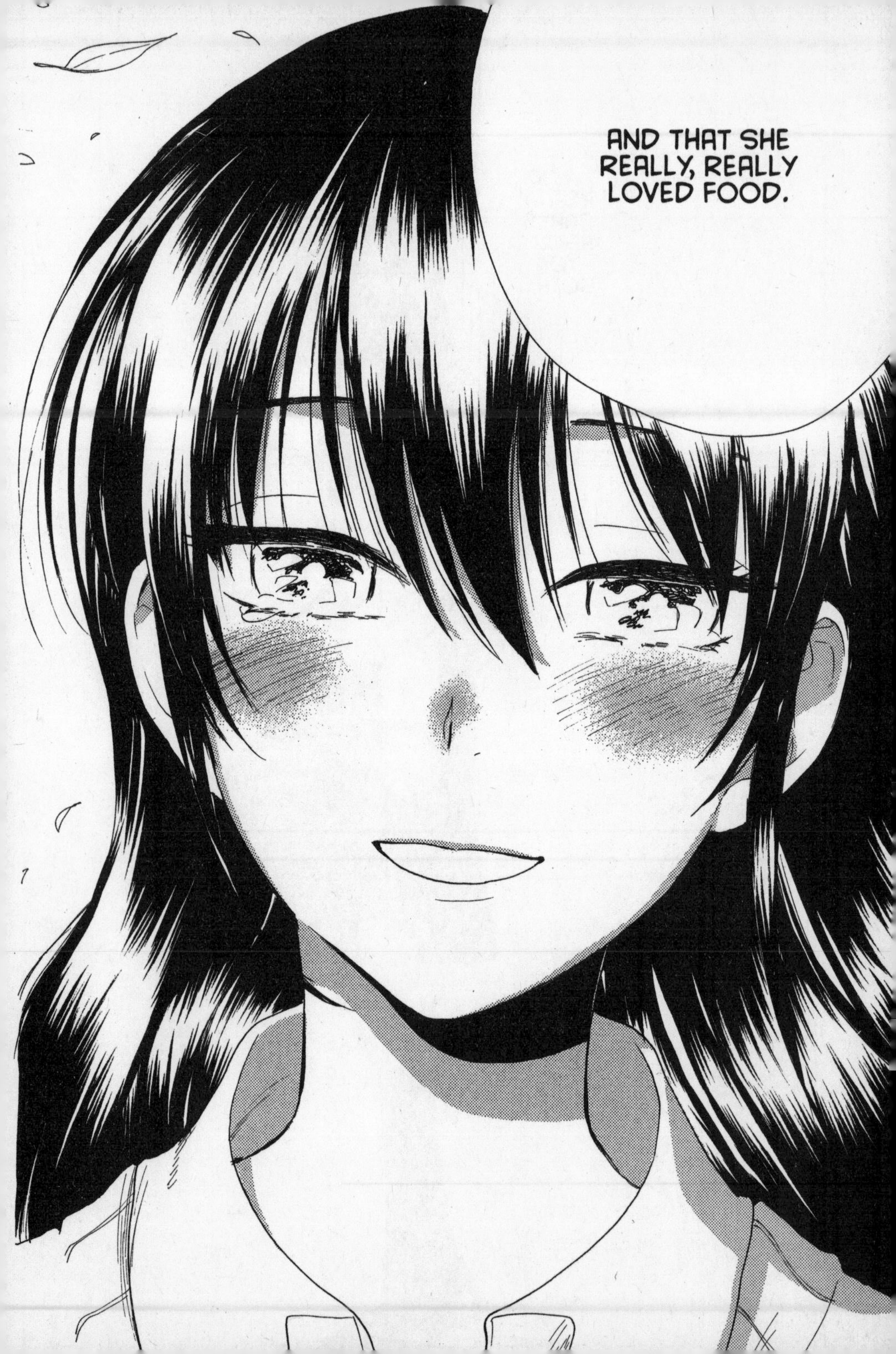
AND THAT SHE REALLY, REALLY LOVED FOOD.

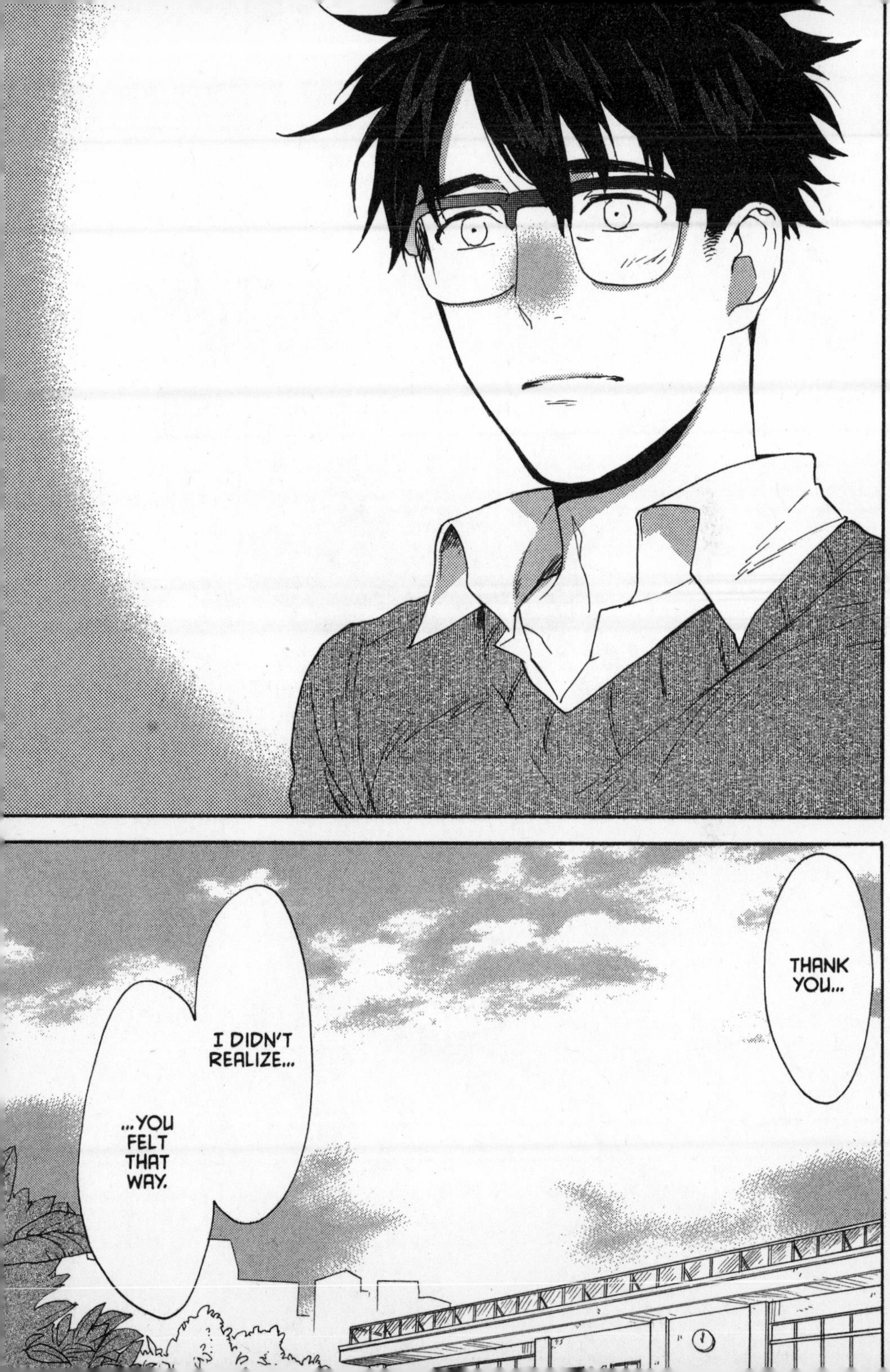
THANK YOU...
I DIDN'T REALIZE...
...YOU FELT THAT WAY.

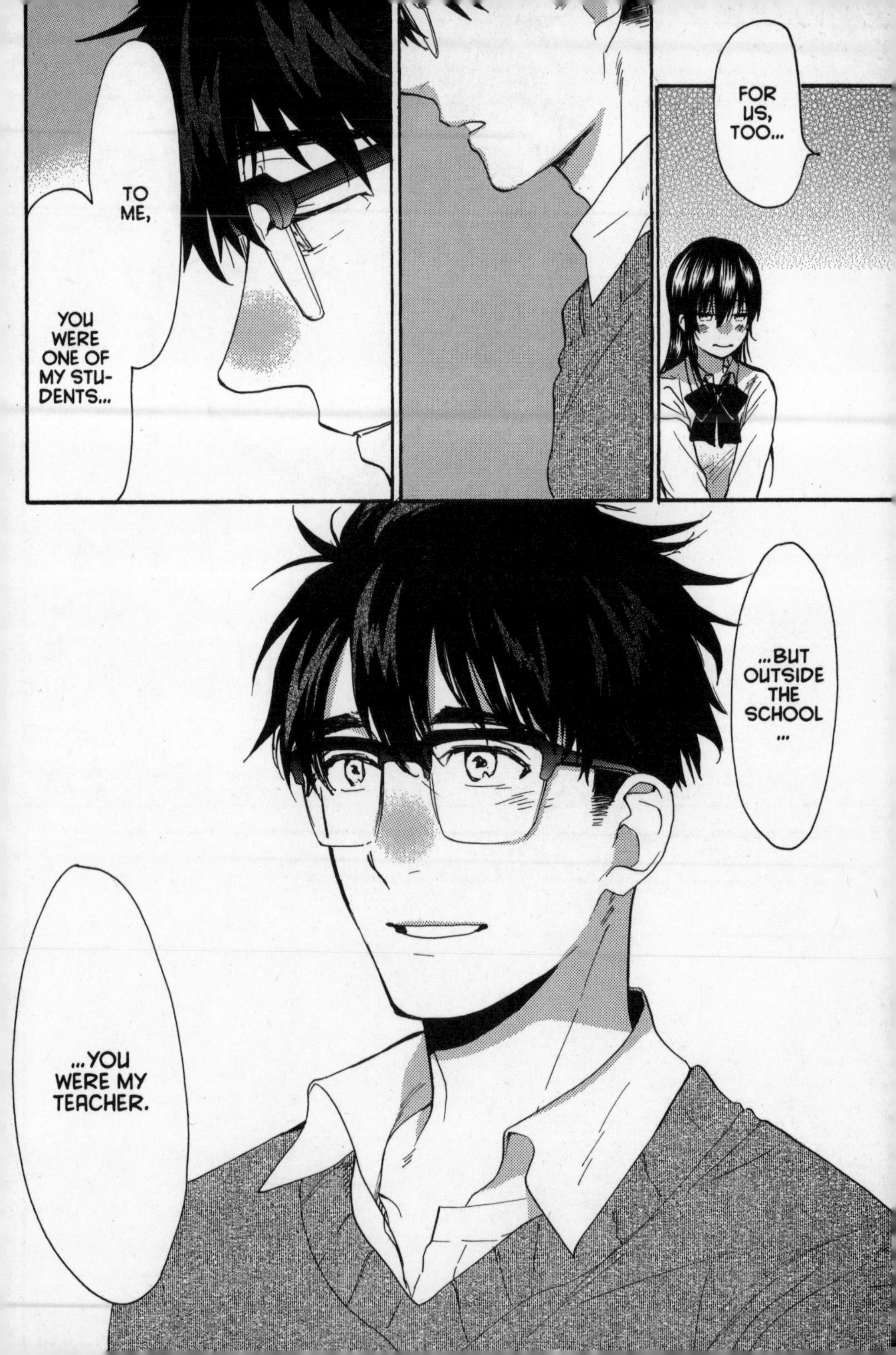
FOR US, TOO...
TO ME,
YOU WERE ONE OF MY STU- DENTS...
...BUT OUTSIDE THE SCHOOL ...
...YOU WERE MY TEACHER.

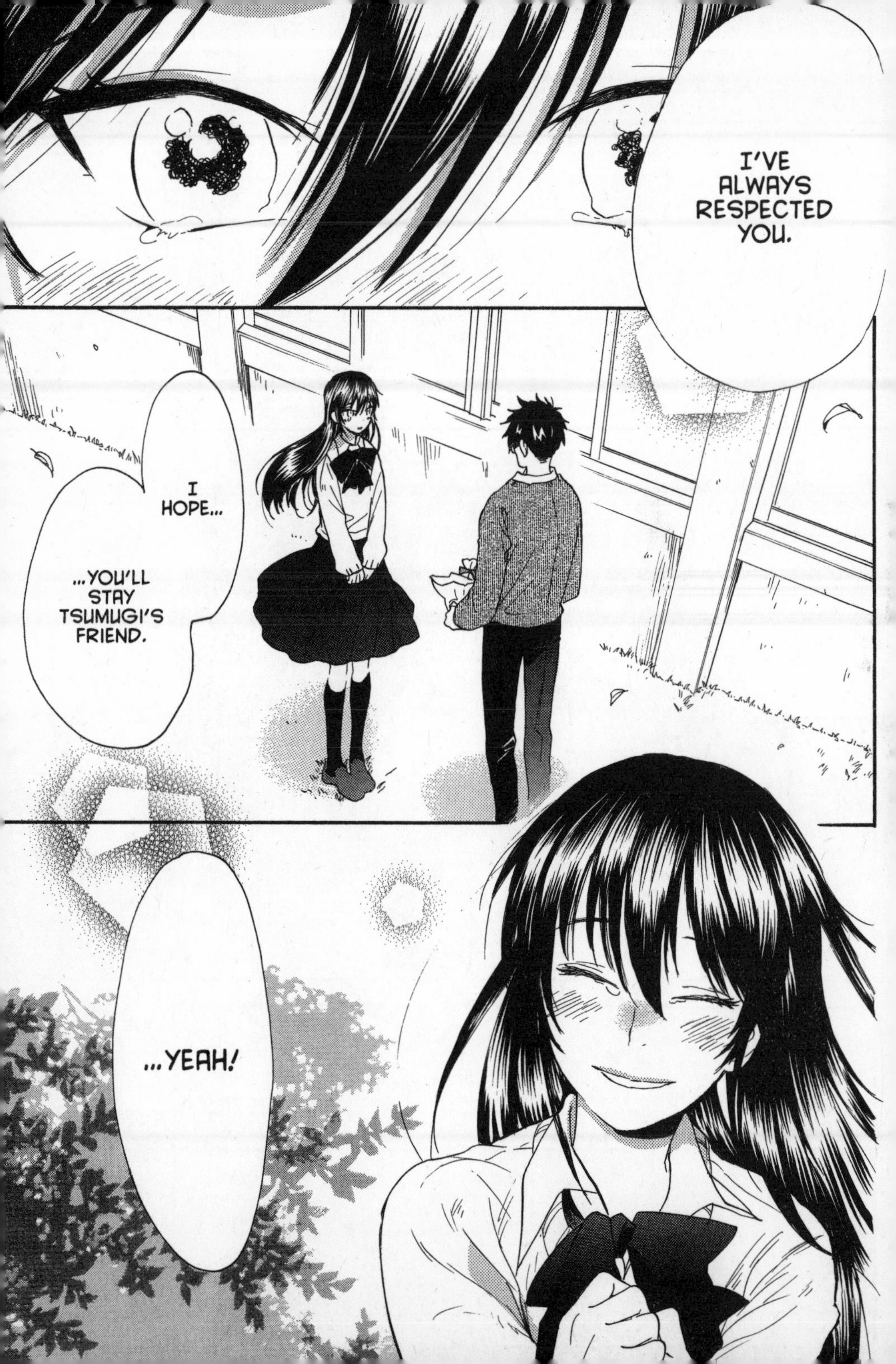
I'VE ALWAYS RESPECTED YOU.
I HOPE... ...YOU'LL STAY TSUMUGI'S FRIEND.
...
...YEAH!

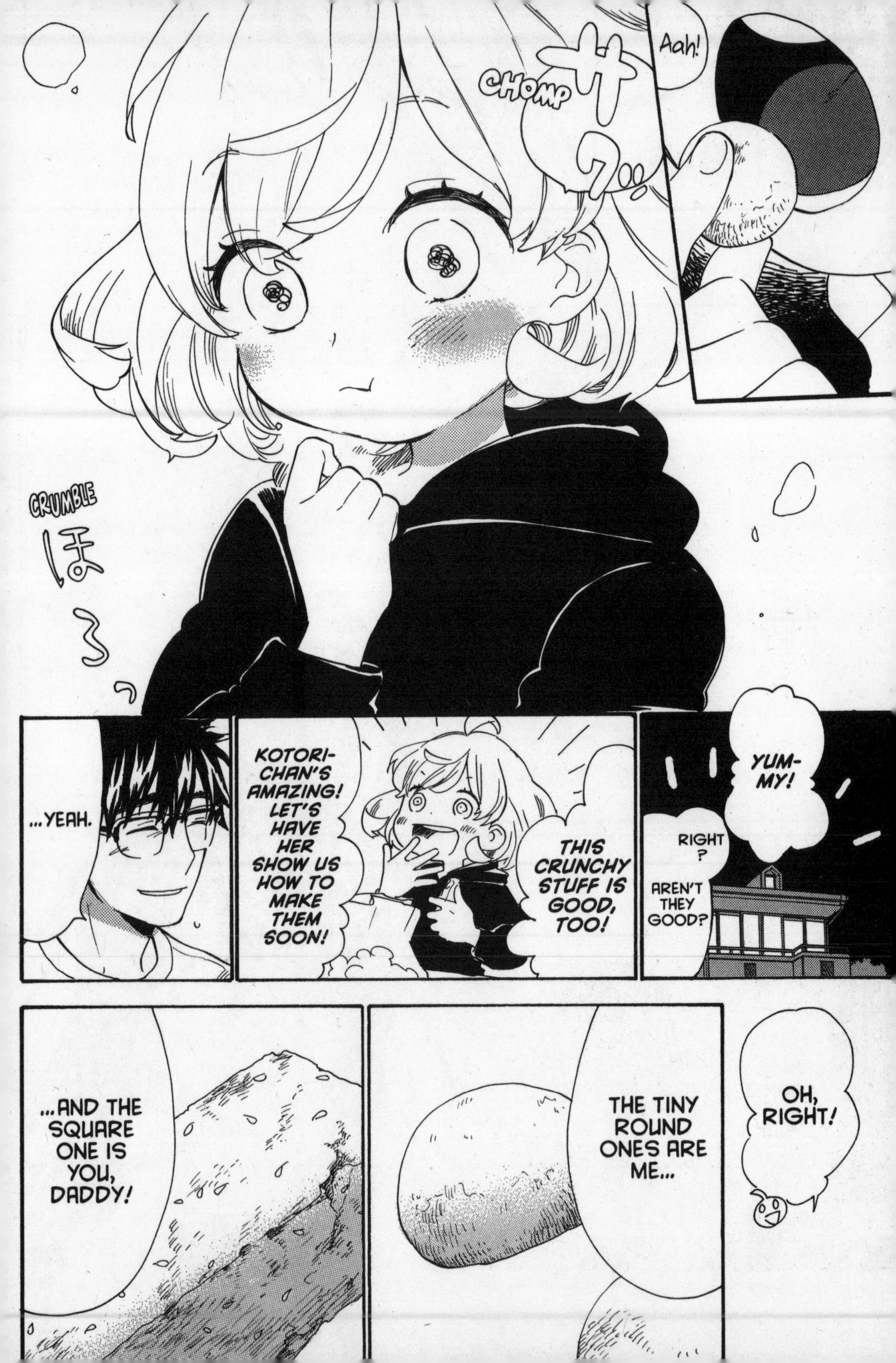
Aah!
CHOMP
CRUMBLE
YUM-MY!
RIGHT?
AREN'T THEY GOOD?
THIS CRUNCHY STUFF IS GOOD, TOO!
KOTORI-CHAN'S AMAZING! LET'S HAVE HER SHOW US HOW TO MAKE THEM SOON!
...YEAH.
OH, RIGHT!
THE TINY ROUND ONES ARE ME...
...AND THE SQUARE ONE IS YOU, DADDY!

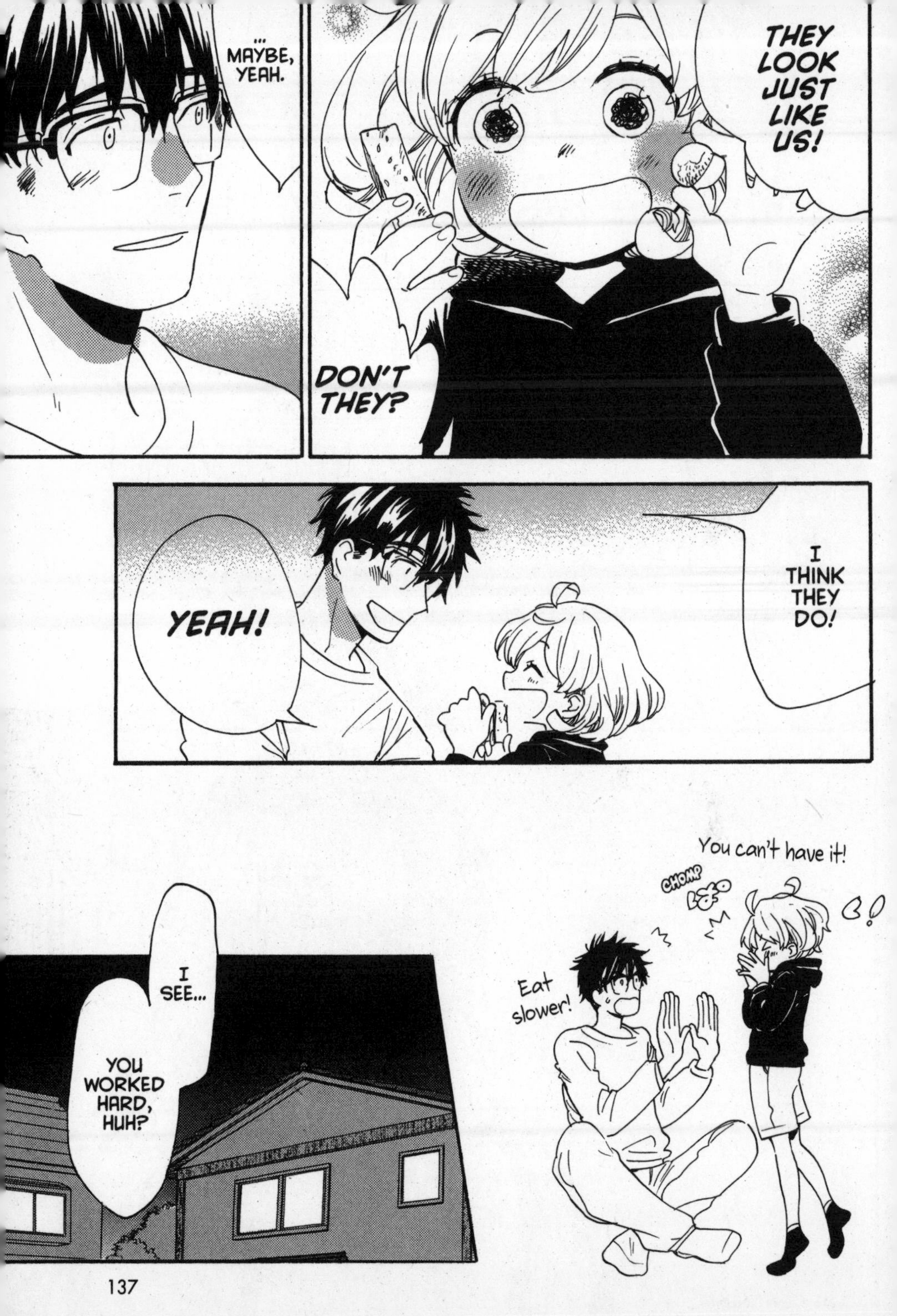
THEY LOOK JUST LIKE US!
DON'T THEY?
... MAYBE, YEAH.
I THINK THEY DO!
YEAH!
You can't have it!
CHOMP
Eat slower!
I SEE...
YOU WORKED HARD, HUH?

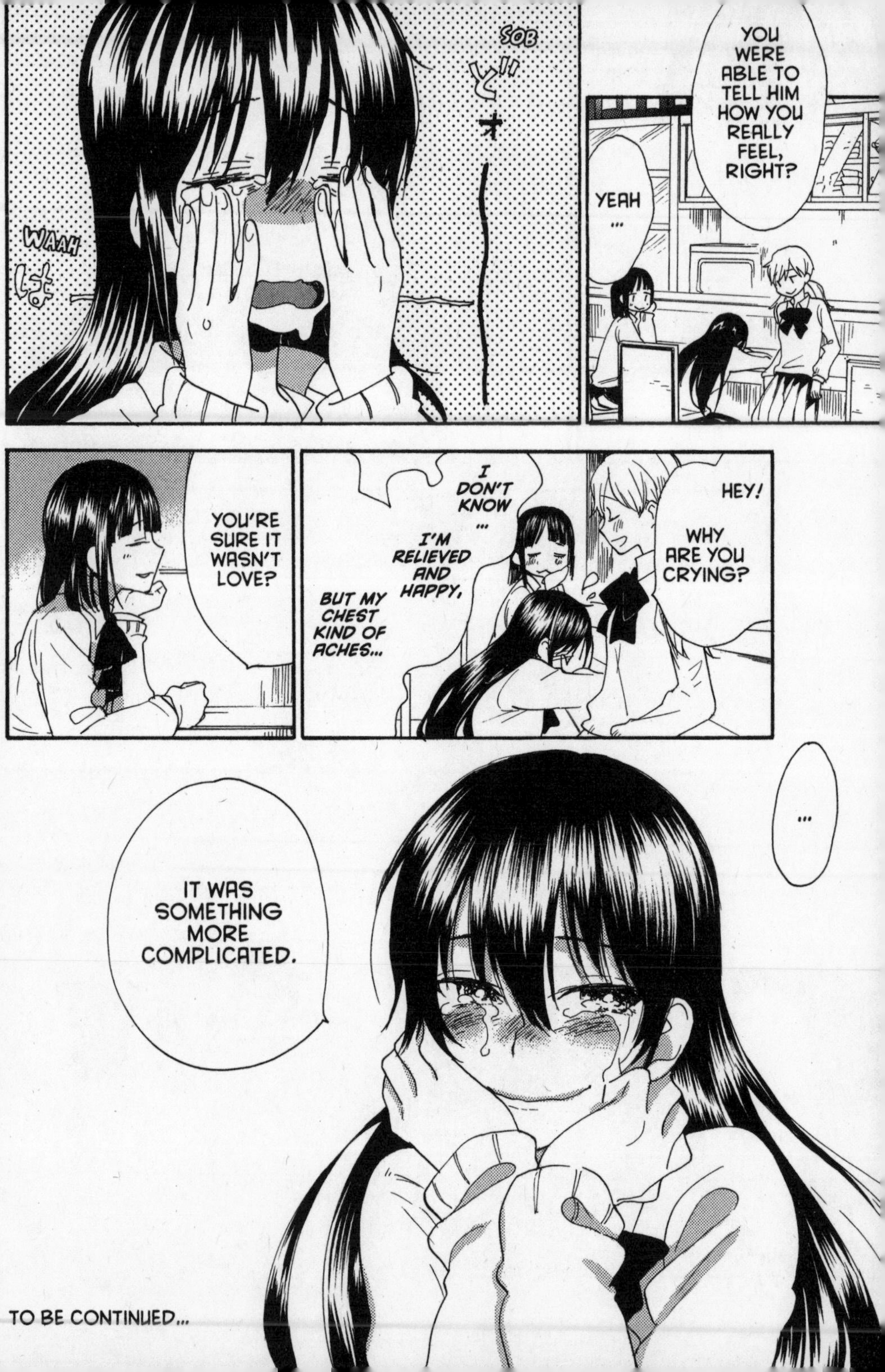
YOU WERE ABLE TO TELL HIM HOW YOU REALLY FEEL, RIGHT?
YEAH ...
SOB
WAAH
HEY!
WHY ARE YOU CRYING?
I DON'T KNOW ...
I'M RELIEVED AND HAPPY,
BUT MY CHEST KIND OF ACHES...
YOU'RE SURE IT WASN'T LOVE?
...
IT WAS SOMETHING MORE COMPLICATED.
TO BE CONTINUED...

SESAME SHORT BREAD

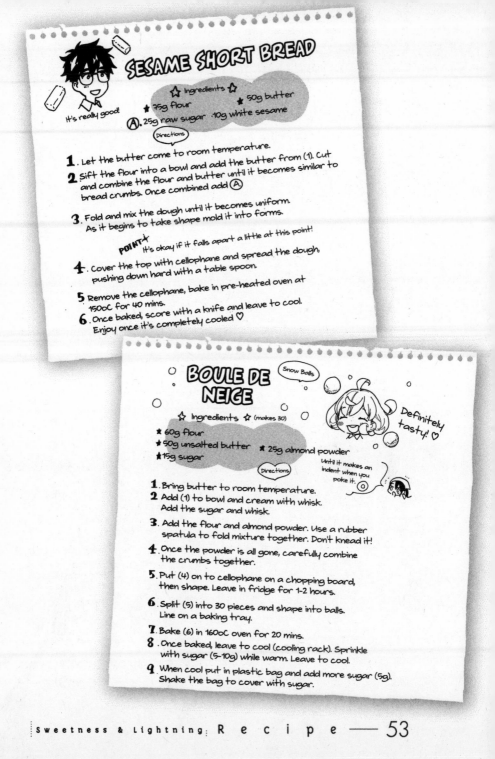

It's really good!

☆ Ingredients ☆

★ 75g flour
★ 50g butter
Ⓐ. 25g raw sugar ·10g white sesame

Directions

1. Let the butter come to room temperature.
2. Sift the flour into a bowl and add the butter from (1). Cut and combine the flour and butter until it becomes similar to bread crumbs. Once combined add Ⓐ
3. Fold and mix the dough until it becomes uniform. As it begins to take shape mold it into forms.

POINT★ It's okay if it falls apart a little at this point!

4. Cover the top with cellophane and spread the dough, pushing down hard with a table spoon.
5. Remove the cellophane, bake in pre-heated oven at 150oC for 40 mins.
6. Once baked, score with a knife and leave to cool. Enjoy once it's completely cooled ♡

BOULE DE NEIGE

Snow Balls

Definitely tasty! ♡

☆ Ingredients ☆ (makes 30)

★ 60g flour
★ 50g unsalted butter
★ 15g sugar
★ 25g almond powder

Directions

Until it makes an indent when you poke it.

1. Bring butter to room temperature.
2. Add (1) to bowl and cream with whisk. Add the sugar and whisk.
3. Add the flour and almond powder. Use a rubber spatula to fold mixture together. Don't knead it!
4. Once the powder is all gone, carefully combine the crumbs together.
5. Put (4) on to cellophane on a chopping board, then shape. Leave in fridge for 1-2 hours.
6. Split (5) into 30 pieces and shape into balls. Line on a baking tray.
7. Bake (6) in 160oC oven for 20 mins.
8. Once baked, leave to cool (cooling rack). Sprinkle with sugar (5-10g) while warm. Leave to cool.
9. When cool put in plastic bag and add more sugar (5g). Shake the bag to cover with sugar.

Those cookies were delicious! You made them to look like me and dad, right!?
Huh? The shape!? Uhm. Yeah. Sure... I did...
That wasn't inten- tional!

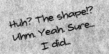

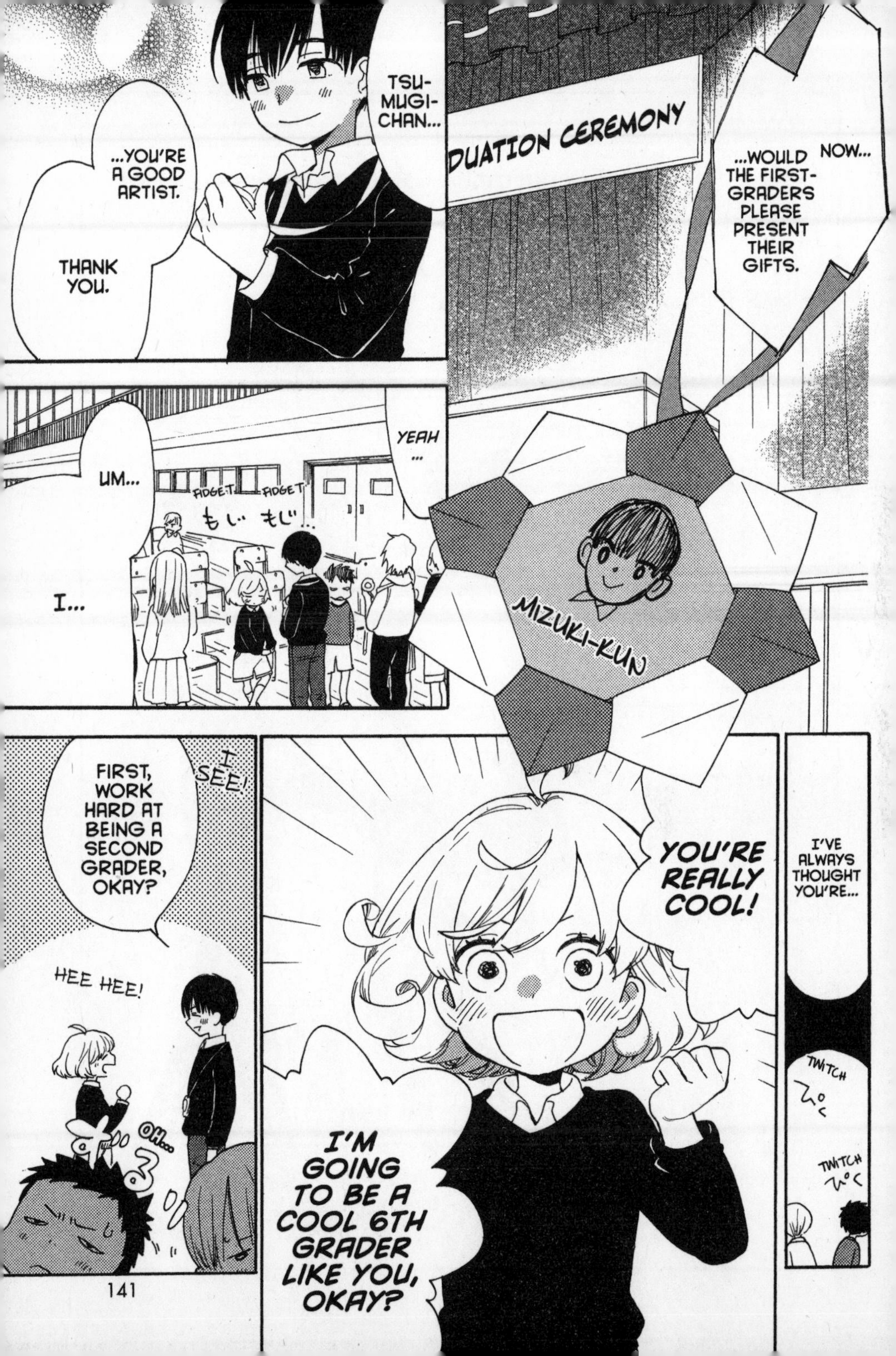
DUATION CEREMONY
NOW...
...WOULD THE FIRST-GRADERS PLEASE PRESENT THEIR GIFTS.
MIZUKI-KUN
TSU-MUGI-CHAN...
...YOU'RE A GOOD ARTIST.
THANK YOU.
YEAH...
UM...
I...
FIDGET FIDGET
もじ もじ...
I'VE ALWAYS THOUGHT YOU'RE...
TWITCH
ぴく
TWITCH
ぴく
YOU'RE REALLY COOL!
I'M GOING TO BE A COOL 6TH GRADER LIKE YOU, OKAY?
I SEE!
FIRST, WORK HARD AT BEING A SECOND GRADER, OKAY?
HEE HEE!
OH...

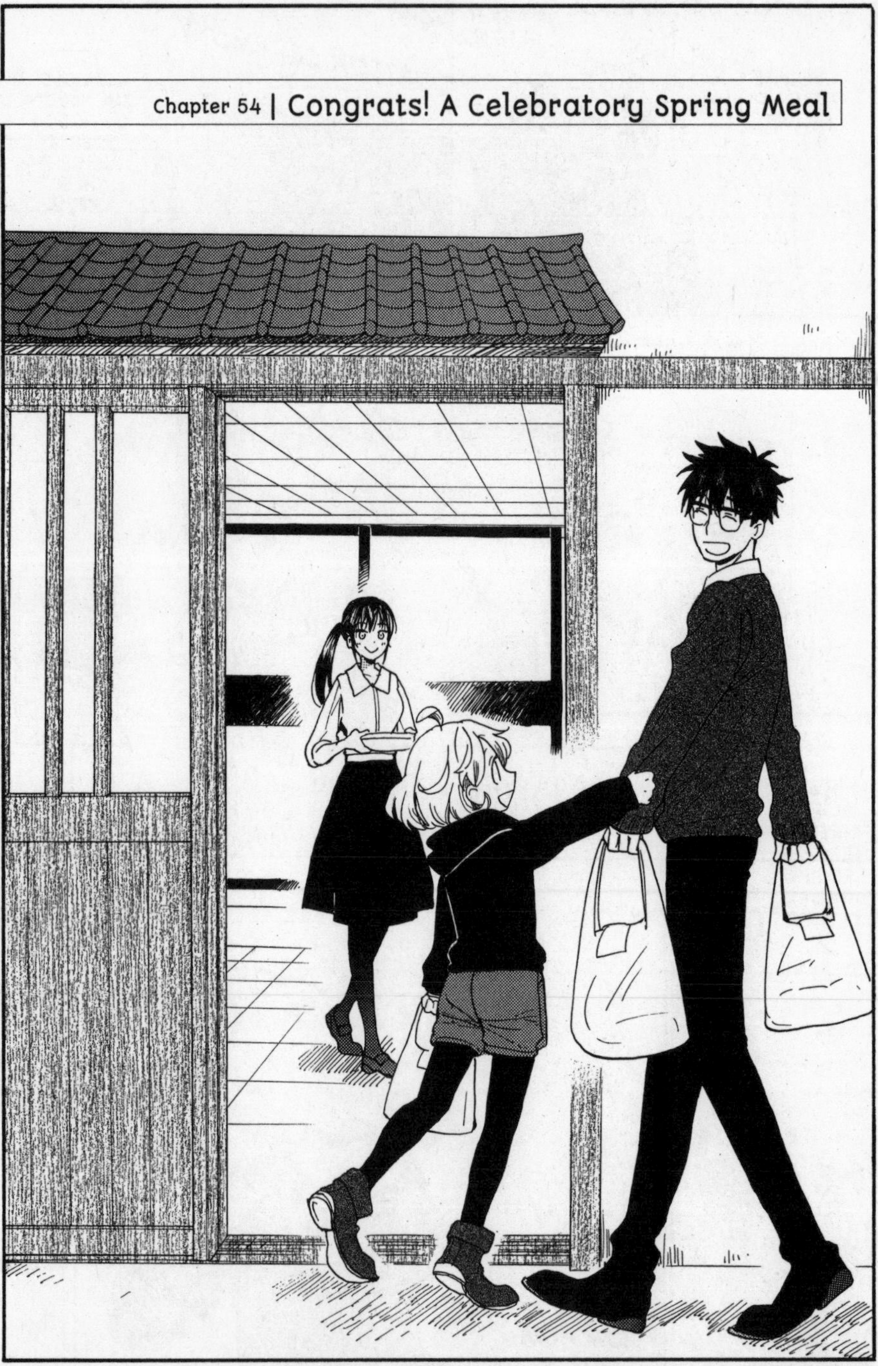
Chapter 54 | Congrats! A Celebratory Spring Meal

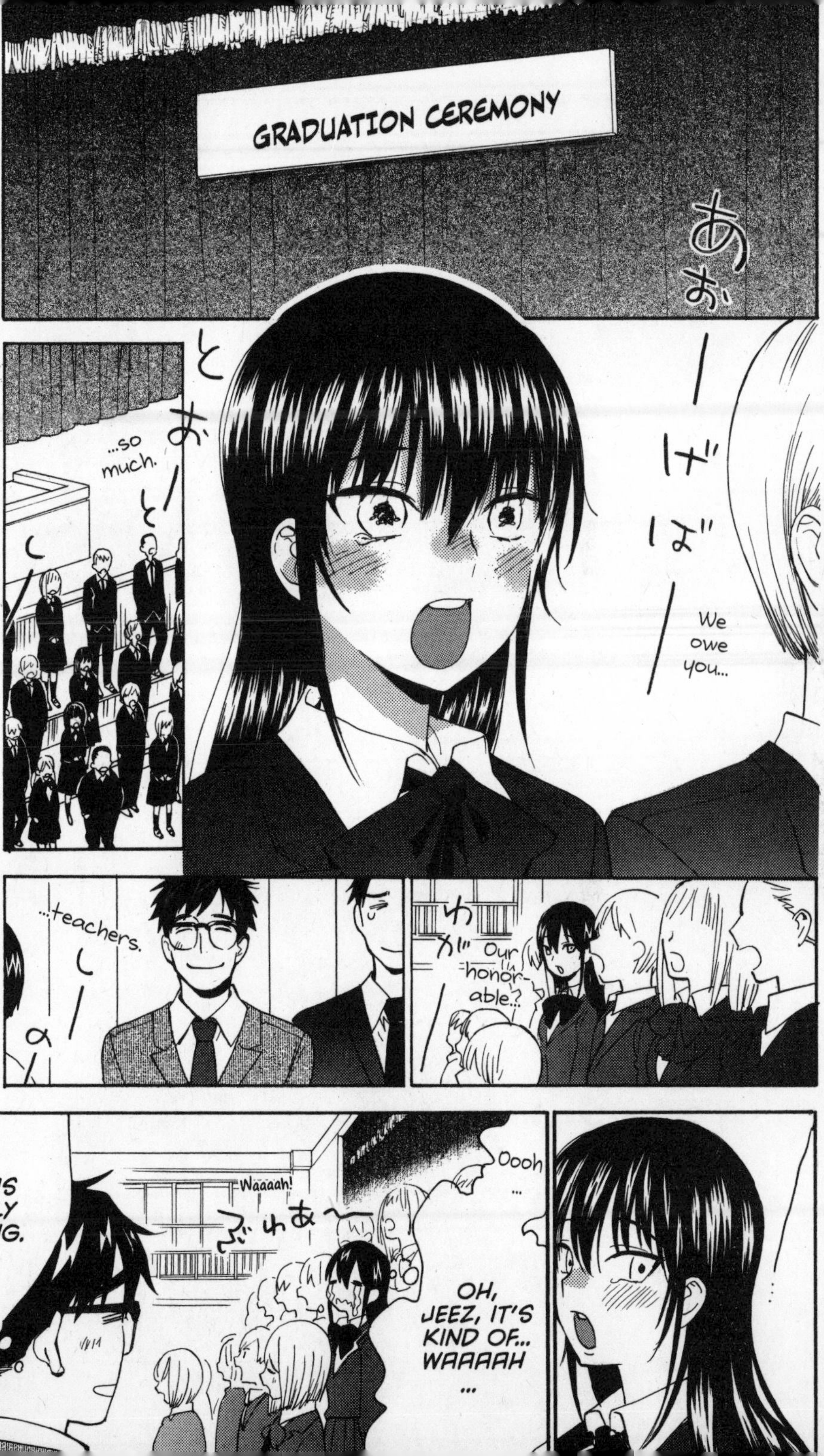

GRADUATION CEREMONY
あお
ーげばー
We owe you...
とおーとー
し
...so much.
わが
Our honorable...?
...teachers.
しーのー
Oooh ...
OH, JEEZ, IT'S KIND OF... WAAAAH ...
Waaaah!
ぶわあ～
THIS IS REALLY MOVING.

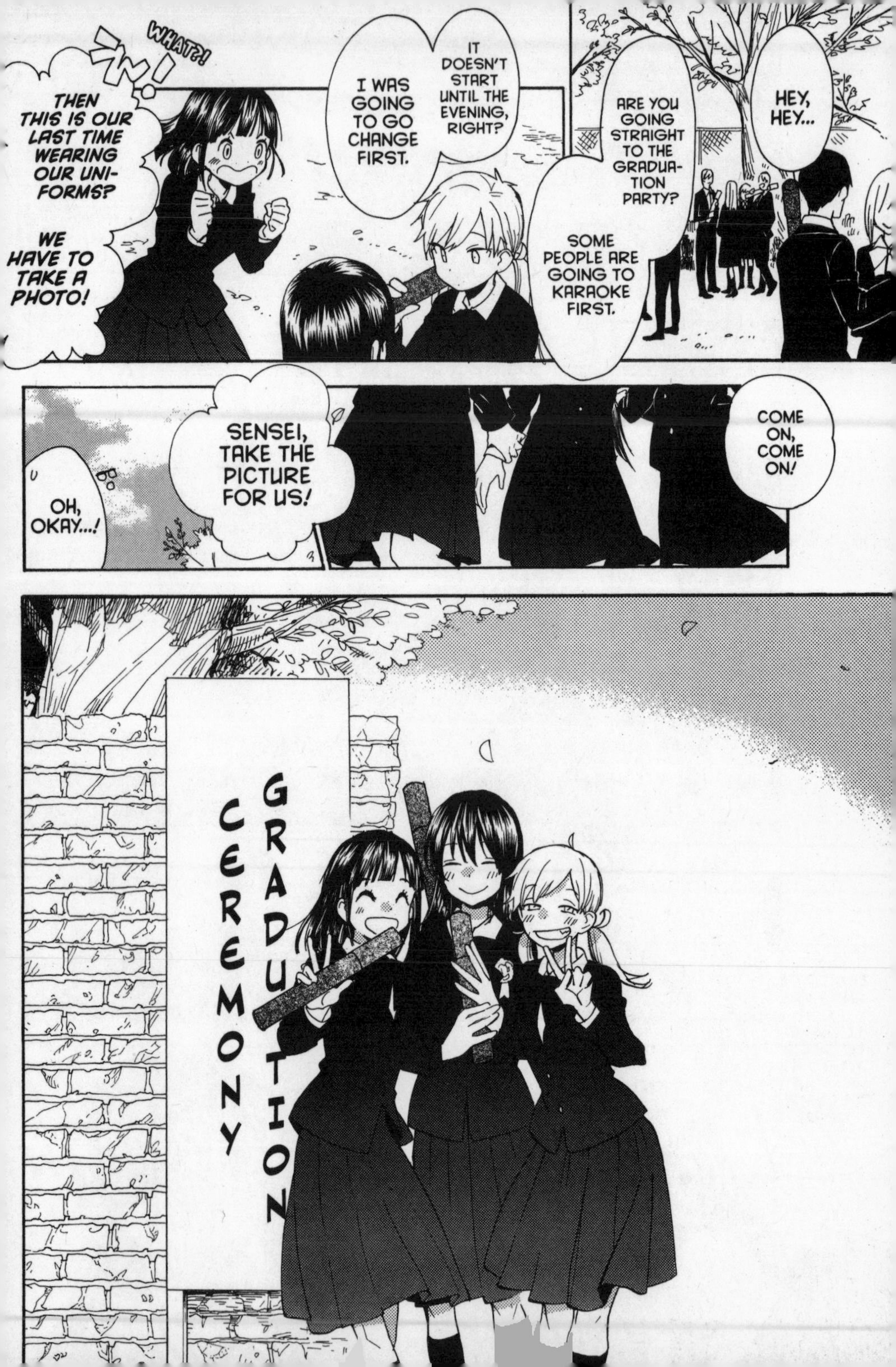
HEY, HEY...
ARE YOU GOING STRAIGHT TO THE GRADUATION PARTY?
SOME PEOPLE ARE GOING TO KARAOKE FIRST.
IT DOESN'T START UNTIL THE EVENING, RIGHT?
I WAS GOING TO GO CHANGE FIRST.
WHAT?!
THEN THIS IS OUR LAST TIME WEARING OUR UNIFORMS?
WE HAVE TO TAKE A PHOTO!
COME ON, COME ON!
SENSEI, TAKE THE PICTURE FOR US!
OH, OKAY...!
GRADUATION
CEREMONY

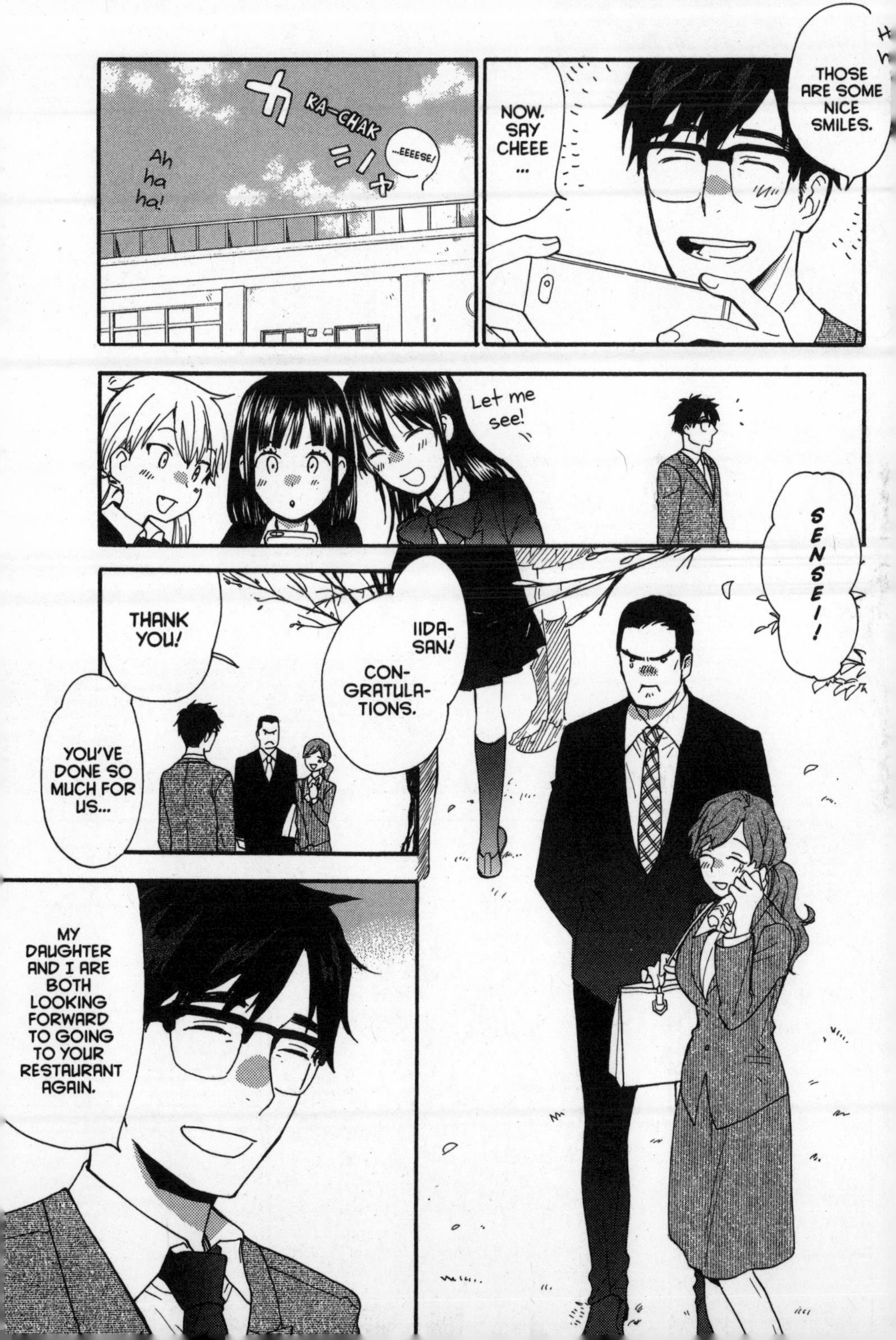
THOSE ARE SOME NICE SMILES.
NOW. SAY CHEEE ...
KA-CHAK
...EEEESE!
Ah ha ha!
SENSEI!!
Let me see!
IIDA-SAN! CON-GRATULA-TIONS.
THANK YOU!
YOU'VE DONE SO MUCH FOR US...
MY DAUGHTER AND I ARE BOTH LOOKING FORWARD TO GOING TO YOUR RESTAURANT AGAIN.

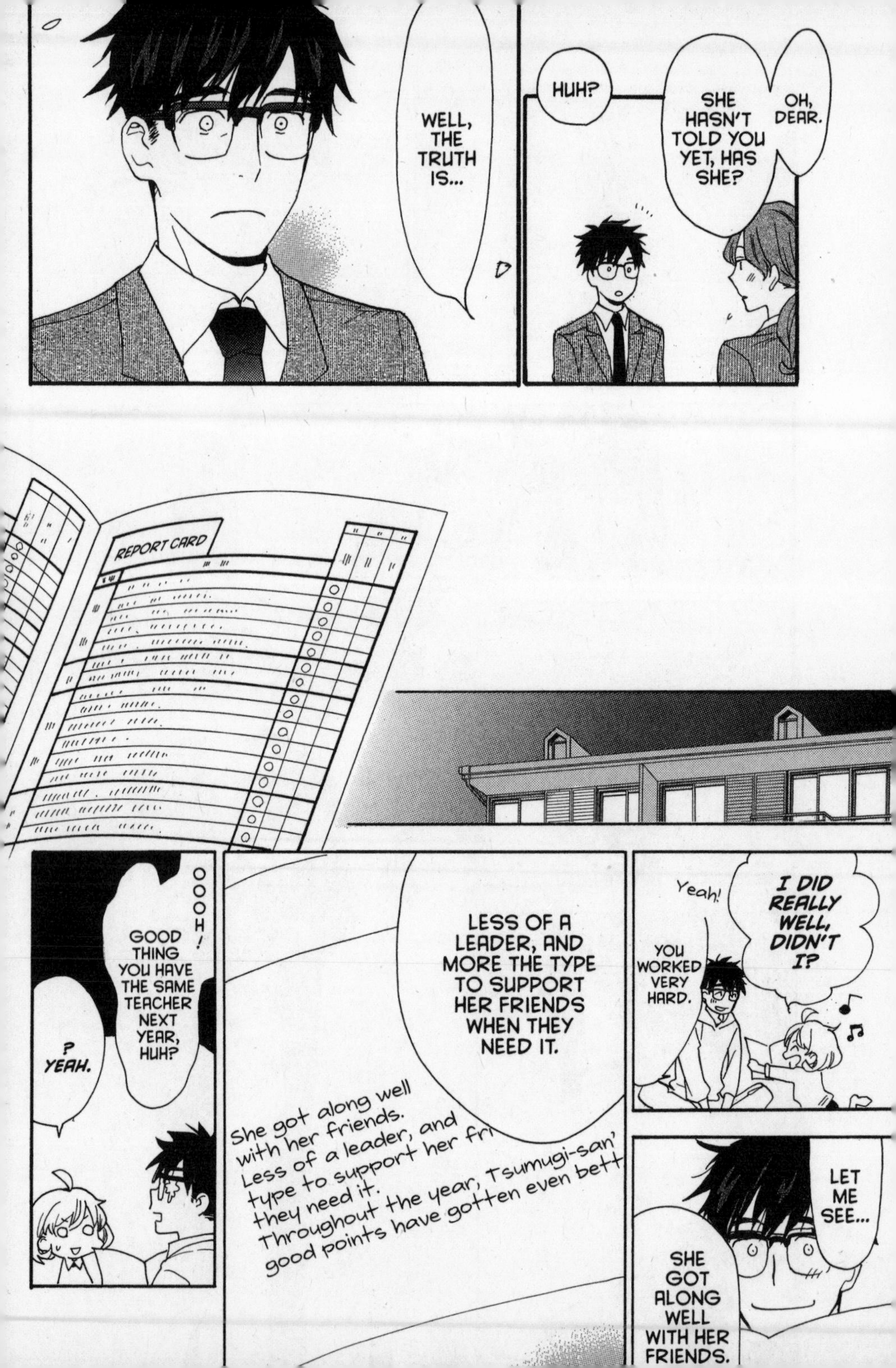
OH, DEAR.
SHE HASN'T TOLD YOU YET, HAS SHE?
HUH?
WELL, THE TRUTH IS...
REPORT CARD
I DID REALLY WELL, DIDN'T I?
Yeah!
YOU WORKED VERY HARD.
LET ME SEE...
SHE GOT ALONG WELL WITH HER FRIENDS.
LESS OF A LEADER, AND MORE THE TYPE TO SUPPORT HER FRIENDS WHEN THEY NEED IT.
She got along well with her friends. Less of a leader, and type to support her fri they need it. Throughout the year, Tsumugi-san' good points have gotten even bett
OOOOH!
GOOD THING YOU HAVE THE SAME TEACHER NEXT YEAR, HUH?
? YEAH.

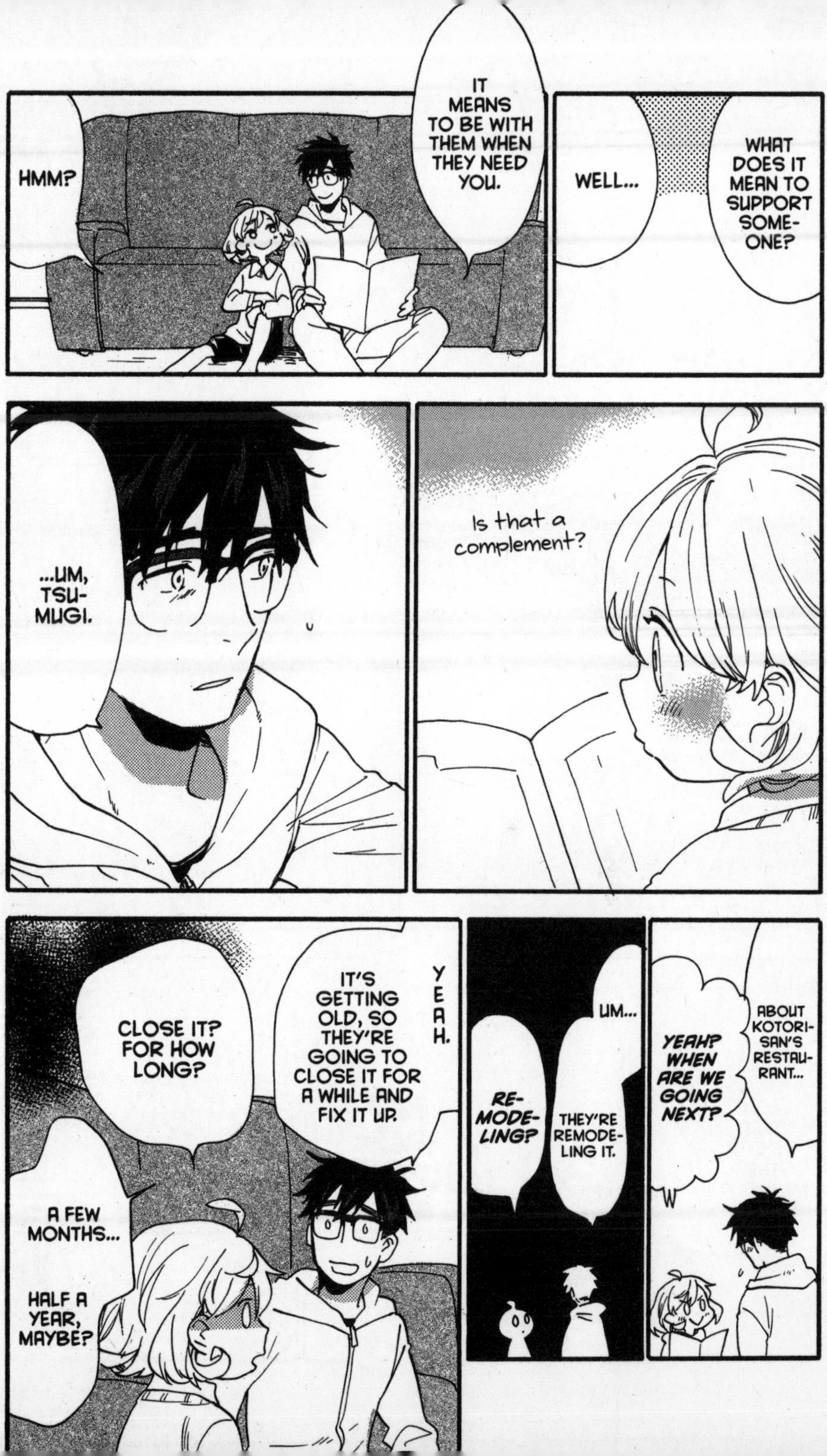
WHAT DOES IT MEAN TO SUPPORT SOME-ONE?
WELL...
IT MEANS TO BE WITH THEM WHEN THEY NEED YOU.
HMM?
Is that a complement?
...UM, TSU-MUGI.
ABOUT KOTORI-SAN'S RESTAU-RANT...
YEAH? WHEN ARE WE GOING NEXT?
UM...
THEY'RE REMODE-LING IT.
RE-MODE-LING?
YEAH.
IT'S GETTING OLD, SO THEY'RE GOING TO CLOSE IT FOR A WHILE AND FIX IT UP.
CLOSE IT? FOR HOW LONG?
A FEW MONTHS...
HALF A YEAR, MAYBE?

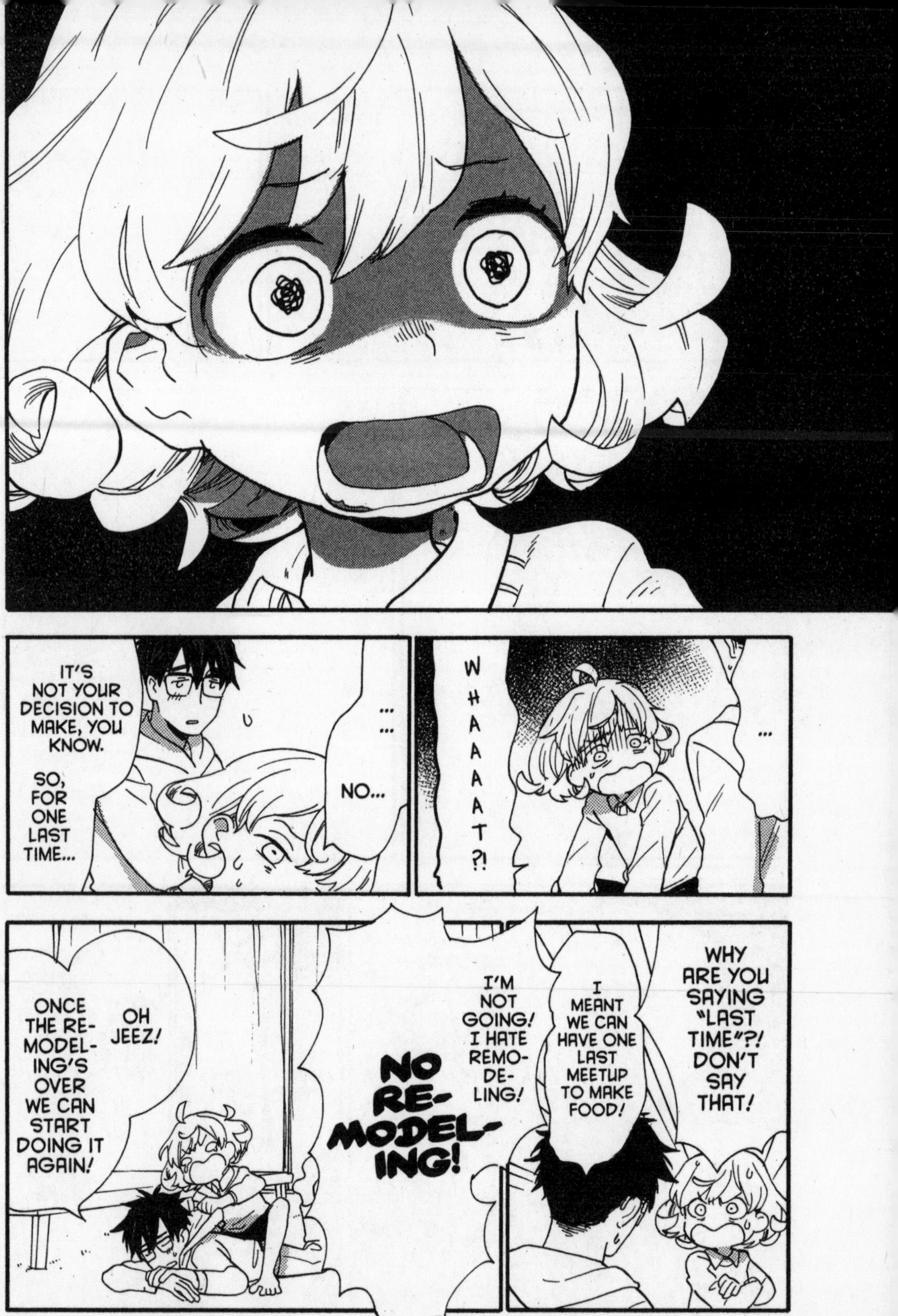
...
WHAAAAAT?!
......
NO...
IT'S NOT YOUR DECISION TO MAKE, YOU KNOW.
SO, FOR ONE LAST TIME...
WHY ARE YOU SAYING "LAST TIME"?! DON'T SAY THAT!
I MEANT WE CAN HAVE ONE LAST MEETUP TO MAKE FOOD!
I'M NOT GOING! I HATE REMODELING!
NO REMODELING!
OH JEEZ!
ONCE THE REMODELING'S OVER WE CAN START DOING IT AGAIN!

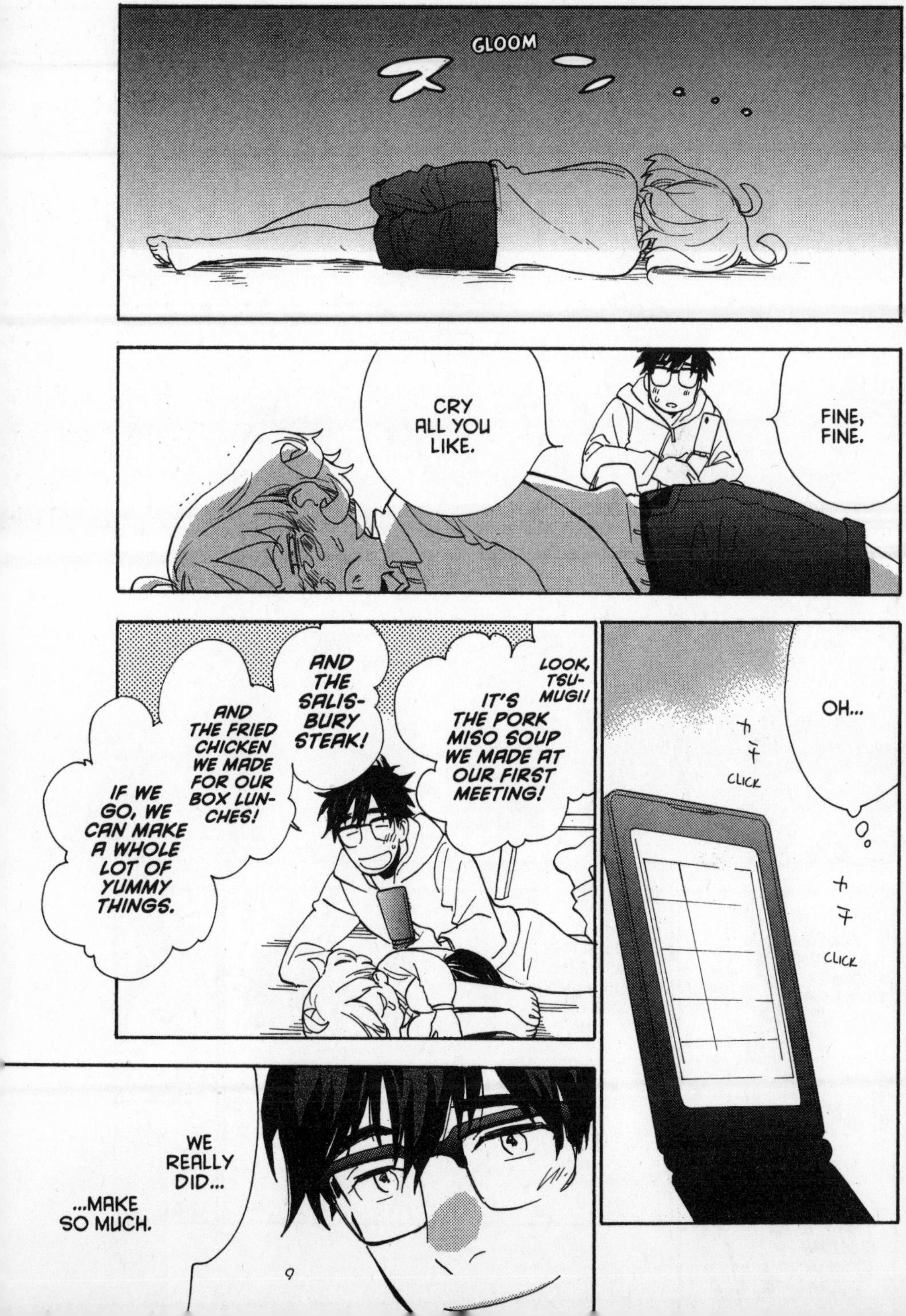
GLOOM
FINE, FINE.
CRY ALL YOU LIKE.
OH...
カチ
CLICK
カチ
CLICK
LOOK, TSUMUGI!
IT'S THE PORK MISO SOUP WE MADE AT OUR FIRST MEETING!
AND THE SALISBURY STEAK!
AND THE FRIED CHICKEN WE MADE FOR OUR BOX LUNCHES!
IF WE GO, WE CAN MAKE A WHOLE LOT OF YUMMY THINGS.
WE REALLY DID...
...MAKE SO MUCH.

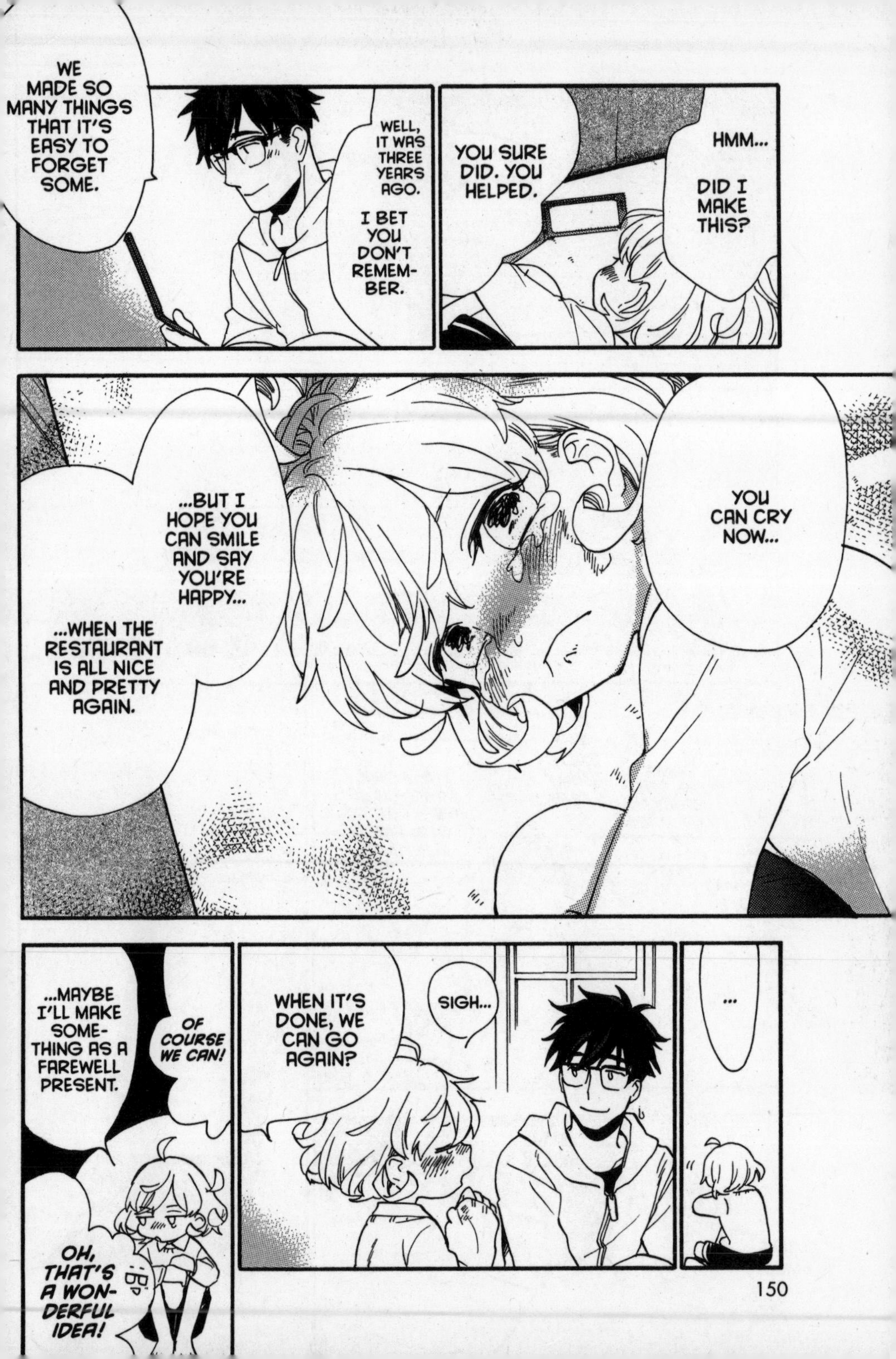
HMM... DID I MAKE THIS?
YOU SURE DID. YOU HELPED.
WELL, IT WAS THREE YEARS AGO. I BET YOU DON'T REMEMBER.
WE MADE SO MANY THINGS THAT IT'S EASY TO FORGET SOME.
YOU CAN CRY NOW...
...BUT I HOPE YOU CAN SMILE AND SAY YOU'RE HAPPY...
...WHEN THE RESTAURANT IS ALL NICE AND PRETTY AGAIN.
...
SIGH...
WHEN IT'S DONE, WE CAN GO AGAIN?
OF COURSE WE CAN!
...MAYBE I'LL MAKE SOMETHING AS A FAREWELL PRESENT.
OH, THAT'S A WONDERFUL IDEA!

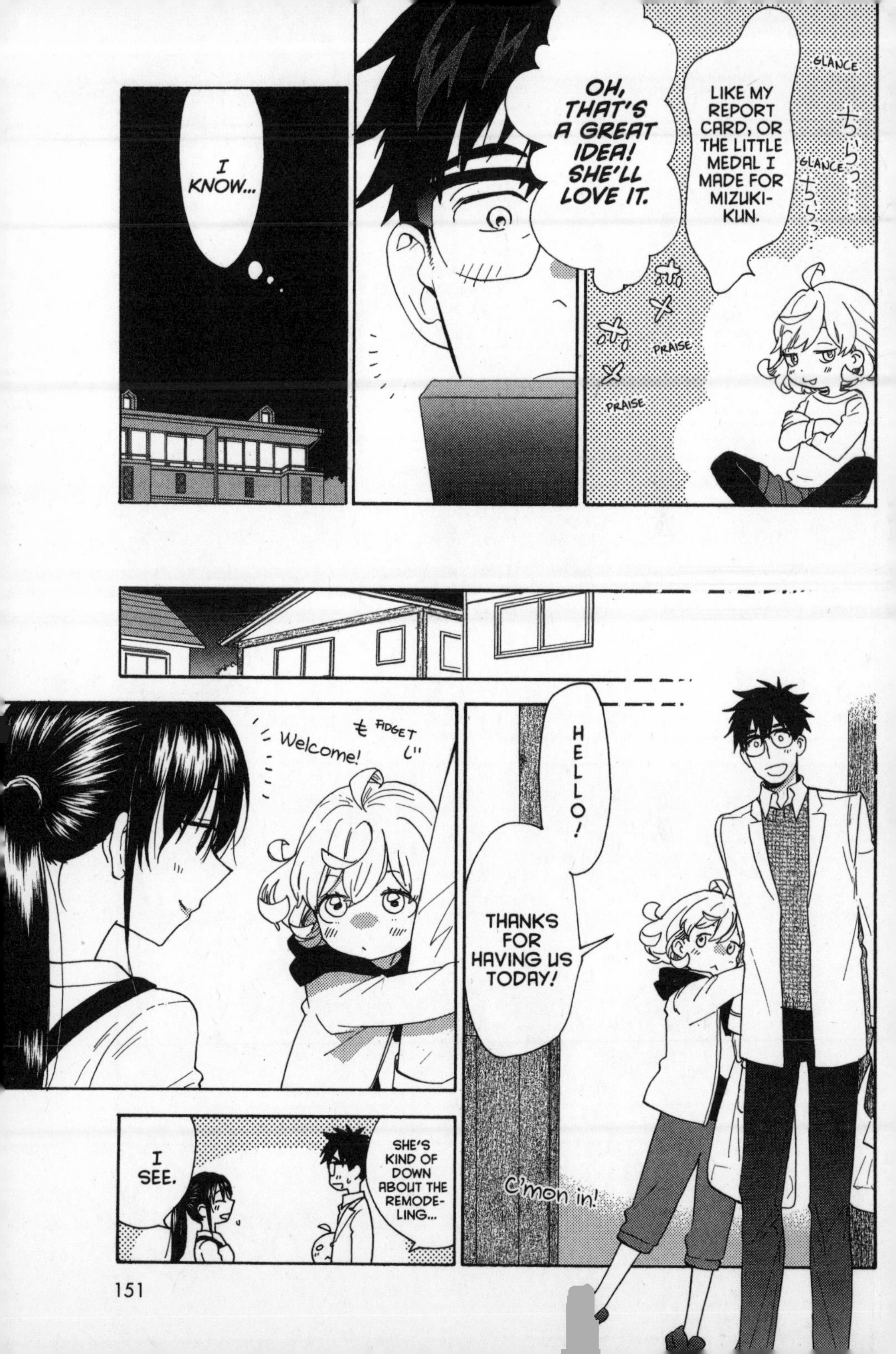
GLANCE
ちらっ
GLANCE
ちらっ
LIKE MY REPORT CARD, OR THE LITTLE MEDAL I MADE FOR MIZUKI-KUN.
PRAISE
PRAISE
OH, THAT'S A GREAT IDEA! SHE'LL LOVE IT.
I KNOW...
HELLO!
THANKS FOR HAVING US TODAY!
C'mon in!
Welcome!
FIDGET
もじ
SHE'S KIND OF DOWN ABOUT THE REMODELING...
I SEE.

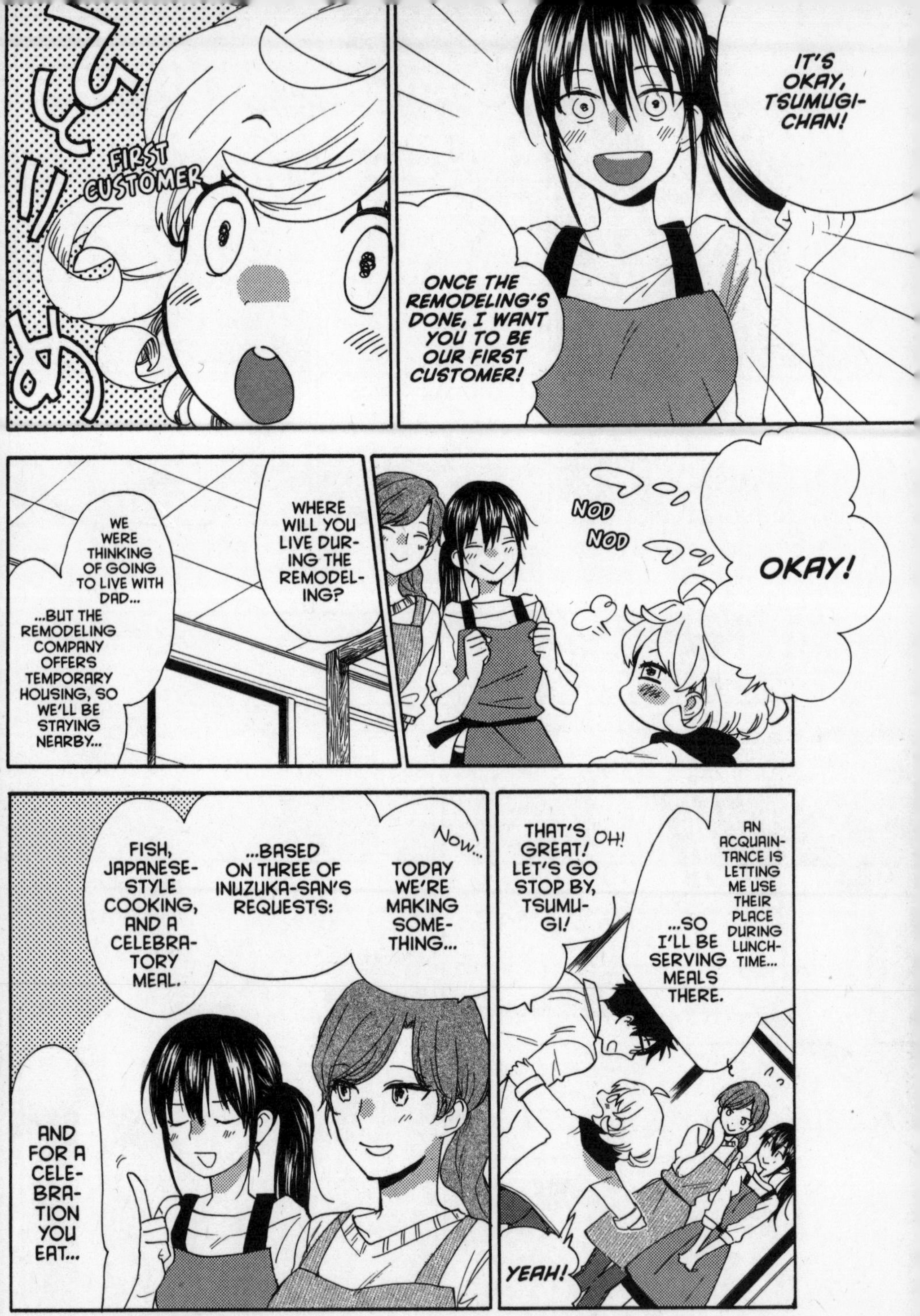
IT'S OKAY, TSUMUGI-CHAN!
ONCE THE REMODELING'S DONE, I WANT YOU TO BE OUR FIRST CUSTOMER!
FIRST CUSTOMER
NOD NOD
OKAY!
WHERE WILL YOU LIVE DURING THE REMODELING?
WE WERE THINKING OF GOING TO LIVE WITH DAD...
...BUT THE REMODELING COMPANY OFFERS TEMPORARY HOUSING, SO WE'LL BE STAYING NEARBY...
AN ACQUAINTANCE IS LETTING ME USE THEIR PLACE DURING LUNCHTIME...
...SO I'LL BE SERVING MEALS THERE.
OH!
THAT'S GREAT! LET'S GO STOP BY, TSUMUGI!
YEAH!
Now...
TODAY WE'RE MAKING SOMETHING...
...BASED ON THREE OF INUZUKA-SAN'S REQUESTS:
FISH, JAPANESE-STYLE COOKING, AND A CELEBRATORY MEAL.
AND FOR A CELEBRATION YOU EAT...

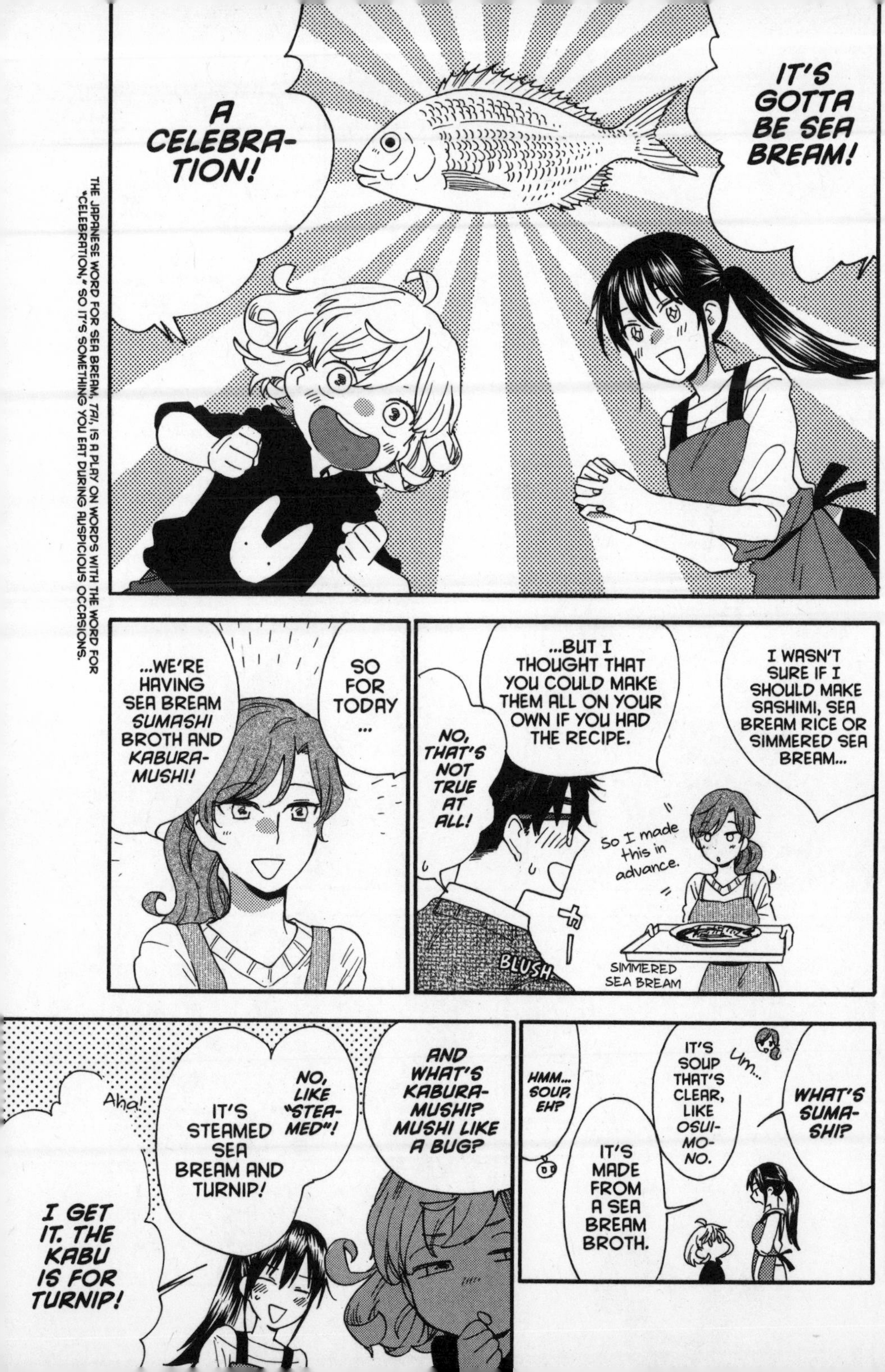
IT'S GOTTA BE SEA BREAM!
A CELEBRATION!
I WASN'T SURE IF I SHOULD MAKE SASHIMI, SEA BREAM RICE OR SIMMERED SEA BREAM...
...BUT I THOUGHT THAT YOU COULD MAKE THEM ALL ON YOUR OWN IF YOU HAD THE RECIPE.
NO, THAT'S NOT TRUE AT ALL!
So I made this in advance.
BLUSH
SIMMERED SEA BREAM
SO FOR TODAY...
...WE'RE HAVING SEA BREAM SUMASHI BROTH AND KABURA-MUSHI!
WHAT'S SUMA-SHI?
Um...
IT'S SOUP THAT'S CLEAR, LIKE OSUI-MO-NO.
IT'S MADE FROM A SEA BREAM BROTH.
HMM... SOUP, EH?
AND WHAT'S KABURA-MUSHI? MUSHI LIKE A BUG?
NO, LIKE "STEA-MED"!
IT'S STEAMED SEA BREAM AND TURNIP!
Aha!
I GET IT. THE KABU IS FOR TURNIP!

THE JAPANESE WORD FOR SEA BREAM, *TAI*, IS A PLAY ON WORDS WITH THE WORD FOR "CELEBRATION," SO IT'S SOMETHING YOU EAT DURING AUSPICIOUS OCCASIONS.

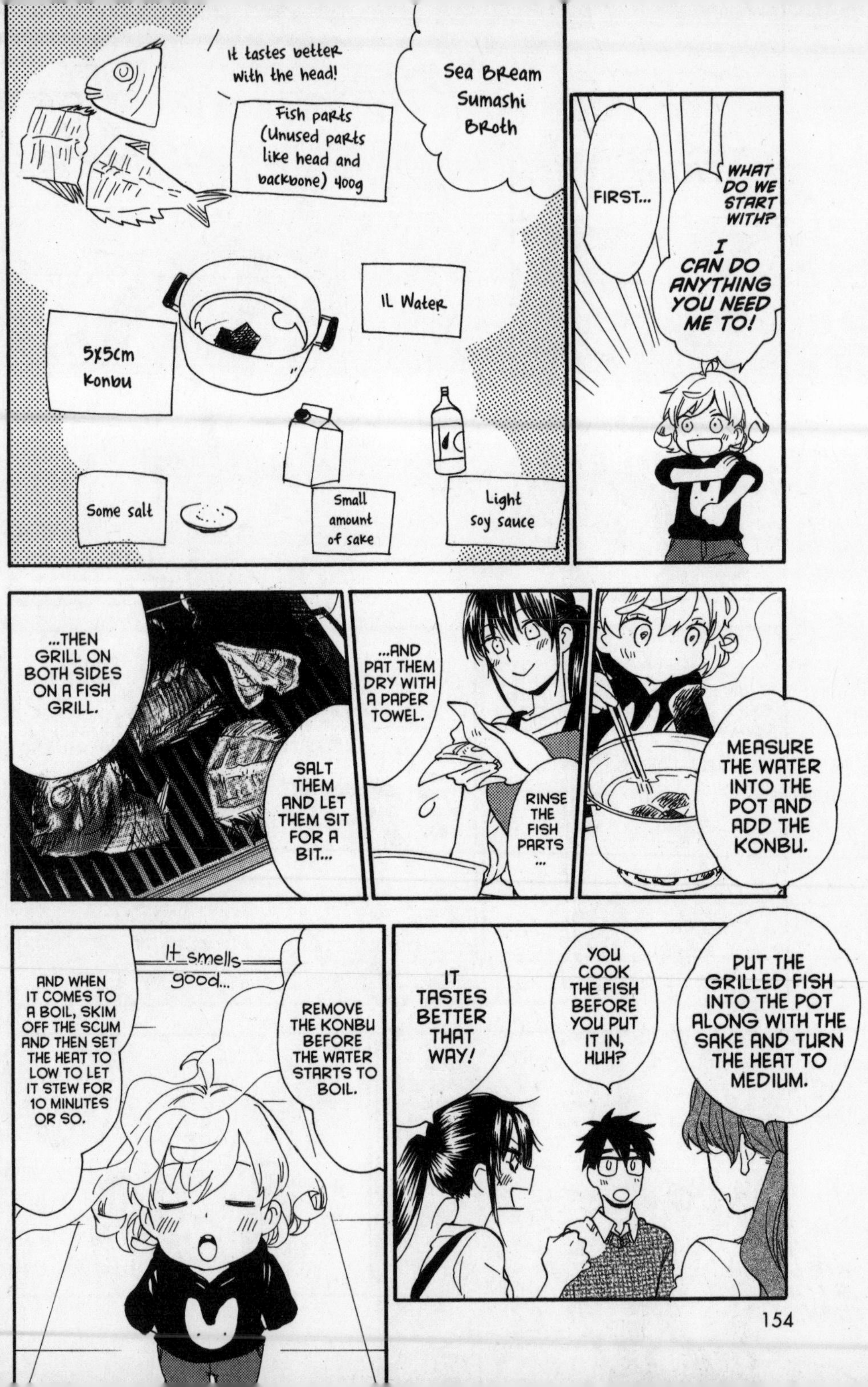
WHAT DO WE START WITH?
I CAN DO ANYTHING YOU NEED ME TO!
FIRST...
Sea Bream Sumashi Broth
It tastes better with the head!
Fish parts (Unused parts like head and backbone) 400g
1L Water
5x5cm Konbu
Light soy sauce
Small amount of sake
Some salt
MEASURE THE WATER INTO THE POT AND ADD THE KONBU.
RINSE THE FISH PARTS...
...AND PAT THEM DRY WITH A PAPER TOWEL.
SALT THEM AND LET THEM SIT FOR A BIT...
...THEN GRILL ON BOTH SIDES ON A FISH GRILL.
PUT THE GRILLED FISH INTO THE POT ALONG WITH THE SAKE AND TURN THE HEAT TO MEDIUM.
YOU COOK THE FISH BEFORE YOU PUT IT IN, HUH?
IT TASTES BETTER THAT WAY!
REMOVE THE KONBU BEFORE THE WATER STARTS TO BOIL.
It smells good...
AND WHEN IT COMES TO A BOIL, SKIM OFF THE SCUM AND THEN SET THE HEAT TO LOW TO LET IT STEW FOR 10 MINUTES OR SO.

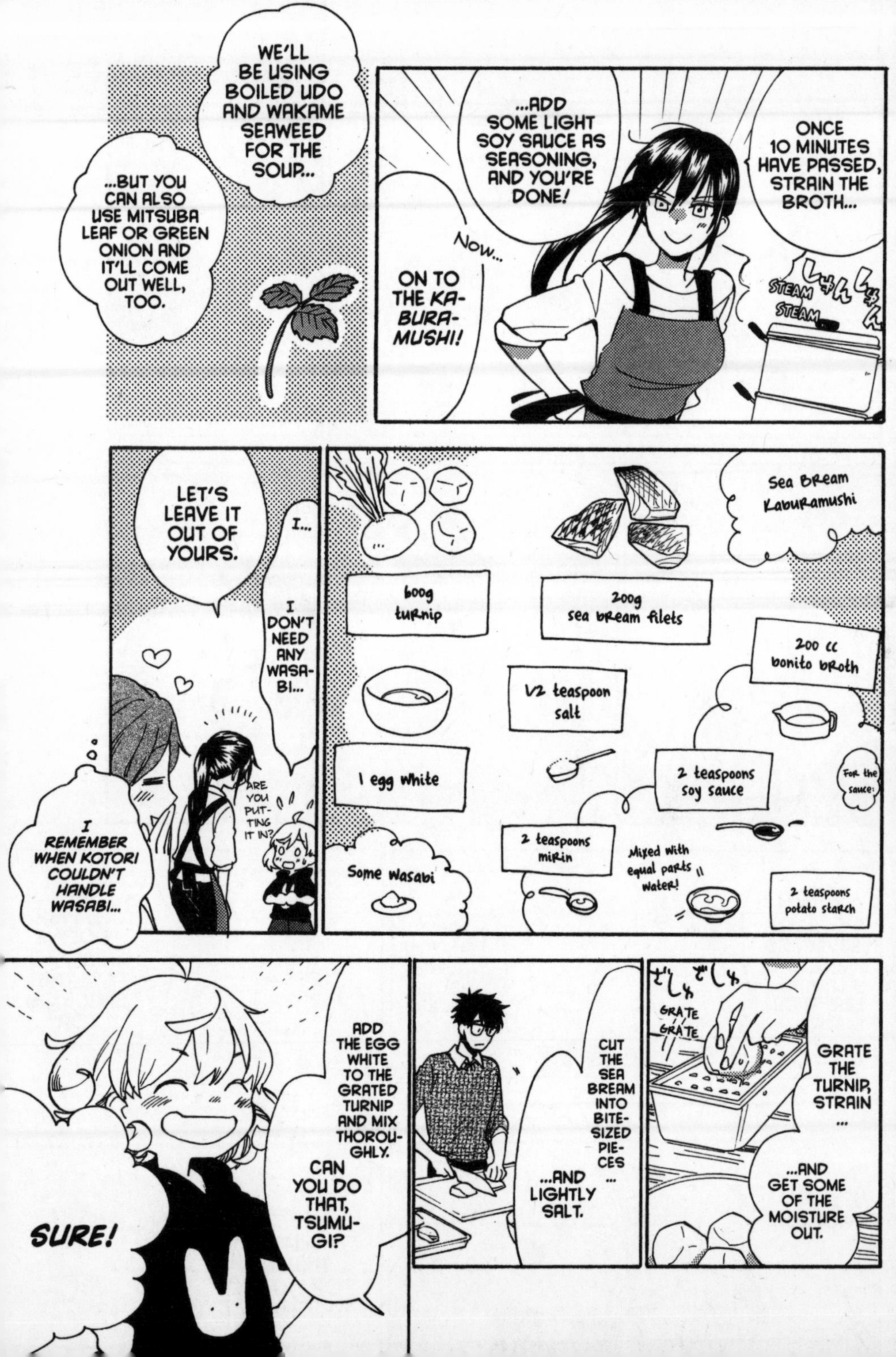
ONCE 10 MINUTES HAVE PASSED, STRAIN THE BROTH...
STEAM
STEAM
...ADD SOME LIGHT SOY SAUCE AS SEASONING, AND YOU'RE DONE!
Now...
ON TO THE KABURAMUSHI!
WE'LL BE USING BOILED UDO AND WAKAME SEAWEED FOR THE SOUP...
...BUT YOU CAN ALSO USE MITSUBA LEAF OR GREEN ONION AND IT'LL COME OUT WELL, TOO.
Sea Bream Kaburamushi
600g turnip
200g sea bream filets
200 cc bonito broth
1/2 teaspoon salt
1 egg white
2 teaspoons soy sauce
For the sauce:
2 teaspoons mirin
Mixed with equal parts water!
2 teaspoons potato starch
Some wasabi
LET'S LEAVE IT OUT OF YOURS.
I...
I DON'T NEED ANY WASABI...
ARE YOU PUTTING IT IN?
I REMEMBER WHEN KOTORI COULDN'T HANDLE WASABI...
GRATE
GRATE
GRATE THE TURNIP, STRAIN...
...AND GET SOME OF THE MOISTURE OUT.
CUT THE SEA BREAM INTO BITE-SIZED PIECES...
...AND LIGHTLY SALT.
ADD THE EGG WHITE TO THE GRATED TURNIP AND MIX THOROUGHLY.
CAN YOU DO THAT, TSUMUGI?
SURE!

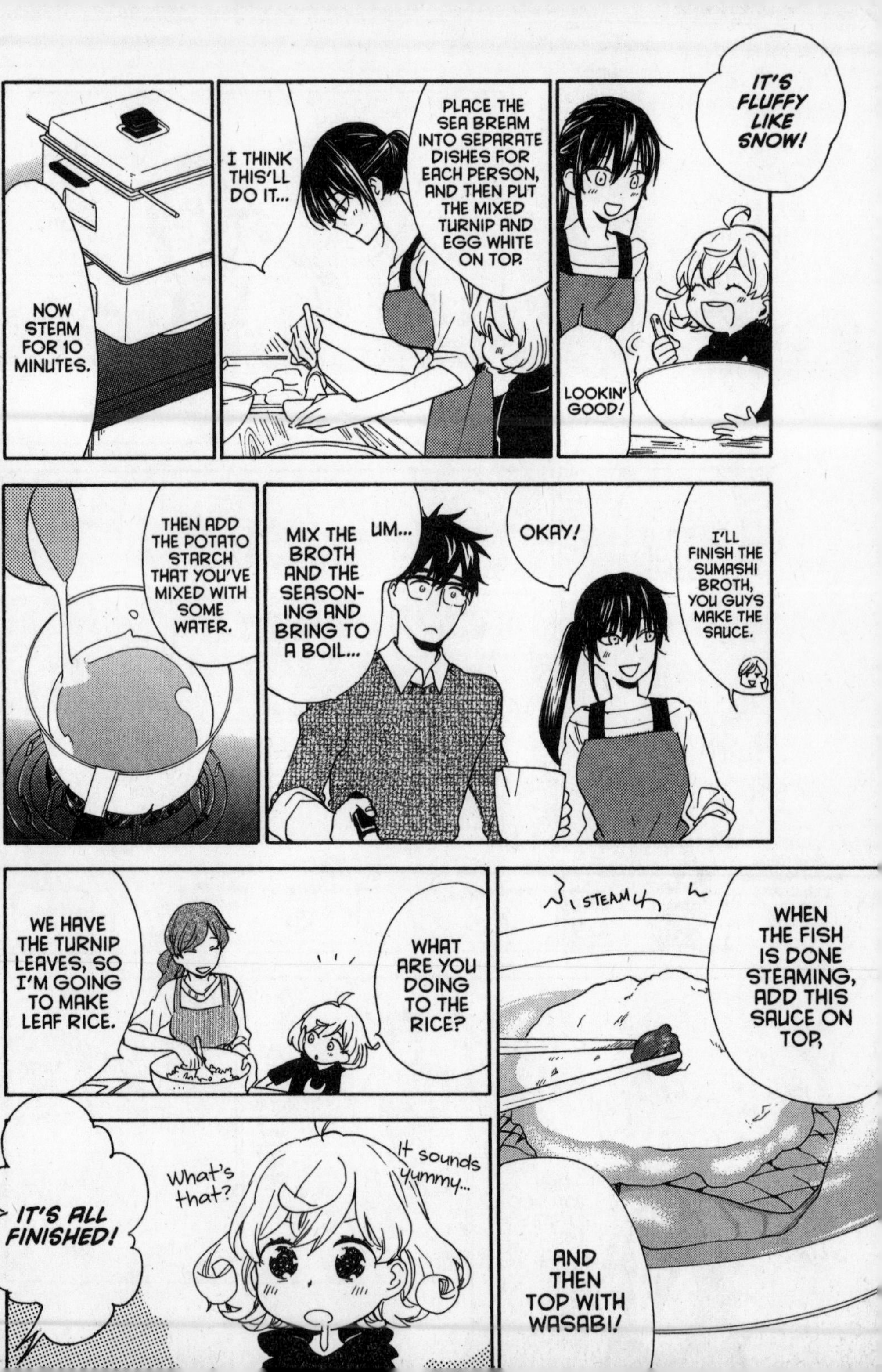
IT'S FLUFFY LIKE SNOW!
LOOKIN' GOOD!
PLACE THE SEA BREAM INTO SEPARATE DISHES FOR EACH PERSON, AND THEN PUT THE MIXED TURNIP AND EGG WHITE ON TOP.
I THINK THIS'LL DO IT...
NOW STEAM FOR 10 MINUTES.
I'LL FINISH THE SUMASHI BROTH, YOU GUYS MAKE THE SAUCE.
OKAY!
UM...
MIX THE BROTH AND THE SEASON-ING AND BRING TO A BOIL...
THEN ADD THE POTATO STARCH THAT YOU'VE MIXED WITH SOME WATER.
STEAM
WHEN THE FISH IS DONE STEAMING, ADD THIS SAUCE ON TOP,
AND THEN TOP WITH WASABI!
WHAT ARE YOU DOING TO THE RICE?
WE HAVE THE TURNIP LEAVES, SO I'M GOING TO MAKE LEAF RICE.
It sounds yummy...
What's that?
IT'S ALL FINISHED!

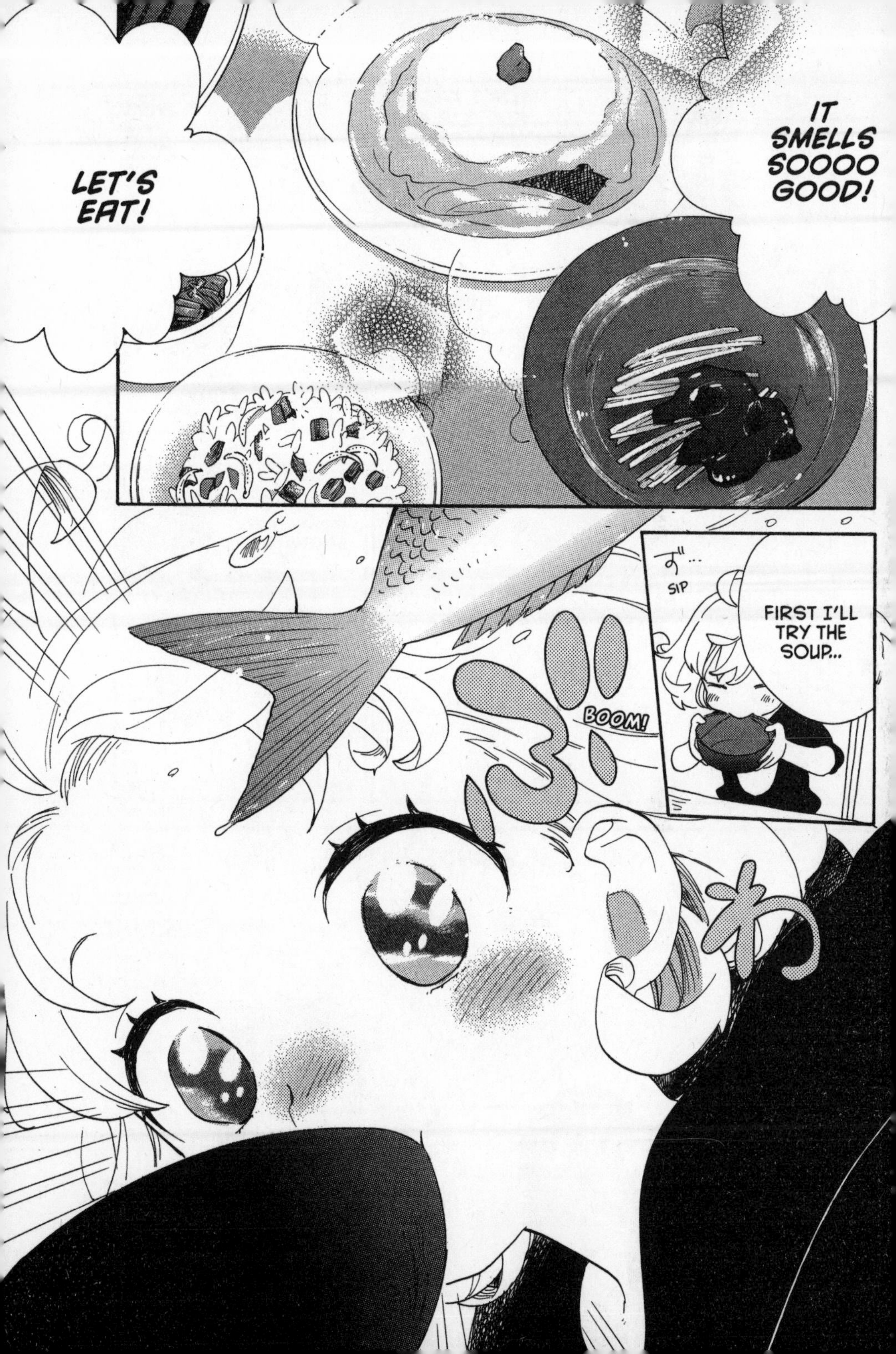
IT SMELLS SOOOO GOOD!
LET'S EAT!
FIRST I'LL TRY THE SOUP...
ず...
SIP
BOOM!

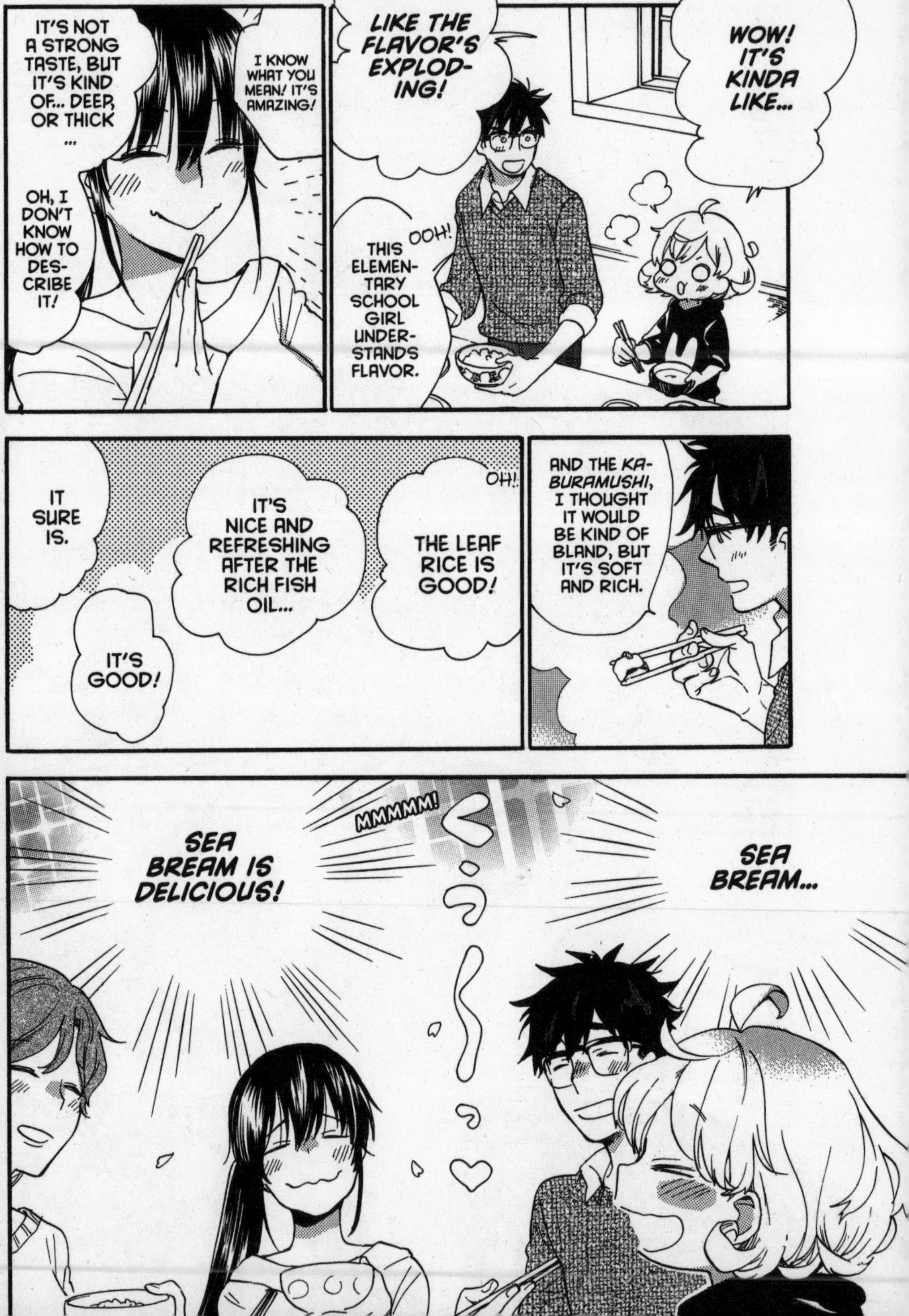

WOW! IT'S KINDA LIKE...
LIKE THE FLAVOR'S EXPLOD-ING!
OOH!
THIS ELEMENTARY SCHOOL GIRL UNDERSTANDS FLAVOR.
I KNOW WHAT YOU MEAN! IT'S AMAZING!
IT'S NOT A STRONG TASTE, BUT IT'S KIND OF... DEEP, OR THICK ...
OH, I DON'T KNOW HOW TO DES-CRIBE IT!
AND THE *KABURAMUSHI*, I THOUGHT IT WOULD BE KIND OF BLAND, BUT IT'S SOFT AND RICH.
OH!
THE LEAF RICE IS GOOD!
IT'S NICE AND REFRESHING AFTER THE RICH FISH OIL...
IT SURE IS.
IT'S GOOD!
SEA BREAM...
MMMMM!
SEA BREAM IS DELICIOUS!

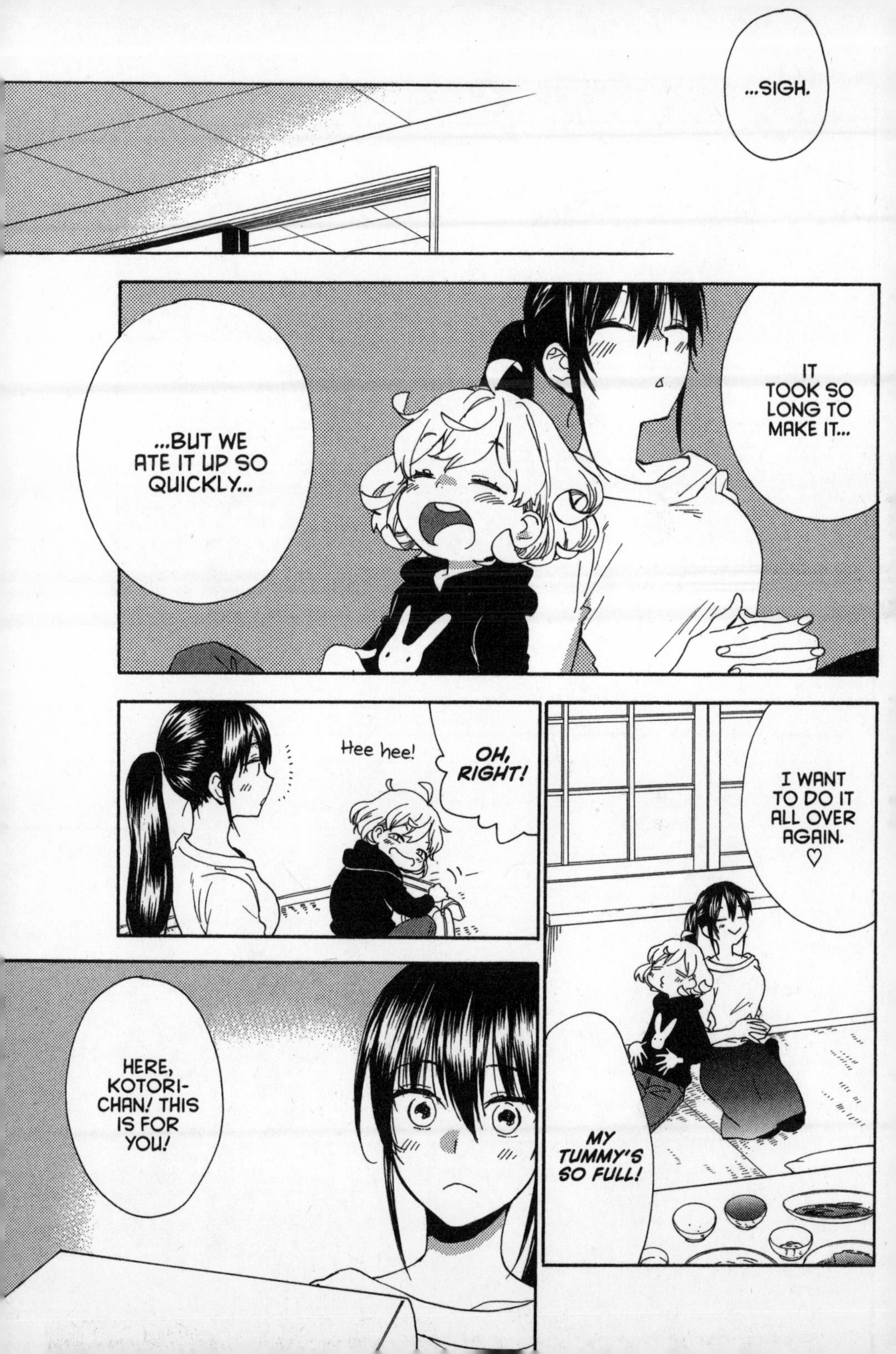
...SIGH.
IT TOOK SO LONG TO MAKE IT...
...BUT WE ATE IT UP SO QUICKLY...
I WANT TO DO IT ALL OVER AGAIN. ♡
MY TUMMY'S SO FULL!
OH, RIGHT!
Hee hee!
HERE, KOTORI-CHAN! THIS IS FOR YOU!

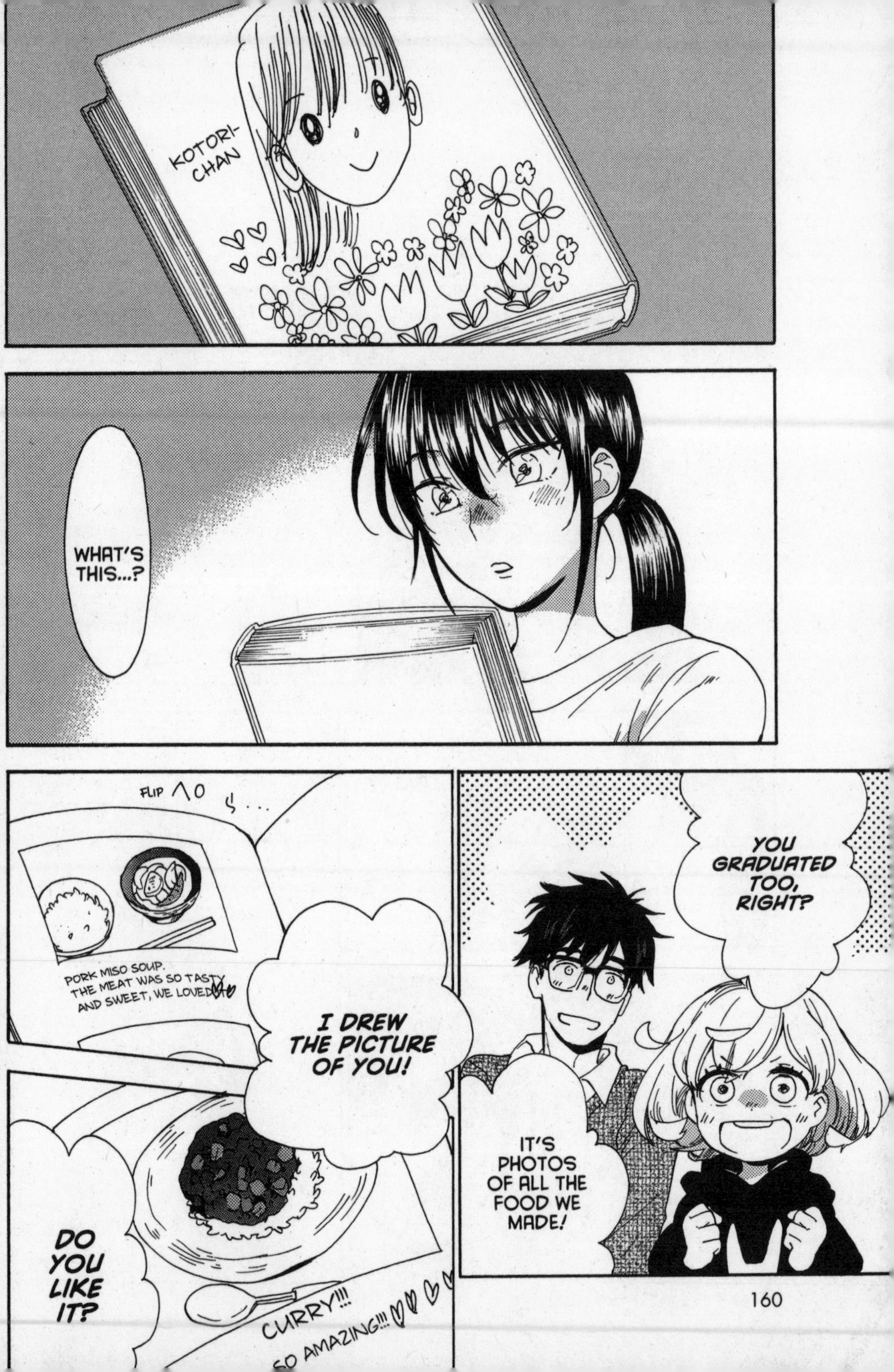

KOTORI-CHAN
WHAT'S THIS...?
YOU GRADUATED TOO, RIGHT?
IT'S PHOTOS OF ALL THE FOOD WE MADE!
FLIP
I DREW THE PICTURE OF YOU!
PORK MISO SOUP. THE MEAT WAS SO TASTY AND SWEET, WE LOVED
DO YOU LIKE IT?
CURRY!!! SO AMAZING!!!

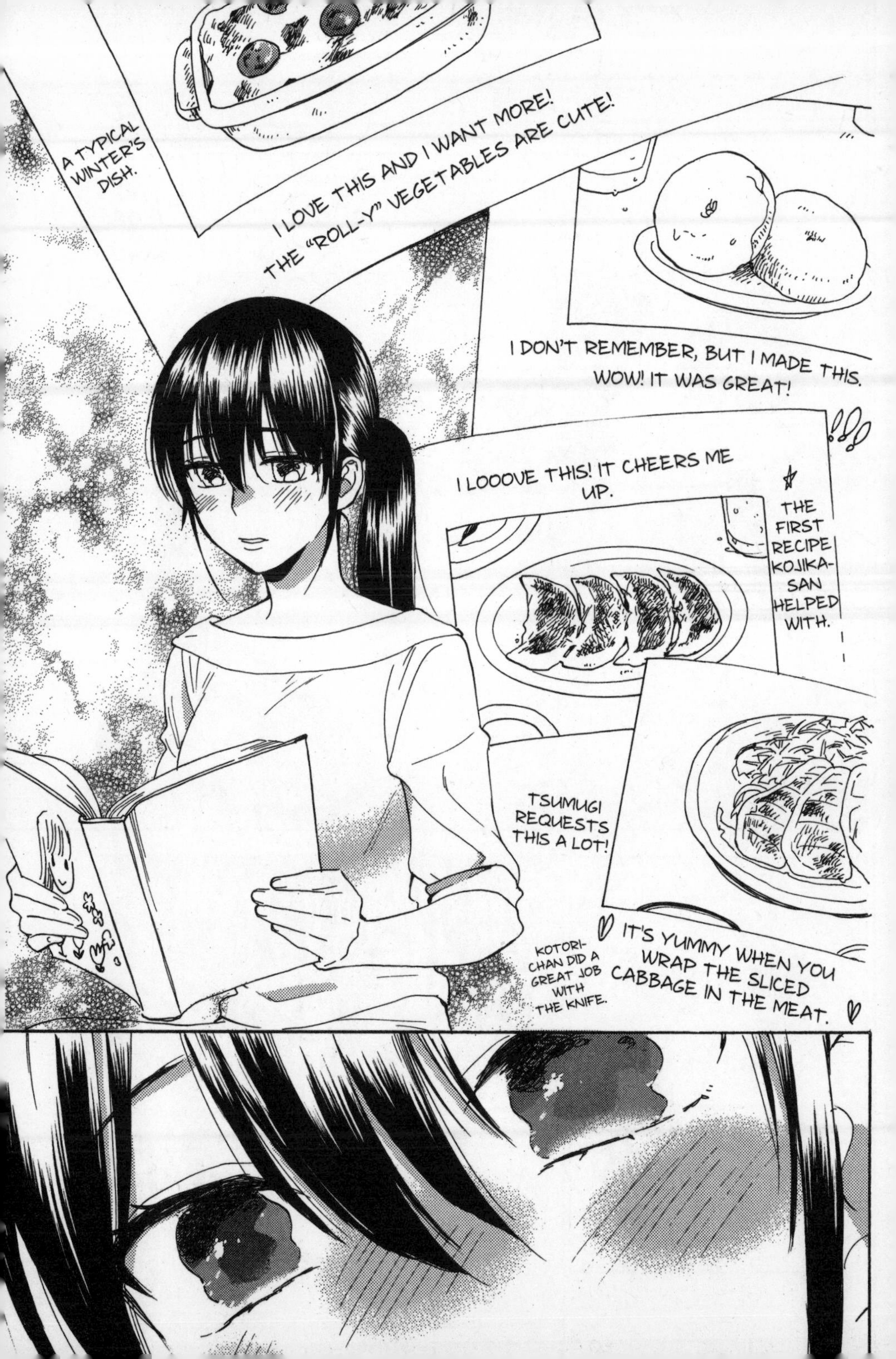
I LOVE THIS AND I WANT MORE! THE "ROLL-Y" VEGETABLES ARE CUTE!
A TYPICAL WINTER'S DISH.
I DON'T REMEMBER, BUT I MADE THIS. WOW! IT WAS GREAT!
THE FIRST RECIPE KOJIKA-SAN HELPED WITH.
I LOOOVE THIS! IT CHEERS ME UP.
TSUMUGI REQUESTS THIS A LOT!
IT'S YUMMY WHEN YOU WRAP THE SLICED CABBAGE IN THE MEAT.
KOTORI-CHAN DID A GREAT JOB WITH THE KNIFE.

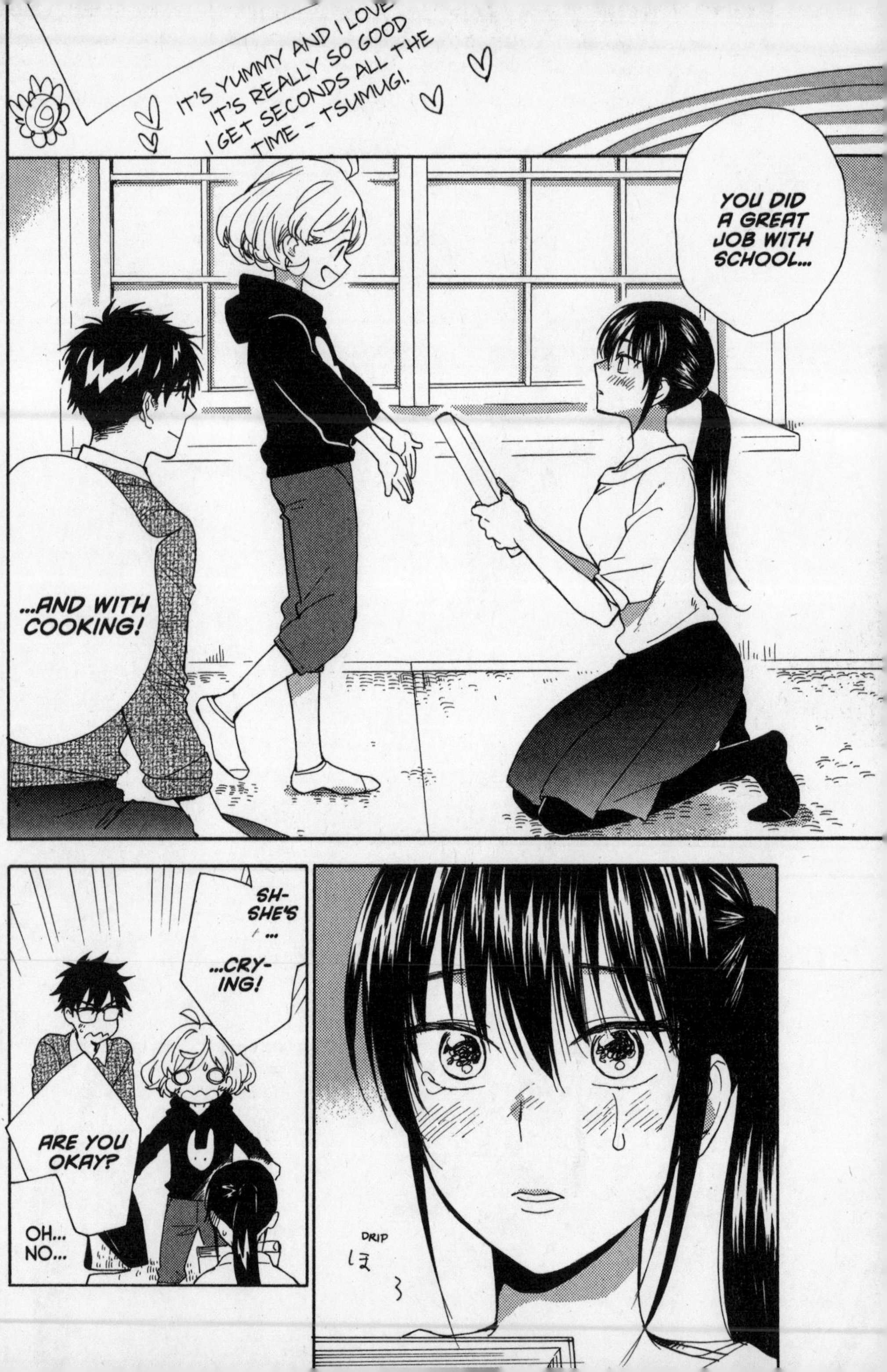
IT'S YUMMY AND I LOVE IT'S REALLY SO GOOD I GET SECONDS ALL THE TIME - TSUMUGI.
YOU DID A GREAT JOB WITH SCHOOL...
...AND WITH COOKING!
DRIP
ほろ
SH-SHE'S ...
...CRY-ING!
ARE YOU OKAY?
OH... NO...

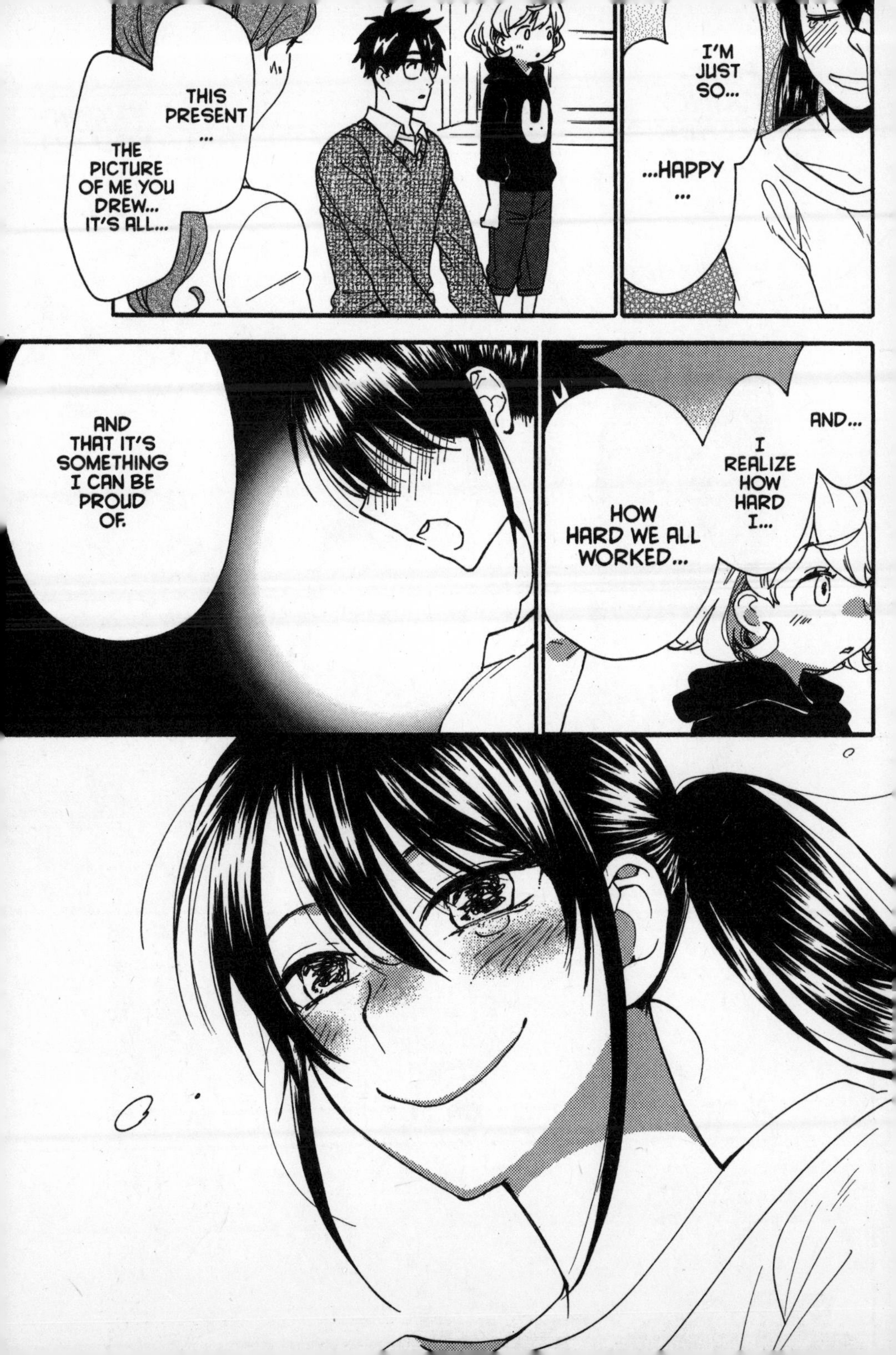
I'M JUST SO...
...HAPPY ...
THIS PRESENT ...
THE PICTURE OF ME YOU DREW... IT'S ALL...
AND...
I REALIZE HOW HARD I...
HOW HARD WE ALL WORKED...
AND THAT IT'S SOMETHING I CAN BE PROUD OF.

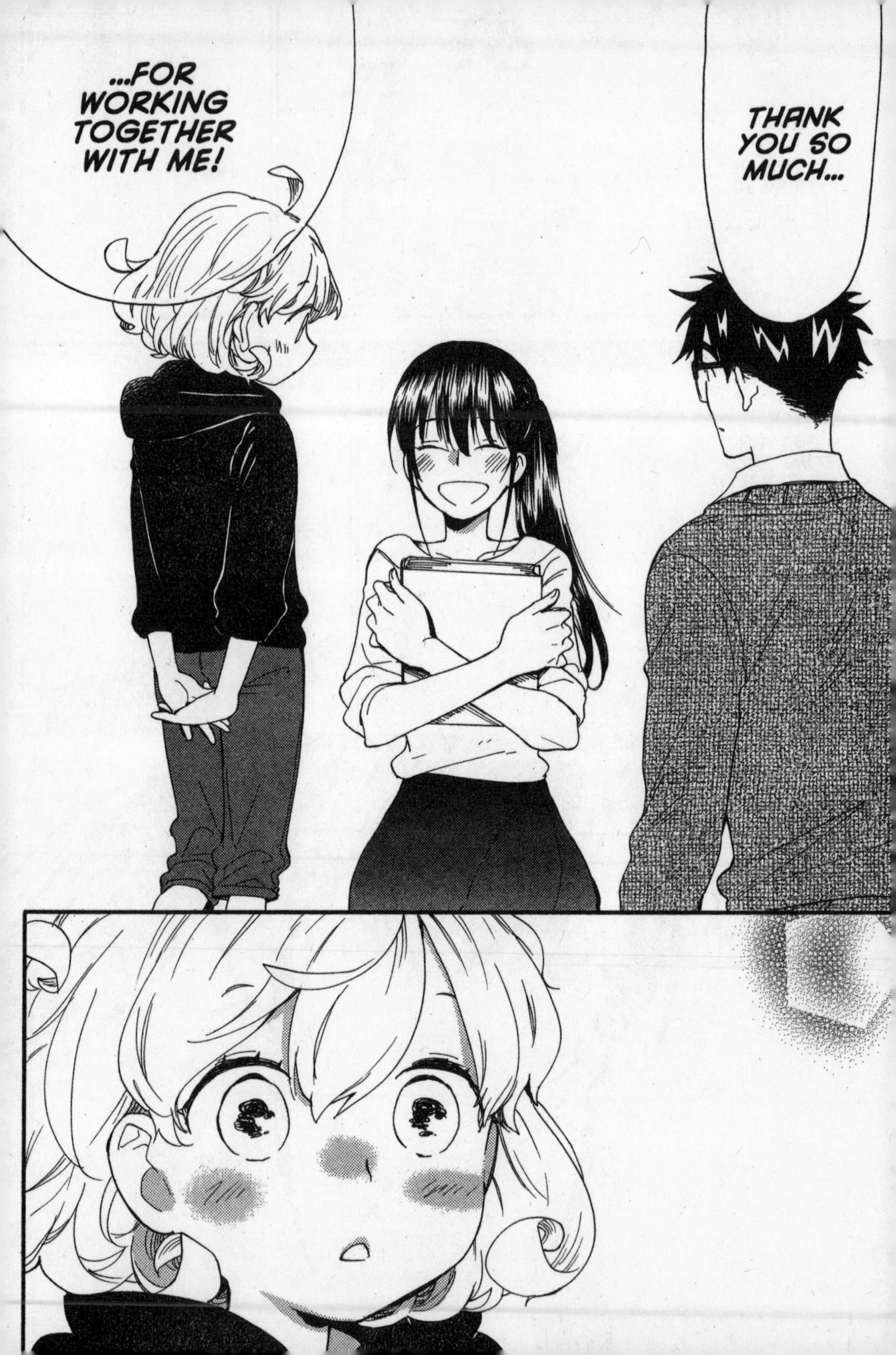
THANK YOU SO MUCH...
...FOR WORKING TOGETHER WITH ME!

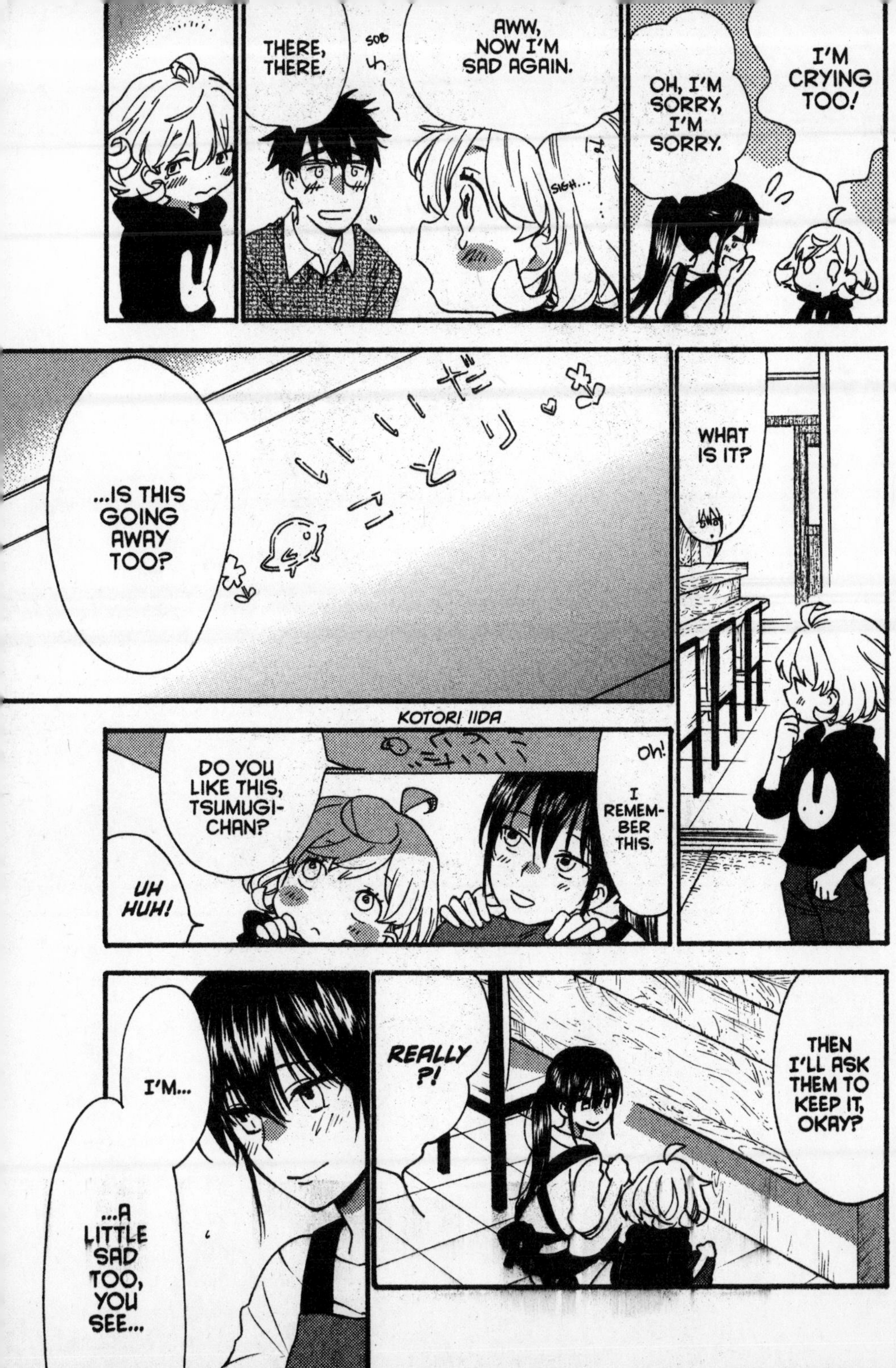
I'M CRYING TOO!
OH, I'M SORRY, I'M SORRY.
AWW, NOW I'M SAD AGAIN.
SIGH...
SOB
THERE, THERE.
WHAT IS IT?
...IS THIS GOING AWAY TOO?
KOTORI IIDA
Oh!
I REMEMBER THIS.
DO YOU LIKE THIS, TSUMUGI-CHAN?
UH HUH!
THEN I'LL ASK THEM TO KEEP IT, OKAY?
REALLY?!
I'M...
...A LITTLE SAD TOO, YOU SEE...

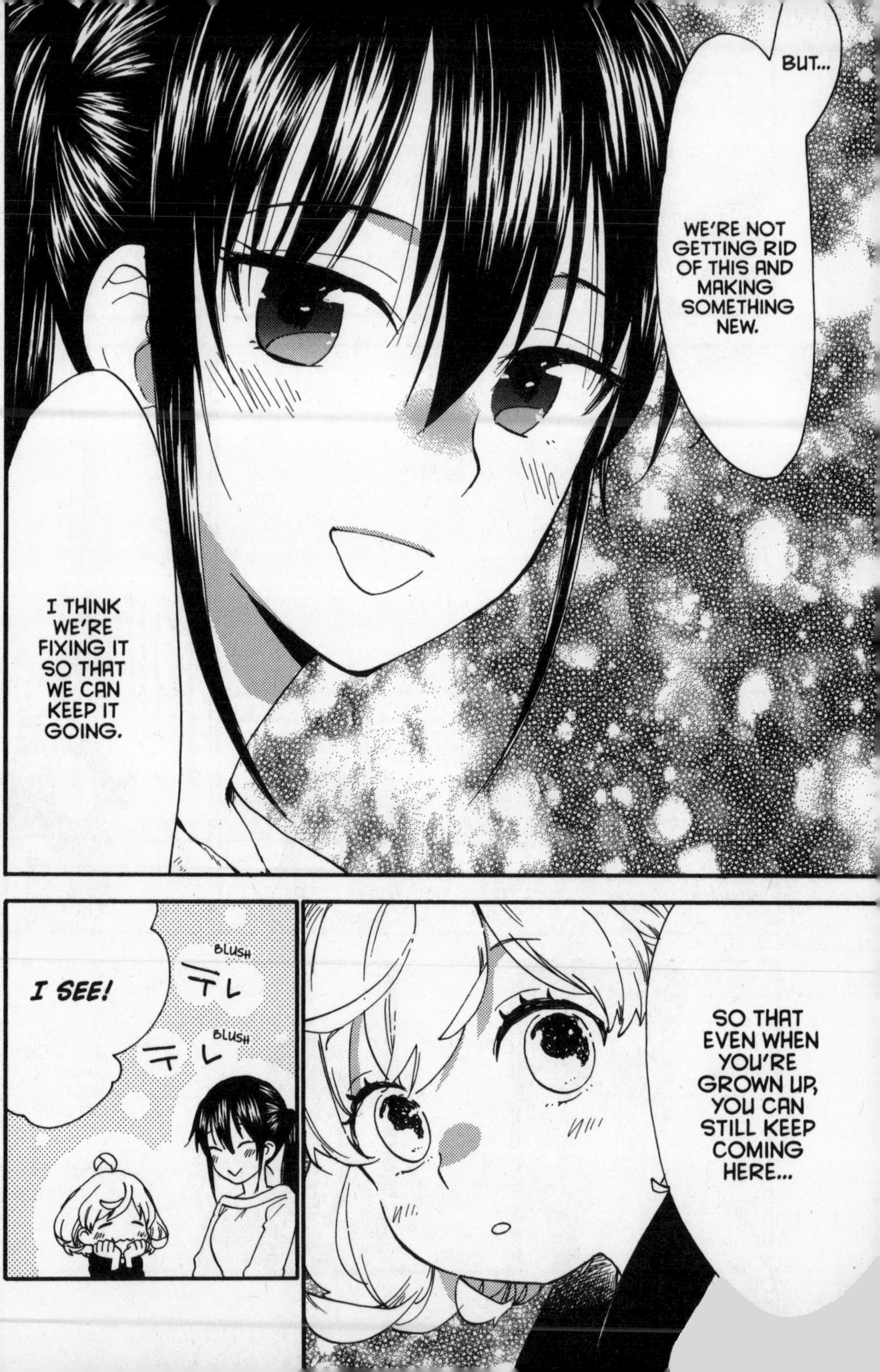
BUT...
WE'RE NOT GETTING RID OF THIS AND MAKING SOMETHING NEW.
I THINK WE'RE FIXING IT SO THAT WE CAN KEEP IT GOING.
SO THAT EVEN WHEN YOU'RE GROWN UP, YOU CAN STILL KEEP COMING HERE...
I SEE!
テレ BLUSH
テレ BLUSH

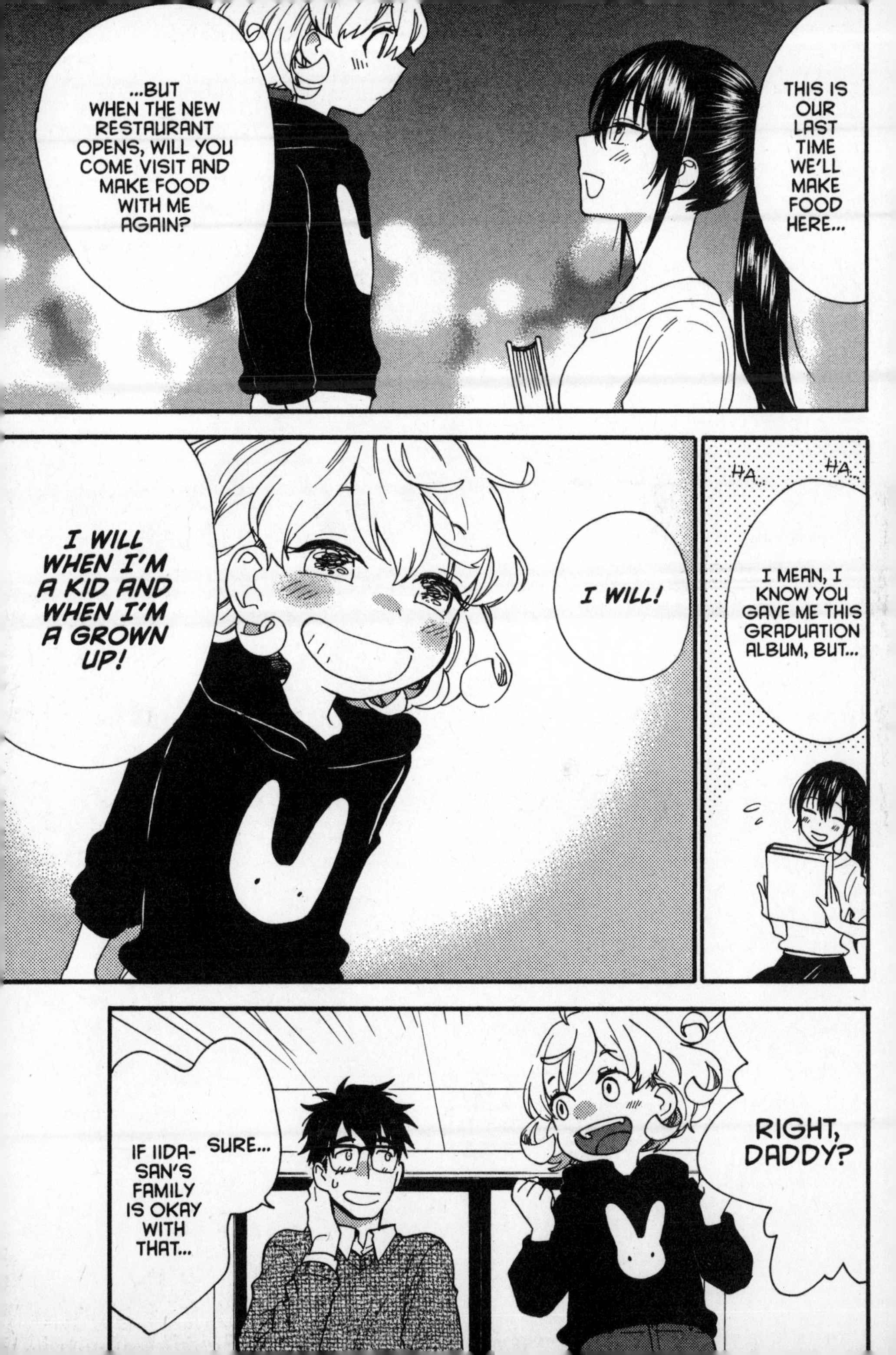
THIS IS OUR LAST TIME WE'LL MAKE FOOD HERE...
...BUT WHEN THE NEW RESTAURANT OPENS, WILL YOU COME VISIT AND MAKE FOOD WITH ME AGAIN?
HA... HA...
I MEAN, I KNOW YOU GAVE ME THIS GRADUATION ALBUM, BUT...
I WILL!
I WILL WHEN I'M A KID AND WHEN I'M A GROWN UP!
RIGHT, DADDY?
SURE...
IF IIDA-SAN'S FAMILY IS OKAY WITH THAT...

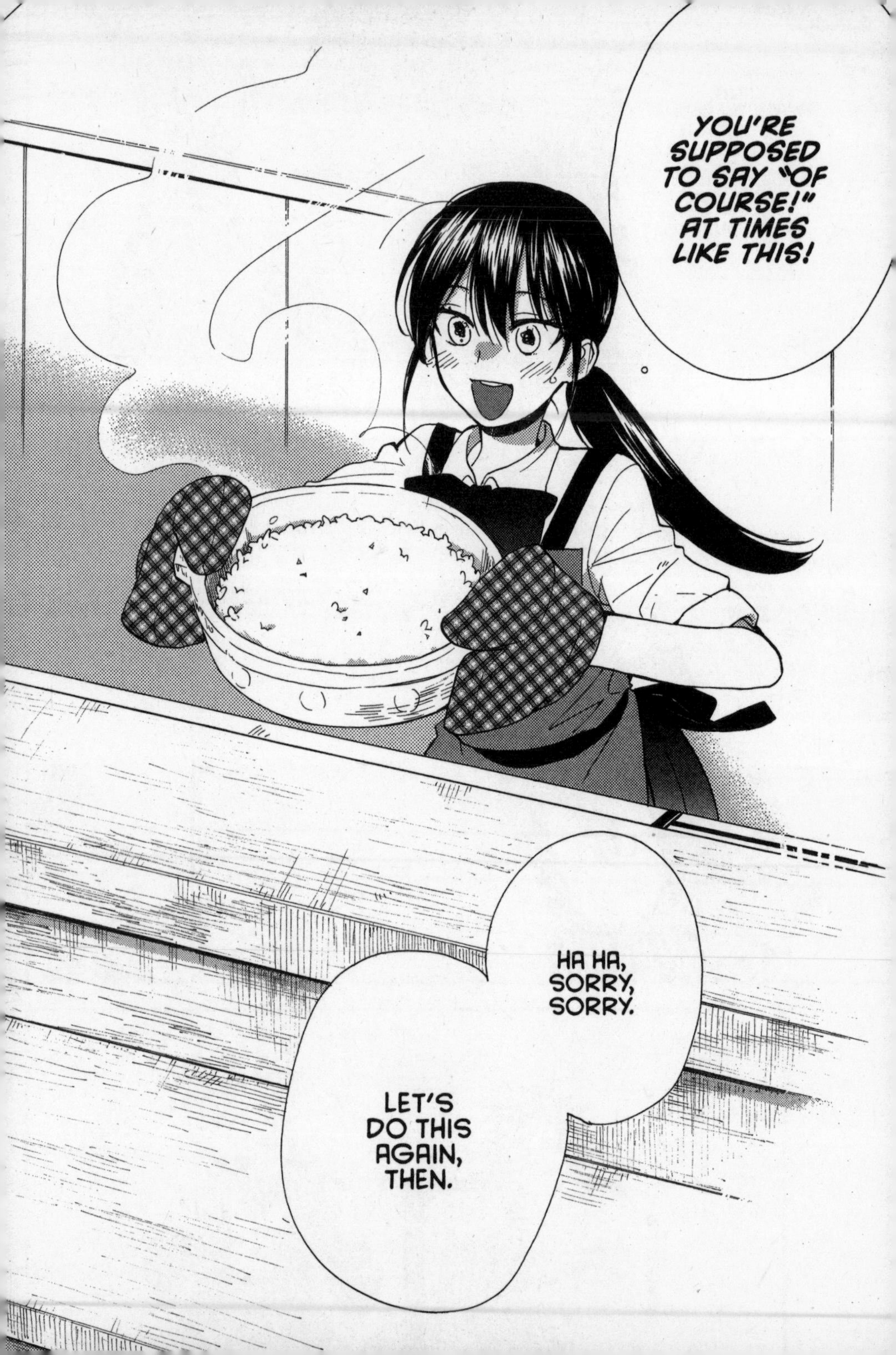
YOU'RE SUPPOSED TO SAY "OF COURSE!" AT TIMES LIKE THIS!
HA HA, SORRY, SORRY.
LET'S DO THIS AGAIN, THEN.

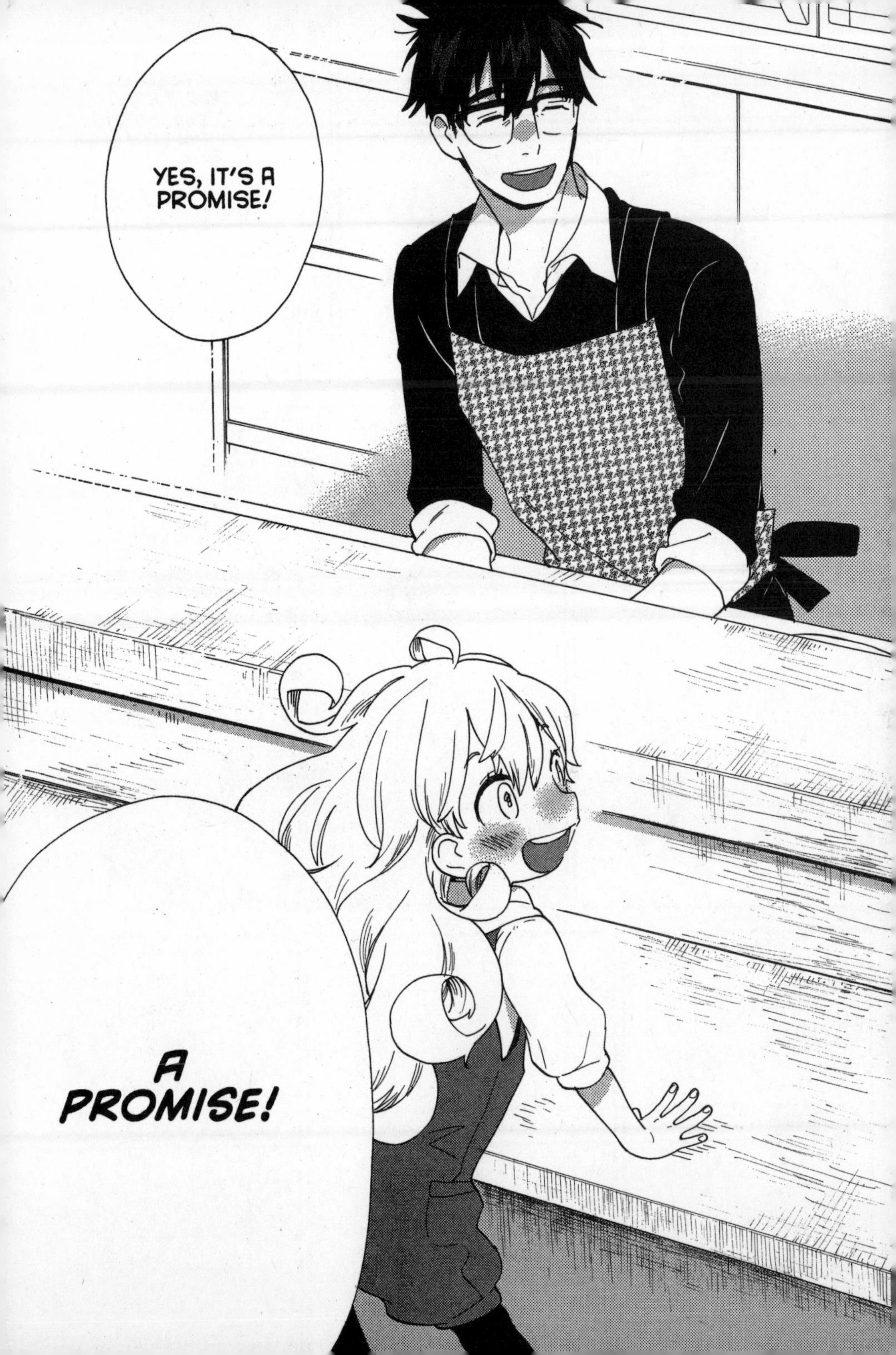
YES, IT'S A PROMISE!
A PROMISE!

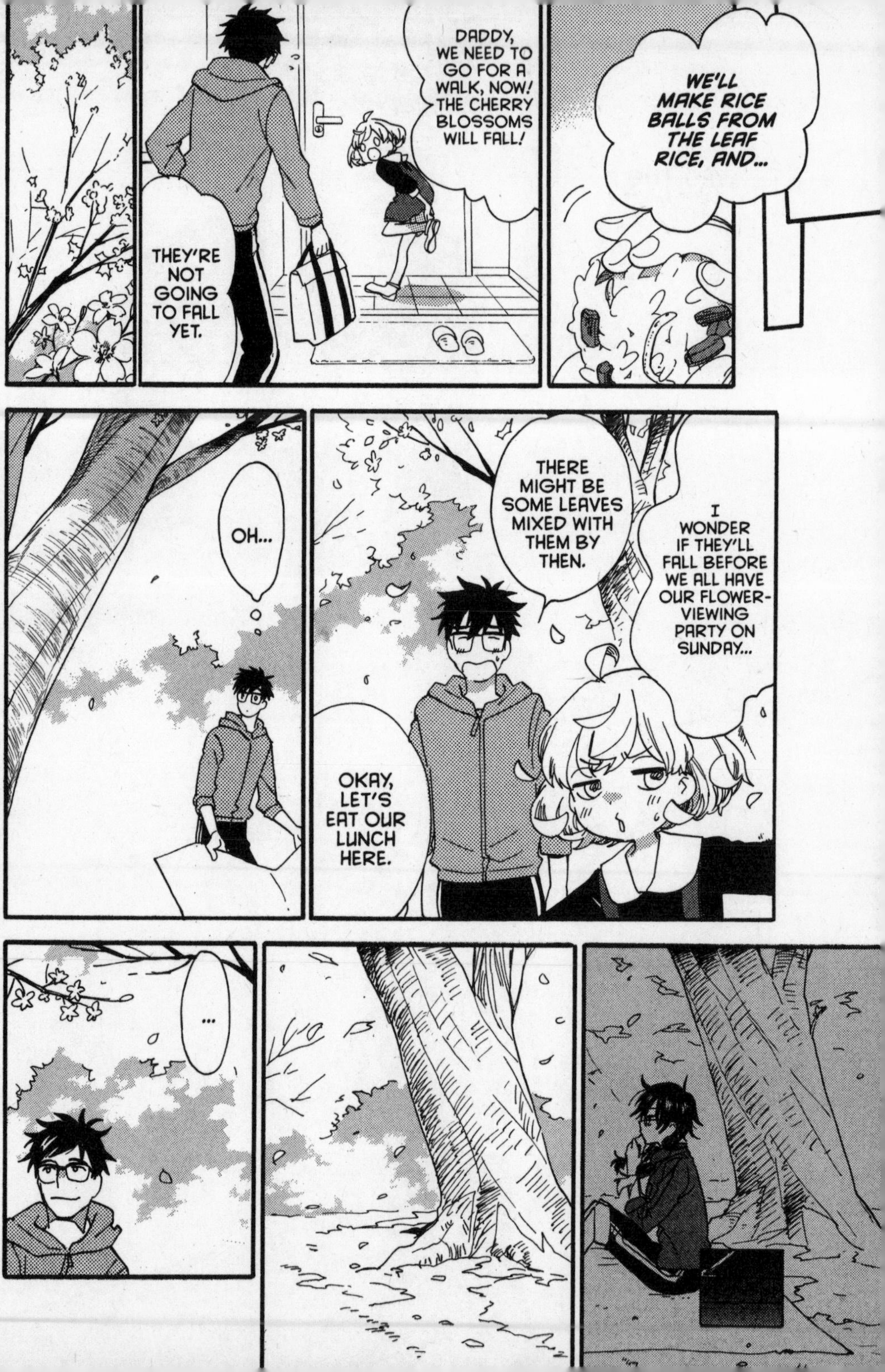

WE'LL MAKE RICE BALLS FROM THE LEAF RICE, AND...
DADDY, WE NEED TO GO FOR A WALK, NOW! THE CHERRY BLOSSOMS WILL FALL!
THEY'RE NOT GOING TO FALL YET.
I WONDER IF THEY'LL FALL BEFORE WE ALL HAVE OUR FLOWER-VIEWING PARTY ON SUNDAY...
THERE MIGHT BE SOME LEAVES MIXED WITH THEM BY THEN.
OKAY, LET'S EAT OUR LUNCH HERE.
OH...
...

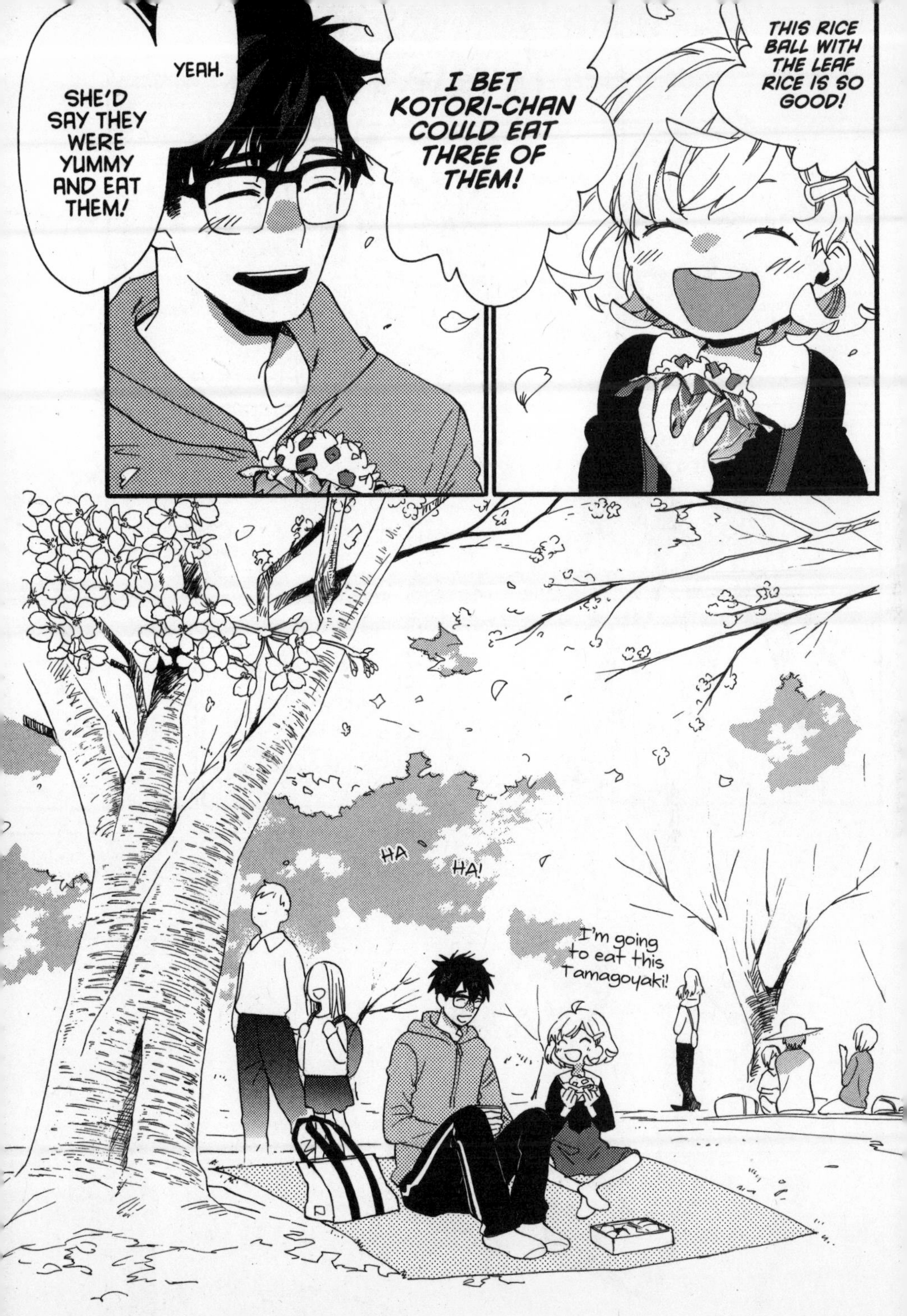
THIS RICE BALL WITH THE LEAF RICE IS SO GOOD!
I BET KOTORI-CHAN COULD EAT THREE OF THEM!
YEAH.
SHE'D SAY THEY WERE YUMMY AND EAT THEM!
HA HA!
I'm going to eat this Tamagoyaki!

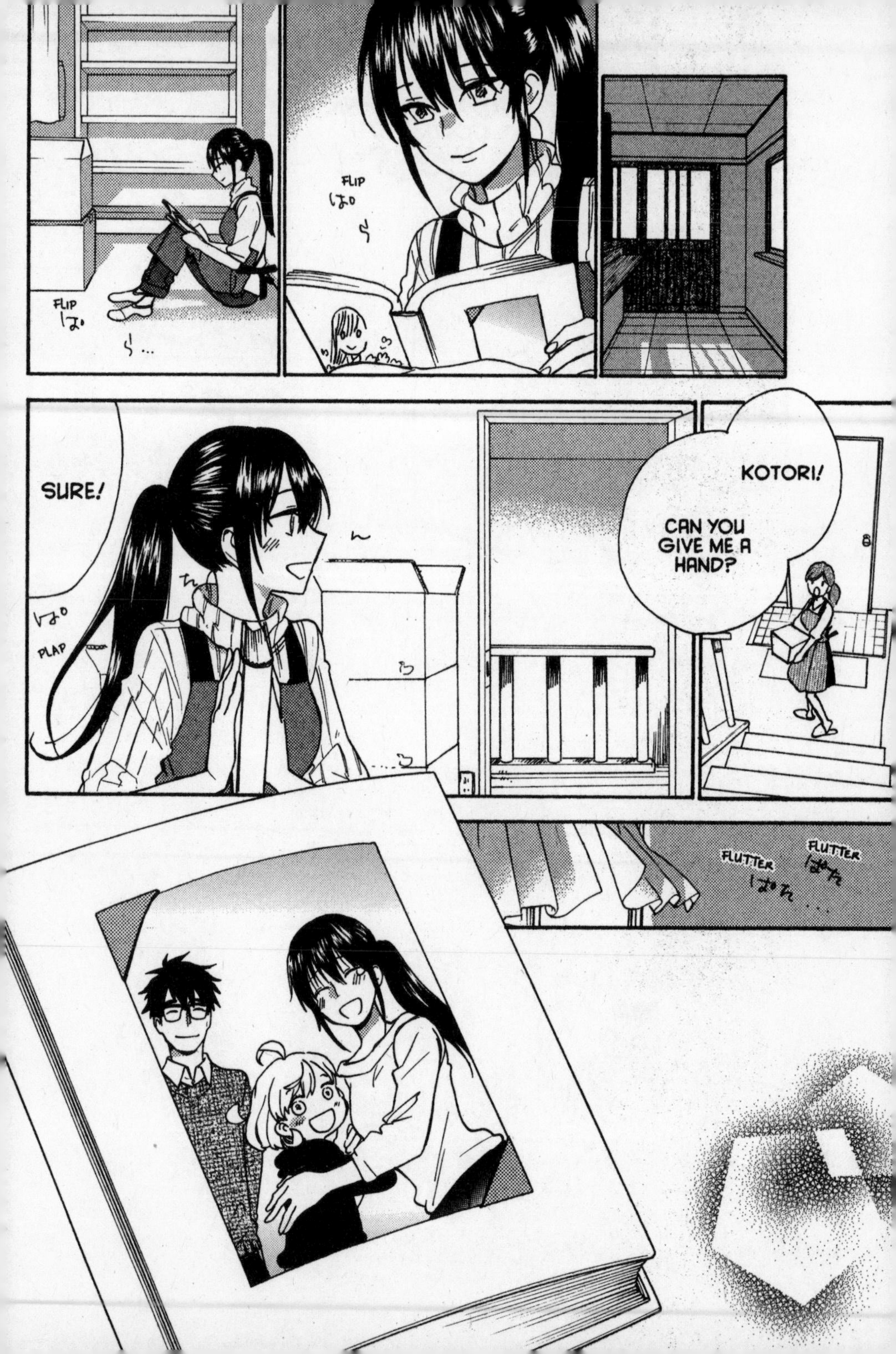
FLIP
FLIP
KOTORI!
CAN YOU GIVE ME A HAND?
SURE!
PLAP
FLUTTER
FLUTTER

SPRING VEGETABLE RICE

☆ Ingredients ☆ (Serves 4)

★ 150g turnip leaves   ★ 50g Japanese parsley leaves
★ 1-15 tsp salt   ★ 2 cups uncooked rice

*15% salt concentration

▽ Directions ▽

1. Boil plenty of water in a pan. Season with salt (not from ingredients). Remove the well washed turnip leaves from the stork, boil for 2 minutes. Rinse with plenty of cold water. Squeeze out water. Chop into 5mm.

2. Boil parsley for 10 seconds, rinse and cut the same way.

3. Combine (1) and (2). Just before the rice is finished mix in the salt. Leave for 5 minutes for remaining moisture to evaporate.

4. Mix (3) into the rice, and it's done! Adding sesame or dried whitebait is good too! ♡

SEA BREAM SOUP

☆ Ingredients ☆ (Serves 4)

★ 400g sea bream (no head or tail)   ★ Dash of sake
★ 1L water   ★ Some 5cmx5cm kombu   ★ Low sodium soy sauce to taste

Directions

1. Put water into pan and add kombu.

2. Rinse the sea bream and pat dry with paper towel. Lightly salt and leave to sit. Then broil on both sides.

3. Add (2) and vinegar to (1), remove kombu before it boils. Remove scum after boiled, lower heat and simmer for 10 mins.

4. Remove the scum again. Add the soy sauce for taste!

♥ POINT♥
Add seasonal fragrances! Parsley & ginseng in spring, bamboo shoots & wakame, etc.

STEAMED TURNIP SEA BREAM

☆ Ingredients ☆ (Serves 4)

★ 2 sea bream fillets (200g)   ★ 600g turnip
★ 1 egg white   ★ ½ tsp salt   ★ pinch wasabi

☆ Paste ☆
• 200cc bonito stock   • 2 tsp low sodium soy sauce
• 2 tsp mirin   • 2 tsp potato starch (dissolved in 2 tsp water)

Directions

1. Grate turnip, put in sieve. Use your hands to push the moisture out.

2. Remove bones from sea bream, cut into 4. Sprinkle with salt and let sit.

3. Add egg white to (1) and mix well.

4. Divide (2) into bowls for each person. Put (3) on top. Steam for 10 minutes.

5. Put (A) into pan and simmer. Add potato starch and make into paste.

6. Top (4) with (5) once steamed. Add wasabi and done. ♡

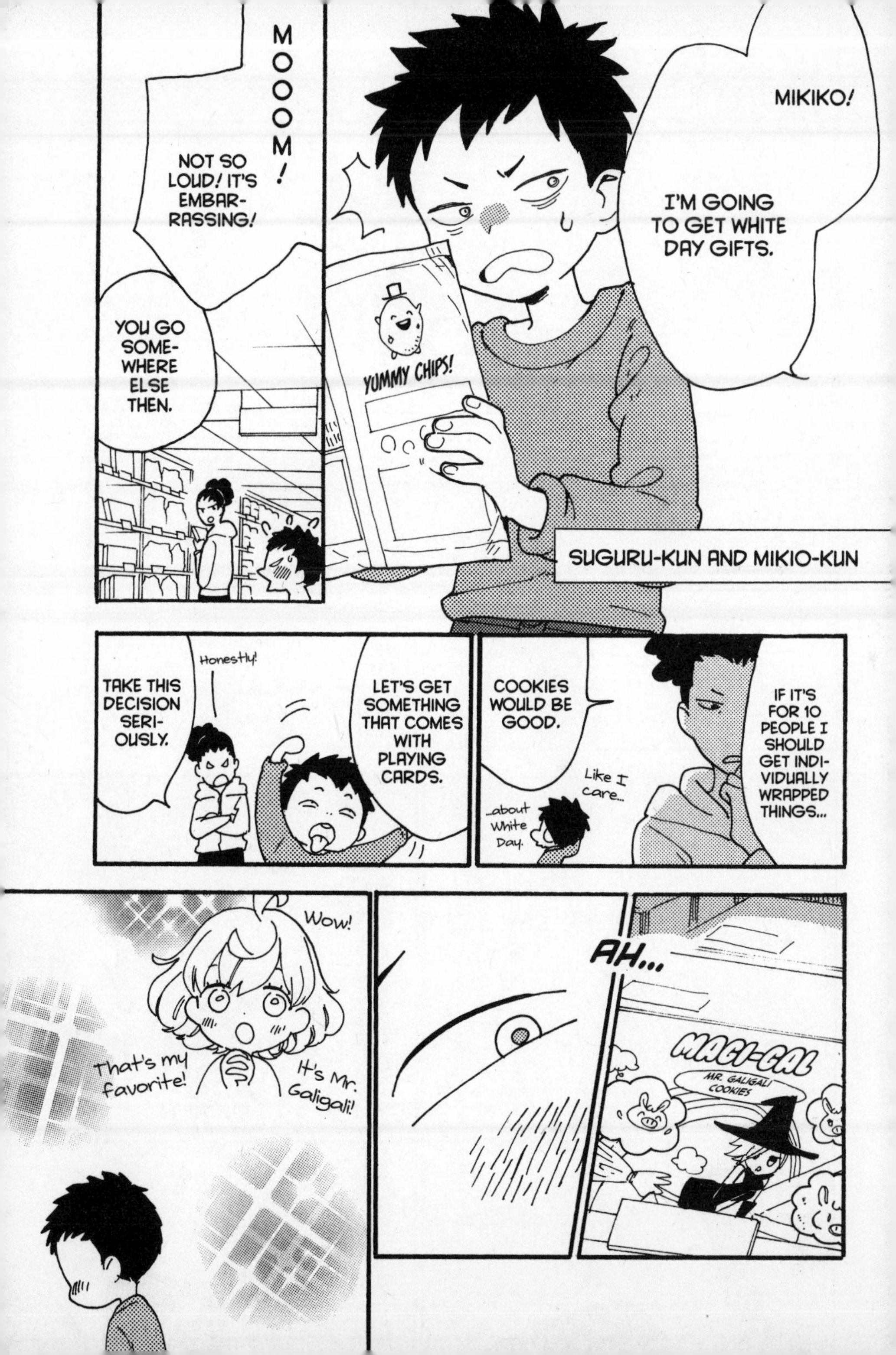
MIKIKO!
I'M GOING TO GET WHITE DAY GIFTS.
YUMMY CHIPS!
SUGURU-KUN AND MIKIO-KUN
MOOOM!
NOT SO LOUD! IT'S EMBARRASSING!
YOU GO SOMEWHERE ELSE THEN.
IF IT'S FOR 10 PEOPLE I SHOULD GET INDIVIDUALLY WRAPPED THINGS...
COOKIES WOULD BE GOOD.
Like I care...
...about White Day.
LET'S GET SOMETHING THAT COMES WITH PLAYING CARDS.
Honestly!
TAKE THIS DECISION SERIOUSLY.
AH...
MAGI-GAL
MR. GALIGALI COOKIES
Wow!
It's Mr. Galigali!
That's my favorite!

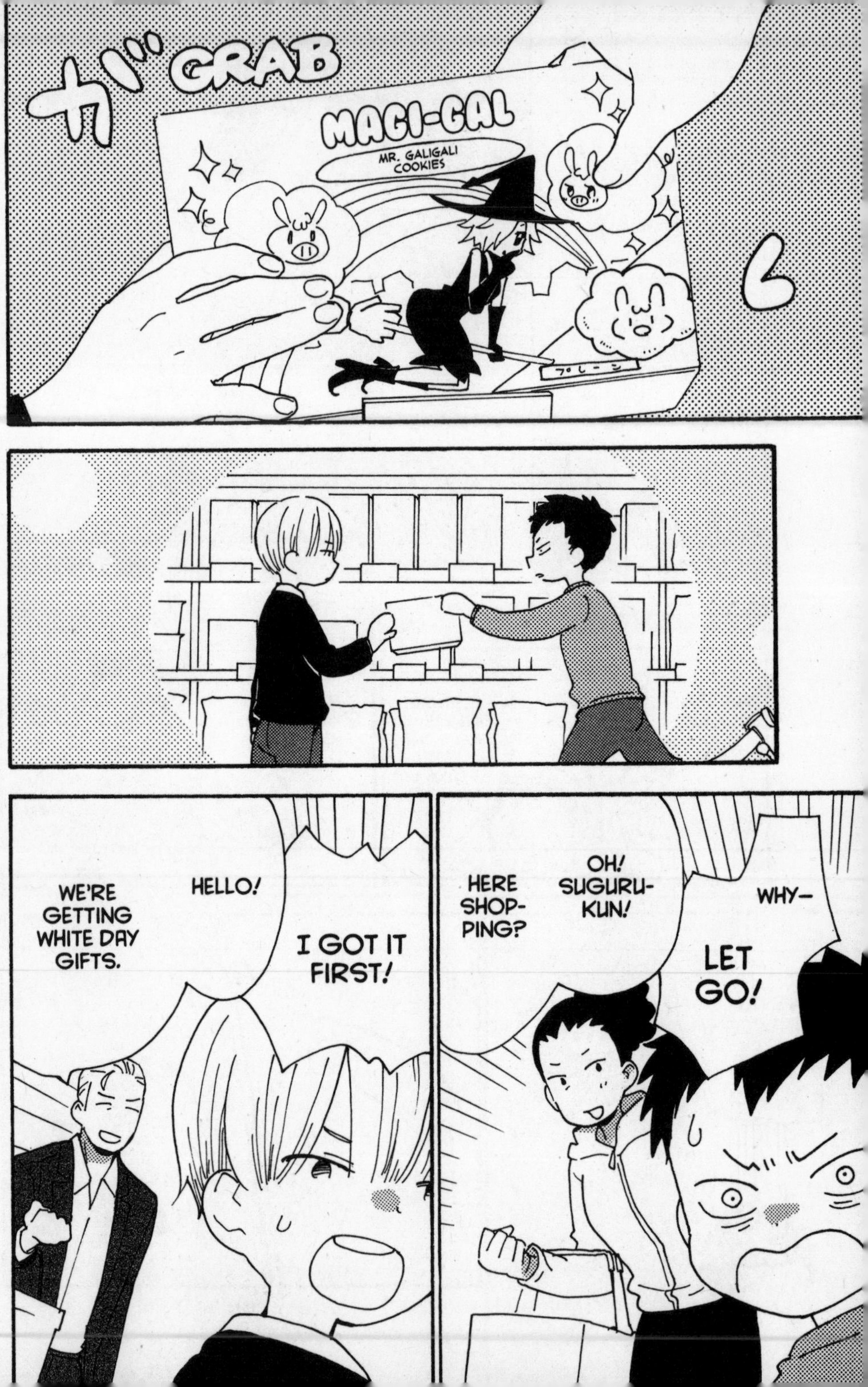
カ゛ GRAB
MAGI-GAL
MR. GALIGALI COOKIES
プレーン
し
WHY—
OH! SUGURU-KUN!
HERE SHOPPING?
LET GO!
HELLO!
WE'RE GETTING WHITE DAY GIFTS.
I GOT IT FIRST!

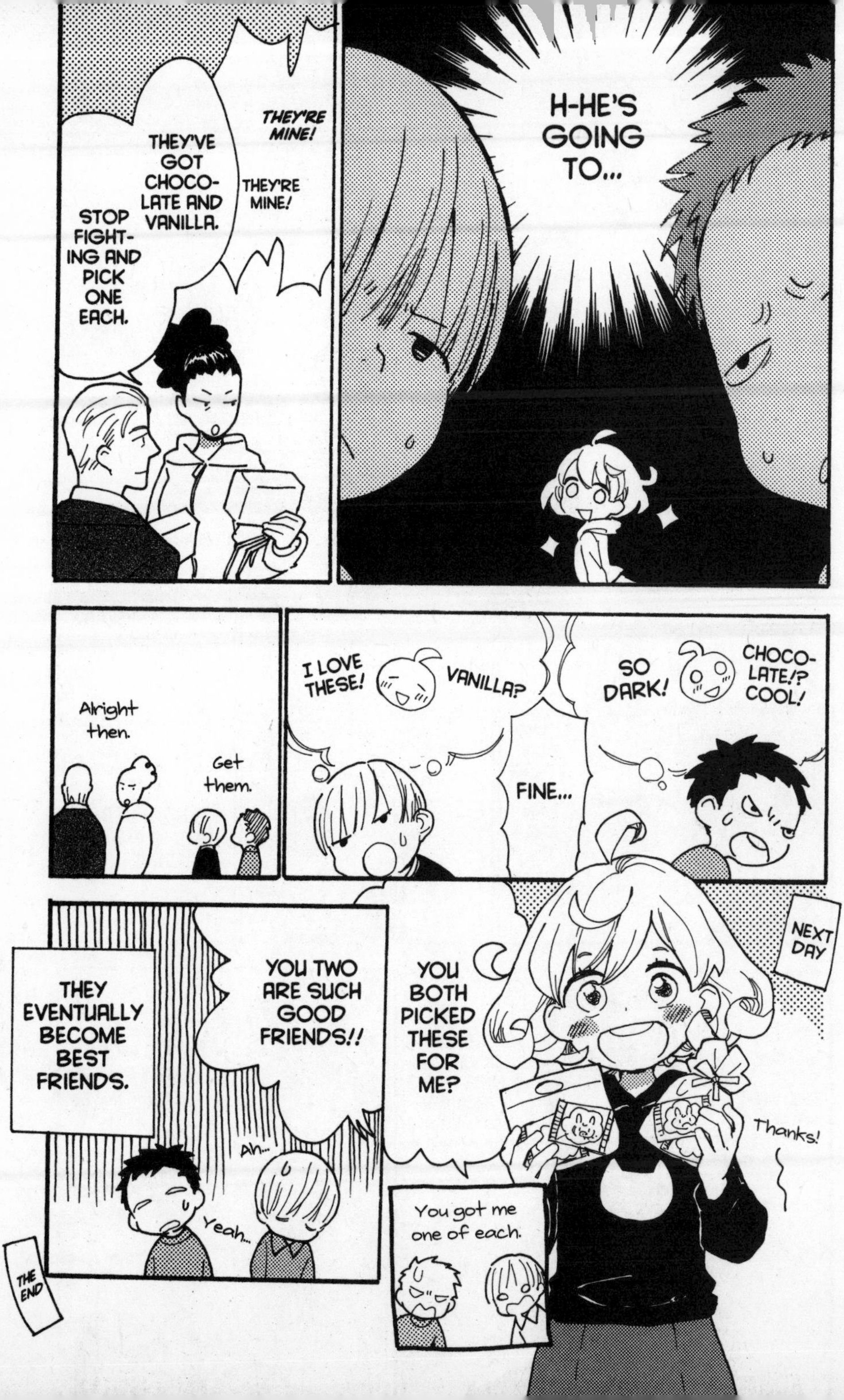
H-HE'S GOING TO...
THEY'RE MINE!
THEY'RE MINE!
THEY'VE GOT CHOCO-LATE AND VANILLA.
STOP FIGHT-ING AND PICK ONE EACH.
CHOCO-LATE!? COOL!
SO DARK!
FINE...
VANILLA?
I LOVE THESE!
Alright then.
Get them.
NEXT DAY
YOU BOTH PICKED THESE FOR ME?
Thanks!
You got me one of each.
YOU TWO ARE SUCH GOOD FRIENDS!!
THEY EVENTUALLY BECOME BEST FRIENDS.
Ah...
Yeah...
THE END

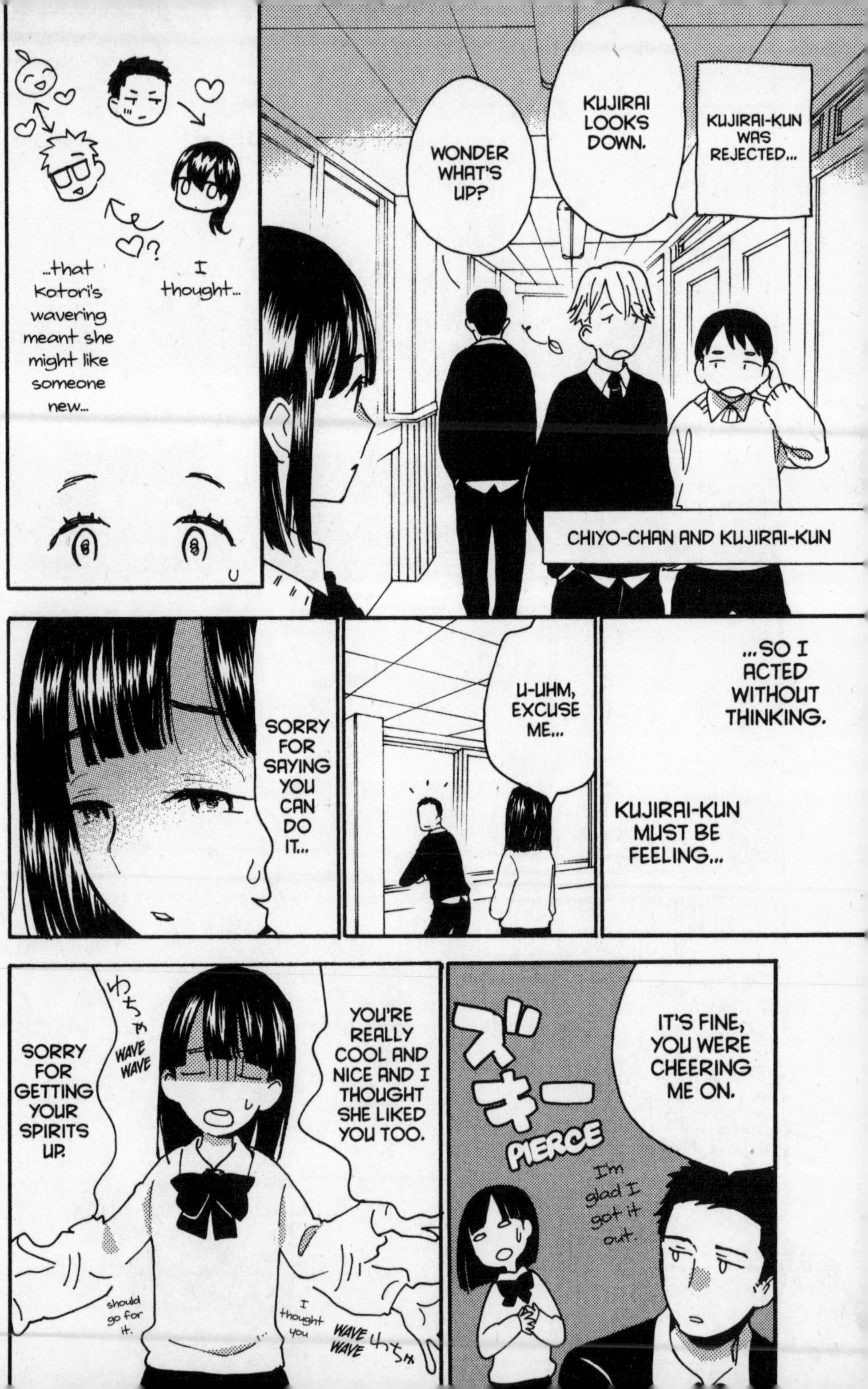
KUJIRAI-KUN WAS REJECTED...
KUJIRAI LOOKS DOWN.
WONDER WHAT'S UP?
CHIYO-CHAN AND KUJIRAI-KUN
I thought...
...that Kotori's wavering meant she might like someone new...
...SO I ACTED WITHOUT THINKING.
KUJIRAI-KUN MUST BE FEELING...
U-UHM, EXCUSE ME...
SORRY FOR SAYING YOU CAN DO IT...
IT'S FINE, YOU WERE CHEERING ME ON.
ズキー
PIERCE
I'm glad I got it out.
YOU'RE REALLY COOL AND NICE AND I THOUGHT SHE LIKED YOU TOO.
SORRY FOR GETTING YOUR SPIRITS UP.
わちゃ
WAVE WAVE
I thought you should go for it.
WAVE WAVE
わちゃ

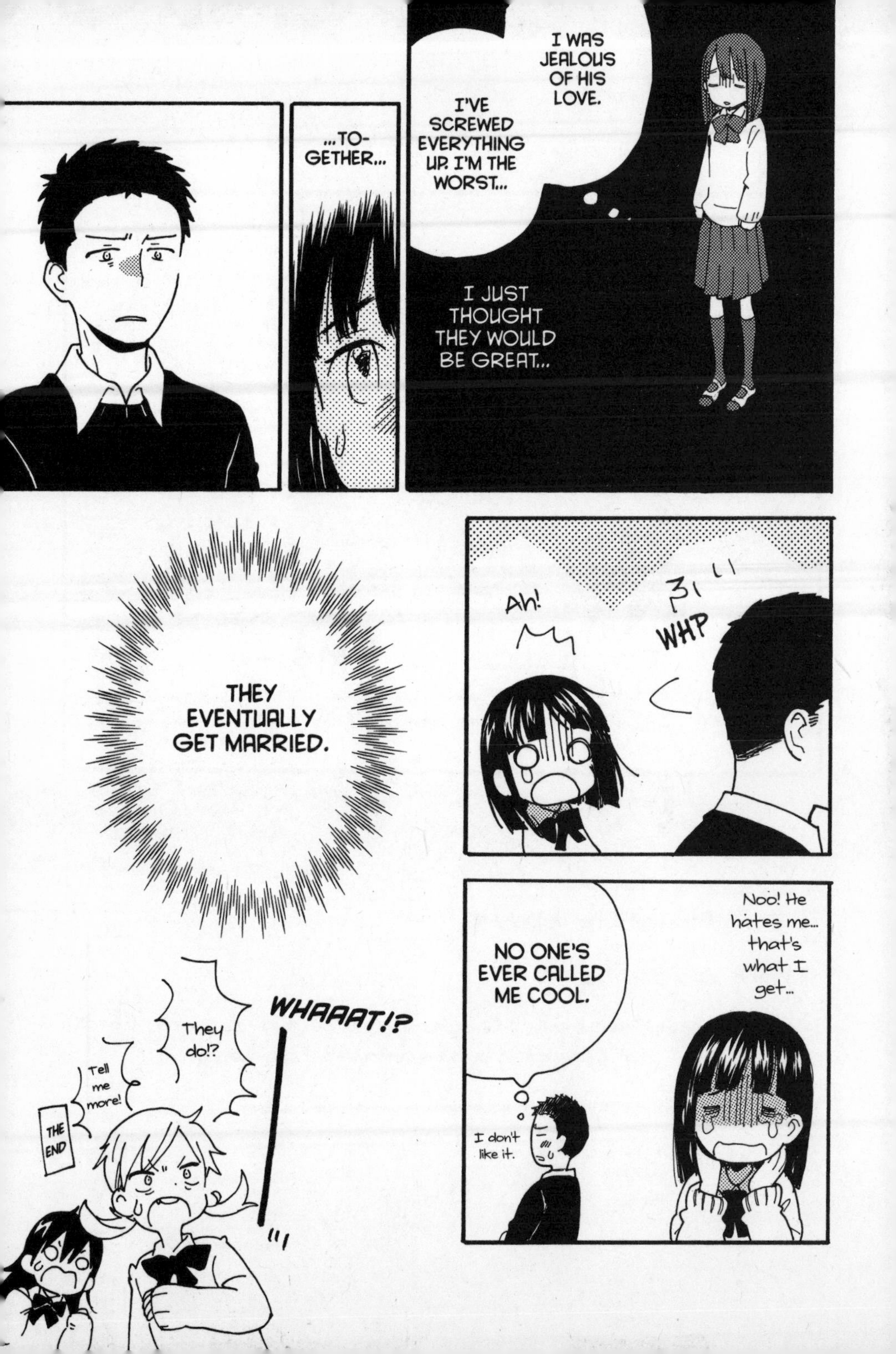

I WAS JEALOUS OF HIS LOVE.
I'VE SCREWED EVERYTHING UP. I'M THE WORST...
I JUST THOUGHT THEY WOULD BE GREAT...
...TO-GETHER...
WHP
Ah!
Noo! He hates me... that's what I get...
NO ONE'S EVER CALLED ME COOL.
I don't like it.
THEY EVENTUALLY GET MARRIED.
WHAAAT!?
They do!?
Tell me more!
THE END

Afterword

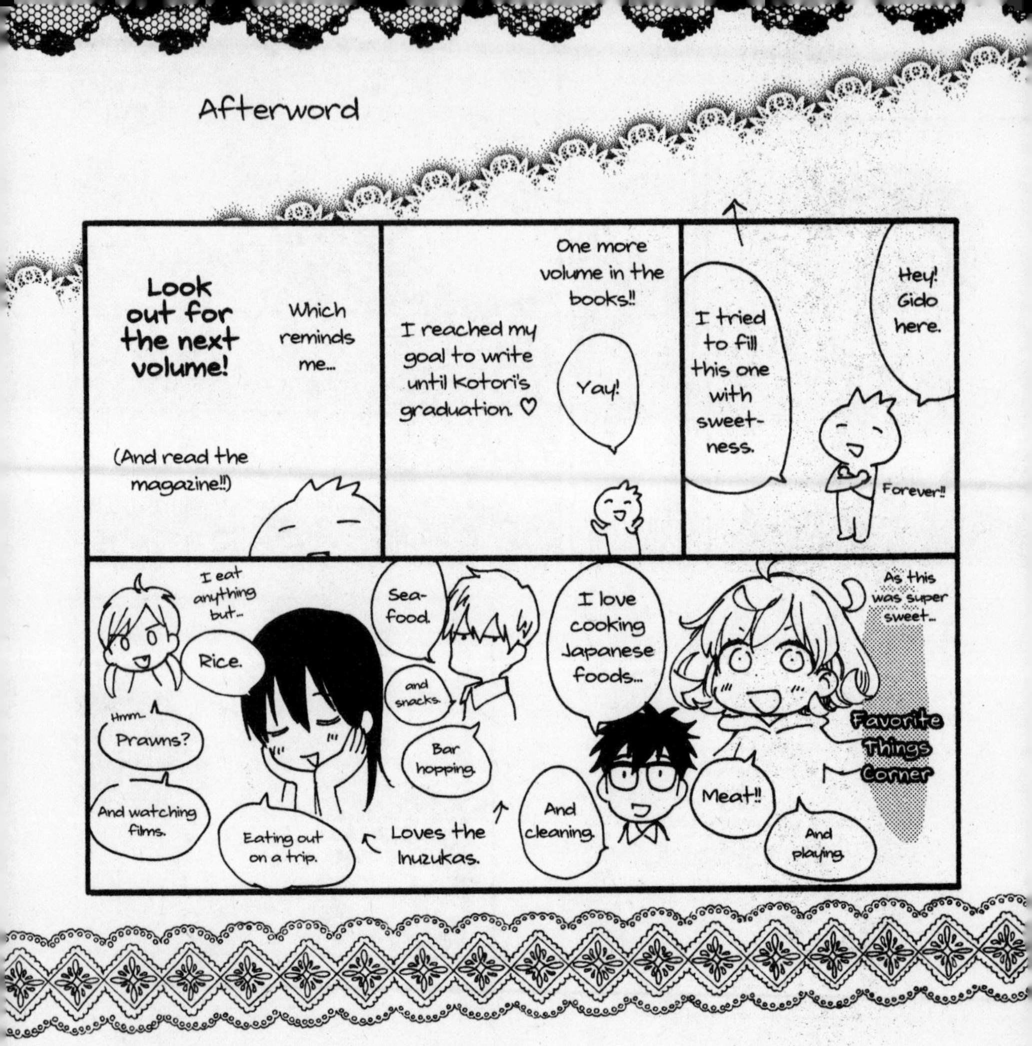
Hey! Gido here.
I tried to fill this one with sweet-ness.
Forever!!
One more volume in the books!!
Yay!
I reached my goal to write until Kotori's graduation. ♡
Which reminds me...
Look out for the next volume!
(And read the magazine!!)
As this was super sweet...
Favorite Things Corner
I love cooking Japanese foods...
Meat!!
And playing.
And cleaning.
Sea-food.
and snacks.
Bar hopping.
Loves the Inuzukas.
I eat anything but...
Rice.
Hmm...
Prawns?
And watching films.
Eating out on a trip.

! Looking forward to Volume 12 !

♥ Thank You So Much ♥

W-Yama-san, Tsuru-san, GON-chan, M-chan, Chii-chan, my family.
T-Dai-sama, K-Yama-sama, Abe Jun-sama

★ Gathering Reference Pictures: Rabou-sama from the restaurant.

★ Editing the Food: Obiryoku You-sama

Amagakure Gido

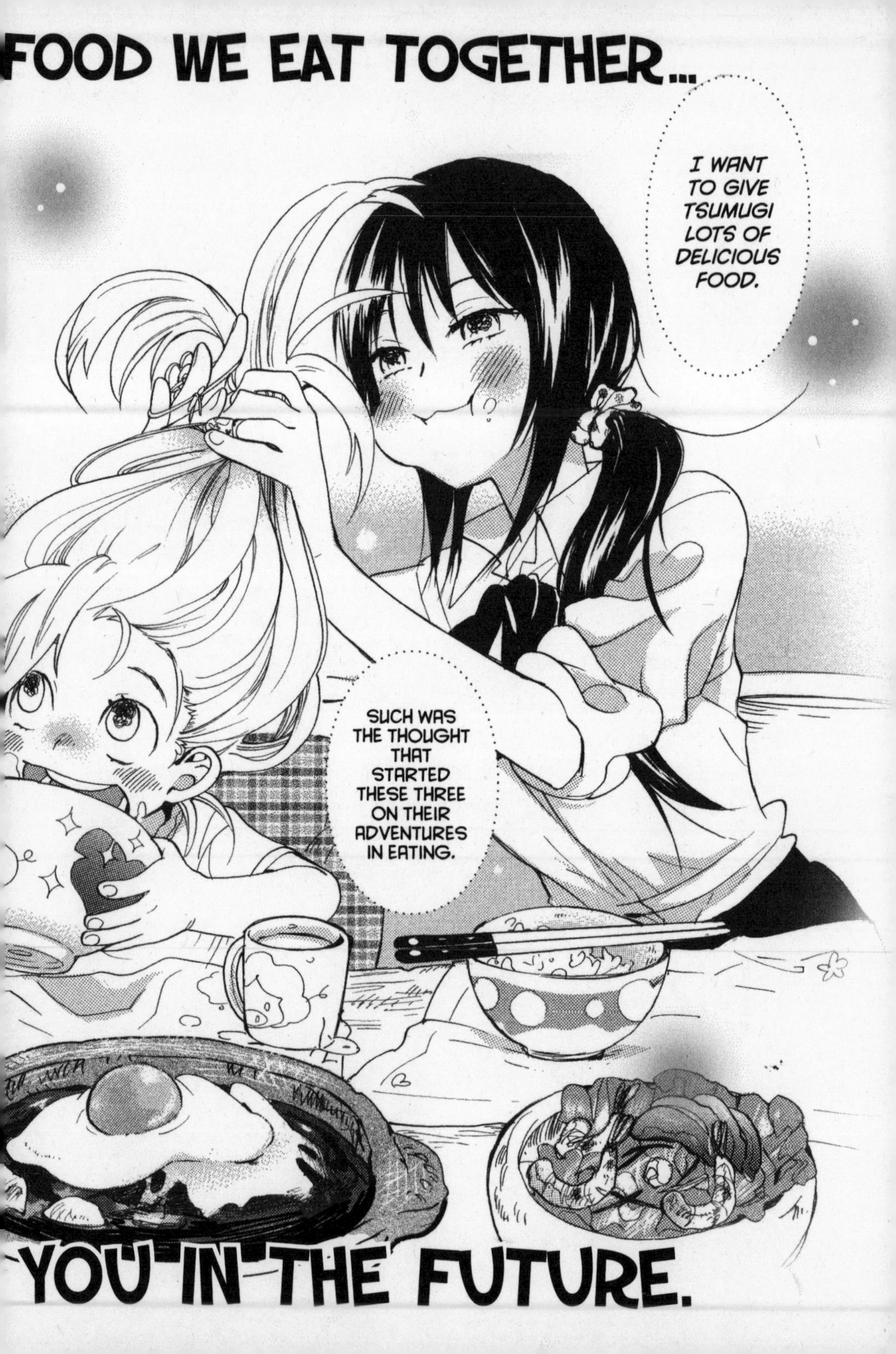
FOOD WE EAT TOGETHER...
I WANT TO GIVE TSUMUGI LOTS OF DELICIOUS FOOD.
SUCH WAS THE THOUGHT THAT STARTED THESE THREE ON THEIR ADVENTURES IN EATING.
YOU IN THE FUTURE.

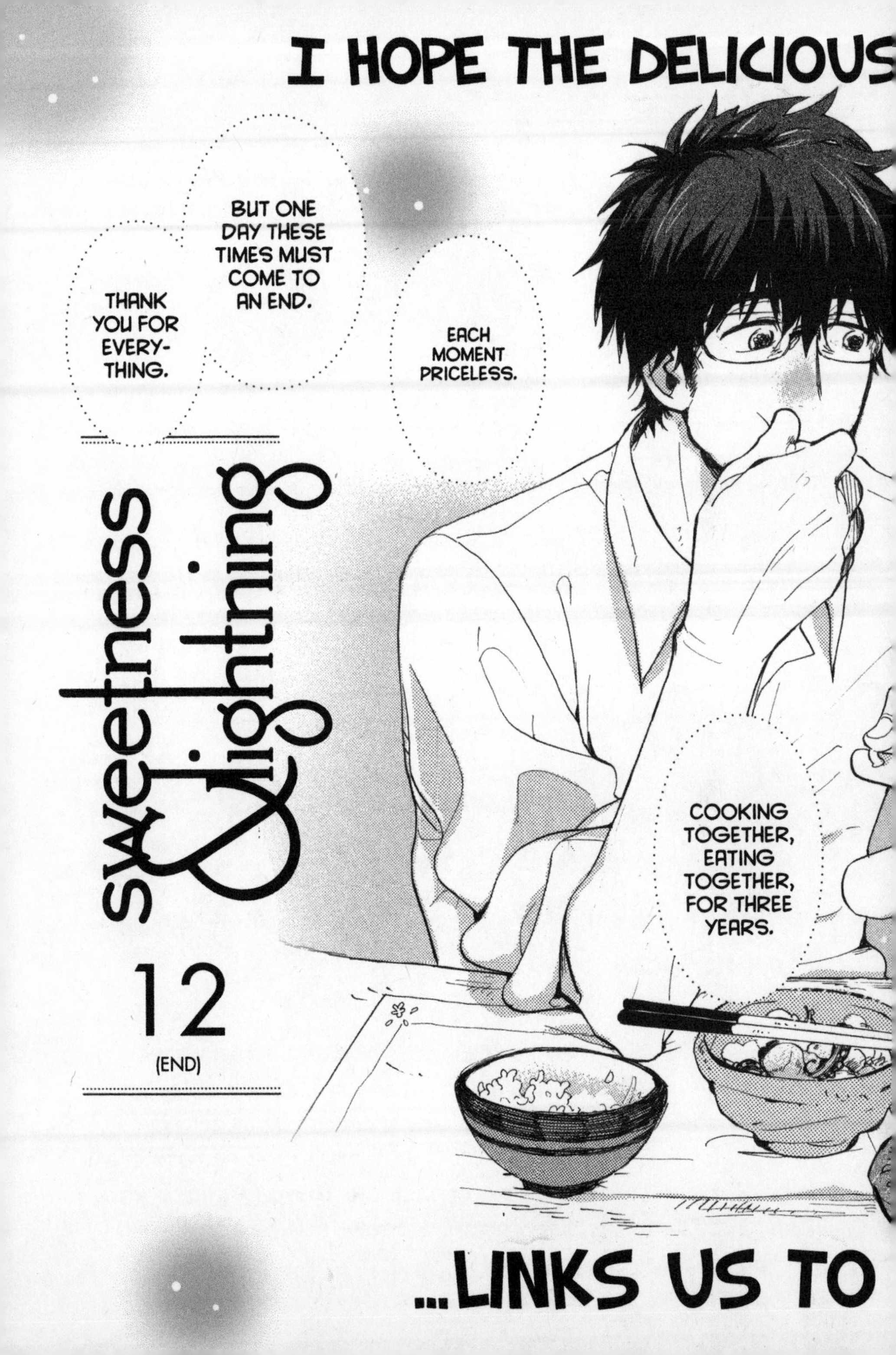
I HOPE THE DELICIOUS
COOKING TOGETHER, EATING TOGETHER, FOR THREE YEARS.
EACH MOMENT PRICELESS.
BUT ONE DAY THESE TIMES MUST COME TO AN END.
THANK YOU FOR EVERY-THING.
sweetness & lightning
12
(END)
...LINKS US TO

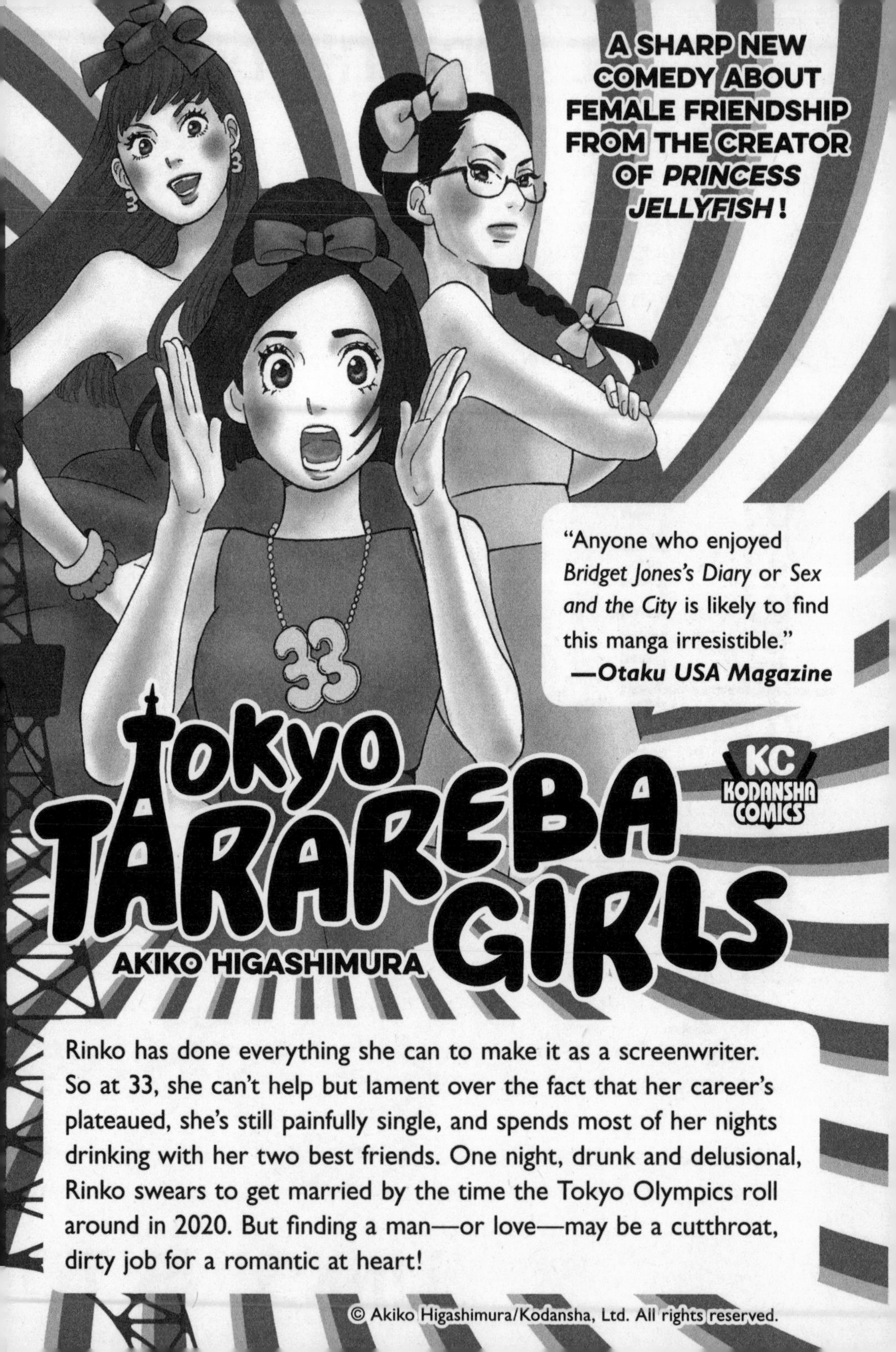

33

Tokyo TARAREBA GIRLS

AKIKO HIGASHIMURA

KC KODANSHA COMICS

Rinko has done everything she can to make it as a screenwriter. So at 33, she can't help but lament over the fact that her career's plateaued, she's still painfully single, and spends most of her nights drinking with her two best friends. One night, drunk and delusional, Rinko swears to get married by the time the Tokyo Olympics roll around in 2020. But finding a man—or love—may be a cutthroat, dirty job for a romantic at heart!

In love, there are no save points.

NOW AN ANIME!

ヲタクに恋は難しい

WOTAKOI:
LOVE IS HARD FOR OTAKU
by FUJITA

Narumi has had it rough: Every boyfriend she's had dumped her once they found out she was an otaku, so she's gone to great lengths to hide it. At her new job, she bumps into Hirotaka, her childhood friend and fellow otaku. When Hirotaka almost gets her secret outed at work, she comes up with a plan to keep him quiet. But he comes up with a counter-proposal: Why doesn't she just date him instead?

Princess Jellyfish

Akiko Higashimura

**ALSO
AN ANIME!**

"One of the best
manga for beginners!"
—*Kotaku*

Tsukimi Kurashita is fascinated with jellyfish. She's loved them from a young age and has carried that love with her to her new life in the big city of Tokyo. There, she resides in Amamizukan, a safe-haven for geek girls where no boys are allowed. One day, Tsukimi crosses paths with a beautiful and fashionable woman, but there's much more to this woman than her trendy clothes...!

KC
KODANSHA
COMICS

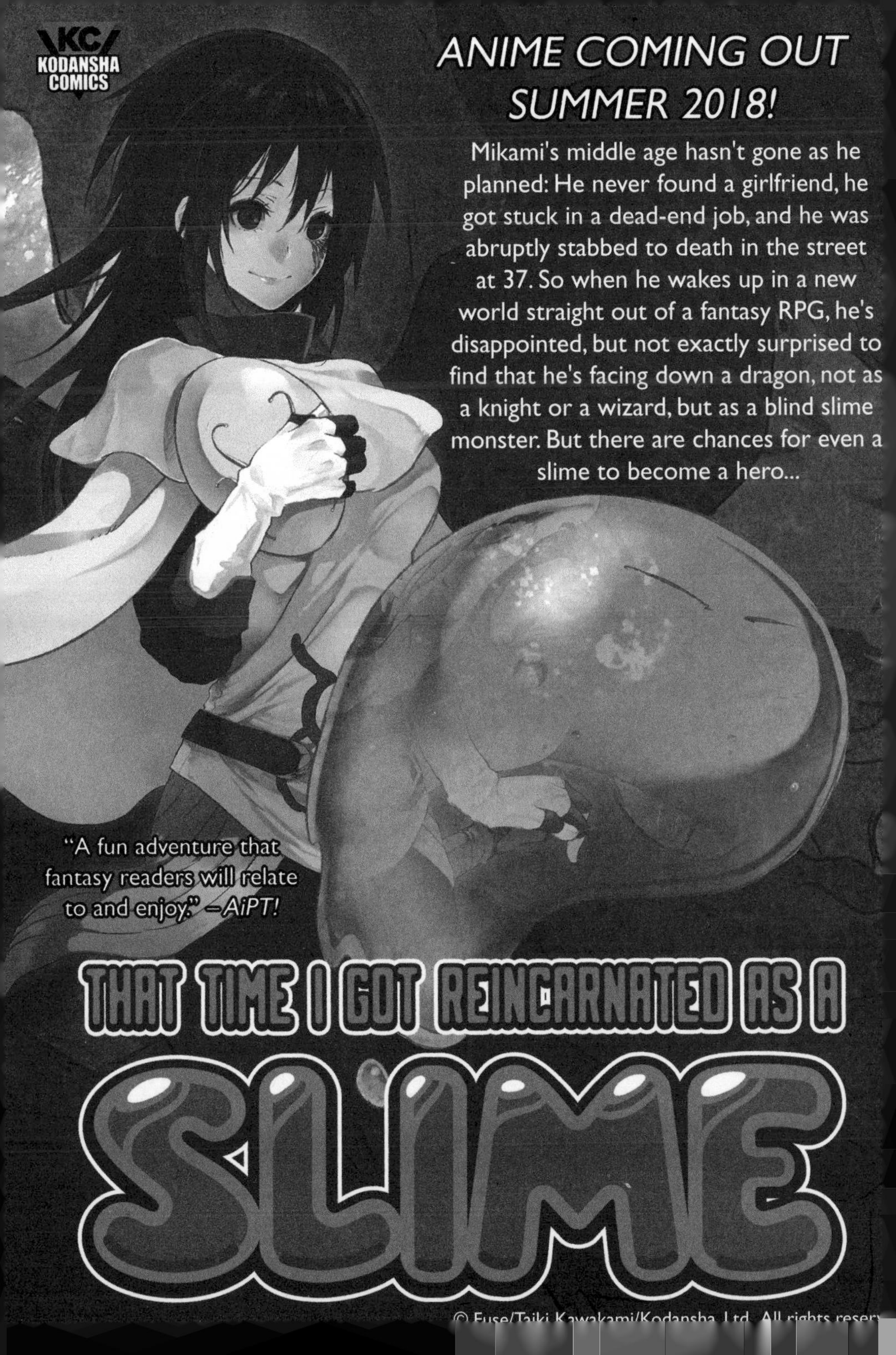
KC KODANSHA COMICS
ANIME COMING OUT SUMMER 2018!
Mikami's middle age hasn't gone as he planned: He never found a girlfriend, he got stuck in a dead-end job, and he was abruptly stabbed to death in the street at 37. So when he wakes up in a new world straight out of a fantasy RPG, he's disappointed, but not exactly surprised to find that he's facing down a dragon, not as a knight or a wizard, but as a blind slime monster. But there are chances for even a slime to become a hero...
"A fun adventure that fantasy readers will relate to and enjoy." –AiPT!
THAT TIME I GOT REINCARNATED AS A
SLIME
© Fuse/Taiki Kawakami/Kodansha Ltd. All rights reserv

Based on the critically acclaimed classic horror manga

The first new *Parasyte* manga in over 20 years!

NEO PARASYTE f

BY ASUMIKO NAKAMURA, EMA TOYAMA, MIKI RINNO, LALAKO KOJIMA, KAORI YUKI, BANKO KUZE, YUUKI OBATA, KASHIO, YUI KUROE, ASIA WATANABE, MIKIMAKI, HIKARU SURUGA, HAJIME SHINJO, RENJURO KINDAICHI, AND YURI NARUSHIMA

A collection of chilling new *Parasyte* stories from Japan's top shojo artists!

Parasites: shape-shifting aliens whose only purpose is to assimilate with and consume the human race... but do these monsters have a different side? A parasite becomes a prince to save his romance-obsessed female host from a dangerous stalker. Another hosts a cooking show, in which the real monsters are revealed. These and 13 more stories, from some of the greatest shojo manga artists alive today, together make up a chilling, funny, and entertaining tribute to one of manga's horror classics!

The prince in his dark days

By **Hico Yamanaka**

A drunkard for a father, a household of poverty... For 17-year-old Atsuko, misfortune is all she knows and believes in. Until one day, a chance encounter with Itaru-the wealthy heir of a huge corporation-changes everything. The two look identical, uncannily so. When Itaru curiously goes missing, Atsuko is roped into being his stand-in. There, in his shoes, Atsuko must parade like a prince in a palace. She encounters many new experiences, but at what cost...?

The Black Museum The Ghost and the Lady

By Kazuhiro Fujita

Deep in Scotland Yard in London sits an evidence room dedicated to the greatest mysteries of British history. In this "Black Museum" sits a misshapen hunk of lead—two bullets fused together—the key to a wartime encounter between Florence Nightingale, the mother of modern nursing, and a supernatural Man in Grey. This story is unknown to most scholars of history, but a special guest of the museum will tell the tale of The Ghost and the Lady...

Praise for Kazuhiro Fujita's Ushio and Tora

"A charming revival that combines a classic look with modern depth and pacing... **Essential viewing both for curmudgeons and new fans alike.**" — Anime News Network

"**GREAT!** The first episode of Ushio and Tora captures the essence of '90s anime." — IGN

Japan's most powerful spirit medium delves into the ghost world's greatest mysteries!

Story by Kyo Shirodaira, famed author of mystery fiction and creator of *Spiral*, *Blast of Tempest*, and *The Record of a Fallen Vampire*.

Both touched by spirits called yôkai, Kotoko and Kurô have gained unique superhuman powers. But to gain her powers Kotoko has given up an eye and a leg, and Kurô's personal life is in shambles. So when Kotoko suggests they team up to deal with renegades from the spirit world, Kurô doesn't have many other choices, but Kotoko might just have a few ulterior motives...

IN/SPECTRE

STORY BY KYO SHIRODAIRA
ART BY CHASHIBA KATASE

KC
KODANSHA
COMICS

complex age

yui sakuma

26-year-old Nagisa Kataura has a secret. Transforming into her favorite anime and manga characters is her passion in life, and she's earned great respect amongst her fellow cospayers. But to the rest of society, her hobby is a silly fantasy. As demands from both her office job and cosplaying begin to increase, she may one day have to make a tough choice— what's more important to her, cosplay or being "normal"?

KC
KODANSHA
COMICS

A new series from the creator of *Soul Eater*, the megahit manga and anime seen on Toonami!

"Fun and lively... a great start!"
    -Adventures in Poor Taste

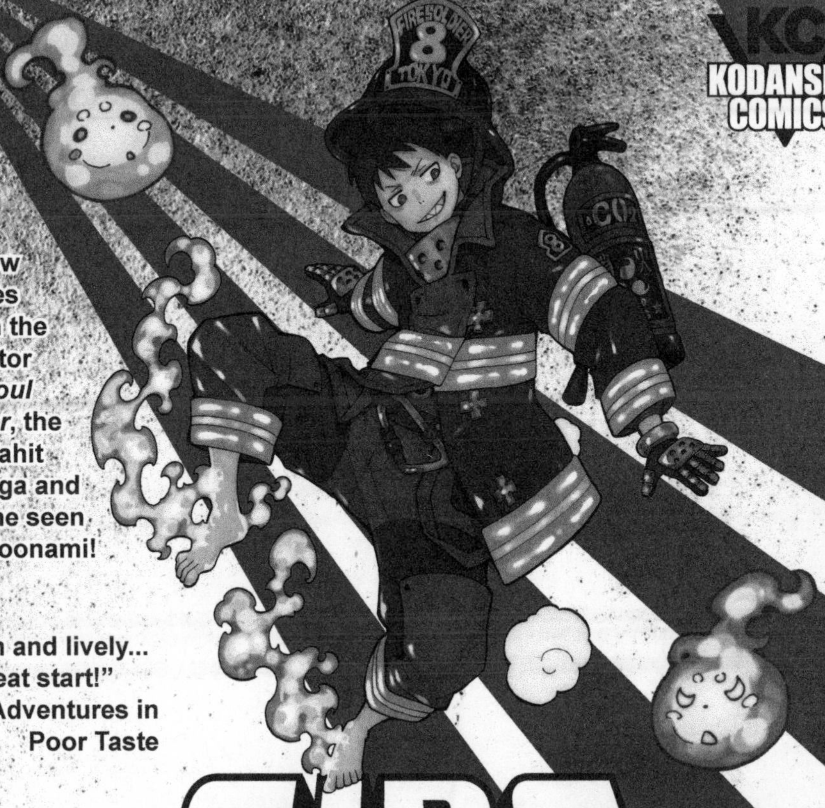

FIRE FORCE

By Atsushi Ohkubo

The city of Tokyo is plagued by a deadly phenomenon: spontaneous human combustion! Luckily, a special team is there to quench the inferno: The Fire Force! The fire soldiers at Special Fire Cathedral 8 are about to get a unique addition. Enter Shinra, a boy who possesses the power to run at the speed of a rocket, leaving behind the famous "devil's footprints" (and destroying his shoes in the process). Can Shinra and his colleagues discover the source of this strange epidemic before the city burns to ashes?

KC
KODANSHA
COMICS

New action series from Hiroyuki Takei, creator of the classic shonen franchise Shaman King!

In medieval Japan, a bell hanging on the collar is a sign that a cat has a master. Norachiyo's bell hangs from his katana sheath, but he is nonetheless a stray — a ronin. This one-eyed cat samurai travels across a dishonest world, cutting through pretense and deception with his blade.

Nekogahara

STRAY CAT SAMURAI

By
Hiroyuki Takei

Sweetness & Lightning volume 11 is a work of fiction. Names, characters, places, and incidents are the products of the author's imagination or are used fictitiously. Any resemblance to actual events, locales, or persons, living or dead, is entirely coincidental.

A Kodansha Comics Trade Paperback Original.

Published in the United States by Kodansha Comics,
an imprint of Kodansha USA Publishing, LLC, New York.

Publication rights for this English edition arranged through Kodansha Ltd., Tokyo.

First published in Japan in 2018 by Kodansha Ltd., Tokyo, as *Ama-ama to Inadzuma* volume 11.

ISBN 978-1-63236-570-5

Printed in the United States of America.

www.kodanshacomics.com

9 8 7 6 5 4 3 2 1

Translation: Adam Lensenmayer
Additional Translation: Jennifer O'Donnell
Lettering, chapters 50-53: Carl Vanstiphout
Lettering, chapter 54: Miriam Esteban Rossi and Massimo Stella
Additional Lettering: Paige Pumphrey
Editing: Paul Starr
Editorial Assistance: Tiff Ferentini
Kodansha Comics Edition Cover Design: Phil Balsman